MW00804984

THE LIGHT OF KAILASH

VOLUME THREE

Jiri Rys

The LIGHT of KAILASH

A History of Zhang Zhung and Tibet

VOLUME THREE
The Later Period: Tibet

CHÖGYAL NAMKHAI NORBU

Translated from the Tibetan and edited by
Donatella Rossi

English editing by
Nancy Simmons

Shang Shung Publications
Merigar
58031 Arcidosso (GR)
Italy
shop.shangshungfoundation.com

Original title: *Zhang bod kyi lo rgyus ti se'i 'od*

Copyright © 2015 Shang Shung Publications
All rights reserved. No portion of this book may be reproduced by any means
without prior written permission from the publisher.

ISBN 978-88-7834-145-6

Cover calligraphy: Chögyal Namkhai Norbu
Editor: Nancy Simmons
Cover and interior design: Daniel Zegunis and Fulvio Ferrari
Layout: Tiziana Gottardi
Graphics: Fulvio Ferrari

IPC - 838EN15 - Approved by the International
Publications Committee of the Dzogchen Community
founded by Chögyal Namkhai Norbu.

339EN

Contents

Translator's Foreword

CHÖGYAL NAMKHAI NORBU (born 1938), former professor of Tibetan and Mongolian Language and Literature at the University of Naples L'Orientale, has dedicated his academic career to the study of Tibetan culture and has published a number of works, in particular, on its origin.[1] In his findings, the cradle of Tibetan culture is to be looked for in the ancient realm of Zhang Zhung and in the Bon spiritual traditions which flourished within and spread from that kingdom.

According to relevant textual sources, the ancient kingdom of Zhang Zhung, prior to the advent of Buddhism in the seventh century, encom-

---

This is an updated version of the Translator's Foreword found in Volume One.

1   Among these figure *Bod kyi lo rgyus las 'phros pa'i gtam g.yung drung nor bu'i do shal*, Library of Tibetan Works and Archives, Dharamsala, 1981; *La Collana di Zi, Storia e cultura del Tibet*, translated in Italian from the Tibetan and edited by Adriano Clemente, Shang Shung Edizioni, Arcidosso, 1997; *The Necklace of gZi. A Cultural History of Tibet*, LTWA, Dharamsala, 1981 (*Bod rigs gzhon nu rnams la gros su 'debs pa gZi yi phreng ba*, LTWA, Dharamsala, 1982); *The Necklace of Zi, On the History and Culture of Tibet*, translated in English from the Italian by Barrie and Nancy Simmons, Shang Shung Edizioni, Arcidosso, 2004; *Gans ti se'i dkar chag. A Bon-po Story of the Sacred Mountain Ti-se and the Blue Lake Ma-pan*, edited by Chögyal Namkhai Norbu, revised, collated, and completed by Ramon Prats, excerpts in English translated by Chögyal Namkhai Norbu and Ramon Prats, Serie Orientale Roma, LXI, IsMEO, 1989; *sGrung lde'u bon gsum gyi gtam e ma ho*, LTWA, Dharamsala, 1989. For a list of the works of Chögyal Namkhai Norbu until 1995, see his *Drung, Deu and Bön. Narrations, symbolic languages and the Bön tradition in ancient Tibet*, translated, edited, and annotated by Adriano Clemente, LTWA, Dharamsala, 1995, pp. 295-297.

passed a vast area including Western and Northern Tibet, with the revered and majestic Mount Kailash as its center and heart. Thus, the author's choice of title for his work is meaningful per se, in that it symbolizes and at the same time emphasizes the rich cultural origin of the Land of Snows.

Tibetan studies have a long and honored history, though only in the second half of the last century did scholars begin to take an interest in the Tibetan Bonpo culture.[2] The reasons for this delay lie primarily in the previous lack of access to textual sources, and in the prevalence of orthodox Buddhist views which not only greatly influenced the attitude of modern Bonpo adherents, but have also been adopted by Western scholars as the unquestioned basis for the study of Tibetan culture as a whole. That attitude resulted in a simplistic view, still maintained by some, according to which Tibet was a savage land before the adoption of Buddhism, even lacking a written language.

Fortunately, a change in the status quo took place in the 1960s, when Professor David Llewellyn Snellgrove invited a group of knowledgeable representatives of the Bon tradition[3] from their refugee settlement in India, and undertook the pioneering task of letting this tradition speak for the first time in its own voice to the Western world.[4]

Soon after, Professor Samten Gyaltsen Karmay published the translation of an outstanding work on the history of Bon, compiled by the famed Bonpo master and scholar, Shar-rdza bKra-shis rGyal-mtshan (1859-1934), which became a seminal text of reference for research

---

2 See for example, Helmut Hoffmann, *Quellen zur Geschichte der tibetischen Bon-Religion*, Akademie der Wissenschaften und der Literatur in Mainz, F.S. Verlag, Wiesbaden, 1950.

3 Lopon Tenzin Namdak, Ven. Sangye Tenzin, and Samten G. Karmay.

4 See *The Nine Ways of Bon. Excerpts from the* gZi brjid, London Oriental Series, Vol. 18, Oxford University Press, 1967. A volume dedicated to Prof. Snellgrove, entitled *Bon: the Everlasting Religion of Tibet. Tibetan Studies in Honour of Professor David L. Snellgrove* (papers presented at the International Conference on Bon, 22-27 June 2008, Shenten Dargye Ling, Château de la Modetais, Blou, France, New Horizons of Bon Studies 2, Samten G. Karmay and Donatella Rossi eds.) has been published in EAST AND WEST, IsIAO, as Vol. 59, nos. 1-4, 2009.

studies;[5] and in 1974, Professor Emeritus Per Kværne published a study of the Bonpo Canon (*bka' 'gyur*), based on a nineteenth century text.[6]

During the 1980s, two sets of the Bonpo Canon (154 and 192 volumes, respectively) were reprinted in Eastern Tibet (present day Sichuan Province, People's Republic of China), while in the late 1990s, a collection of 300 volumes of ancillary texts (*bka' brten*) of the Bonpo Canon was published in Lhasa by the Venerable Tenpai Nyima.

The availability of this extensive literature has paved the way for a series of analytic cataloguing, research studies, field work, seminars, and so on, that have contributed dramatically to improve understanding about the Bon tradition as a whole.[7] *The Light of Kailash, A History of Zhang Zhung and Tibet* can be considered a highly significant contribution to this body of knowledge.

---

5 *The Treasury of Good Sayings: A Tibetan History of Bon*, London Oriental Series, Vol. 26, Oxford University Press, London, 1972.

6 "The Canon of the Tibetan Bonpos," *Indo-Iranian Journal*, Vol. 16, Part One, pp. 18-56, Part Two, pp. 96-144.

7 See mainly the following works, produced under the aegis of Prof. Yasuhiko Nagano: *Mandalas of the Bon Religion*, Bon Studies 1, Tenzin Namdak, Yasuhiko Nagano and Musashi Tachikawa eds., Senri Ethnological Reports 12, National Museum of Ethnology, Osaka, 2000; *New Horizons in Bon Studies*, Bon Studies 2, Samten G. Karmay and Yasuhiko Nagano eds., Senri Ethnological Reports 15, National Museum of Ethnology, Osaka, 2000; *New Research on Zhangzhung and Related Himalayan Languages*, Bon Studies 3, Yasuhiko Nagano and Randy J. LaPolla eds., Senri Ethnological Reports 19, National Museum of Ethnology, Osaka, 2001; *A Catalogue of the New Collection of Bonpo Katen Texts*, Bon Studies 4, Samten G. Karmay and Yasuhiko Nagano eds., Senri Ethnological Reports 24, National Museum of Ethnology, Osaka, 2001; *A Catalogue of the New Collection of Bonpo Katen Texts—Indices*, Bon Studies 5, Samten G. Karmay and Yasuhiko Nagano eds., Senri Ethnological Reports 25, National Museum of Ethnology, Osaka, 2001; *The Call of the Blue Cuckoo. An Anthology of Nine Bonpo Texts on Myths and Rituals*, Bon Studies 6, Samten G. Karmay and Yasuhiko Nagano eds., Senri Ethnological Reports 32, National Museum of Ethnology, Osaka, 2002; *A Survey of Bonpo Monasteries and Temples in Tibet and the Himalaya*, Bon Studies 7, Samten G. Karmay and Yasuhiko Nagano eds., Senri Ethnological Reports 38, National Museum of Ethnology, Osaka, 2003; *A Catalogue of the Bon Kanjur*, Bon Studies 8, Dan Martin, Per Kværne and Yasuhiko Nagano eds., Senri Ethnological Reports 40, National Museum of Ethnology, Osaka, 2003; *Feast of the Morning Light. The Eighteenth Century Wood-engravings of Shenrab's Life-stories and the Bon Canon from Gyalrong*, Bon Stud-

The text was originally conceived as a set of university lectures that Chögyal Namkhai Norbu was invited to give at the University of Nationalities in Beijing (Minzu Daxue, former Zhongyang Minzu Xueyuan) in 1988. The contents of the lectures formed a first abridged version of *The Light of Kailash*, which was subsequently enlarged and expanded by the author after further research, until the manuscript, written in his unique calligraphy, became a work of 1,900 pages, divided in three volumes.

The first volume, "The Early Period, the History of Ancient Zhang Zhung," considers the rise of early human generations and the Bon lineages of ancient Zhang Zhung, its dynasties, language, and culture.

The second volume, entitled "The History of the Intermediate Period: Tibet and Zhang Zhung," is focused upon human generations, the Bonpo lineages, the spread of Bon during the lifetimes of the first Tibetan monarchs, the dynasties, written language, and civilization of ancient Tibet, as well as upon the reigns of specific kings, the Bon religion, and Bonpo religious figures (Dran-pa Nam-mkha' in particular) of Zhang Zhung during that period.

The third volume, "The History of the Later Period: Tibet," is concerned with an assessment of the genealogies, Bonpo lineages, royal dynasties (from the first monarch gNya'-khri bTsan-po until the forty-fifth monarch Khri-dar-ma 'U-dum-btsan), language, and civilization of Tibet.

In the translator's view, this summa of Chögyal Namkhai Norbu's researches is dedicated, first and foremost, to his fellow countrymen and

ies 9, Samten G. Karmay ed., Senri Ethnological Reports 57, National Museum of Ethnology, Osaka, 2005; *Bonpo Thangkas from Khyungpo*, Bon Studies 10, Tenpa Yundrung, Per Kværne, Musashi Tachikawa and Yasuhiko Nagano eds., Senri Ethnological Reports 60, National Museum of Ethnology, Osaka, 2006; Pasar Tsultrim Tenzin, Changru Tritsuk Namdak Nyima, Gatsa Lodroe Rabsal, *A Lexicon of Zhangzhung and Bonpo Terms*, Bon Studies 11, Yasuhiko Nagano and Samten G. Karmay eds, Senri Ethnological Reports 76, National Museum of Ethnology, Osaka, 2008. For iconographic and artistic perspectives, see Per Kværne, *The Bon Religion of Tibet. The Iconography of a Living Tradition*, Serindia Publications, London, 1995, and *Bon, The Magic Word, The Indigenous Religion of Tibet*, Samten G. Karmay and Jeff Watt eds., Rubin Museum of Art, New York, and Philip Wilson Publishers Ltd, London, 2007.

women, and to Tibetan youth in particular. *The Light of Kailash* through meticulous selection and a critical use and analysis of a vast array of literary and often unpublished sources, such as dynastic and religious histories and cycles, myths, articles, and so on, offers an open, daring, holistic, unbiased approach to the study of the cultural and spiritual heritage of Tibet and to the understanding of the origin of this fascinating and endangered civilization. It is my hope that scholars will appreciate the import and interested readers enjoy the content of this amazing trilogy.

In conclusion, I wish to express deep gratitude above all to Chögyal Namkhai Norbu for the invaluable opportunity for study and reflection that this work offered, and also for his great patience in aiding me with the interpretation of difficult or obscure passages. My heartfelt thanks go also to Ponlop Trinley Nyima Rinpoche, the Director of the Dialectic School of New Menri Monastery in Dolanji (Himachal Pradesh, India), for his precious clarifications.

I greatly thank Adriano Clemente for his excellent advice and Enrico Dell'Angelo for permitting me to consult his dissertation, in itself a pioneering work.[8] I am especially grateful to Nancy Simmons for her unremitting support and wonderful editing throughout the project. Marta Sernesi has my gratitude for her precision in checking the Indexes and Tiziana Gottardi, Igor Legati, Maurizio Mingotti, and Dan Zegunis for their accurate production work.

In terms of sponsorship, I thank the International Shang Shung Institute, particularly Laurie Marder, Jacqueline Gens, and the late and loved Andrea Sertoli (United States branch), Luigi Ottaviani (Italian branch), and Oliver Leick (Austrian branch); the David Sharpe Bequest; Dick Drury for his unstinting generosity and exceptional commitment to this work; Benedetta Tagliabue who with great bounty underwrote the printing of the first volume; Mark Farrington; and Mark Fulton. At the onset of this project these individuals and institutions made its launching possible.

---

8 *Srid pa'i spyi mdos: Contributo allo Studio dell'Insegnamento di gShen rab Mi bo che* [Contribution to the study of gShen rab Mi bo che's teaching], MA dissertation, Istituto Universitario Orientale di Napoli, Naples, 1982.

The finalization of this ultimate volume of The Light of Kailash trilogy was made feasible by a Fellowship of the International Consortium for Research in the Humanities "Fate, Freedom and Prognostication. Strategies for Coping with the Future in East Asia and Europe" (supported by the Federal Ministry of Education and Research) at the University of Erlangen-Nuremberg, Germany.

My whole-hearted appreciation goes to Prof. Dr. Fabrizio Pregadio, Institute of Sinology, Friedrich-Alexander-Universität Erlangen-Nürnberg for his friendly encouragement. Many other people helped in both tangible and intangible ways; I hope they will consider the realization of this work as the token of my recognition for their kindness and support.

Donatella Rossi
November 2014
Erlangen, Germany

A TECHNICAL NOTE ON THE TRANSLATION

The translation is based on the original Tibetan manuscript (*Zhang bod kyi lo rgyus ti se'i 'od*). The Light of Kailash was published in the People's Republic of China in 1996 in block print form.[9] The text printed in China presents some omissions and imprecisions and for that reason was not used as a main source, though at times it was consulted.

The transliteration used follows the Wylie system. It has been preferred as the most accurate method, despite its notorious difficulty for nonspecialists, since reader-friendly solutions, though more accessible, are notably misleading. A combination of the two seemed cumbersome, in view of the great number of names and terms contained in the text. To facilitate reading by nonspecialists, personal and geographical names have been hyphenated while textual sources and technical terms are written in italics. The name of the ancient kingdom of Zhang Zhung has not been hyphenated in view of the explanation provided by the Author in the text. Similarly the word Bonpo has not been hyphenated, in this case because of its common usage.

Bibliographic references in the text appear as in the original. They are self-explanatory in that they follow a consistent structure: a first syllable for the publishing place, volume letter or number, page or folio number, and line number. The relevant sources can be found in the bibliographies that follow each of the three volumes.

Translator's notes have been added when deemed necessary and are enclosed in brackets [...]. Similarly, names or terms translated or quoted appear in square brackets in the body of the text.

Responsibility for any defect, error, or imperfection rests solely with the translator.

---

9 *Zhang bod kyi lo rgyus ti se'i 'od*, Chinese title: *Gudai xiangxiong yu tufan shi*, The China Tibetology Publishing House, Beijing. Other works by Chögyal Namkhai Norbu have also been published in the People's Republic of China: see *Nam mkha'i nor bu'i gsung rtsom phyogs bsgrigs* (Selected Works of Namkhai Norbu, Tibetan Edition), The China Tibetology Publishing House, Beijing, 1994.

Brian Beresford/Nomad Pictures

The LIGHT
of KAILASH

VOLUME THREE

I

Identifying the Human Generations
of Ancient Tibet

Tibetan Buddhist scholars have endorsed two divergent opinions concerning the genesis of the ancestral lineages of Tibet.

1. THE FIVE SONS OF KING sKYA-SENG

An example of the first of those opinions is found in the *Deb ther sngon po* [The Blue Annals] (Si, sTod, 60, 10):

> Master Shes-rab Go-cha [Ācārya Prajñāvarman] said, "At the onset of the kaliyuga before the appearance of the Teacher Muni when the Five Sons [of King] sKya-seng [sKya-seng Bu-lnga][10] conducted a war leading a military force of twelve or thirteen units, a king named Rūpati and the troops he commanded suffered a defeat. [Rūpati and the rest of his soldiers] fled disguised as women; [they eventually] arrived within a snowy mountain region and settled there. Nowadays, Rūpati's lineage is known as Bod."
>
> The old documents of the past say, "Formerly the name of the country was Pu-rgyal; later on it was called Bod." That is in line with the account of Master Shes-rab Go-cha.

---

10   *skya seng bu lnga.* King sKya-seng is known as Pāṇḍu in Sanskrit; he had five sons, the five Pāṇḍava brothers: Nakula, Yudhiṣṭhira, Bhīma, Arjuna, and Sahadeva [Tib. rNa-can, g.Yul-ngor-brtan, 'Jigs-sde, Srid-sgrub, and lHar-bcas].

Thus the fact that the troops of Rūpati were driven out of India
into Tibet or in other words that they escaped from that country
and sought refuge in the Land of Snows where they settled, would
represent the justification for saying that Tibetans descend from the
line of Rūpati who came from India and also for the meaning of the
word *bod*—actually *bud* [to escape]—the name by which the country
was known afterward.

In this regard, an article published in the *mTsho sngon slob gso* [Blue
Lake Education Review] (6–1983), titled *Bod kyi rus khungs thog ma'i tshan
dpyod* [Investigation on the Original Lineages of Tibet], affirms (51, 19):

> When Rūpati ran away, he was followed by a retinue of a
> thousand [soldiers] who fled disguised in women's clothes. Most
> probably there was not even one woman with them. Only about
> a thousand men arrived. Even if they had been a hundred thou-
> sand, they would gradually have become extinct; how could
> they possibly have proliferated? That marriageable women were
> present in the place they reached after fleeing means that human
> beings already existed there. Hence, how could Rūpati's retinue
> be reckoned as the original lineage?

What is written here makes perfect sense. Furthermore, as we have read,
the new appellation of *bod* was subsequently attributed to the Land of
Snows—formerly known as Pu-rgyal—because it was the place where
Rūpati's army fled; it is difficult to see that as a valid reason, since
phonetically speaking *bud*, as in *yul bud pa* [escaped to the country],
and *bod*, which derives from *bod pa* or *'bod pa* [to call, summon], are
fundamentally distinct from each other.

In spite of this, one should recognize that general statements such
as "Scriptures and reason do not disprove that Tibet, India, and similar
countries, people, and so on arose in the kalpa of existence"[11] are made
in good faith as they are totally consistent with conventional historical
points of view.

---

11 [*gnas pa'i bskal pa* is the second of the four eons (*bskal pa bzhi*), following the
one during which the universe is formed and preceding the eon of destruction;
the last of the four eons is that of nothingness.]

A slightly different version of the first way of seeing is contained in the *lHo brag chos 'byung* [Religious History of Lhodrak] that says (Pe, 158, 5):

> In the commentary of the text titled *In Praise of the Gift from the Gods*[12] by Shes-rab Go-cha it is said, "When in former times the Five Sons [of King] sKya-seng fought with twelve military units a king called Rūpati and [his] retinue of a hundred [soldiers] fled into [the region of] the Snowy Mountains disguised as women. In these days [his] line of descent is known as Bod." However, this is not the origin of all the Tibetan people: it is a contradiction, because even if Rūpati is considered [to be] gNya'-khri bTsan-po, it is known that many people already existed before him; and in any case it is a mistake because another royal lineage linked to the Śākyas existed in Tibet.

As the excerpt indicates, some Tibetan historians did not attribute much credibility to that theory.

2. THE MONKEY MEDITATOR BODHISATTVA AND THE CRAG-DEMONESS

The second theory refers to a legend universally famed in Tibetan Buddhist circles according to which the ape offspring born from the union of the Monkey Meditator Bodhisattva [sPrel-sgom Byang-chub Sems-dpa']—emanation of the sublime Avalokiteśvara—and the Crag-Demoness [Brag Srin-mo], emanation of the goddess Tārā, gradually evolved from the condition of monkeys into that of human beings. The *bKa' chems ka khol ma* [The Will of King Srong-btsan] affirms (Kan, 47, 10):

> In the three upper territories [sTod-khams-gsum] of Tibet, the Land of Snows—[that is to say,] in the ranges of snow-covered, rocky, and slate mountains—lived various species of carnivorous animals, such as lions, jackals, and so forth, and of wild [herbivorous] animals, such as deer, antelope, sheep [argali, Ovis ammon], and so on.

---

12 *lha las phul byung*: a praise of the Buddha, king of the Śākya, written by the Indian Paṇḍita bDe-byed bDag-po.

The three middle territories [Bar-khams-gsum]—[that is to say,] the areas of boulders, pastures, and forests—were inhabited by all kinds of animals, such as wild boars, monkeys, bears, and so on.

In the three lower territories [sMad-khams-gsum]—[that is to say,] the areas of jungles, lakes, ponds, and grasslands—lived different kinds of animals, such as birds, elephants, hippopotami, buffaloes, and so on.

There was not a single human being; for that reason, the time for spiritual conversion had not [yet] come.

This excerpt shows that the vast region of snowy Tibet was a desolate land where not a single being of the human species existed. Further on in the text we read (Kan, 48, I):

At that time, in Lang-ka Pu-ri [Sri Lanka], the Country of the Ogres [Srin-po, Skt. Rākṣasa], [the king of the] Srin-po Lang-ka mGrin-bcu [Ten Necks, Skt. Rāvaṇa] and the king of the gods Ramaṇa were disputing over the goddess gZi-ldan-ma.

The monkey champion of the battle called Ha-nu-ma-da, disciple of a manifestation of Avalokiteśvara, went to Avalokiteśvara on the Potala Mountain. Avalokiteśvara said to the monkey, "Monkey, do you have the ability to meditate on the snow-covered rocky mountains of the north?"

The monkey replied, "Yes, I do have the ability to meditate in the rocky snow mountains of Tibet." Since he replied in that way, the sublime and greatly compassionate Avalokiteśvara taught him how to meditate on the abhorrence [of transmigration], conferred upon him the religious vows for laypeople,[13] gave him vast and profound religious instructions, and renaming him Monkey Bodhisattva [sPre'u Byang-chub Sems-dpa'], sent him to meditate in the snowy mountains of the north.

---

13   *dge bsnyen gyi sdom pa.* Laypeople can take vows for individual liberation [*so thar lugs*, Skt. *prātimokṣa*] in six different ways. They consist in taking only the vow of refuge, only one of the five vows, several vows, most of the vows, or all the vows, and the vow of chastity. [The vows for laypeople, apart from the refuge vow, consist in not killing, stealing, pursuing sexual misconduct, lying, and becoming intoxicated.]

That is how the Monkey Meditator Bodhisattva went to meditate in the snowy mountains after having received instructions from the sublime Avalokiteśvara. Then (Kan, 48, 13):

> The Monkey Meditator Bodhisattva arrived magically in the snowy northern region of Tibet. While he was meditating inside a cave [situated] in the middle of a gorge, a Crag-Demoness disguised as a monkey in female garments came to him; she exhibited her sexual organs, threw herself on the ground, gestured in a way that expressed desire, and went away. She behaved in that manner for the length of seven days; however, since Monkey was meditating on the abhorrence [of transmigration], he did not let her desire waver his mind.
>
> On the eighth day the Crag-Demoness, transformed into a ravishing fully adorned woman, came to him. Monkey watched her expose her sexual organs, make lustful signs, and throw herself on the ground; on that account, his meditation [altered as if a subtle] wind had blown through the cracks [in a wall].[14] He thought of bringing the iniquitous one under control, but remained doing nothing whatsoever.
>
> The Crag-Demoness said, "Let's get married, you and I." Monkey Meditator replied, "I am a religious devotee of the sublime and greatly compassionate Avalokiteśvara dBang-phyug Āryapalo; it would be improper for me to do so." The woman, who was the Crag-Demoness in disguise, said, "In that case, I will be furious with you; and if I die in that state, I will be reborn over and over again in the [three] bad rebirths of the lower realms of existence."
>
> Monkey Meditator thought, "If I get together with her, I will break my vows. If I don't, she will wander into the lower realms and that would constitute a heavy negative action." Therefore, considering that [refusing her] would amount to a debasement of [his] conduct as a Bodhisattva, Monkey Meditator generated loving-kindness. Nevertheless, although he stared at the face of the Crag-Demoness for an entire day, he was completely at a loss [as to what he was supposed to do].

---

14 *ser kar rlung 'jug:* this means that a slight thought breaches the state of peaceful contemplation like a subtle wind circulating inside the cracks on the surface of a wall.

Thus, the Crag-Demoness encouraged Monkey Meditator in all delicate and coarse ways to have intercourse with her. And also (Kan, 49, 17):

> Monkey realized that at that point he had to ask the sublime and greatly compassionate Avalokiteśvara Āryapalo for some advice, and magically transported himself to Mount Potala. When he arrived, he spoke to the sublime and greatly compassionate Āryapalo in this way, "Oh Sublime Āryapalo, I have gone to the snowy [region] and was meditating inside a cave [situated] in the middle of a gorge, when a Crag-Demoness appeared in front of me and said, 'Let's get married, you and I.' I ask, is that allowed or not?" The sublime Āryapalo said, "Do get married" and gave him three gifts. He [also] gave [him] five different varieties of grains and blessings for discovering mines of precious gems. Then He said, "Monkey Meditator, your sons and grandsons will become Buddhas." Also the venerable goddess Tārā, who was sitting in front of him, said, "Very good. Well done."

This is the way in which the Monkey Meditator Bodhisattva obtained a command from the greatly compassionate Avalokiteśvara and the sublime Tārā. Then, (Kan, 50, 11):

> Monkey Meditator, fearing that the Crag-Demoness would die, quickly returned to the gorge in Tibet by way of magical means and married [her] as promised. On the tenth moon, the Crag-Demoness generated a son who did not look like his father and did not look like his mother; he had no fur on his body nor a tail; his face was red, he consumed red meat as food and warm blood as beverage. Then both the child and the mother became hungry; therefore, in order that the child have something to eat, the father Monkey took him and carried him into the forest of the birds, leaving him in the company of the numerous monkeys that were living there.
>
> The following year, thinking, "What is that son of mine doing?" [he] went into the forest, and when he arrived and looked, [he saw] that restless[15] and lusty female monkeys had given birth to four hundred offspring. Also those children did

---

15 *dal rgyags byas*: an expression used to indicate lack of contentment even when the stomach is full and satiated.

not look like their grandfather Monkey Meditator. They did not look like their father either, nor like their monkey mothers. They did not have fur nor tails. They [apparently] did not know how to gather nourishment from the trees, since their red mouths were clean; [nonetheless,] they stayed there and [appeared] on the verge of dying. Grandfather Monkey Meditator felt loving-kindness for them; he collected fruits, nourished them, and just barely managed to save them.

This excerpt shows how the Monkey Meditator and the Crag-Demoness initiated the first human lineage of Tibet. And also (Kan, 52, 11):

The Sublime One said, "For what concerns those who have become your progeny, [there is] one [group among them that] forms the paternal line and one that represents the maternal line. Out of these two [groups of] descendants, those belonging to the paternal line have great faith, great respect, great loving-kindness, great wisdom, great diligence, and great tolerance. Fearless, they especially wish [to realize] the meaning of the profound dharma of Emptiness. They are not satisfied by the accumulation of a scant amount of merit, nor are they gratified by [performing] meager deeds of virtue. They possess a vast intelligence. Their hands are diligent and they create objects out of little stones and sticks. They are always gazing everywhere. They will become the lineage of those called the Bodhisattvas-Who-Have-A-Great-Mind. Their descendants will make the doctrine of the Teacher flourish and will perform the deeds of great Bodhisattvas.

As for those who belong to the maternal line, they have little faith, little respect, little loving-kindness, little wisdom, little diligence, little tolerance, great attachment, great animosity, great pride, great jealousy, and great ignorance. They do not like to be charitable. They like to eat red meat and drink warm blood. They concentrate on doing business and making profits. They like to speak in an arrogant voice. They hate to hear about their defects, but enjoy hearing about the short-comings of others. They hold themselves in high esteem and despise everyone else. They have little virtue. They are depraved. They have great physical strength and evil thoughts. They are unsuitable, difficult to tame. They will become the lineage of those called the Carnivorous-Lice-Eating-Barbarians. Nourish them. Protect them. I will also protect them; and by virtue of my protection, they will conquer the king[s] on the frontiers."

This excerpt shows the nature of the first Tibetan lineages. And also (Kan, 54, 1):

The greatly compassionate and sublime Avalokiteśvara said, "Monkey Meditator, the food to share among your sons, grandsons, and great-grandsons is this. Take it." Saying that, [Avalokiteśvara] took out five different types of grain: barley, wheat, unhusked rice, beans, and lentils. The Monkey Meditator, taking the five kinds of grains, looked in the direction of the snowy land of Tibet.

Then the Sublime One, holding a handful of gold dust, spoke thus, "Monkey Meditator, your sons, grandsons, and great-grandsons will have precious gold as their supreme support. From time to time, bypassing the various stages [of the Path], they will also become [perfectly realized] Bodhisattvas.

This indicates the mythic origin of grain farming in Tibet based upon Avalokiteśvara's gifts of five different grains to be shared as food and of gold to the first Tibetan lineages. And also (Kan, 55, 8):

Then, during the three summer months, [Monkey Meditator] went to the forest of the birds to attend to his sons and grandsons and to instruct them on how to plant the five different kinds of grains and on [the use of] the gold.

The five different kinds of grains grew and ripened quickly. Then [Monkey Meditator] said to his sons and grandsons, "Sons and grandsons, the food that the sublime and greatly compassionate Āryapalo has given you to share is this. Eat." Therefore, the four hundred children and grandchildren of Monkey Meditator were joyous. For the inhabitants [of this area] the place had come to be [known as] Yar-lungs Zo-thang [Food Valley].

Eating corn and the like, they found them delicious. They counted the number of grains on the stalks and [saw] thousands and thousands of seeds. For that reason [the place] is also called Yar-lungs Khri-thang [the Valley of a Thousand Seeds].

Then they took the most delicious ones and ate [them]; because of that, they were satisfied. They became playful and therefore had fun; for that reason [the place] came to be called Yar-lungs rTses-dang [the Valley of Amusement].

Furthermore, they ate the stalks of the grains. They became vigorous and started to race; for that reason [the place] came to be known as Yar-lungs 'Ol-kha rGyug-thang [the Valley of Racing].

The excerpt explains the manner in which the first Tibetan lineages started farming and how the various names referring to the place came to be, depending on the different events. And also (Kan, 56, 4):

Afterward the monkey children [started to] disagree with each other and fought. They were not afraid of one another and split into four groups. In this regard, the forefather Monkey Meditator examined his children, grandchildren, and great-grandchildren: he found that one group happened to have prominent noses [*sna ldong*], so he named them the Clan of the lDong. The lDong came to be known as the Eighteen Big Clans [Rus-chen-po bCo-brgyad].

The next group happened to have gaunt [literally, hollow, *stong*] cheeks, so he named them the Clan of the sTong. The sTong came to be known as [the Clan of] the Four Lords and Eight Servants [rJe-bzhi Khol-brgyad].

The next group happened to have grayish hair [*mgo se*], so he named them the Clan of the Se. The Se came to be known as [the Clan of those with] Many Eyes ['Jug-le sPyan-dgu].

The next group happened to have a dark [*smug*] lower part of the face, so he named them the Clan of the sMu. They came to be known as [the Clan of the] Eight Shrewd Ones [Ko-le'i 'Phra-brgyad].

lDong and sTong and Se and sMu were known to each other as the Four Original Clans [Mi'u-rigs-bzhi]: those were the first people of the snowy country of Tibet.

This clarifies how the first Tibetan generations disbanded and divided into four distinct main tribes. This explanation has definitely become the basis or foundation for the majority of historical narrations dealing with the rise and development of the Tibetan lineages.

Many other important documents, such as the *Ma ṇi bka' 'bum* and so on, contain narrations akin to the ones quoted above, but I think that the explanation in the *bKa' chems ka khol ma* excerpts offers a sufficient understanding of the basic viewpoint.

Accounts that relate how the first human lineages of Tibet descended from apes and monkeys or other kinds of similar sentient beings are perfectly acceptable. As a consequence of the mutation of different factors that affected the conditions of the world during long periods of time, the ancestors of humanity underwent many transformations in their shape, intellectual power, way of thinking, and so on, gradually emerging from the condition of animals into that of human beings. In fact, also a number of famed contemporary scientists endorse the theory according to which some kinds of beings similar to apes and monkeys would be the first ancestors of humanity. The history concerning those transformations and changes is a scientific explanation of the process underwent by the human species in primeval times. In that regard, the story maintaining that human beings as such appeared all at once, or that some of them partially completed their evolution as humans in some regions of the world but were generated as humans from monkeys and apes in other remote areas is completely unsustainable.

An example of that type of story is found in the *lHo chos 'byung blo gsar rna ba'i rgyan* ('Brug, 36, 18, 5) which says:

> In the male Iron Monkey year about a century after the *parinirvāṇa* of the Teacher in [a place where] the sea had gradually decreased and a forest of Sal trees[16] appeared, the monkey and the crag-demoness, emanations of Avalokiteśvara and Tārā, united in marriage in a rocky shelter of the Yar-klungs region. From the union of the father and the mother numerous offspring were generated. These [offspring] gradually turned into human beings and gave birth to the Tibetan generations.

The *rGya bod yig tshang chen mo* (Si, 122, 12) affirms:

---

16 [*Shorea robusta.*]

In early records we read as follows, "At first, there were no human beings in Tibet. [The country] was populated by a myriad of nonhuman beings ruled by Lord Srid-pa Phywa'i-mkhan-rje. Afterward [the country] was ruled by rMu-rje bTsan-po, by the demon Ma-tram Rutra, by the flesh-eating demon Yakṣa De-ba, and by the king of the Klu.

At that time in the Western Realm of Pure Bliss in the retinue of the Buddha of Infinite Light [Amitābha] was the best of Bodhisattvas, the sublime and glorious Avalokiteśvara. The Victorious Amitābha told him, 'In the eastern World of Endurance called 'Dzam-bu'i-gling a Tathāgata called Śākya Thub-pa has the intention of entering *nirvāṇa*.

In the past, the Wheel of Dharma has not been turned for the sentient beings of the snowy country of Tibet. Therefore, go [there], appeal to that Buddha, and see [to it] that he does not fulfill his intention [for the time being].'

The Sublime One went [as requested] and thus beseeched Buddha Śākya Thub-pa: 'I pray You to turn the Wheel of Dharma for the sentient beings of the snowy Tibet and to fulfill your intention [only] after you have done so.' The Buddha Śākya Thub-pa replied, 'Son of noble descent, the sentient beings of the Land of Snows are extremely difficult to tame because they are not yet ready to mature. Bodhisattvas like yourself will tame them in a future time.'

Immediately the Sublime returned to the Land of Pure Bliss and reported to the Victorious Amitābha what had been said. The latter proclaimed, 'Son of noble descent, in accordance with that, attract the hostile sentient beings of the Land of Snows by means of the four attitudes,[17] and having done that, in the end guiding them to this realm of Pure Bliss, come into my presence.'

Then the sublime, glorious, and greatly compassionate Avalokiteśvara arrived in 'Dzam-bu-gling, the World of Endurance. Facing the northern direction from the top of the Potala Mountain, [he] contemplated the liberation of the sentient beings of the Land of Snows, looking into the six parts of day and night. For what concerned the Land of Snows, [he

---

17 [Giving, speaking kindly, adapting to disciples' conditions, and acting congruently.]

saw that] it was the worst of the five or nine big regions of
'Dzam-bu'i-gling: the Buddha had not conquered it with his
lotus feet; the light rays of the Buddha's Word did not encom-
pass it; there was no Teaching; no beings to be tamed. It was
a total obscurity."

What is said here is repeated in the *bKa' chems ka khol ma*; also the majority of important Tibetan religious and dynastic histories, such as the
rGyal rabs gsal ba'i me long, and so on, hold this view.

The origins of the narrative can be deduced from the context of
the *Deb ther dpyid kyi rgyal mo'i glu dbyangs* where we read (Pe, 10, 12):

> Those viewpoints are taken from [the words of] the totally
> accomplished paṇḍita [Atiśa] Dīpaṃkara Śrījñāna [982-1054]
> that appear in the edict carved on the northern side of the
> pillar with a design of tree leaves around its capital [of the
> gTsug-lag-khang temple in Lhasa]. They have become wide-
> spread in the Land of Snows [through documents] such as
> the *Ma ṇi bka' 'bum* and so forth, in which the numerous cycles
> focused on Avalokiteśvara present the same idea, speaking [about
> the Tibetans] as the descendants of the carnivorous, red-faced
> children generated by the union of the Monkey and the Crag-
> Demoness.

If we examine the ideas expressed in the above-mentioned excerpts, it
appears that when the Buddha of the royal Śākya lineage was alive—a
little over 2,500 years ago according to the well-known School of the
Elders [Skt. Sthavira nikāya]—still no human beings existed in Tibet.
Then, the Bodhisattva Monkey Meditator and the Crag-Demoness
united in marriage; from their union, and only then, human beings
started to exist in the Land of Snows. This assumption contradicts
real knowledge. In this respect, I have written as follows in the *Bod kyi
lo rgyus las 'phros pa'i gtam nor bu'i do shal* (Dha, 2 ,9):

> When the Lotus-Holder Protector of the World [Avalokiteśvara]
> turned the Wheel of Dharma for the three lineages,[18] [he] prom-
> ised to convert the Land of Snows with as much kindness as
> possible.

---

18   [Śrāvakas, Pratyekabuddhas, and followers of the Mahāyāna path.]

Be that as it may, at a time when the cultures of Zhang Zhung, India, and China were all blooming, the old Tibetan monkey had not lost its tail and was lagging behind. What went wrong?

Even in these few words of comment one can see that the proposition is an illogical one.

This illogical proposition is not an erroneous account of the *Ka khol ma* and of the *Ma ṇi bka' 'bum*: it serves the purpose of establishing the authenticity of the viewpoint contained in the *Ka khol ma* and in the *Ma ṇi bka' 'bum*. It is possible that readers and students without a proper historical perspective wrongly interpreted the ideas contained in ancient documents that were copied one after the other over more than a thousand years; but it is also possible that the editors of those original documents planted the seeds of error by presenting as factual something that was not so.

The gist of the main topic contained in this kind of elaborate history is as follows: at a time when the Buddha was physically living in India, a ray of light beamed toward the north from the circle of hair between the eyebrows on the Teacher's forehead. When the sublime Avalokiteśvara or another of the several Bodhisattvas said to be present at Bodhgaya asked what was the reason for that phenomenon, the Buddha prophesied, "In the future the waters of the northern snowy region will decrease and a world [*snod*] will arise. There, from the descendants generated from the union of a monkey and a crag-demoness, emanations of yours, Bodhisattva Avalokiteśvara, and of the goddess Tārā, the Tibetan generations will gradually spread. They will exist as the sentient beings [*bcud*] [of that world].

When the [proper] conditions of that world and of its sentient beings are achieved, the Buddhadharma will flourish and develop in that region." A vast array of versions also explain how the sublime Avalokiteśvara made his promise in accordance with the Buddha's revelation and generated compassion.

If we grant veracity to the meaning of these basic points, we can discern that when the Teacher Buddha was alive in India, a ray of light beamed toward the north from the circle of hair between the eyebrows on the Teacher's forehead. When the sublime Avalokiteśvara asked the reason for that phenomenon, the Buddha made a prophecy saying that in ancient times the region of Tibet was covered with snow and water and that no human beings existed there. Subsequently, however, the Tibetan generations would be born from the union of a monkey and a crag-demoness, emanations of the Bodhisattva Avalokiteśvara and of the goddess Tārā; because of that, the auspicious circumstances for the future spreading and flourishing of the Buddhadharma in the Land of Snows would have been established and the land would have turned into the specific conversion field of Avalokiteśvara. The meaning of the prophecy must definitely be that, also since this interpretation would not be mistaken even from a historical viewpoint. Consequently, since the interpretations contained in the *bKa' khol ma* and in the *Ma ṇi bka' 'bum* do not transcend that framework, they automatically become exempt from all possible contradictions.

3. THE TIBETANS AS DESCENDANTS OF THE CHANG ETHNIC GROUP

The *rGya'i thang yig gsar rnying* [[Old and New Chronicles of the Chinese Táng 唐 dynasty] claim that the Tibetan race descended and developed from the ethnic group of the Chang [Chin. Qiāng 羌]. A meticulous examination of this topic is found in an article titled *Bod mi'i 'byung khungs che long tsam brjod pa* [A Preliminary Essay about the Origin of the Tibetan People] (*Bod ljongs zhib 'jug*, 1-1985), where we read (5, 3):

> The affirmation of contemporary scholars according to which the Tibetan people developed from the ethnic group of the Qiāng 羌 is based upon [information contained in Chinese sources such as] this: "At the time of the Eastern Han [Tung Han, Chin. Dōng Hàn 东汉] (25-220 CE) the Qiāng 羌 were looting the Hàn 汉 territories and the area around Lake Kokonor [mTsho-sngon]; for that reason, the Chinese emperor of the Hàn 汉 oppressed and massacred them in such an un- bearable and fearsome way that the survivors fled south and west. Some of them escaped to the lHa-sa region where they

developed the Qiāng 羌 lineage and established the so-called kingdom of Tǔbō 吐蕃 [Tib. Thu-bhod]."

Also the *rGya'i thang yig gsar rnying Chronicles*, concurring with the above statement, say that the Tibetan people descend from the Qiāng 羌. Some present day scholars have adhered to this viewpoint and we have seen a great increase in [the production of relevant] literature. However, since such a statement does not appear at all in Tibetan historical documents, how could it possibly be valid without a reliable textual and logical analysis?

This discourse reveals an unequivocal and pragmatic point: to say that at the time of the Chinese Hàn 汉 emperor there were still no human beings in the Tibetan dBus-gTsang area has no value beyond being an unrealistic pronouncement. If such an historical event had definitely taken place, it would have been totally impossible for the Tibetans not to know it and for Tibetan historical sources not to contain even a casual reference to it. The article continues (ibid., 5, 18):

> Moreover, not only were there numerous human beings in the Tibetan region at the time of the Chinese emperor of the Eastern Hàn [Dōng Hàn 东汉, Tung Han], but also Tibetans existed even before then, as it is stated in the *'Dul ba lung* and in the *Dus 'khor*. Tibet existed also at the time of Buddha Śākyamuni.

The truth of what the article's author affirms can be appraised in greater detail by reading the Early Period volume of *The Light of Kailash* trilogy where I discuss the rise of the generations of ancient Zhang Zhung [Chapter I] and the Intermediate Period volume where I discuss the royal lineages of ancient Tibet [Chapter III].

In addition, some ancient historical writings from Burma ['Bar -ma] relate that the first Burmese generations originated from people who descended to the valley areas from the high mountains of Tibet; that is proven by the presence in the Burmese language of not a few Tibetan archaic terms, some of which are still in use at present. If all this evidence is properly examined, it can indeed be established that the Tibetan race is not a race that materialized at approximately the time of the Chinese Hàn 汉 emperors, but rather, is a very old one. Moreover, we read (ibid., 5, 26):

> Even if we assume that the Qiāng 羌, who fled at the time of the Eastern Hàn [Dōng Hàn 东汉], arrived in dBus-gTsang as soon as political authority was restored in the year 25 CE, not only did a Tibetan kingdom already exist in Tibet then, but also, a long time had elapsed since the arrival of King gNya'-khri bTsan-po in Tibet (Wood Mouse year, 417 BCE). Unless those refugees had paid homage to the king of Tibet and become his subjects, there would have been no way for the Thu-bhod [Tŭbō 吐蕃] kingdom, which turned into a Tibetan lineage as a development of the Qiāng 羌 ethnicity, to establish itself a little before the year 200 CE.
>
> The Qiāng 羌 who fled at the time of the Chinese Hàn 汉 emperors sought refuge and settled in the areas of present day Yúnnán 云南, Sìchuān 四川, Gānsù 甘肃, and Qīnghǎi 青海. The branch of the Qiāng 羌 who fled to Gānsù 甘肃 (also known as Lǒngxī 陇西) occupied that territory.
>
> Then, in the year 384 CE, during the time of the Eastern Jìn [Tun Cin] (Dōng Jìn 东晋 [317-420 CE]) dynasty, a state [of Qiāng 羌 ethnicity] called Chin (Qín Guó 秦国) was also founded; its dynasty ruled for a period of thirty years [until 417 CE].
>
> Additionally, the Qiāng 羌 who fled to the Qīnghǎi 青海 area encountered the tribes ruled by the so-called Bud-med Thang-mo [Amazons]. These tribes started to fight the Qiāng 羌 with frightening military force. It is said that the Qiāng 羌 then fled to Zong-cu (Sōngjiě 松解, which corresponds to Song-phan County [Sōngpān Xiàn 松潘县] of present day Sìchuān Province [Sìchuān Shěng 四川省]). There is not the slightest mention of [the Qiāng 羌] escaping in the direction of Central Tibet [dBus-gTsang]. Nevertheless, the fact that also some contemporary scholars agree in identifying the so-called Western Qiāng 羌 [Tib. Nub Chang] territory precisely with present day dBus-gTsang is inconceivable.
>
> Even if it is true that at the time of the Eastern Hàn [Dōng Hàn 东汉], the areas that are now called Gānsù 甘肃 and

Qīnghǎi 青海 were called 'the West,' the area of Western Qiāng 羌 [Xī Qiāng 西羌] was not called dBus-gTsang. Why? Because at that time the Qiāng Róng 羌戎 [Chang Rong] were called the Western Qiāng [Tib. Nub Chang] (Xī Qiāng 西羌); sometimes the Western Qiāng 羌 (Xī Qiāng 西羌) were also known as Zhis Rong (Xī Róng 西戎) or [simply] Róng (戎). Since those who were called Western Qiāng 羌 were the Qiāng Róng 羌戎, it is not logically viable to maintain that the Western Qiāng 羌 [area] referred to Tibet and that the Tibetan people descended from the Qiāng 羌 lineage, because that is a distorted, prejudiced representation.

This quotation clarifies that the Central Tibetan [dBus-gTsang] lineages do not descend from the Qiāng 羌. The actual meaning of the word *chang* is *byang* [north]. The article entitled *Mi nyag gi skor rags tsam gleng ba* [General discussion about Mi-nyag] (*Bod ljongs zhib 'jug*, 3-1986) says (5, 21):

> The tribes of Tibetan descent separated into three main groups: Bod, Byang, and lHo. The Tibetans called Byang-pa the tribes who lived in the northern part of Tibet; those living in the southern part were called lHo-pa. It is known that the Byang-pa and lHo-pa tribes did not call themselves Byang and lHo, but simply used their own names. Because the Central Tibetans pronounced the word *byang* (*zhang*) like *chang*, the Chinese adopted the sound *chang* (Qiāng 羌) as the main one in their historical writings, even though the meaning of the word is *byang* [that is, north].

This excerpt shows that the meaning of the words *chang* and *byang* is one [north]; similarly, it is easy to understand that also the words *rong* and *lho*, even if they are combined in different ways, mean the same thing [south]. For what concerns the words *byang* and *rong*, in an article entitled *Byang gi 'byung khungs la dpyad pa'i thog ma'i bsam tshul* [Preliminary Ideas for an Analysis of the Origins of the Byang], (*Bod ljongs zhib 'jug*, 2-1986) we read (69, 4):

> Because the terms *byang* (qiāng 羌) and *rong* (róng 戎) date back to the time of the ancient Chinese dynasties of the Shāng 商 [c. 1600-c. 1046 BCE] and the Zhōu 周 [c. 1045-256 BCE]

and the term *byang* was found even on Chinese bone inscriptions, one could ask if these two different names indicate [distinct] lineages of the Byang and the Rong. The answer is no.

The Chronicles of the Hàn 汉 say, "The Byang (Qiāng 羌) are an ordinary [group of] people of Western Rong (Nub Rong, Xī Róng 西戎)."

The Venerable Ku'u-cas-kang said, "Western Byang and Western Rong are general names."

The *sNyug byang la bkod pa'i lo tshigs* says, "As for the Spring and Autumn period [Chūnqiū Shídài 春秋 时代, 770-476 BCE] and that of the Warring States [Zhànguó Shídài 战国 时代, 475-221 BCE], since those were times during which the Western Rong were requesting much bigger disbursements, the western troops had to interrelate with them; as a consequence of that, the Byang and Rong became known as 'Western Rong' [Nub Rong]." These elements prove in a straightforward manner that [Nub Rong] is the name of the same lineage as the Byang and Rong, or, alternatively, that it is a synonym referring to the same ethnic group.

The excerpt indicates that although the terms *byang* and *rong* are distinct, in reality they are simply different designations for the same ethnic group. Furthermore, we read (ibid., 69, 21):

> The name Rong gradually became less and less popular with the passing of time, while the designations Byang and Ded Byang (Dī Qiāng 氏羌) became renowned.
>
> In ancient times, Byang and Ded Byang were the names of a tribal group belonging to the Rong. Later on, the power of the Byang tribal group reached its zenith, and because they were always at war with the Chinese, when the name of the Byang tribe became widespread in China, it was recorded as such in historical documents.
>
> A similar example is that of the Ded Byang (Dī Qiāng 氏羌) of the sBal-lung gTsang-po [River] lineage of Cal-ling in Upper gTsang [gTsang-stod]: at the beginning of the Hàn 汉 dynasty, they were called Bod-mi-byang (Bái Mǎ Qiāng 白马羌); during the time of the Western Jìn [Jin Nub-ma, Xī Jìn

西晋, 265-316 AD], they were called Bod-mi'i-ded (Bái Mǎ Qiāng 白马枪 [sic]).

The Chinese characters 'pe ma' [bái mǎ] are used to reproduce the words 'bod mi' [Tibetan people]; [but] the way in
which those characters are pronounced in the Chinese spoken
language is [only] partially accurate. It is possible to understand
this point by comparing the way in which the words 'bod mi'
are pronounced in the lHa-sa and A-mdo dialects: in the lHasa dialect, the words are pronounced 'bod mi;' in the A-mdo
dialect, they sound more or less like 'pod mis.'

As for the way in which the designation Byang was known to the
Chinese people, the article says (ibid., 78, 7):

The Historical Records of the Chin Dynasty [清朝 Qīng
Cháo, 1644-1912] say, "Tibet consists of [the territories of]
the Tibetan region proper [Bod-ljongs], Qīnghǎi 青海, Sìchuān
四川, Gānsù 甘肃, and Yúnnán 云南. In that respect a distinction is made between the Byang nationality (Qiāng zú 羌族)
[Byang-rigs] and the lHo nationality (Luò zú 落族) [lHo-rigs].

In Tibetan, 'Byang' (Qiāng 羌) means 'the tribes of the
north', while 'lHo' (Luò 落) means 'the tribes of the south.'"

One is thus able to understand that Byang (Qiāng 羌) is the
name of a tribal group of northern Tibet. Rong and Byang are
the names of a tribal group that descends from a single lineage;
they are not names of distinct ethnic groups.

The quotation shows how even in China the words Byang and lHo
were known from earlier times as the names of tribal groups of Tibetan
nationality. Likewise, we read (ibid., 79, 4):

After gNya'-khri bTsan-po, the first of the Tibetan kings, arrived
[in Tibet] to be the ruler of Bod-ka g.Yag-drug, the name of
that little kingdom was known as Bod. Later on, when all the
land and people of Tibet were brought under control by his
descendants, 'Bod' gradually became the general name for the
country, so Byang and Rong, the names of some tribal groups
or people inside the kingdom called Bod, gradually became
less popular.

Before the word Bod was used, the name of our country was
Rong and Byang. When the name Bod became a general name

for the country, due to the fact that also [the names] Byang and Rong gradually lost their acclaim, the Chinese recognized [in those names] an isolated ethnic group. That is why these days the Byang are considered as an ethnic group distinct from the Tibetan one. Thinking about it, one can clearly understand that such a distinction is a historical contradiction.

There exist also other ethnic groups, such as the 'Jang (Nàxī zú 纳西族), the lHo-pa, the Mon-pa, the Shar-pa, the sTeng-pa, and so on; historically speaking, they are Tibetans. Today, however, they are classified as different nationalities. Such a distinction is a bewildering one.

Similarly, also the Khams-pa, the A-mdo-ba, the gTsang-pa, the dBus-pa, the rTse-pa, the lHa-sa-ba, and so on, are unquestionably classified as different groups, although their names bear the same connotation as the previous ones: the lHo-pa are Tibetans who live in the south; the Mon-pa are Tibetans who live in Mon-yul; the Shar-pa are Tibetans who live in the east; the sTeng-pa are Tibetans who live in Upper Tibet. I want to ask why, on what basis, are such distinctions made?

These words represent the eloquent elucidation of a knowledgeable scholar who is serious and competent. As far as I am concerned, I agree one hundred percent with what he says.

The reason for my agreement that what this scholar says is right is before our eyes: in the past, all ethnic groups of the world have experienced many sorts of different situations under diverse spatiotemporal circumstances, and Tibet has not been an exception in that respect. For example, it is difficult to understand the conditions of the Rong and Byang during the Early Period in comparison with the prominent history of Zhang Zhung. We only know that, most probably, Sum-pa and 'A-zha existed at that time.

During the Intermediate Period, Zhang Zhung and Tibet separated. The Twelve Minor kings [rGyal-phran bCu-gnyis] and the Forty Principalities [Sil-ma bZhi-bcu], which had appeared and become known in former times, were successively placed under Tibet's rule. A new kingdom, that of Tibet, came into being.

During the Later Period, apart from the Rong, the Byang, and all the people who were living in Tibetan areas under Tibet's rule, there were also other non-Tibetan ethnic groups in many localities and regions, such as Xīnjiāng (新疆) and so on, who became Tibetan subjects. For that reason the political influence of Tibet experienced a time of expansion which is confirmed by an array of old historical sources.

Nevertheless, when the power of the Tibetan kings disintegrated, the Tibetan territory was split among several Tibetan ethnic groups. The link among the peoples became progressively smaller and weaker due to the extension of the territory. In present times, however, Tibetans of most areas can understand each other's speech and writing, representing a unifying factor for them. Awareness of this circumstance is priceless; and that [possibility] is something to be grateful for.

On the other hand, in some regions with peculiar [geo-political] characteristics Tibetan ethnic groups representing the minority of the population lost awareness of their invaluable cultural history because for hundreds of years they were not able to adequately interact with the rest of the Tibetan people and because the only language used was the local idiom. Consequently, they were identified not only as non-Tibetan ethnic groups, but also were regarded as backward people of a primitive nature who did not even possess a written language of their own.

In the meantime, many localities known in antiquity as Zhang Zhung Phug-pa, the region situated at the western border of Tibet, fell under the dominion of Kashmir; their inhabitants were never converted to the ancient Bon tradition, nor were they affected by the subsequent spread of Buddhism. Under the influence of the Kashmiri language and religious system, they became separated from other Tibetans and lost their connection with them. Since this state of affairs continued for many centuries, those people are now not considered Tibetans. Besides, many other Tibetan groups who were living on the western Tibetan border in what was formerly a region of ancient Tibet have undergone similar astonishing changes and have been integrated with the peoples of Russia, Afghanistan, and Pakistan, once cradle of the ancient country of O-rgyan [Skt. Oḍḍiyāna].

Ethnic groups or nationalities are recognized on the basis of the human rights accorded them. From a certain viewpoint, the explanations given for their classification are correct and constructive. Those explanations are applicable as long as one is dealing with an actual ethnic group that existed from ancient times, but are not at all suited for those who are not certain of their historical and cultural foundations.

However, when an ethnic group is fully aware of its history and qualifications, it deserves such a designation, regardless of its dimension and degree of development. In that regard, it is indeed totally correct and thoroughly constructive to recognize a nationality by respecting and paying attention to its history and culture and by preserving its assets and promoting its diversity.

From another viewpoint, it is not correct and constructive to do so: it is not merely incorrect and counterproductive, under the pretense of respecting their rights, to identify people such as the Zhang Zhung Phug-pa who were completely cut off and separated from their main group for several centuries, or people such as the lHo-pa, Mon-pa, Shar-pa, and sTeng-pa who became ignorant of their own history and culture because they lost their connection, as different from the Tibetan nationality; or else, to regard people of the present time, with more than 3,900 years of history, as backward and primitive, alien to their own culture, and even deprived of a written language. If perpetrated, such an approach would also become dangerous in that it could elicit the entire destruction of small ethnic groups.

II

Identifying the Bon Lineages
of Tibet in the Later Period

E ver since the Buddhist historical perspective became predominant
in Tibet, a variety of opinions have emerged about the origins of
the Tibetan Bon traditions.

1. REVEALED BON, DERIVED BON, TRANSFORMED BON

One of those opinions is remarkable in its own right. It was formulated by the 'Bri-gung master 'Jig-rten mGon-po [1143-1217] in his
'Jig rten mgon po'i gsung bzhi bcu pa, a treatise which is part of the *dGongs
gcig* collection (Bir, Vol. I, 291, 20, 1):

> There have been three traditions of Bon: the first is the Bon
> 'revealed' by gShen-rab Mi-bo [*rdol bon*]; the second is the Bon
> 'derived' from the bad theories of the extremists [*'khyar ba'i bon*];
> the third is the Bon 'transformed' by evil spirits with the intent
> of destroying the [Buddhist] Teachings [*bsgyur ba'i bon*].
>
> Concerning the first, at the time of Khri-lde bTsan-po—the
> sixth ruler of the dynasty founded by Lord gNya'-khri bTsan-
> po—in a place called Ngam-shod-'on of dBus, a thirteen-year-
> old boy who belonged to the gShen clan was carried off by
> spirits and for thirteen years was transported to all the regions
> of Tibet. When he was twenty-six, he was brought back among
> human beings.

Owing to the power of nonhuman beings, he had obtained
the capacity of knowing what kind of deity or spirit inhabited
a given place, what kind of benefit or harm they could do,
and all the ways in which rituals for making offerings and for
relinquishing ritual substances had to be performed.

He took Khri-lcam, the daughter of Kong-rje dKar-po, as
his wife, but she was abducted by a disciple. Since he had not
[duly] analyzed [circumstances], the three karmic enemies [las
kyi dgra gsum] arose: not having [duly] examined his disciples,
one of them became the karmic enemy who stole his wife. Not
having [duly] examined his wife, she became the karmic enemy
who abandoned him. Not having [duly] examined his friends,
the bTsan Ya-ba rKya-cig became the karmic enemy who suppressed the old Bon, tore his drum and broke his bell [shang].
However, he [gShen-rab Mi-bo] knew the life-essence [mantra]
of the gTsang bTsan, practiced it, and displayed its efficacy.

This episode, the one related to the construction of the
palace of Sham-po lHa-rtse, and other events are said to be
described in detail in the dhāraṇī pertaining to the practice of
the gTsang bTsan.

Afterward, when King Gri-gum bTsan-po was murdered by
his subject Long-ngam rTa-rdzis, [gShen-rab Mi-bo] was invited
to perform the funerary ritual for the dead [gri gshid]. But he
is reported to have said, "Even though my Bon teachings are
diversified, they can be classified into three [categories]: [ritu-
als for] suppressing evil spirits below; rituals for worshipping
the ancestral deities above; and rituals to defend the domestic
hearth in the middle. Apart from those, I do not possess other
teachings. Hence I do not know how to perform the funerary
rituals for the dead." These teachings are also known as the Bon
of the Cause [rgyu bon] and as the Black Waters [chab nag]. They
are all Revealed Bon [rdol bon].

As for the second tradition called Derived Bon ['khyar ba'i
bon]—because it is derived from the poor theories of the extremists—Bon texts say that in the beginning there was the emptiness
of primordial Nonbeing from which Primordial Being came
somewhat into existence; then whitish frost formed and so on;
and finally, Existence was created from an egg through a creative

act of the gods of the Phya, dBang-phyug [Īśvara], and so on. All these are derived from the theories of the extremist followers of dBang-phyug. The philosophical view of the eternalists is the basis from which the four abominable practices derived: conquering wild spirits [*rgod 'dur ba*][19] and other kinds of funerary practices; the ability to handle searing iron[20] and to cut iron with bird feathers; divine responses,[21] *ju thig* [divination], and scapulimancy;[22] and the sacrifice of sheep and horses.

Since gShen-rab Mi-bo did not know how to perform funerary practices for the death of King Gri-gum bTsan-po who was assassinated [*gri bshid*], three Bon-pos from Kha-che, Brusha, and Zhang Zhung were invited in order to perform them. One of them, as a result of his practice of Ge-khod, Khyung, and Me-lha [Fire Deity], displayed the powers of flying in the sky riding a drum, handling scorching iron, cutting iron with bird feathers, and so on. One of them, by practicing the *ju thig* and *lha bka'* divinations and scapulimancy [*sogs (sic) dmar*], could distinguish good from bad. One of them knew how to perform various kinds of funerary rituals, such as those for liberating the deceased person from obstacles [*gshin po 'dur ba*] and for appeasing the spirit of murdered people [*gri 'dul*], and so on. Before they arrived, Bon did not have a philosophical view, but from then on, a Bon philosophical view based upon worshipping deities, conquering Sri spirits, and so on took hold.

Thus, as a result of the negative karma matured through the cult of deities, spirits, and demons as well as through wrong views, the followers of this Bon accumulated impure causes. These are all Derived Bon [*'khyar ba'i bon*].

---

19 *rgod 'dur ba*: funerary practices for conquering wild spirits polluted by death and for recollecting the soul, consciousness, and mind of the deceased person in order to transfer him or her to a happy condition.

20 *gtar ba len pa*: a sign of accomplishment of mantric power.

21 *lha bka'*: oracular trance associated with important Phywa deities such as Phuwer, involving practitioners of those deities or boys and girls of good ancestry.

22 *sog dmar*: a type of divination which reveals good or bad omens based on the shape of cracks produced on the shoulder blades of sheep burned in a fire. [See Volume One, Chapter V, pp. 199-202.]

The third aspect, Transformed Bon [*bsgyur ba'i bon*], consists of three phases: the first transformation, the intermediate transformation, and the final transformation.

The first transformation: [it is said that] the Paṇḍita Sham-sngon-can was punished by King Indrabodhi for his lustful behavior, so the Paṇḍita decided to harm the Buddhist teachings. In order to do that, he mingled in a malevolent spirit with the Buddhists, became the king's officiating Bla-ma, and maintained that if monks were beheaded they would obtain the fruit of enlightenment. He then transformed many Buddhist teachings into Bon ones and concealed them near a reliquary belonging to the king.

[The second transformation:] at the time of the sovereign Khri-srong lDe'u-btsan, Slob-dpon Padma and other paṇḍitas and translators as well as ministers who favored Buddhist doctrines such as mGos-rgan occupied the right row [at court], while the Bon-pos, such as gShen Dran-pa Nam-mkha', Khyung-po Dun-tse, and others, together with the [ministers who were] supporters of Bon—such as Ngam sTag-ra Glu-gong and others—occupied the left row.

The king, seated in the middle, commanded that [the two groups] perform a debate. The Buddhists won. Later on the king said, "Compete with your magical powers." Everyone gathered around the corpse of Ngam sTag-ra Glu-gong to perform the funerary rituals. gShen Dran-pa Nam-mkha' summoned the soul of the deceased and brought the minister back to life. He said, "This is the power that Bon-pos have." [Seeing that,] the king conveyed the implication to the Teacher [Slob-dpon Padmasambhava] that he was not the only powerful one. The Teacher asked, "Does the king [really] believe [that]?" The king replied, "I believe it very much, since the minister is actually here."

[Then] the Teacher blocked [the ghost] with a hand gesture and forced him to answer his questions. [The ghost said, "I answered] correctly every time, but did not know [his] secret name. At that point the Teacher expelled me with the force of the *vajra*." The Bon-pos were humiliated. The king realized that [their power] was not stable and resolved to tender obeisance to the teachings of Slob-dpon.

The king said, "They [the Buddhists] have won the debate; [they have shown that] their magical power is greater [than yours]. You do not possess the knowledge of ultimate enlightenment; they do. Now everyone will follow the Buddhadharma." Then he said to rGyal-ba Byang-chub, "You will go and listen to the Buddhadharma from Ācārya Rin-chen-mchog." But rather than listening to Rin-chen-mchog's teachings, rGyal-ba Byang-chub said, "I prefer to read books" and refused to comply. The king punished him with exile.

rGyal-ba Byang-chub, angered, joined the Bon-pos and transformed some of the Tathāgata's teachings into Bon. He substituted gShen-rab Mi-bo for Sangs-rgyas bCom-ldan-'das [Bhagavān Buddha]; *bon* for *chos* [*dharma*]; *bon sku* for *chos sku* [*dharmakāya*]; Yum-chen-mo Sa-tri E-sang [*sic*] for Yum-chen-mo Shes-rab-kyi Pha-rol-tu Phyin-ma [Mahāmātṛ Prajñāpāramitā]; Kun-tu bzang-po for *longs sku* [*sambhogakāya*]; gShen-lha 'Od-dkar for Vairocana [rNam-par sNang-mdzad]; Srid-pa Sangs-po 'Bum-khri for *sprul sku* [*nirmāṇakāya*]; Ye gshen for Sangs rgyas [Buddha]; gShen sras for dGra-bcom [Arhat]; gTo-bu 'Bum-sras [*sic*][23] for Sha-ri'i-bu [Śāriputra], Yid-kyi Khye'u-chung for Me'u 'Gal-gyi-bu [Maudgalyāyana], Rig-pa'i Khye'u-chung for Kun-dga'-bo [Ānanda], Te'u-tong for sGra-gcan-'dzin [Rāhula], gSal-ba 'Od-ldan for Rab-'byor [Subhūti], g.Yung-drung Sems-dpa' for Byang-chub Sems-dpa' [Bodhisattva], Bya-ru-can brgyad for Sems-dpa' brgyad [the Eight Bodhisattvas],[24] *bon gab-pa* [hidden Bon] for *rdzogs pa chen po*, dBal-gyi Phur-nag for rDo-rje Phur-ba [Vajrakīlaya], gTsug-gshen rGyal-ba for Slob-dpon 'Phags-pa

---

23   [That is, gTo-bu 'Bum-sangs. According to the Bon tradition, gShen-rab Mi-bo-che, the founder of the Everlasting Bon (g.Yung-drung Bon) manifested himself as four different teachers: gTo-bu 'Bum-sangs, a teacher of rituals, was one of them. The historical Buddha was a member of this group as well.]

24   [According to the *Dharmasaṅgrahaḥ* (Excellent Collection of Doctrines), a short text on Buddhist terminology attributed to the philosopher Nāgārjuna, these are: Maitreya, Gaganagañja (Treasure of the Sky or Thunder of the Sky) or, according to other sources, Maitreya, Avalokiteśvara, and Samantabhadra, Vajrapāṇi, Mañjuśrī, Sarvanīvaraṇaviṣkambhī (Eliminator of All Obscurations), Kṣitigarbha (Essence of the Earth), and Khagarbha (Essence of the Sky).]

[Ācārya Āryadeva], dBal-bon sTag-la Me-'bar for Slob-dpon
Padma [Ācārya Padma], and so on, transforming as many other
words as possible. When the King heard about that, he ordered
all those beheaded who had transformed the teachings of the
Buddha into Bon. Since many encountered this fate, the Bon-pos,
terrified, concealed the transformed texts, including incomplete
ones, in secret locations. Afterward these concealed texts came
to be known as Bon[-po] treasure texts [gter ma].

The final transformation occurred at a later date when the
remnants of the Buddhist teachings were undergoing a revival
in Eastern Tibet [mDo-smad]. In the Upper Nyang region of
gTsang, [a Bon-po] named gShen-sgur Klu-dga',[25] having spent a
long time cultivating a friendly relation with the caretaker of the
Chu-mig Ring-mo Temple, offered [him] a huge recompense and
transformed the place into a Bon center called Dar-yul sGro-lag.

There he transformed the rGyas pa [the long version of
the Prajñāpāramitā] into the Khams chen; the Nyi shu rtsa lnga
pa [the 25,000 verse version of the Prajñāpāramitā] into the
Khams chung;[26] the gTan la phab pa series [of the twelve sections
of Buddha's precepts] into the Bon Sūtra series [Bon mdo]; and
the Five Dhāraṇī Series [gZungs sde lnga] into the 100,000 Black,
White, and so forth Klu [cycle] [Klu 'bum dkar nag khra gsum]. He
concealed the transformed texts in a white rock at mTsho-lnga
Dre'u-chung. Later he retrieved them, pretending he had discovered them. Having incurred all sorts of misfortunes, [eventually]
he died and his body was torn to pieces. Until now, Bon-pos
like Khyung-po Bon-zhig[27] and others have not ceased to pla-
giarize [Buddhist texts]. These [traditions] are the Transformed
Bon [bsgyur ba'i bon].

---

25 [gShen-chen Klu-dga' or gShen-sgur Klu-dga' (Crooked gShen) (996-1035)
is considered the leading textual discoverer (gter ston) of the entire Bonpo tradition, although he was not the first one. His discoveries took place in 1017. He
was called Crooked, because according to a story he related about his life, his
body became crooked when he was eighteen years old.]
26 [These two texts are, respectively, the long and middle-length versions of the
Bonpo Prajñāpāramitā.]
27 [Bon-zhig Khyung-nag (1103-1183) is considered a manifestation of Dran-
pa Nam mkha' and of a teacher who received textual transmissions from the
female deity-protector Srid-pa'i rGyal-mo.]

> The Transformed Bon [in its] earlier, intermediate, and later [phases] is called the White Waters [*chab dkar*] and Bon of the Fruit [*'bras bu'i bon*].

As the excerpt shows, all Bon teachings were classified under the three categories of Revealed Bon [*rdol bon*], Derived Bon [*'khyar ba'i bon*], and Transformed Bon [*bsgyur ba'i bon*]. Revealed Bon would have appeared at the time of the Tibetan king Gri-gum; Derived Bon, even if the time frame of its origin is not explicitly mentioned, presumably originated from the Shaivist traditions which were greatly widespread in India. As for the three phases of Transformed Bon, the first indicated is the one carried out by Paṇḍita Sham-sngon-can; the second transformation, even if the real initiator is not specified, involved rGyal-ba Byang-chub and other Bon-pos. The third transformation named is that carried out by gShen Klu-dga' and Khyung-po Bon-zhig.

Since 'Bri-gung sKyobs-pa 'Jig-rten mGon-po was a highly important Tibetan scholar who lived during the years 3060-3134 of the first *sMe-phreng* of the eighteenth *sMe-'khor* (1143-1217), Tibetan historians who came after him adhered to and adopted his views about Bon. This is especially true for Thu'u-bkwan [Blo-bzang Chos-kyi Nyi-ma, 1737-1802], who reproduces 'Jigs-rten mGon-po's account almost verbatim in his *Grub mtha' shel gyi me long*—except for condensing certain passages and calling Revealed Bon *'jol bon* instead of *rdol bon* (Kan, 380, 9):

> The three [kinds of] Bon that became widespread in Tibet were Revealed Bon [*'jol bon*], Derived Bon [*'khyar bon*], and Transformed Bon [*bsgyur bon*].
>
> The first one [Revealed Bon, *'jol bon*]: at the time of Khri-lde bTsan-po—the sixth ruler of the dynasty founded by gNya'-khri bTsan-po—in a place called dBus-sam Shang-'on [*sic*], a thirteen-year-old boy who belonged to the gShen clan was [abducted] by spirits [and] for thirteen years was taken to all the regions of Tibet. When he was twenty-six he was brought back among humans. Owing to the power of nonhuman beings, he was able to say what kind of deity or spirit inhabited a given place, what kind of benefit or harm they could do, and which rituals for offerings and for relinquishing ritual substances would be good to perform.

Although dynastic histories that cover the period from gNya'-khri bTsan-po to the twenty-sixth dynasty of Khri-rje Thog-btsan do not say anything about Bon except that it was predominant in the country, evidently the beginning of the diffusion of Bon in Tibet started from there. Nevertheless, the Bon-pos of that time—apart from [rituals for] suppressing evil spirits below, rituals to worship the ancestral deities above, and rituals to defend the domestic hearth in the middle—did not have a defined philosophical view.

Some religious and dynastic histories say that the diffusion of Bon started from the time of Gri-gum bTsan-po. These [traditions] are also known as the Bon of the Cause [rgyu'i bon] [and] as the Black Waters [chab nag].

The second [transformation], Derived Bon ['khyar bon]: since the Tibetan Bon-pos did not know how to perform funerary practices [to allay] the slaying [gri gshin] of King Gri-gum bTsan-po, three Bon-pos from Ka-che, Bru-sha, and Zhang Zhung were invited to perform them.

One of them, as a result of his practice of Ge-khod, Khyung, and the Me-lha [Fire Deity], displayed the powers of flying in the sky riding a drum, handling searing iron, cutting iron with bird feathers, and so on.

One of them, by practicing Ju thig and lHa ka [sic] divination and scapulimancy [sog dmar], could determine good from bad.

One of them knew how to perform various kinds of funerary rituals, such as those for liberating the deceased person from obstacles [gshin po 'dul ba], for appeasing the spirit of the murdered [gri 'dul], and so on.

Before their arrival, Bon did not have a definite philosophical view, but from then on, a Bon-po philosophical view, said to be a blend derived from extremist Shaivist doctrines, took hold.

The third aspect of Transformed Bon [bsgyur bon] is three-fold. The first transformation is said to have been carried out by Paṇḍita Sham-thabs sNgon-po-can who combined Buddhist teachings with Bon-po ones, concealed them all, and then re-trieved them.

The second intermediate transformation: at the time of Khri-srong lDe'u-btsan it was decreed that the Bon-pos had to convert to Buddhism. rGyal-ba'i [sic] Byang-chub was requested to attend and listen to the teachings of Rin-chen-mchog, but he refused to do so. Because the king punished him, he, angered, joined the Bon-pos and transformed into Bon some of the Tathāgata's teachings. The king, hearing that, ordered the beheading of all those who had transformed the teachings of the Tathāgata in Bon. Since many heads fell, the Bon-pos were terrified and concealed the transformed texts, including incomplete ones, in secret locations. Afterward, the concealed texts were brought to light and were said to be Bon[-po] treasure texts [gter ma].

The third and final transformation: after [King] Lang-dar[-ma] [died 842 CE] suppressed the Buddhadharma, at Nyang-stod in gTsang in a Bon-po center called Dar-yul sGro-lag, a certain gShed-rgur Klu-dga' [sic] co-opted many of Buddha's teachings, claiming them as Bon-po doctrine: [for example] he renamed the Khams chen series the Yum [sic] rGyas pa; the Khams chung series, the Nyi shu lnga pa [sic]; the gTan la phab pa series, the Bon Sūtras [Bon mdo]; and the Five Dhāranī Series, the 100,000 Black and White Klu [cycle] [Klu 'bum dkar nag]. He altered various other Buddhist technical terms and expressions and having done so, concealed the texts in the rock of Tsho-lnga 'Bri'u-chung [sic]. Later on he retrieved them, pretending he had discovered them.

After him, also Khyung-po Bon-zhig and other Bon-pos appropriated many [Buddhist texts] in the same way. The Transformed Bon [in its] earlier, intermediate, and later [phases] is called the White Waters [chab dkar] and Bon of the Fruit ['bras bu'i bon].

The lHo brag chos 'byung says (Pe, Vol. I, 164, 8):

At 'On in the dBus region in the place of the gShen called Bon-mo Lung-ring, a boy of the gShen clan had donkey ears. At twelve he was abducted by spirits, and for twelve years met no human beings. When he returned after twelve years, he knew everything about autochthonous spirits and how to worship them. In order to hide his donkey ears he wore a woolen turban. Thus, Revealed Bon [rdol bon], the cult of spirits, spread.

This excerpt is based on sKyobs-pa 'Jigs-rten mGon-po's *gSungs bzhi bcu pa*; although the author uses the term *rdol bon*, in reality, this and the so-called *'jol bon* described in the *Shel gyi me long* have the same meaning. There are no other major discrepancies in the *mKhas pa'i dga' ston*'s version, except for the fact that the boy with donkey ears is one year younger and his abduction lasts one year less. The learned sKyobs-pa 'Jigs-rten mGon-po does not reveal the source of his account. Perhaps he put into writing the hearsay of some aged Buddhists who despised Bon, or he may have found documentation in different records; but on the basis of what he writes, we can conclude that most probably he limited himself to reporting the stories of some old biased Buddhists.

The *Chos 'byung dpag bsam ljon bzang* [composed in 1748] says (Dhi, 75):

> gNya'-khri bTsan-po, the first king of Tibet resided at the Yum-du Bla-sgang [*sic*] palace. At that time the Bon of Sum-pa arrived.
>
> His descendants were Mu-khri bTsan-po, Ding-khri, So-khri, Mer-khri, and Srib-khri bTsan-po. At the time of the last of the Seven Khri of the Sky [gNam-gyi Khri-bdun] 'Jol Bon arrived.

The excerpt shows that at the time of gNya'-khri bTsan-po the Bon of Sum-pa arrived in Tibet; apart from this information the text does not present big differences when compared to the narration by Thu'u-bkwan. The *Chos 'byung* also clarifies that (ibid., 75):

> At the time of Gri-gum bTsan-po, son of Srib-khri, the Bon of funerary practices (*dur bon*) spread from Zhang Zhung and Bru-sha.
>
> At the time of Bya-Khri, or sPu-de Gung-rgyal—one of the three sons of Gri-gum—*sgrung*, *lde'u*, and the great gShen-po [of the] Bon [of the] Sky [gNam Bon] appeared.

The last sentence of this quotation is nothing more than a reference to the affirmation contained in the *lHo brag chos 'byung* [composed in the fifteenth century] according to which (Pe, Vol. I, 164, 8), "[...t]he great gShen-po of the Bon of the Sky as well as Bon texts appeared."

The definition *rdol bon* became customary during the later diffusion of Bon due to the revelations that many *gter ston* [treasure revealers] received as aural transmissions [*snyan rgyud du rdol ba*] or because texts were brought to light [*rdol*] from significant places, such as rocks and so on. As a matter of fact, in a fourteenth century text titled *Khro bo dbang chen ngo mtshar rgyas pa'i rnam bshad gsal ba'i sgron ma* we read (Thob, 55, 13, 7):

> The third [part explains] the threefold way in which [Bon] spread, declined, and was revealed [*rdol*].

It is possible that other types of definitions for the Bon traditions similar to the ones found in the above-mentioned sources exist, but if the meaning of the words and the definitions to which they refer are examined with an impartial perspective, one arrives at the following conclusions: that *rdol bon* or *'jol bon* [Revealed Bon], *'khyar bon* [Derived Bon], and *bsgyur bon* [Transformed Bon] are names attributed only in later times by Tibetan Buddhists on the basis of their own judgment or way of thinking; and that they are not in the least definitions known in Bon and to the Bon-pos, nor authentic names originating from a standpoint connected with the real state of things.

Ever since the Buddhadharma was instituted in Tibet, Buddhists rancorously defamed Bon and the Bon-pos in all possible ways: more than a few examples of such slandering are contained in historical documents. Similarly however, also Bon-pos of various historical periods composed numbers of defamatory works against Buddhism and the Buddhists, with the pretense of supporting their own teachings. An example of this type of literature is found in the *rGyal rabs bon gyi 'byung gnas*, where we read (Thob, 146, 73, 2):

> At that time in the dBus region of Tibet several illnesses, famine, frost, and hail appeared. Since nothing done helped to improve the situation, a divination was requested of the expert Pe-ne-gu. His response was, "In this place lives a fatherless boy. He is the one who creates all these troubles."
>
> When asked what the boy looked like, the diviner replied, "You can recognize him through the following clues: he is a

fifteen-year old boy with a reddish complexion, arched eyebrows, and a fine set of white teeth." Asked what would be of benefit to do, the diviner replied, "It would be beneficial if Bon-pos from twelve different clans performed the Great Sky Exorcism [*gnam sel chen po*], have the boy ride a reddish-brown bull, and banish him to a country with different languages." They did as advised and exiled him to Kha-che. The boy, surmounting the dangers of wild animals, bridges, and difficult passes, finally reached Kha-che where the Teacher Padma was residing and went to meet him. With him he studied the Dharma, became knowledgeable, and was given the name Bo-dhi-sa-twa.[28]

Then, since he much resented the Tibetan Bon-po diviner who had him sent into exile, he described [Bon] negatively to the King, saying, "Bon is difficult to learn, but there exists a true sacred teaching, which is the [Buddha]dharma. Hence, Bon should be abolished and Buddhism should be adopted." The King said, "If Bon were to be abolished, would it not be like the sun and the moon disappearing?" and for a while he did not take the matter to heart. However, important ministers who favored Buddhism, like g.Yu-sgra [sNying-po] and others, petitioned the king in this way, "Oh Lord! In order to drink beer [*chang*], one must first brew it in water. In order to eat meat, one must first kill animals. If you are willing to surpass your forefathers, you must first abolish Bon and establish the Buddhadharma. You need to bring the Dharma from India by inviting Buddhist teachers. If you succeed in accomplishing that, the signs that you have surpassed your forefathers will appear more clearly than the light of the sun and the moon: you will be like a mule sired by a donkey [or] like a *mdzo* sired by a bull."

It has become customary for all Bonpo historians to repeat over and over again this tale and similar ones that would see a boy involved in the suppression of Bon. Here the Tibetan boy in question is none other than the prodigious scholar Śāntarakṣita [mKhan-chen Zhi-ba-'tsho, 725-788], who seemingly went to Kashmir and met with Teacher

---

28 [This is the name with which the famous master Śāntarakṣita who visited Tibet during the reign of King Khri-srong lDe'u-btsan was known. Cf. *Drung*, p. 239, note 44.]

Padmasambhava, became an expert in all Sūtra and Tantra teachings, then returned to Tibet determined to take vengeance for what the Bon-pos had done to him.

Furthermore, Bonpo texts frequently recriminate that Bonpo teachings have been plagiarized and incorporated in Buddhist ones. As examples we can quote the *Srid pa rgyud kyi kha byang*, where we read (Thob, 152, 77, 5):

> Bon [teachings] were coercively transformed into Buddhist teachings: many Bon teachings of the Mind Series [*Sems phyogs*] were transformed into the Buddhist Mind Series; the Bon-po *g.Yung drung khams brgyad* teachings were transformed into the Buddhist *sTong phrag brgya pa* [*Prajñāpāramitā*] ones.

And also the *Dar rgyas gsal sgron*, which says (Thob, 678, 92, 1):

> The *g.Yung drung ye khyab* teachings were transformed into the Marvelous Dharma [*chos rmad du byung ba, Adbhuta Dharma*] Buddhist teachings. The Bon *sGrags pa thugs kyi pe'u tse* teachings were transformed into the Buddhist *mNgon pa mdzod* [*Abhidharma*] teachings.

Concerning the polemics surrounding the mutual plagiarism of teachings, even if it is possible that some transformations or adaptations occurred, it is not correct to assume that on the basis of a few occurrences it was the case for the teachings as a whole. It would be like endorsing the proverb that says, "thief one day, thief forever," or rejecting the one that says, "because one man is a thief, it does not mean that one hundred men will become thieves."

Whenever research is undertaken, one must completely eschew narrow-mindedness in order to find the truth and be able to see the authentic face of history; otherwise it will be extremely difficult to study the subject matter properly. To completely eschew narrow-mindedness means that it is necessary to arrive at the truth by seeing with one's own eyes the limited viewpoint and attitude that both parties have. This does not mean that we hold ourselves the judges of whether the Bonpos or the Buddhists possess the truth and it does not mean that we simply uphold one or other of the sides. How else can one come to conclusions and settle critical key questions of such a nature without pursuing a research with these qualifications? For centuries Buddhists and Bonpos have criticized each other; but if their mutual criticism is looked at from a duly neutral standpoint, one can clearly see that tales such as the one of the child are utterly ridiculous.

2. The Mutual Criticism of Bon-pos and Buddhists

Guru Padmasambhava, the great Teacher who knows and sees the real condition of all phenomena and showed total and immeasurable kindness toward the Tibetan people, never spoke of Bon as being devoid of a precise origin, nor of Derived Bon, Revealed Bon, and so on. As a matter of fact, he settled the question of Bon's nature in the *Blon po bka'i thang yig*, which contains a description of how sTon-pa gShen-rab himself, contemplating the benefit of sentient beings, descended from the pure dimension of 'Og-min, and transforming himself into a cuckoo, entered the womb of the deity Byams-ma gNam-phyi Gung-rgyal (Pe, 494, 7):

> The way in which the Teacher gShen-rab Mi-bo descended from the palace of 'Og-min in order to produce benefits for sentient beings:
>
> Everything was transformed into lights of the five colors and the lights completely filled the physical worlds. Then [he] alighted on the top of a *shing-shol*[29] tree, [taking the form of a] turquoise cuckoo, the king of all birds. This cuckoo had a body the color of lapis lazuli. The splendid king of all birds spread his melodious sound for the joy of the sentient beings of the three realms. Then—with [its] clarity not obscured by the distinction between *saṃsāra* and *nirvāṇa*—[it] descended on the crown of the head of Shes-rab Byams-ma gNam-phyi Gung-rgyal and flapped its wings. It shook [itself] three times, and from its genitals two clear and sparkling lights, one white and one red, entered the crown of the mother's head and descending

29 This is said of a tree that has a type of wood that is hollow inside like bamboo. *Shing-shol* also refers to a bird with a slight body.

inside, dissolved in her womb. When [the child] exited [from the mother's womb], he was [already] able to speak.

This ancient story is also contained in the *Srid pa mdzod kyi mdo 'khor 'das khams kyi rtsa ba g.yung drung las rnam par dag pa'i rgyud* (mDo, KA, 496, 4, 4):

> The arrival of the Teacher gShen-rab Mi-bo from 'Og-min for the benefit of sentient beings:
>
> A light of all colors magically appeared and shone every-where, completely filling the physical worlds. Then, by generating the intention in [his] heart, [he] descended on a throne of light to liberate all sentient beings. He alighted on the top of a *shing shon* [*sic*] tree [taking the form of a] turquoise cuckoo, the king of all birds. This cuckoo had a body the color of lapis lazuli. This most splendid [of all birds] spread its melodious sound for the joy of sentient beings in the three realms. [Its] clarity was not obscured by the distinction between *saṃsāra* and *nirvāṇa*. With its power, it conquered all false [views]. With its excellence, it pointed out the path in a marvelous way. Performing its feats, it emanated unobstructed wisdom. Its behavior emerged from the sphere of Method and Wisdom. It did not act with conceit. Manifesting itself in such a way, [it] descended on the crown of the head of Shes-rab Byams-ma, also called gNam-phyi Gung-rgyal. It flapped its wings and shook [itself] three times, and from its genitals, two clear and sparkling lights, one white and one red, [entered] the head of the mother and from there descended inside, dissolving in her womb. The mother who knew that an emanation would come purified her body with lustral ablutions [*lha yi tshan*] and rubbed it with various medicines, awaiting [the epiphany] in a shady garden of a secluded island of precious stones.

Many old Bonpo texts relate the story of this event clearly and in detail, and with uniformity of content. Furthermore, the *Blon po bka'i thang yig* says (Pe, 494, 18):

> [sTon-pa gShen-rab Mi-bo] had four visions [before] his arrival. He saw in which country he would make his arrival, who would be his father and mother, what teaching [had to be taught], and the field [of recipients]. First, [he saw himself] in the three

realms and arrived [there]. Secondly, he arrived at the great Turquoise Garden. Thirdly, he chose [a family] of high lineage and pure karma. Finally, [out of the] six spheres [of existence,] he chose the human beings of the world.

The *mDo 'dus*, the shortest version of gShen-rab Mi-bo's life, relates this event in a more or less similar way, although it speaks of five visions instead of four (mDo, SA, 26, 1):

> Considering the continents, [he chose] 'Dzam-bu-gling. Considering the place, [he chose] 'Ol-mo Lung-ring, and from there, the mountain g.Yung-drung dGu-rtse [and] the castle of Bar-bo So-brgyad. As for the lineage, he considered a royal one. As for the time, [he considered] the time when the lifespan was one hundred years. As a father, [he chose] King Thod-dkar; as a mother, [he chose] Yo-phyo rGyal-bzhad.

In the *Blon po bka'i thang yig* we also read (Pe, 495, 1):

> [The teachings of] Bon [are] vast and profound like the depths of the ocean. They are collected in the 84,000 portals [*sgo mo*] and in the 360 treasure caves [*mdzod mig*]. They are [the teachings of] the Four Bon of the Cause [*rgyu'i bon bzhi*] and of the Four Bon of the Fruit [*'bras bu'i bon bzhi*] and the Eight [teachings of the Waters], Four of the River [*chu bo bzhi*] and Four of the Streams [*chu bran bzhi*].
>
> For entering the state of contemplation, [the Teacher taught] three types of practices [*las ka rnam pa gsum*]. Any of the Nine Vehicles [*theg dgu*] is suitable to enter [the path]. As a practice for the body, [he taught] the symbol [*phyag rgya*], which is difficult to learn. As a practice for the voice, [he taught] the essence [*snying po*], which is difficult to learn. As a practice for the mind, [he taught] meditative concentration [*ting 'dzin*], which is difficult to learn and is said to consist of 100,000 branches. In synthesis there are five [groups of teachings in all].
>
> The Nine or Ten Vehicles of Bon are: the Vehicle of the gShen of Phya [*phya gshen*], the Vehicle of the gShen of the Phenomenal Universe [*snang gshen*], the Vehicle of the gShen of Magic Power [*'phrul gshen*], the Vehicle of the gShen of Existence

[*srid gshen*], the Vehicle of the gShen of Virtue [*dge gshen*], the Vehicle of the gShen hermits [*gshen gyi drang srong*], the White A Vehicle [*gshen gyi a dkar*], the Vehicle of the Primordial gShen [*ye gshen*], [the Vehicle of the] Great Difference [*khyad par chen po*]. [The tenth vehicle] is *ma khu pa*.[30]

[The teachings of the] *Phya gShen* include the 360 series [*sgo*] of *gTo* rituals and the 84,000 series of medical diagnosis [*dpyad rigs*].

The *sNang gShen* includes four series for summoning [*gyer sgo bzhi*], the nine melodies [*skad kyi lcong dgu*], and worshipping Gar-babs bTsan-po.

The *'Phrul gShen* [utilizes] thirteen great [types of] magic [*rdzu 'phrul chen po bcu gsum*] and six great methods [*thabs chen drug*] through which one meditates on sBas-gsas rNgam[-pa].[31]

The *Srid gShen* [comprises] 360 methods for coping with death and four main series of funerary practices [*'dur sgo chen po bzhi*] [linked to the deity] rMa-bo.

The *dGe gShen* [comprises the methods of] the four joys [*dga' ba bzhi*], the two purities [*dag pa gnyis*], and the three antidotes [*gnyen po gsum*], which are the Magic King Who Knows All [Kun-shes 'Phrul-rgyal-po].

The *Drang Srong* [Vehicle includes] the ten rules [*shad pas bcu*] and the two weapons [*mtshon pa gnyis*], the two trainings [*sbyangs pa gnyis*], the three accomplishments [*sgrub gsum*], [and] Everlasting life [*g.yung drung tshe*].

The *A dkar* has eighteen branches of practice [*sgrub pa'i yan lag bco brgyad*], the nine sacred portals [*gnyan po'i sgo dgu*], and the 'Gi-nga deity of action [*las kyi lha*].

The *Ye gShen* has four series [*'jug pa rnam pa bzhi*] which include sixty branches of meditative absorption [*ting 'dzin yan lag drug bcu*] and sixteen signs [of accomplishments] [*rtags bcu drug*].

[In the Vehicle of] the Great Difference [*Khyad par Chen po*] [the names of] the three deities [have] one single essence.

The highest Ma-khu-ba [*sic*] has nine ways of conquering [*gdul dgu*].

---

30   *ma khu pa* signifies secret seal [*gsang ba'i rgya*].

31   [One of the deities associated with the *sPyi spungs* cycle.]

[The first] Seven Vehicles merge with the Vehicle of the Primordial gShen [*ye gshen*].

In the language of rGyal-sdong, [*ma khu ba*] is called I-yang. In the sMar language of Zhang Zhung, it is called U-ya Ag-tham. In the Tibetan language of sPur-rgyal, it is called gSang-ngo Kha-tham.

This excerpt clearly illustrates the way in which the various series of Bon teachings are arranged. Some of its passages are difficult to interpret. I will try to clarify a few of them by utilizing information found in Bonpo sources.

First of all, one can immediately infer from what is said afterward that "the three types of practices" [*las ka rnam pa gsum*] in the sentence "For entering the state of contemplation, [the Teacher taught] three types of practices," refer to practices related to body, speech, and mind.

As for "the four series for summoning" [*gyer sgo bzhi*] of the *sNang gShen*, the *Legs bshad skal bzang mgrin rgyan* affirms (Bod, 162, 14):

> The four series of summoning [are]: the exorcism [rituals] of the River of Black Waters; the series of White Waters [to suppress] the 'Dre and Sri [spirits]; the 'Phen-yul series of ransoms of equal exchange, and the dPon-gsas series of *gTo* rituals [for] the Phya [and] gNyan [entities].

The so-called "nine melodies" [*skad kyi lcong dgu*] are described as follows in the above-mentioned text (Bod, 168, 4):

The nine melodies are:

[1.] the melody of the Roar of the Turquoise Dragon that convenes the hordes of deities;

[2.] the chirping melody of the female Khyung that exhorts the wrathful deities to action [*bdar*];

[3.] the melody of the Duck that has lost its offspring, through which the positive force [*phya*] of human beings is summoned;

[4.] the melody of the Peacock displaying [its] tail feathers that summons prosperity in terms of livestock;

[5.] the melody of the Cuckoo that delights deities and demons [*lha srin*];

[6.] the melody of the Lark that sends ransoms [and] ritual objects [*glud yas*];

[7.] the shrieking melody of the Parrot that communicates with deities and demons;

[8.] the melody of the Hungry Crow that notes the presence of Sri [spirits];

[9.] the buzzing melody of the Hornet[32] that controls calamities caused by Sri [spirits].

"Worshipping Gar-babs bTsan-po": the main deity of the *sNang gShen* is called Gar-gsas bTsan-po; therefore Gar-babs is to be intended as Gar-gsas. Concerning the "thirteen great [types of] magic of the 'Phrul gShen" [*rdzu 'phrul chen po bcu gsum*], the *sKal bzang mgrin rgyan* affirms (Bod, 170, 10):

The thirteen [types of] magic [bound to an] oath are:

[1.] not to abandon [the recitation] of magic formulae;

[2.] not to interrupt the offering of flesh and blood sacrificial cakes [*gtor-ma*];

[3.] not to let the [flow of] nectar dry;

[4.] not to give up the practice of actions [linked to the] magic force;

[5.] not to stop eliminating enemies [of the teaching];

[6.] not to be deprived of compassion;

[7.] performing the practice in an exact way;

[8.] not to oppress the innocent;

[9.] not to abandon the blessing that derives [from the practice] of ritual offerings [*tshogs 'khor, ganacakrapuja*];

---

32 *stag brang*: a large and imposing insect of the wasp family that hovers noisily.

[10., 11., 12.] not to open the portals of the positive force, long life, and prosperity outside of a ritual setting;

[13.] in particular, discretion about one's practice.

The six great methods [*thabs chen drug*] through which one meditates on sBas-gsas rNgam—that is to say dBal-gsas rNgam-pa, the main deity of the 'Phrul gShen—consist, as the *sKal bzang mgrin rgyan* specifies, in eighteen important methods of accomplishment, of which six are related to the knowledge of the Base, six to the Path, and six to the Fruit [*gzhi lam 'bras gsum*] (Bod, 203, 11):

The eighteen branches of accomplishment:

[1.] the accomplishment of the sense of the intermediate limit [*bar mtshams don*],

[2.] the precise creation of miniature paintings [*tsa ka li*],

[3.] the throne offering blessing,

[4.] the invitation wisdom,

[5.] prostration, invocation, and aspiration, and

[6.] purification and repentance are the six accomplishments related to the Base.

[1.] The secret accomplishment of expansion and absorption ['*phro 'du*], [which is] the blessing of the secret limit [*gsang mtshams*],

[2., 3., 4.] encouraging the consort [*phyag rgya*], the upper body, and the messenger,

[5.] the [manifested] signs of the deities, and

[6.] the accomplishment of the fundamental heart promise are the six accomplishments related to the Path.

[1.] practicing top quality offerings [*phud*] and reciting the mantras of the deity, [which is] the real accomplishment [*dngos grub*],

[2.] preparing sacrificial cakes [*gtor-ma*],

[3.] performing [burial sorcery by] quashing [entities under-ground and] dancing [above the spot to impede their exit], and

[4., 5., 6.] establishing the flow of differentiation and conflu-ence of the positive force, long life, and prosperity are the six accomplishments of the Fruit.

The "four main series of funerary practices" [*'dur sgo chen po bzhi*] refer to the funerary practices for elderly people [*bkra 'dur*], young adults [*stag 'dur*], children [*sri 'dur*], and murdered people [*gri 'dur*]. In this regard the *Dri med gzi brjid* says (Thob, GA, 53, 27, 4):

> For elderly people one should perform the variegated funerary rituals [*bkra 'dur*]. If they are well done, benefit for others will develop.
>
> For young adults one should perform the funerary rituals of the Tiger [*stag 'dur*]. If they are well done, long life and wealth will increase.
>
> For children one should perform the funerary rituals of the Sri [spirits]. If they are well done, the lineage will develop.
>
> For murdered people one should perform the funerary rituals for the slain [*gri 'dur*]. If they are well done, the Sri [that haunt] the youngsters will be controlled.

The deity rMa-bo corresponds to the main deity of the *Srid gShen* called 'Dur-gsas rMa-bo, as it is clearly pointed out in the *sKal bzang mgrin rgyan* (Bod, 171, 4):

> The deity is 'Dur-gsas rMa-bo, the Lord of Death.

As far as the four joys [*dga' ba bzhi*] and the two purities [*dag pa gnyis*] of the *dGe gShen* are concerned, I have not found any information about the four joys in texts that deal with the Vehicle of the Virtuous Adherers [*dGe bsnyen theg pa*]. However, Sa-skya Paṇḍita [1182-1251] said, "Because something is not seen, it does not mean that it can be negated"; so I cannot say that none exists only because I did not see any, given that I am not totally familiar with the vast amount of Bonpo sources and my possibility for consulting them is limited. The *sKal bzang mgrin rgyan* specifies that the two purities—that is to say, the two basic points upon which meditation of the *dGe gShen* is focused—are (Bod, 201, 3):

> Meditation on the truly pure Essence of Reality [*bon nyid*] and meditation on the image of the deity [which represents the] relative [pure] vision.

Concerning "the three antidotes [*gnyen po gsum*] which are the Magic King Who Knows All [Kun-shes 'Phrul-rgyal-po]," I think that the sentence may be adequately elucidated by a passage concerning behavior contained in the *sKal bzang mgrin rgyan* (Bod, 201, 7):

> With the three powerful and excellent forms of behavior, one enjoys benefits for oneself and others. The view: meditating on the Essence of Reality will [make it] appear also to others. By accomplishing [that], [one will] carry to completion the benefit for oneself and others.

"The ten rules [*sbad pas bcu*] and the two weapons [*mtshon pa gnyis*] of the *Drang Srong*": the ten rules certainly refer to the ten forms of behavior [*spyod pa bcu*] that the Buddhist Kriyatantra [*bya ba'i rgyud*] and the Bon Vehicle of the Virtuous Adherers [*dGe bsnyen gyi theg pa*] consider in a similar fashion as the most important forms of behavior. They are the ten virtuous actions that need to be practiced to counteract the ten nonvirtuous ones and that are related to an overall intention of always performing pure actions. In this respect, the *gZi brjid* affirms (Thob, GA, 487, 243, 3):

> The ten nonvirtuous actions must be abandoned. The ten virtuous actions must be adopted. I also must wish for virtue. [I] also must aspire to and practice virtue. Others must be persuaded [to practice] virtue. They must also be put in [the condition of practicing] virtue.

The meaning of the two weapons [*mtshon pa gnyis*] is clarified in the *gZi brjid* in the following manner (Thob, GA, 496, 247, 1):

> In reality [they are] two: outward appearance and internal discipline.

[Like] the sun disk and [its] light, like the Wish-fulfilling [Tree] and [its] branches and leaves, Methods and Compassion [are like] the land and the soil.

If the sun did not have its rays, how could sentient beings of the six spheres get warm?

If the Wish-fulfilling Tree did not have leaves and fruits, how could all wishes and benefits be obtained?

If Compassion did not have Method, how could sentient beings be tamed?

If [internal] discipline did not have an external expression, who would know that an essence exists?

If gold did not reveal its radiance, it could not be distinguished from many [other] yellow objects.

If precious gems did not have a receptacle, faulty karmic traces would be covered by dust.

For that reason, [external] appearance [*tshul*] and [internal] discipline must be combined together.

The excerpt shows how important it is not to separate internal discipline from outward behavior and since the *Drang Srong* Vehicle considers these two as powerful tools of conduct they are given the designation of weapons. The Buddhist Tantras of Conduct [*spyod pa'i rgyud*] conform to the precepts of the Kriyatantra for what concerns behavior, and for what concerns the View they adhere to the principles of the Yogatantra; for this reason they are also called "Tantras of the Two" [*gnyis ka'i rgyud*, Caryātantra or Ubhayātantra].

Similarly, also in the Bon tradition the followers of the *Drang Srong* Vehicle conform to the precepts of the Vehicle of the Virtuous Adherers [*dGe bsnyen gyi theg pa*] for what concerns behavior and to the principles of the Mantra Vehicle of the White A [*A dkar sngags kyi theg pa*] for what concerns the View. For this reason I think that the term "appearance" [*tshul*] mentioned in the citation should be understood in connection with the discipline of behavior.

The "two trainings [*sbyangs pa gnyis*]" refer to the two mental trainings on the absolute and the relative perceptions. In this respect, the *sKal bzang mgrin rgyan* affirms (Bod, 206, 2):

For those who maintain that the absolute is without inherent nature and without diversification, the relative is in the appearance of the real characteristics. [These two are] spoken of [as] nonduality; but in fact, due to the hindrance of intellectual antidotes, appearance is viewed as defective and for that reason [they are seen as] diametrically opposite. Tantras do not possess specific characteristics. All that which is nonexistent appears in all sorts of ways. All that which is appearance is that which does not [inherently] exist. It is like, for example, a mirage or a fantasy.

As for "the three accomplishments [*sgrub gsum*]," I suppose they refer to the accomplishments pertaining to the three [tantric] aspects of development, perfection, and nonduality, since the above-mentioned text affirms (Bod, 206, 13):

> [At the time of] the Development Stage [*bskyed rim*], one meditates upon the *maṇḍala* of the deity without being hindered by [specific] characteristics. At the time of the Perfection Stage [*rdzogs rim*], one meditates upon Emptiness without pursuing conceptuality. During the Nondual Stage [*gnyis med*], one meditates upon illusion [as being] true Emptiness.

As for "Everlasting life [*g.yung drung tshe*]," it is easy to understand that it refers to obtaining the signs of immortality as a result of having accomplished the three stages.

"The eighteen branches of accomplishment" [*sgrub pa'i yan lag bco brgyad*] of the White A [*A dkar*] are clearly defined in the *gZi brjid* (Thob, GA, 53, 27, 4):

> The eighteen branches of accomplishment, known as the eighteen perfect ones, are the six branches related to the Primordial Base [*thog mar gzhi*], the six branches related to the marvelous Path [*ngo mtshar lam*], and the six branches related to the ultimate Fruit [*mthar phyin 'bras bu*].
>
> Explanation of the single branches: the six branches related to the Base [*gzhi*] are the accomplishment of the condition of the Nature-itself [*bdag nyid*] [at the] moment [of practice]; accomplishment of the *mudrās* during the practice; accomplishment in the self-liberation of the five poisons; accomplishment in inviting nondual wisdom; accomplishment in reverence, aspira-

tion, and prostrating; accomplishment in respectfully repenting for one's errors.

The six branches of the Path [*lam*]: accomplishment in the secret eradication of afflictions; accomplishment in benefiting from the blessing of wisdom; accomplishment in the extent of the secret expansion and collection [*'phro 'du*]; accomplishment in the dance with the secret *mudrā*; accomplishment in [visualizing] the throne, the characteristics, the *mudrās*, and the body color [of the deity]; accomplishment in [recognizing] the mutable characteristics of peaceful and wrathful deities.

The accomplishments of the ultimate Fruit [*mthar phyin 'bras bu*]: accomplishment in the attainment of the true essence; accomplishment in the promise of the inseparability of the three times; accomplishment in the treasuring of inexhaustible nectar; accomplishment in powerfully suppressing suffering; and accomplishment in the meaning of differentiated and unified wisdom.

As for the meaning of "the nine sacred portals" [*gnyan po'i sgo dgu*], the *gZi brjid* affirms (Thob, 52, 26, 7):

> The nine foundations of recitation [*bsnyen pa*] are the three external recitations of preliminary practices, the three recitations done internally, and the three recitations performed through the promise, the foundation, and the action.
>
> First [come] the three external recitations that are the recitation to the teacher and to the deity, the recitation for the abode of the Wisdom-Holders, and the recitation for qualified helpers.
>
> The three recitations done internally are the recitation for the implements, the recitation for supplementing lacks in liberating ransom [rituals], and the recitation for the selection of external supports.
>
> The three recitations performed through the promise, the foundation, and the action are the outer recitation for defining the protection, the inner recitation for the displaying of the dimension of the *maṇḍala*, and the secret recitation in which the doors [*sgo*] are differentiated and merged together.

On the basis of what is clarified here, the word *gnyan po* [literally, fierce] in the name of the nine sacred portals [*gnyan po'i sgo dgu*] appears to be a mistake, since we know that recitation [*bsnyen pa*] is involved.

As for the 'Gi-nga deity of action [*las kyi lha*], the *sKal bzang mgrin rgyan* says (Bod, 209, 18):

> The deity to be worshipped is the supreme chief of the wrathful [deities], called 'Chi-med sKyes-nas-btsan [the King Immortal from Birth].

I presume that this refers to the main deity of the Vehicle of the White A [*a dkar theg pa*].

For what concerns "the four series of the *Ye gShen*" [*'jug pa rnam pa bzhi*], if we take into account the essential meaning of the detailed explanations about the teachings of the Primordial gShen found in the *Dri med gzi brjid*, I think that they could refer to the four teachings related to Method [*thabs*], with or without characteristics [*mtshan can dang mtshan med*], and to the Creation [*bskyed rim*] and Perfection Stages [*rdzogs rim*].

About "the sixty branches of meditative absorption" [*ting 'dzin yan lag drug bcu*], we first read in the *gZi brjid* (Thob, DA, 168, 84, 2):

> When entering the Vehicle of the Primordial gShen, by meditating on the Pure-and-Perfect-Mind [*byang chub kyi sems*], if one is diligent and practices with awareness, from the unaltered condition of equality [*ma bcos mnyam pa'i ngang*]—the essential Suchness [*ngo bo de bzhin nyid*], the Mind-itself [*sems nyid*]—the branches of meditative absorption, which are endowed with eighty-five [characteristics], will remove [all] obscurations within the essence of the instant presence [*rig pa'i snying po*], the way of being of the Mind [*sems kyi gnas lugs*], [and] will eliminate the darkness of ignorance, becoming the glory that tames deluded sentient beings.

The text proceeds with the explanation of each of the eighty-five characteristics and it briefly deals with the sixty branches saying (Thob, DA, 209, 105, 2):

> The light rays of the sixty branches of meditative absorption radiate forth, by emanating and reabsorbing [them].

The sixteen signs [of accomplishment] [*rtags bcu drug*] certainly refer to sixteen different specific experiential signs related to meditative absorption, but I have not found precise statements about them in the Bonpo texts that I have consulted. Nonetheless, the *gZi brjid* says (Thob, DA, 158, 79, 6):

> Experiences related to Emptiness [*stong pa'i nyams*] arise as [inner] heat and [other] signs: [one can] fly in the sky [like a] bird; walk on water; move mountains; manipulate earth and stones like kneaded dough; be unattached to anything; and untie the knots of greed.

And also (ibid., 160, 80, 1):

> Experiences related to clarity [*gsal ba'i nyams*] arise as [inner] heat and [other] signs: the *maṇḍala* with its characteristics is perfected in the essence of the Mind-itself [*sems nyid*]; the body of the deity arises in the pure realm [*zhing khams*] of the circle [*thig le*] and seed syllable [*yig 'bru*]; in visions [in] the dark, the characteristics become visible [through] the seed syllables.

And also (ibid., 161, 81, 5):

> The degree of progress [related to the experience of] Bliss [*bde ba*] is the burning of the warm fire of inner heat [*gtum mo'i me drod*]; attachment is reversed and appearances are transformed; defects develop [into] virtuous qualities; there is no clinging to what is contemplated; [one can] tether and control the great planets; the afflictions of ignorance are seized with the lasso of compassion.

This explains the main ways in which experiential signs can arise. I think that from them one can acquire a general idea of the sixteen major ones.

For what concerns the expression "[in the Vehicle of] the Great Difference the three deities [have] one single essence" [*khyad par chen po lha gsum don dam gcig*], the Great Difference [*khyad par chen po*] indicates that this Vehicle is the most sacred and special of all. In the Bon tradition it is known as [the Vehicle of] the Great Primordial gShen [*ye gshen chen po*] or the Unsurpassable Vehicle [*bla med kyi theg pa*]. As for the three deities who are one [*lha gsum don dam gcig*], the *gZi brjid* offers the following explanation (Thob, DA, 221, 111, 1):

In the View [*don*] of the Unsurpassable Great Vehicle [*bla med theg pa chen po*], no benefit can derive from the so-called deities [*lha*], nor can harm derive from the so-called hindrances [*bgegs*]. [The View is] uncompounded, beyond harm and benefit. [It is] the Everlasting Body [*g.yung drung sku*], the King Immortal from Birth ['Chi-med sKyes-btsan (*sic*)].

We can understand from what is said here that the three deities upon which the practices of the Vehicles of Virtuous Adherers, Ascetics, and Primordial gShen are focused are truly perfected in the nature of self-originated awareness.

Finally, the expression *ma khu ba* refers to profound essential instructions on secret focal points. This secretive aspect is confirmed by the fact that the text clearly says, "In the Tibetan language of sPur-rgyal, it is called gSang-ngo Kha-tham" [secret and sealed].

In the *Blon po bka'i thang yig* we also read (Pe, 496, 2):

It is the infallible Bon of the Cause and of the Fruit descended from the sky. The teacher 'Chi-med gTsug-phud differentiated [it] into nine Cuckoos and twenty-seven paths. [It reveals the] infinite clarity [of] gShen-lha 'Od-dkar.

The *sKal bzang mgrin rgyan*, a scriptural transmission related to the Bonpo text titled *Rig pa'i khu byug*, allows us to understand the above-mentioned quotation (Bod, 172, 4):

The Cuckoo proclaiming the divinations of the *Phya gShen* is not focused on anything, because healing rituals are devoid of characteristics.

The Cuckoo proclaiming the ritual chants of the *sNang gShen* is not focused on anything, because meditations and rituals are devoid of characteristics.

The Cuckoo proclaiming the power of the *'Phrul gShen* is not focused on anything, because magical displays are devoid of characteristics.

The Cuckoo proclaiming the funerary rituals of the *Srid gShen* is not focused on anything, because funerary practices are devoid of characteristics.

The *Blon po bka'i thang yig* also says (Pe, 496, 4):

> The way in which the Bon-po teachings were established.
>
> Ta Bu-sbyid Ming-ske [*sic*] established the divination teach-ings of the *Phywa gShen* [and entrusted them] to the divine king sKye-bu-ri.
>
> sNang-ba [sNang-gshen gTsug-phud], having established the Bon for the deities, for human beings, and for the royal laws, [entrusted] the proclamation of the *sNang gShen* ritual chants [*gyer*] [to] the deities of Gar-gsas bTsan-po.
>
> The teachings of the *'Phrul gShen* were established by sBas-gsas rNgam-pa.
>
> The teachings of the *Srid gShen* were established by 'Dur-gsas sBa-bo [*sic*].
>
> [The teachings of] the Virtuous Adherers [*dGe bsnyen*] were established by Ye-mkhyen 'Phrul-rgya.
>
> As for the teachings on monastic discipline for the Ascetics [*Drang srong*], these were established by the King of Everlasting Life [of] the Sixth Vehicle [g.Yung-drung-tshe'i rGyal-po].
>
> The teachings of the White A [*A dkar*] were established by gSang-ba 'Dus-pa.
>
> Those of the Primordial gShen [*Ye gshen*] were established by g.Yung-drung Ye-dbang rGyal-po.
>
> The Bon of the Mind of the Ninth Vehicle of the Great Difference [*Khyad par chen po*] was established by gShen-po Tshad-med 'Od-ldan.
>
> The joyful gShen-po Tshad-med 'Od-ldan practiced and meditated intensively on the expanse of space [and] departed leaving no remainder, in union with his consort and with all his retinue.
>
> Then the Bon-po 'Phrul-gshen sNang-ldan practiced and meditated intensively on the top of Mount Meru [and] departed leaving no remainder, in union with his consort and with all his retinue.
>
> [The teachings] declined at the time of King Gri-gum bTsan-po.
>
> From that time onward, the royal political power degenerated.

As we can see, the text not only explains in a precise way the primeval origin of each of the Bonpo Vehicles but also relates the essential teachings of Bon, the teachings on the Mind, and shows how Bon existed and flourished up to the time of the Tibetan King Gri-gum bTsan-po. The information contained in this text is guaranteed by Guru Padmasambhava. If we do not trust him, whom else can we trust?

In this excerpt the name of the initiator of the *Phywa gShen* teachings is Ta Bu-sbyid Ming-ske. He obviously corresponds to Phywa gShen gTsug-phud Legs-rgyal Thang-po, since the history of how the latter requested the teachings of the *Phywa gShen* from sTon-pa gShen-rab is mentioned in many famous Bonpo texts. Furthermore, it is easily inferred that sBas-gsas rNgam-pa refers to the deity dBal-gsas rNgam-pa, and 'Dur-gsas sBa-bo to the deity 'Dur-gsas rMa-bo.

3. THE SUPPRESSION OF BON BY THE DHARMARĀJA
KHRI-SRONG LDE'U-BTSAN

The great Master Padmasambhava accepted Bon as a correct teaching. Although a contradiction seems to exist between his pronouncement and the abolishing of Bon by the Dharmarāja Khri-srong lDe'u-btsan, in reality two distinct reasons and purposes brought the Dharmarāja Khri-srong lDe'u-btsan to act in that way.

The first reason: the testament of the forefather Srong-btsan sGam-po inscribed on a copper strip reads, "From myself until the time of the king called Khri and lDe [*khri dang lde*], who is the fifth in the descent line, the sacred Dharma [will] flourish. With the arrival of many paṇḍitas the Buddhadharma will expand.

Khri-lde gTsug-brtan Mes-ag Tshoms-can, the father of the Dharmarāja Khri-srong lDe'u-btsan, thought that the Khri and lDe king mentioned in the inscription was himself. For that reason he dispatched Bran-kha Mu-le-ko and gNyags Dznyā-na Ku-ma-ra to invite the Paṇḍitas Sangs-rgyas gSang-ba and Sangs-rgyas Zhi-ba who resided at Mount Kailash. The two paṇḍitas declined the invitation but sent as a present copies of the Five Mahāyāna Sūtra Series [*theg pa chen po'i mdo sde lnga*]. The king sponsored the construction of five temples to accommodate the texts at Brag-dmar Ka-ru, Kha-che 'Phrin-bzang, lHa-sa Kha-brag, 'Phyin-phu Nam-ral, and Mang-gong Khri-rtse, and performed many other activities for the teaching. Some of his ministers, Bonpo ministers who disliked the Dharma, resented that. In the end the king was treacherously killed by two of his ministers, Lang Mes-gzigs and 'Bal sDong-tshab.

When the Dharmarāja Khri-srong lDe'u-btsan was young the political power was still held by some Bonpo ministers who disliked the Dharma. Since the Dharmarāja incurred many hardships, as clearly described in the Tibetan dynastic and religious histories and particularly on stone pillars, when he was finally able to take full control of the political power as king of Tibet, he punished many Bonpo ministers who hated the Dharma; needless to say, many Bon gShen-pos related to those Bonpo ministers were also penalized. Due to the circumstances a law was declared, as we can read in the *Padma bka'i thang yig* (Si, 400, 1):

> No one said that Bon is heretic. The Bon-pos have been exiled to a place where bSam-yas cannot be seen. Those who went to sKyid-shod settled at Yog-thang. Those who went to gTsang established their settlement at dBen-tsa-kha.

This citation reflects mainly a demonstration of political power transformed into a royal command, rather than a ban of Bon as an intrinsically incorrect view. For example, an excerpt from the sixteenth chapter of the *Khrims yig blang dor gsal bar byed pa'i drang thig dwangs shel me long nyer gcig pa* [Guidelines for Government Officials] authored by the Regent [sDe srid] Sangs-rgyas rGya-mtsho [1653-1705] shows how such an attitude became part of the political strategy of the government (Gangs can Rig mdzod, 7, 255, 1):

> In this northern region, which is the conversion field of the great incomparable Tsong-kha-pa, the types of monks who believe in different doctrines—like the hands of evil spirits ['Dre] that should not reach into the land of the gods—do not consider fitting and appropriate to act for the benefit of beings; hence they do anything they can, from stealing to collecting money by force, and so on.

Apart from hatred for the Bonpos, various Buddhist schools are well-known to have fought against each other in all possible ways to establish their individual dominion and power. In reality, that behavior had nothing to do with the Dharma of the Buddha or the Bon taught by gShen-rab: it was simply the proof of an extremely narrow-minded way of seeing.

At the time Guru Padmasambhava set his lotus feet in Tibet, some Bonpos harbored wrong forms of conduct. A quotation from the *gSol 'debs bar chad lam sel* [Invocation for Clearing the Path of Interruptions] clearly tells us how he abolished those incorrect Bonpo teachings and how he spread the pure and precious teachings of the *dharmakāya* (bKa' thang, SI, 788, 12):

> [He] abolished the harmful Bon teachings [and] taught the precious, immaculate [precepts of the] *dharmakāya*.

However, this was not just a feat of the Teacher Padmasambhava; before him, also the Teacher gShen-rab put an end to the wrong practices of Bonpos such as the bDud-bon, bTsan-bon, gDon-bon, and so on who performed animal and blood sacrifices; he substituted those offerings with all sorts of adequate ransom objects made of clay, of dough, and that had the shape of sentient beings. That is clearly recorded in the *Srid pa spyi mdos* and in proclamation texts dealing with ransom offerings for higher beings.[33]

In ancient times blood offerings were customary not only in Zhang Zhung but also in other countries of the world and it is worth noting that around four thousand years ago, at the time of gShen-rab Mi-bo-che, experts in those kind of offerings were everywhere. Needless to say, the fact that in that time period gShen-rab Mi-bo-che was able to develop ransom methods to substitute for blood offerings and to establish such a custom is an amazing accomplishment.

Although gShen-rab Mi-bo-che established the custom of substitute ransoms and his followers renounced harming the life of sentient beings—and using those methods created the circumstances for

---

33 *smrang gzhung*: early ritual texts of ransom proclaiming the power of truth linked to natural and supernatural forces.

the benefit and happiness of themselves and others, distinctly styling themselves *g.Yung drung Bon* [Everlasting Bon]—it is impossible that the bDud-bon, gDon-bon, bTsan-bon, and so on, who personified widespread ancient beliefs, and the experts who used sanguinary offerings simply disappeared as soon as the Everlasting Bon spread in Zhang Zhung and Tibet. Even at later times some Bonpos performed blood offerings in areas of Zhang Zhung and Tibet; even nowadays it is attested that in the border areas of Tibet there are priests who cut the throats of birds and goats and ritually offer their blood. Taking that into consideration, let us read another passage from the *Padma bka'i thang yig* (SI, 473, 4):

> At that time it was said that the Bon-po [ritual of the] Deer with Branched Antlers [*sha ba rwa rgyas*] had to be performed [as a] healing ceremony for the king. The Bon-pos did not seize a live deer but sang ritual hymns. "Divine tools are needed," they declared, slaughtering yaks and sheep.
>
> The Translators and Paṇḍitas reckoned as misdeeds that and other similar actions by the Bon-pos. The Paṇḍitas, single-mindedly, with the intercession of the Translators, pleaded with the king [as follows]: "The precepts of the Dharma and the Bon system are incompatible. [The first are] extraordinary, [the latter] coarse and harmful. If this state of affairs persists, we will return to our countries. It is not good to have two masters for one teaching. It is unsuitable to have two methods for one religion.

The Bon of the Deer with Branched Antlers [*bon shwa ba ru rgyas*], an especially widespread tradition of the Bon series known as the *Dur gShen* endowed with weapons [*Dur gshen mtshon cha can*], refers to an order of priests who performed sanguinary offerings in ancient times. Since they were eventually associated with the Bonpo tradition as a whole, it is easy to see how all the Bonpos were unjustly accused on the basis of the conduct of some Bonpos who performed ransom rituals belonging to the ancient system of the Deer with Branched Antlers. That clearly provides proof for the proverb that says, "because one man is a thief, it does not mean that one hundred men will become thieves."

Furthermore, in the *Padma bka'i thang yig* we read (SI, 472, 14):

> gShen Li-shu sTag-ring, Thang-nag Bon-po, and Tshe-mi
> g.Yung-drung came from the country of Zhang Zhung.
>   gShen-bon Dran-pa Khod-spungs, Mi-lus bSam-lhag [*sic*],
> sTag-lha Me-'bar, Thar-bon Gru-bskyal, rTa-bon Byon-khri-
> nag, 'Phrul-bon gSang-ba Ngang-ring, and others gathered at
> the Āryapalo Temple to translate Bon [cycles].

The fact that Zhang Zhung scholars and translators had been invited
to Tibet and had started to translate Bon cycles into Tibetan did not
please the paṇḍitas who had been invited from India, China, and other
places, nor the Tibetan translators. Since they complained to the king,
saying that "it was not good to have two masters for one teaching,"
and that "it was unsuitable to have two methods for one religion," the
king was irritated; it is related that many circumstances took place that
were unavoidable.

     The gShen-pos Li-shu sTag-ring, Khod-spungs Dran-pa Nam-
mkha', and the others mentioned here were famous Bon-gShen in Zhang
Zhung, but they were active during the Intermediate Period, so it is
impossible that they were present at that time.

     Nonetheless, Buddhist history has customarily utilized names of
famous siddhas and wisdom-holders of the past and has connected
them to subsequent times, as is the case for a previous 'Jam-dpal bShes-
gnyen, who was one of the main disciples of the Teacher dGa'-rab
rDo-rje, and a later 'Jam-dpal bShes-gnyen, who was a teacher of Guru
Padmasambhava. Therefore, due to the fact that Li-shu sTag-ring was
endowed with the *siddhi* of immortality from birth, it is considered that
he and other similarly prominent figures of the Bon tradition were still
alive when the Dharmarāja Khri-srong lDe'u-btsan abolished Bon. That
could be possible if viewed within the context of pure vision, but it does
not seem reasonable from the ordinary, mundane viewpoint of history.

     In the *Padma bka'i thang yig* we also read (SI, 473, 17):

> The flag of the Dharma is small. Bon is mighty. Hence it is
> imperative that many scholars and translators be banished.

When the Dharmarāja was young, the power of the Buddhists was feeble compared with that of the Bonpos; but it was also vulnerable when the king seized political power and the time had come to spread the Buddhist doctrine in earnest. Consequently the king had to find some reasons to justify his abolition of Bon teachings. One of those reasons was as follows (ibid., 474, 4):

> At that time, when the Buddhists and the Bon-pos performed the vase [purification] ritual [*bum chog*] for the death of the mother of rGyal-ba'i Blo-gros and Minister Ta-ra Klu-gong, the king believed the Buddhists and doubted the Bon-pos.
>
> When they competed in magical chants at Don-mkhar-thang, the king believed the Buddhists and doubted the Bon-pos.
>
> When the Teacher Padma and Thang-nag Bon-po presented their respective doctrines and refuted that of the other, the king believed the Buddhists and doubted the Bon-pos.
>
> When Bo-dhi-sa-twa and Sha-ri dBu-chen presented their respective doctrines and refuted that of the other, the king believed the Buddhists and doubted the Bon-pos.
>
> When Bi-ma Mi-tra and Li-shu sTag-ring presented their respective doctrines and refuted that of the other, the king believed the Buddhists and doubted the Bon-pos.
>
> When the translators engaged in establishing and refuting [the meaning of] the Bon-po and of the Buddhist Nine Vehicles, the king believed the Buddhists and doubted the Bon-pos.

This shows how the debates between Buddhists and Bonpos took place. Moreover, a doctrinal debate on the intrinsic meaning of the Nine Vehicles of the Buddhists and of the Bonpos also shows that the designation of Nine Vehicles [*theg pa rim pa dgu*] already existed in Bon at that time.

As we understand from this excerpt, the fact that the Dharmarāja Khri-srong lDe'u-btsan believed the Buddhists and doubted the Bonpos was dependent on six intrinsic causes. Those causes resulted in the abolishment of Bon and the subsequent propagation of Buddhism. The *Padma bka'i thang yig* describes clearly and in detail how Bon was abolished (SI, 474, 17):

All the Bon-pos were subjected to the authority of the king. Everywhere in the kingdom [*khams gsum na gar*], the Bon-po appurtenance could be recognized [by the following]: they were named after their fathers and their plaited hair was wrapped around their heads.

They wore fox skin hats and carried a half drum [*phyed rnga*] in their hands.

They were clad in blue clothes and were given unhusked grains as their staple food.³⁴

All the evil and corrupt Bon-po customs were abolished. Except for the *lha g.yang skor gsum*,³⁵ all rituals were abolished, including the Bon that averts sudden mundane obstacles, that of the wooden-headed deer with branched antlers, and the rites involving dough effigies of yaks and sheep.

The gShen-Bons were given donkeys as pack animals.

The followers of g.Yung-drung Bon were given live cattle as a means of survival.

The [King's] subjects escorted them [to] Bye-ma g.Yung-drung [the Eternal Deserts] [of] Upper gTsang [gTsang-stod].

They were exiled to the regions of rTsa-mi, Shing-mi, lJang-mo Mig-dgu, and the land of the Sog-pos [where people are] clad in monkey skins.

These circumstances are related not only in the *Padma bka' thang*, but also in most chronicles, in the hagiography of mKha'-'gro Ye-shes mTsho-rgyal titled *rGyud mang dri za'i glu phreng*, and in other textual sources.

The sentence "All the evil and corrupt Bon-po customs were abolished" implies that the Dharmarāja Khri-srong lDe'u-btsan explicitly abolished Bon customs of blood sacrifices and similar offerings, but not that he implicitly abolished correct Bonpo teachings as well.

In recent times some Bonpo textual cycles, such as those related to the earlier traditions of the Zhang Zhung Aural Transmission [*Zhang zhung snyan rgyud*] and to the Oral Transmission of Zhang Zhung Me-ri

---

34 *lhad zas*: unhusked grains such as a mixture of oats, beans, and buckwheat.
35 *lha g.yang skor gsum*: the lustral aspersion rituals for purifying the [images of the] deities, fumigation rituals to purify contaminations and obscurations, and rituals to summon good fortune and prosperity.

[*Zhang zhung me ri bka' ma*] have become available; those texts contain the teachings as well as confirm the history of those that were not abolished. Nonetheless, due to the catastrophic circumstances of that time, all Bonpos suffered, regardless of their relation to corruption. As the text clearly demonstrates:

> The gShen-Bons were given donkeys as pack animals.
> The followers of g.Yung-drung Bon were given live cattle as a means of survival.
> The [King's] subjects escorted them [to] Bye-ma g.Yung-drung [the Eternal Deserts] [of] Upper gTsang [gTsang-stod].

The famous Gu-ru Nga-'dra-ma statue of Padmasambhava at Samye. Photo taken by HRH the Queen Mother of Sikkim, rGyal-yum Kun-bzang bDe-chen mTsho-mo rNam-rgyal, when visiting Tibet in 1935.

Identifying the Royal Lineages
of Tibet in the Later Period

Most historians of the Later Period who researched the history of the Intermediate Period adhered to the Buddhist viewpoint; for that reason they associated the origin of the ancient Tibetan kings with Indian royal lineages. This widespread assumption on the part of Buddhists scholars was also shared by the New Bonpos whose historical works contain a number of similar theories.

1. THE ROYAL LINEAGES FROM KING gNYA'-KHRI bTSAN-PO TO THE DHARM ARĀJA SRONG-BTSAN

The *Bu ston chos 'byung* says (Zhol, YA, 123, 1):

> The Tibetan royal line according to some [originated from] the fifth son of Prasenajit [gSal-rgyal, c. sixth century BCE], the king of Kosala; some say that [it originated from] the fifth son of sTobs-chung, the younger son of King Bimbisara;[36] some say that when the Tibetans were oppressed by [the ruling] demons and Yakṣas [gNod-sbyin] of the Twelve Minor Principalities [rGyal-phran bCu-gnyis], the King of Pad-sa-la [Vatsa], 'Char-

---

36 Tib. gZugs-can sNying-po, ruler of the Magadha Empire and firm supporter of the Buddha, reigned 542-492 BCE.

byed [Udayana], generated a son with webbed fingers and eyelids closing [from below]. Terrified, [the king had him] put into a copper pot and thrown into the river Gang-gā [Gaṅgā]. He was found and raised by peasants and when he grew older he was told his story; he ran away in distress to the Himalayas and from there, he gradually reached the lHa-ri Yol-ba Pass and then arrived at bTsan-thang sGo-bzhi.

All the Bon-pos, [thinking that he had descended on] the magic dMu cord and dMu ladder said that he was a god. When they asked, "Who are you," he replied, "bTsan-po [I am a king]." When they asked, "Where do you come from," he pointed a finger toward the sky. They did not comprehend his language; [nevertheless, they] placed him on a wooden throne carried by four men at neck [height] and said, "He must be our king" and called him gNya'-khri bTsan-po.

He was the earliest king.

As we have seen, the origin of the first Tibetan king is attributed to three different Indian royal lineages. The *rGyal rabs 'phrul gyi lde mig* affirms (Dhi, 16, 5):

> As for the [Tibetan] royal line, the *Bu ston chos 'byung* says that it originated either from the fifth son of [King] Prasenajit or from the fifth son of sTobs-chung, son of [King] Bimbisara, or from the son of 'Char-byed, king of Pad-sa-la [Vatsa], who had the marks of a superior individual, and that all three correspond to Lord gNya'-khri bTsan-po. While it is certain that the first two cannot be confirmed as part of the Śākya clans, it is right to say that the last one can be.

In this textual source a compromise is reached because it is determined that the Śākya clans were involved. The *Deb ther sngon po* adds (Si, Vol. I, CHA, 61, 2):

> Even though it seems incompatible that gNya'-khri bTsan-po may belong to any of the Śākya clans—Śākya Chen-po, Śākya Ri-brag-pa, and Śākya Li-tsa-byi—in the root Tantra of 'Jam-dpal [*Mañjuśrīmūlatantra*] a clear prophecy [referring to the royal lineages] from Srong-btsan to [Lang-]dar-ma says, "[They will]

arise from the Li-tsa-byi lineage." This is proof that at issue is the Li-tsa-byi clan.

In this way it is established that the Śākya clans were involved and it is demonstrated that not just any Śākya clan was involved, but that of the Licchavi; in reality, it is evident that every possible effort has been made to prove that the Tibetan kings not only descended from a great Indian royal lineage, but also from the same lineage and king related to the Teacher Śākyamuni.

The foundation used by Buddhist historians to develop their theories concerning the origin of the ancient Tibetan kings is clearly shown by the author of the essay titled *sPu rgyal gdung rabs kyi rtsa ba'i 'byung khungs skor la cung zad dpyad pa* [A Brief Analysis of the Primary Origin of sPu-rgyal's Lineage] (*Bod ljong zhib 'jug*, 4-1986, 29, 25):

> In the *rGyal po'i bka' thems shog gril las ngos bshus pa*, at the end of the extensive citation regarding the Indian Śākya lineage, it is written (page nine of the old manuscript), "The lineage of the Sugarcane One [*bu ram shing pa'i rgyud*] [the Buddha] belongs to the royal castes of which there was a great number. At the time of the victorious Siddhartha [several] extremely famous kings existed: at the royal court there was King Bimbisara; at Kosala, King Prasenajit; at Pad-ma-can, King Pad-ma Chen-po; and at Pad-ma Sa-la [Vatsa], King 'Char-byed [Udayana]. His son was Shar-pa; Shar-pa's son was dMag-rgyal; the son of dMag-rgyal was exiled to Yangs-pa-can [Vaiśālī], but he escaped to the mountains and then reached lHa-ri Gyang-tho. He was known as gNya'-khri bTsan-po. He was the first king of Tibet."
>
> A slightly longer version of this story is found in the *rGyal po'i bka' thems bka' bkol ma* (old Sa-skya manuscript, pp. 16-17) that says, "The son of King Udayana was Shar-pa. Shar-pa had two sons, sKyabs-seng and dMag-brgya-pa. King dMag-brgya-pa generated a son who had eyes like a bird, turquoise-blue eyelids closing from below, teeth like rows of tiny conch shells, and hands with webbed fingers like a swan. The king seeing the child declared, 'This is a bad omen. If we raise him, the kingdom will certainly be destroyed. Kill him.' But the ministers were not willing to kill him, so they put the child in a copper pot and cast it in the Gang-gā [Gaṅgā] River. Some peasants rescued

him from a riverbank at the city of Yangs-pa-can [Vaiśālī] and reared him in the depths of the forest. When the prince asked, 'What are my antecedents?' he was told that [his father was] King dMag-brgya-pa [and that he] had [abandoned him,] jettisoning him in the river.

The prince ran away to the mountains and arrived at lHa-ri rGyang-mtho [sic]; then he saw a crevice in the snowy mountains of the North, headed in that direction, and attained the summit of lHa-ri Rol-mo; from there he descended on the nine-runged dMu ladder, [eventually] reaching bTsan-thang sGo-bzhi."

An extensive version of this story is contained in a bKa' chems ka khol ma woodblock print, but since its meaning is for the most part similar to the above tale, it will not be related here.

Furthermore, in the Ma ṇi bka' 'bum (woodblock print, Vol. I, p. 161, 7) it is written, "At that time in Tibet no distinction existed between lord and subjects. Within the three clans of the Śākya—Śākya Chen-po, Śākya Li-tsa-byi, and Śākya Ri-brag-pa—the small son of King sKyabs-seng of the last-mentioned [sic] [clan] escaped with the army in the direction of the Himalayas; from there he reached Tibet and having crossed the summit of lHa-ri Rol-po, alighted from a divine ladder at bTsan-thang sGo-bzhi in Yar-lung. We requested this king who came from the sky to be our lord. He was seated on a throne [carried] at neck [height] and was called King gNya'-khri bTsan-po."

The sources quoted here constitute the basis for the propagation of similar theories in Tibet. As a matter of fact, in discussing the origin of gNya'-khri bTsan-po, the majority of texts composed after those sources, such as the Chos 'byung bstan pa'i rgyal mtshan, the Bu ston chos 'byung, the Tshal pa'i deb dmar, the rGyal rabs gsal ba'i me long, the Yig tshang mkhas pa dga' byed, the Deb ther sngon po, the Deb ther dpyid kyi rgyal mo'i glu dbyangs, and so on, as well as less renowned historical records and religious histories or documents belonging to specific philosophical schools, have extensively promoted the idea that he came from India and was a descendant of the Śākya lineage, basing their accounts on whichever of the above-mentioned sources seemed suitable.

That Buddhist historians disseminated in many ways the theory of a primeval king of Tibet who descended from an Indian lineage that was also a Śākya one influenced the viewpoint of the Bon gSar-ma [New Bon] tradition so that the latter attributed the origin of the first Tibetan king to the lineage of the mythical King Mang-pos bKur-ba [Mahā Sammata, The Great Elect]. The *Legs bshad rin po che'i mdzod* says (PE, 128, 4):

> Some of the outsiders [non-Bonpos] say that Lord gNya'-khri bTsan-po was the child of Prasenajit; some maintain that he was the child of sGra-ngan; some say that he belonged to the Śākya royal lineage; and some say that he was the son of dMag-rgyal.
>
> In our tradition, according to the *bsGrags byang* and the *Nyi sgron*, he was a child belonging to the lineage either of Khri-bar bDun-tshigs or of Mang-bkur.
>
> According to the *mTho thog* and the *rTsa 'grel*, he was the son of dMag-rgyal, the king of U-rgyan.
>
> Although many discordant versions exist, in the real sense the only certainty about labeling him as the son of any of those kings is that he was not the son of any of them at all, but that he had come from the heavenly realm of the gods to be the lord of the people. In fact, according to the *Byams ma rigs kyi 'jigs skyobs*, he is the son generated from the blessing of the six deities of existence directly summoned through the Mother's [Byams-ma] compassion.
>
> He is also considered to belong to the lineage of Mi-lus bSam-legs and to have been born in that lineage many generations later as the son of King sKya-bseng.
>
> As it is said in the *Byams ma rigs kyi 'jigs skyobs*, since King sKyabs-bseng [*sic*] did not have offspring and fearing that the kingdom would be lost to the many children of his brother Zla-yul 'Khor-skyong, he went to a secluded place in the forest together with the queen; once there, they met with a sage who had obtained the *siddhi* of Byams-ma and was abiding in the meditative absorption of fire.
>
> The king and queen paid their respects to him and asked for his assistance. The sage increased the heat of the fire twice as much; as a result, the hand of the queen was burned and she

cried out in pain, awakening the sage from his *samādhi*. [The sage]
said, "Alas! The royal couple has met with adversity. Why do
you supplicate me?" The king said, "Since I have no children,
I fear that I may lose my kingdom. I request the blessing of a
son." [The sage] gave him a vase containing the special mantra
of Byams-ma [for having a son] along with [other substances]
and said, "Cast this in the sky and submit [yourself] to the
power of the deities who rule existence. Anoint the hand of the
queen [with these contents] and it will be healed."

So the king hurled [the substances] into the sky six times
and summoned the six deities.

The southern king of Everlasting Bon, rGyal-byin, the Sun
[god], [the goddess of] Tha-skar [Aśvinī Lunar Mansion], Yab-
bla, and the Lord of the desire realm bestowed their blessing
upon the queen.

The king's power became so strong [that] a child was conceived without intercourse. [At birth] the child [had] swastikas
at [his] ears, eyes [like] those of a bird, teeth [like] rows of tiny
conch shells, and fingers connected by a web. The queen was
ashamed and without showing the son to the father, put him
in a copper pot and threw him into the Gang-gā [Gaṅgā]. Due
to the power of karma, he arrived in the city of Yangs-pa[-can]
[Vaiśālī]. Everyone was bewildered and he was raised [there].

He displayed many signs of great goodness. When he grew
older he reached Tibet. From lHa-ri Gyang-tho he arrived at
Sog-ka in Yar-lung.

At that moment the prophecy of the divine child who would
descend from the sky was realized in Tibet.

Explaining the way in which the royal gShen Mi-lus bSam-
legs was born, the *Byams ma* says, "The Lord that the gods have
made King of the people called Mang-pos bKur-ba, the Chief
Lord of all the Black Heads [the Tibetan people], was named
Tha-tshan Hi-sangs-skyes prior to becoming the King of the
people."

Although this excerpt presents information which has to do with another tradition, it clearly indicates that gNya'-khri bTsan-po was the

descendant of King sKya-bseng. Concerning Mi-lus bSam-legs, the *Legs bshad rin po che'i mdzod* affirms (Pe, 90, 8):

> The origin of the first Tibetan king would thus be the royal lineage of Mang-pos bKur-ba; in reality this affirmation does not disprove the idea that he descended from the lineage of sKya-seng.

The topic of royal dynasties from the initial king gNya'-khri bTsan-po until the Dharmarāja Srong-btsan sGam-po is discussed in several historical records which were committed to writing during the Later Period; among the many views of the Buddhist historians of that period the one contained in the *Deb ther dpyid kyi rgyal mo'i glu dbyangs* is particularly worth mentioning (Pe, 15, 9):

> Up to that point, although the royal lineages were produced only by the exquisite power of the blessing of the Great Compassionate One, no king was associated with the Dharma; but when the magic emanation lHa-tho-tho-ri gNyan-btsan, glorious, righteous, all-resplendent, and endowed with good vision, was born as the son of Khri-rje Thog-btsan and Ru-yong-bza' sTong-rgyal Na-mo-tsho, the sacred Dharma begun.
>
> During the time of this king, a casket—containing the *dPang bkong phyag brgya pa* [*Sakśipūraṇasudraka*, The Hundredfold Homage for Mending Breaches], a golden stūpa, the Six Syllable [Avalokiteśvara mantra], the essence of the *mDo sde za ma tog* [*Kāraṇḍavyūhasūtra*, The Sūtra Designed as a Jewel Chest], and a Cintāmaṇi [wish-fulfilling jewel]—fell from the sky on the uppermost roof of the Yum-bu Gla-sgang Castle. [At the same time,] a voice resonating from the sky prophesied that in five generations someone who could understand the meaning of these [objects] would appear.
>
> Even if [the king] did not know [the significance of the texts and of the objects], he treated them with veneration, [stored them] in the castle repository, and called them gNyan-po gSang-ba [Secret Powerful Objects]. Due to his devotion [toward these objects], the eighty year old king miraculously regained the youth of an adolescent and lived until he was 120 years old.

It is thus said that the sacred Dharma began at the time of the thir-
tieth Tibetan monarch lHa-tho-tho-ri gNyan-btsan [347-494 CE].
This event would also represent the beginning of the history of the
Later Period; however, historical records have shown that the history
of the Later Period actually began with the thirty-fifth monarch, the
Dharmarāja Srong-btsan sGam-po, who had control of the kingdom.
It was he who established the concrete foundation of the Buddhist
doctrine. The records elaborate profusely upon the way in which a
new written language was acquired; how the words of the Victorious
One and several subsequent scholarly treatises were translated from
the Indian language into Tibetan; how all kinds of sciences from India
and China were propagated in Tibet; and how many different kinds of
relevant histories, annals, religious histories, and ancient stories were
compiled in the new Tibetan language during his reign.

As for the identification of the beginning of the sacred Dharma
with lHa-tho-tho-ri gNyan btsan's lifetime, the *Ma ṇi bka' 'bum* relates
(mTsho, E, 267, 267, I):

> From the celestial palace on the summit of the Potala Mountain
> the noble Lord Avalokiteśvara, the most exalted of [all]
> Bodhisattvas, greatly compassionate and skillful in means, saw
> and considered that the time for converting the snowy kingdom
> of Tibet had come.
>
> When the king of Tibet called lHa-tho-tho-ri sNyan-shal
> was staying at the famous Yum-bu Bla-sgang Castle, by virtue
> of the blessing of the Compassionate One, rainbow-colored
> light rays radiated from the heart center of Avalokiteśvara
> and a precious casket containing golden books written in
> Tibetan with liquefied lapis lazuli [ink] of the *mDo sde za ma*
> *tog* [*Kāraṇḍavyūhasūtra*, The Sūtra Designed as a Jewel Chest], the
> *sPang skong phyag brgya pa* [*Sakṣipūraṇasudraka*, The Hundredfold
> Homage for Mending Breaches], the *dhāraṇī* of the Twelve Links
> of Dependent Origination [*rTen 'brel bcu gnyis kyi gzungs*], and the
> *Sūtra of the Ten Virtues*, traveling on the sunbeams, alighted on the
> roof of the king's residence.
>
> The king opened the casket, saw [the books], and wondered
> whether they were Bon-po or Dharma [texts]. Perceiving their

wondrousness, [nonetheless,] he put them in a box made of gold and silver, called them Secret Powerful Objects [gNyan-po gSang-ba], and placed the box on a golden stand.

The king and his retinue would pay homage to them every day, offering golden beverages [*gser skyems*] and the first draft [*phud*] of beer [*chang*][37] during the daytime, and lighting butter lamps at night so as not to leave them in darkness. At that time the king was aging and his hair was ever more gray; but because of the blessing of the Secret Powerful Objects [gNyan-po gSang-ba], his hair turned a lustrous black again, his wrinkles disappeared, and he regained a youthful appearance. In one body he was able to live two lives.

In his last will he said, "Supplicate the Secret Powerful Objects [gNyan-po gSang-ba] for any physical illness and mental affliction that arise in this snowy kingdom of Tibet. All calamities will be removed and will turn into auspicious and joyful [happenings]. Supplicate them also for all the good that you wish for. All desires will be fulfilled." Then, without leaving a body behind, he vanished in the sky like a rainbow.

The son of King lHa-tho-tho-ri was Khri-gzungs-btsan; the son of Khri-gzungs-btsan was 'Gro-gnyan 'Di-ru; the son of 'Gro-gnyan 'Di-ru was sTag-gu gNyan-gzigs; the son of sTag-gu gNyan-gzigs was gNam-ri Srong-btsan. Also those kings worshipped [the Secret Powerful Objects] as had their ancestors and for that reason they were endowed with all the best qualities.

King sTag-gu gNyan-gzigs was born blind and for that reason he was banished from the capital; but as a result of offering prayers to the Secret Powerful Objects [gNyan-po gSang-ba], his eyes were cured.

Tibetan dynastic and religious histories present many different viewpoints concerning the birth date of lHa-tho-tho-ri gNyan-btsan.

For example the *Bai dkar* [*Baiḍūrya dkar po*], the *Sum pa'i rtsis gzhung ma*, and the *Brag dgon rtsis gzhung* say that he was born in the Wood Dog year of the first *sMe-phreng* of the thirteenth *sMe-'khor* (13/1 - Tibetan year 2171, 254 CE); and the *Bai dkar g.ya' sel* says that he was born in the Water Dragon year of the intermediate *sMe-phreng* of the thirteenth

---

37   *g.yu sngon gyis mchod*, an offering of the best *chang*.

sMe-'khor (13/2, Tibetan year 2249, 332 CE). The *Bai dkar* contains a few contradictions, but since it was composed before the *Bai dkar g.ya' sel* we obviously must rely upon it as the primary source.

According to the religious history compiled by dGe-ye-ba Tshul-khrims Seng-ge [fifteenth century], lHa-tho-tho-ri was born in the Fire Sheep year of the intermediate *sMe-phreng* of the thirteenth *sMe-'khor* (13/2, Tibetan year 2264, 347 CE).

The *Ngor pa'i chos 'byung* says that he was born in the Earth Monkey year of the intermediate *sMe-phreng* of the thirteenth *sMe-'khor* (13/2, Tibetan year 2265, 348 CE).

'Gro-mngon Chos-rgyal 'Phags-pa [1235-1280] says that lHa-tho-tho-ri was born in the year 2,500 after the *parinirvāṇa* of the Buddha, corresponding to the Fire Tiger year of the last *sMe-phreng* of the thirteenth *sMe-'khor* (13/3, Tibetan year 2283, 366 CE).

'Jam-mgon Mi-pham [1846-1912], dPal-sprul Rin-po-che [1808-1887], and others maintain that he was born in the Wood Pig year of the last *sMe-phreng* of the thirteenth *sMe-'khor* (13/3, Tibetan year 2292, 375 CE).

Sa-chen Kun-dga' sNying-po [1092-1158] says that he was born in the Fire Horse year of the last *sMe-phreng* of the thirteenth *sMe-'khor* (13/3, Tibetan year 2323, 406 CE).

According to the *g.Yas ru stag tshang ba'i mkhas pa dga' byed*, he was born in the Earth Sheep year of the last *sMe-phreng* of the thirteenth *sMe-'khor* (13/3, Tibetan year 2336, 419 CE).

As we can see, many different opinions have been expressed about the year in which lHa-tho-tho-ri gNyan-btsan was born; but all sources agree that he was born in the thirteenth *sMe-'khor* and that he received the Dharma books.

Most of the histories are in agreement about the objects received by the king, such as the *mDo sde za ma tog* [*Kāraṇḍavyūhasūtra*, The Sūtra Designed as a Jewel Chest], the *sPang skong phyag brgya pa* [*Sakṣipūraṇasudraka*, The Hundredfold Homage for Mending Breaches], and so on. Some of them, however, show different opinions about the objects received and the manner in which they were received. An approximate idea of these differences can be had by consulting a few sources. For example, the *lDe'u rgya bod kyi chos 'byung* says (Bod, 249, 15):

The golden *sPang skong phyag brgya pa* [*Sakṣipūraṇasudraka*, The Hundredfold Homage for Mending Breaches] and a four-storey turquoise stūpa descended to his hands from the sky.

The *Grags rgyal bod kyi rgyal rabs* says (sDe, TA, 197, 5, 5):

The *sPang skong phyag brgya pa* [*Sakṣipūraṇasudraka*, The Hundredfold Homage for Mending Breaches], a golden stūpa a full cubit [in height], the Six Syllable [*mantra*], and a Cintāmaṇi [wish-fulfilling jewel] mold [*kol phor*] came from the sky.

The *rGyal rabs 'phrul gyi lde mig* says (Dhi, 6, 14, I):

lHa-tho-tho-ri gNyan-btsan was considered an emanation of Kun-tu bZang-po [Samantabhadra]. When he was residing at the 'Um-bu Glang-mkhar Castle, the *mDo sde za ma tog bkod pa* [*Kāraṇḍavyūhasūtra*, The Sūtra Designed as a Jewel Chest], the *sPang skong phyag brgya pa* [*Sakṣipūraṇasudraka*, The Hundredfold Homage for Mending Breaches], and a golden stūpa fell from the sky.

[The king] called them Secret Powerful Objects [gNyan-po gSang-ba] and venerated them; for that reason he obtained [a lifespan of] one hundred twenty years.

He also had a prophetic dream in which he was told, "The meaning of these objects will be understood five generations after yours."

According to Nel-pa [Nel-pa Paṇḍita Grags-pa sMon-lam Blo-gros, thirteenth century], the Bon-pos said that [the objects] had dropped from the sky because the sky [gods were] pleased. In reality they had been brought by the Paṇḍita Blo-sems-mtsho and the translator Li-thi Pes-ches, but since the king did not understand the meaning of the written words, he put the Dharma objects aside and told the Paṇḍita and the translator to return.

Blo-sems-mtsho and Zhi-ba-mtsho are the same person; in previous texts it is explained that the scholar who had been waiting in Nepal at the time of the ninth Tibetan dynasty said that [the texts] were most probably authentic.

During the Intermediate Period it would appear no extensive constructions of royal tombs were made. Not a single history describes the construction of royal tombs until the arrival of lHa-tho-tho gNyan-btsan, except for some approximate information about King sPu-lde Gung-rgyal and his minister Ru-las-skyes building a tomb for King Gri-gum.

As for the tomb of lHa-tho-tho-ri gNyan-btsan, the *rGyal rabs gsal ba'i me long* says (Pe, 60 ,4):

> His tomb was built in his own birthplace. The name of the place
> was Phying-yul Dar-thang. The tomb was an earth mound that
> resembled a black yak hair tent.

This type of tomb in the shape of an earth mound resembling a black yak hair tent is not as imposing as those found in later times; however, the text clearly indicates that a tomb was built. The same source also contains explicit indications about the tomb of Khri-snyan gZung-btsan, son of lHa-tho-tho-ri gNyan-btsan (ibid., PE, 60, 9):

> His tomb was built at Don-'khor-mda'. It had the semblance
> of a heap of soil;

and also about the tomb of Khri-snyan gZung-btsan's son, 'Brong-snyan lDe-ru (ibid., PE, 61, 7):

> The tomb of 'Brong-snyan lDe-ru was built at Zhang-mda'.
> The name of the tomb was gSon-chas Zlum-po.

The name of the tomb indicates that it consisted of a rounded [*zlum po*] structure. The tomb of 'Brong-snyan lDe-ru's son sTag-ri gNyan-gzigs (ibid., PE, 61, 14):

> was built at Don-'khor-mda'. It was situated on the left side
> of Khri-snyan gZung-btsan['s grave]. It had the semblance of
> a heap of soil.

As we can see, most of the tombs were spherical in form and pointed at the top, much like a contemporary hooded rain cape [*char khebs*]. The tomb of gNam-ri Srong-bstan, son of sTag-ri sNyan-gzigs (ibid., PE, 61, 21):

was built at Don-mkhar–mda' [*sic*]. It was situated on the right side of Khri-snyan gZung-btsan['s grave]. It was a big mound [resembling a] shoulder blade.

Examining how this tomb is described, we can understand its form is similar to that of a shoulder blade with a small and narrow upper side and a lower side of larger dimensions, surmounted by a slightly bigger structure similar to a rain cape; such a structure shows that burial notions underwent great improvement from the time of lHa-tho-tho-ri gNyan-btsan.

2. THE THIRTY-FIFTH RULER OF TIBET: SRONG-BTSAN SGAM-PO

Srong-btsan sGam-po is this king's most renowned name; however in the religious history of Bu-ston [1290-1364] and in that of Klong-chen-pa [1308-1364], Pad-ma dKar-po [1527-1592], and the like, the name of this king is Khri-lde Srong-btsan, [whereas] in the *Chos 'byung mkhas pa'i dga' ston* he is called Khri Srong-btsan. This last name is the real one. That is certain because the *Tun hong bod kyi lo rgyus yig rnying* [Old Tibetan Chronicles of Dunhuang] (PI 579, 12, 14) clearly call him "bTsan po [King] Khri-srong-rtsan;" and even if the religious histories of Bu-ston and so on call him Khri-lde Srong-btsan, we can implicitly understand that his name is actually Khri Srong-btsan.

The *Tun hong bod kyi lo rgyus yig rnying* [Old Tibetan Chronicles of Dunhuang] (PI 556, 62) also call him Srong-lde-brtsan. Combining these last two names, Khri-srong-rtsan and Srong-lde-brtsan, we obtain Khri-lde Srong-btsan.

In any case, *khri* is a Zhang Zhung word which in Tibetan means deity or Mind [*thugs*], while *srong* is an archaic Tibetan term which means fair [*drang po*], brave [*mdzangs pa*], and so forth.

The archaic term *brtsan*, which corresponds to the modern *btsan*, can either mean sharp [*rnon po*] or king [*rgyal po*]. To be exact, this name used in modern Tibetan would be Thugs-mdzangs rNon-po or Thugs-mdzangs rGyal-po.

According to ancient Tibetan custom, this name was used by the Bonpos to address the gShens who protected the king [sKu-gshen]; hence, it is evident that [the name] became a mixture of Zhang Zhung and Tibetan.

The *Gleng gzhi bstan pa'i byung khungs* says (IsMEO, 19):

> His son was Srong-btsan sGam-po, who was also called Khri Srong-btsan sGam-po. His sKu-gshen [was] Zhang-zhung Ra-ring.

The *Dar rgyas gsal sgron* says (Thob, 669, 87, 5):

> At that time, gTso-bon gNam-la-skyes and Sum-bon rGyal-la-dbang [who acted] as the Bla-bon [royal master] of the king implored the protectors; the diseases and famine stopped.

All of the sKu-gshens mentioned in the citations attributed this famous name to the king, most probably from when he ascended the throne. This certainty can be gained by reading the following two citations which clearly explain both the reasons and the meaning of the name. The *rGyal rabs gsal ba'i me long* says (Pe, 64, 22):

> By the time the prince reached adulthood, since he was gifted and had become expert in the Five Traditional Sciences [grammar, logic, craftsmanship, healing, and spirituality], art, astrology, and engineering, the ministers said: "This Lord of ours is endowed with manifold skills. His mind is profound [*sgam*]." So they called him Srong-btsan sGam-po.

The *lHo brag chos 'byung* says (Pe, Vol. I, 175, 19):

> He was called Khri Srong-btsan, but since he was endowed with many qualities and his mind was profound, his name became Srong-btsan sGam-po.

Concerning the date of birth of Srong-btsan sGam-po, Tibetan historians agree that the Dharmarāja's birth occurred in an Ox year, but are of two opinions about the element of that year, maintaining that it was either a Fire Ox year or an Earth Ox year.

Generally speaking, old records of ancient history were for the most part accurate in reporting which animal of the twelve-year cycle,

Mouse, Ox, Tiger, and so forth, was involved; but they were not accustomed to calculating which element was to be attributed to a given year. For that reason, when historians of later times were composing new religious and dynastic texts, they contented themselves with reporting the year of birth or death of ancient kings, famous lamas, masters, and important persons indicated in earlier records, but would also decide which one of the five elements, Wood, Fire, Earth, Metal, and Water would better harmonize with the flow of history and in doing so they habitually altered and excised the content of those historical sources. This is why famed religious and dynastic histories as well as historical records present all sorts of mutually contradictory information. Even so, if we consult the various historical records and dynastic histories in an equitable way and search scrupulously for the real sense, it is not impossible that the genuine historical truth fully emerge and that the reasons for the degree and facets of these variances be revealed.

As I have said, the majority of Tibetan historical records show that Srong-btsan sGam-po was born either in the Fire Ox year or in the Earth Ox year. The *Deb ther dkar po* affirms (Si, 109, 10):

> Although many histories indicate that his year of birth was that of the Ox, scholars disagree about the relevant cycle and element.
> The Great Fifth [Dalai Lama Ngag-dbang Blo-bzang rGya-mtsho, 1642-1682] and 'Gos [Lo-tsa-ba gZhon-nu-dpal, 1392-1481] maintain that he was born in the Earth Ox year, while Bu-ston and others say that he was born in the Fire Ox year.

The primary sources for the assumption that Srong-btsan sGam-po was born in an Earth Ox year are the *Deb ther dmar po* which determines the chronology of the king's life by conforming to Chinese historical records and the highly detailed *Deb ther sngon po*. The *Deb ther dkar po* says (Si, 110, 11):

> Even though 'Gos himself and the Chinese annals clearly indicate the year of death of Srong-btsan sGam-po, for some reason they never specify the year of birth.

While that is indeed the case, the author of the *Deb ther sngon po* ['Gos Lo-tsa-ba gZhon-nu-dpal] also constructs the chronology derived from the prophecies concerning the Tibetan kings contained in the root Tantras and says (ibid., Si, Vol. I, 71, 19):

> He ruled the kingdom until he was eighty and lived [until he was] eighty-two.

The author bases his words on a traditional view found in famous histories; perceiving no contradiction between the tantric texts and that renowned traditional view, he agrees that Srong-btsan sGam-po died when he was eighty-two. Concerning the year of death of Srong-btsan sGam-po the *Deb ther dmar po* (Pe, 18, 23) says:

> The Tibetan king Srong-btsan sGam-po died in the male Metal Dog year.

This statement based upon Chinese records identifies the year of death of Srong-btsan sGam-po as the Metal Dog year (Tibetan year 2567, 650 CE).

By subtracting or calculating backward the eighty-two years of Srong-btsan sGam-po's life from that Metal Dog year, we arrive at the female Earth Ox year of the last *sMe-phreng* of the fourteenth *sMe-'khor* (Tibetan year 2486, 569 CE), which explains the reason for 'Gos Lo-tsa-ba's assertion.

The Metal Dog year is therefore the year of death of Srong-btsan sGam-po, a date that tallies with Chinese historical records. If in addition, we consider that Srong-btsan sGam-po lived for eighty-two years, the only suitable date for his year of birth would be the Earth Ox year of the last *sMe-phreng* of the fourteenth *sMe-'khor*.

Nevertheless, 'Gos Lo-tsa-ba's assertion according to which the Earth Ox year of Srong-btsan sGam-po's birth is most probably to be identified with the female Earth Ox year of the fifteenth *sMe-'khor* (Tibetan year 2546, 629 CE) is totally misleading. In this respect the *Deb ther sngon po* says (Si, Vol. I, 94, 14):

> Lo-tsā-ba Rin-chen bZang-po was born in the male Earth Horse year, 329 years after Srong-btsan's birth.

If from the date of birth of Lo-tsā-ba Rin-chen bZang-po [d. 1055] which falls in the male Earth Horse year of the last *sMe-phreng* of the sixteenth *sMe-'khor* (Tibetan year 2875, 958 CE), we subtract or calculate backward 329 years, we arrive at the female Earth Ox year of the first *sMe-phreng* of the fifteenth *sMe-'khor* (Tibetan year 2546, 629 CE). Furthermore, the text says (Si, Vol. 2, 1249, 7):

> A little over 720 years after the birth of the Dharmarāja Srong-btsan sGam-po, the Omniscient Blo-bzang Grags-pa'i-dpal came into this world. He took birth in the region of Tsong-kha in the female Fire Bird year.

If from the year of birth of rJe Tsong-kha-pa—said to be the female Fire Bird year of the first *sMe-phreng* of the nineteenth *sMe-'khor* or of the sixth *rab byung* [1327-1386] (Tibetan year 3274, 1357 CE)—we subtract the 720 years elapsed from the birth of Srong-btsan sGam-po, we arrive at the year 2554 of the Tibetan calendar and at the Western year 637.

The author says, "[O]ver 720 years after the birth of the Dharmarāja Srong-btsan sGam-po..." With an accurate calculation we can see that the word 'over' [*lhag*] implicitly indicates that eight years have been added for practical purposes.

Therefore, since it had been clearly shown that the year of birth of Srong-btsan sGam-po was the Earth Ox year of the first *sMe-phreng* of the fifteenth *sMe-'khor* (Tibetan year 2546, 629 CE), the *Deb ther dkar po* says (Si, 109, 13):

> By considering that Ox [year] as the Earth Ox [year] of the first *sMe-phreng* [of the fifteenth *sMe-'khor*], 'Gos states that Srong-btsan lived for eighty-two years.

This statement seems incongruous and gives rise to doubt; or maybe the author does not accept 'Gos opinion according to which Srong-btsan sGam-po was probably born in the Earth Ox year of the first *sMe-phreng* of the fifteenth *sMe-'khor* (Tibetan year 2546, 629 CE).

In his *Deb ther dpyid kyi rgyal mo'i glu dbyangs* the Great Fifth clearly asserts that the year of birth of Srong-btsan sGam-po was the Earth Ox year (Pe, 18, 8):

> [He] was born in the female Earth Ox year called *'gal ba* in the Byams-pa Mi-'gyur-gling Palace as the son of King gNam-ri Srong-bstan and [Queen] Tshe-spong-bza' 'Bri-ma Thod-dkar, 1508 years after Kun-mkyen Nyi-ma'i-gnyen [The Omniscient, Kinsman of the Sun, that is, Buddha Śākyamuni] entered *parinirvāṇa* in the peaceful dimension of reality [*zhi ba chos dbyings, dharmadhātu*].

To discover the *sMe-phreng* of that Earth Ox year we take into consideration the Phug-pa system of astrological calculation,[38] which determines that Buddha Śākyamuni entered *nirvāṇa* in the male Metal Dragon year (Tibetan year 1037, 581 BCE). If we subtract the 1,508 years of the Buddha's *nirvāṇa* from the female Earth Ox year of the first *sMe-phreng* of the fifteenth *sMe-'khor* (2546), the resulting number will be 1308 (2546−1508=1308), which corresponds to the male Metal Dragon year (Tibetan year 1037, 581 BCE) of the last *sMe-phreng* of the sixth *sMe-'khor*. If we identify that as the year of the Buddha's *nirvāṇa*, reckoning it as the first year of the *nirvāṇa* and add 1508, the only suitable year would be the female Earth Ox year of the first *sMe-phreng* of the fifteenth *sMe-'khor* (Tibetan year 2546, 629 CE). That is why it is accepted that the Earth Ox year in which Srong-btsan sGam-po was born is the one of the fifteenth *sMe-'khor*.

One of the most important traditional sources that considers Srong-btsan sGam-po's birth to have occurred in the Fire Ox year is the *Nyang gi chos 'byung*. The text says (Bod, 167, 6):

> [He] was born painlessly in the third month of the Fire Ox year.

Although mNga'-bdag Nyang-ral Nyi-ma 'Od-zer (1124-1192) does not specify the source of his statement, the scholar Ne'u Paṇḍita Grags-pa sMon-lam (thirteenth century), who came after Nyang-ral

---

38 [The system was devised by Gra-phug-pa Lhun-grub rGya-mtsho and is expounded in his *Pad dkar zhal lung*, compiled in 1447.]

and composed the *sNgon gyi gtam me tog phreng ba* [1283], acknowledged the latter's statement.

During the course of history, the majority of dynastic and religious treatises, such as

- the *Chos 'byung gsung rab rin po che'i mdzod* by Bu-ston Rin-chen-grub (1290-1364),
- the *Chos 'byung rin po che'i gter mdzod* by Klong-chen-pa Dri-med 'Od-zer (1308-1363),
- the *Chos 'byung* (compiled in 1310) of Yar-lung Jo-bo Shakya Rin-chen-sde,
- the *Deb ther dmar po* of Tshal-pa Kun-dga' rDo-rje (1309-1364),
- the *rGyal rabs gsal ba'i me long* composed by Sa-skya-pa Bla-ma Dam-pa bSod-nams rGyal-mtshan (1312-1375),
- the *rGyal rabs me long rnam gsal* composed by the treasure revealer [gter-ston] gTer-chen Ratna Gling-pa (1403-1478),
- the *Chos 'byung mkhas pa'i dga' ston* of dPa'-bo Tsug-lag Phreng-ba (1504-1566),
- the *rGya bod yig tshang chen mo* by sTag-tshang rDzong-pa dPal-'byor bZang-po (1434-?),
- the *rGyal rabs 'Phrul gyi lde mig* of Paṇ-chen bSod-nams Grags-pa (1478-1554),
- the *bsTan rtsis gsal ba'i nyin byed* of Mang-thos Klu-sgrub rGya-mtsho (1523-1596),
- the *lHa thog rgyal rabs* (composed in 1753) by Bya-rog 'Gyur-med rNam-rgyal,
- the *rGyal rabs deb ther dkar po* by dGe-'dun Chos-'phel (1905-1951), and so on have recognized, following mNga'-bdag-nyang and Ne'u Paṇḍita, that the date of birth of Srong-btsan sGam-po was the female Fire Ox year. The identification of that Fire Ox year conforms to the specific outlooks of each individual scholar vis-à-vis the year of the teacher Buddha Śākyamuni's *nirvāṇa*. In actuality, the year should be identified with the female Fire Ox year of the first *sMe-phreng* of the fifteenth *sMe-'khor* (Tibetan year 2534, 617 CE).

Great Tibetan Buddhist scholars consider the most important periods of the dynastic histories in relation to the year of the Buddha's *nirvāṇa*. Several ways of identifying that year exist, even when it has been determined under which sixty-year cycle the Buddha's *nirvāṇa* took place. For that reason it is difficult to reach an exact understanding of the historical stages. Let us consider the most important of them.

According to the reckoning method of Phug-pa, the Teacher Buddha entered the womb in the female Earth Sheep year (Tibetan year 956), took birth in the male Metal Monkey year (957), attained enlightenment in the male Wood Horse year (991), and at the age of eighty-one in the male Metal Dragon year (1037) entered *nirvāṇa* after having taught the Kālachakra Tantra [*Dus kyi 'khor lo'i rgyud*].

According to g.Yung-ston [rDo-rje dPal-bzang, 1284-1365] and sTag[-tshang] Lo[-tsa-ba Shes-rab Rin-chen, b. 1405], the Teacher Śākyamuni took birth in the male Wood Mouse year (961), attained enlightenment in the female Earth Pig year (996), taught the Kālachakra Tantra at the age of seventy-eight in the female Metal Snake year (1038), and when he was eighty in the female Water Sheep year (1040) entered *nirvāṇa*.

According to mTshur[-phu Don-grub 'Od-zer, fourteenth century], the Teacher Śākyamuni took birth in the male Wood Mouse year (961), attained enlightenment in the male Earth Mouse year (985), and at eighty in the female Water Sheep year (1040) taught the Kālachakra and entered *nirvāṇa*.

According to Bu-ston, the Teacher Śākyamuni took birth in the male Fire Horse year (1003), attained enlightenment in the female Metal Snake year (1038), and entered *nirvāṇa* in the male Fire Tiger year (1143).

Any of the chosen years of birth and death of Buddha Śākyamuni has become an historical basis or model for determining the time period in which the Dharmarāja Srong-btsan sGam-po appeared. In this regard, the *Chos 'byung* of Klong-chen-pa is to be considered as an indicative example (Del. Vol. 2, 392, 3):

> At the time of the lHa-mo Dri-med [Immaculate Goddess] prophecy [the Buddha] said, "The year of my *nirvāṇa* [will be the year] 2000. Five hundred [years] after my *nirvāṇa*, the Dharma will appear in the snowy country of the ruddy-faced ones."

The number of years mentioned in the prophecy matches with the arrival of mTho-do sNyan-btsan at Yum-bu Bla-sgang in Yar-lung.

That year exceeds the one of the Nepalese king, which is the male Earth Monkey year.

'Od-zer Go-cha modified the year by [adding] 198 [years to] the Fire Rabbit year, [the first of the] *rab byung*, and said that the year 2000 reckoned in the prophecy [of the Buddha's *nirvāṇa*] and the 700 [years that result from his modification] are antithetical.

Then ten years [after] in the female Fire Ox year, the eleventh year of the *rab byung* [*dbang phyug lo*], the Lord of Tibet, King Srong-btsan sGam-po, was born.

The excerpt shows that no precise calculating method is employed to establish the reckoning of each number of years, apart from a formulation of the time periods based on approximate justifications.

Concerning the time at which the Dharmarāja Srong-btsan sGam-po ascended the throne, many religious and dynastic histories, such as the *lDe'u chos 'byung chen mo* and the like, maintain that Srong-btsan sGam-po was enthroned when he was thirteen years old after his father, gNam-ri Srong-btsan, died. The *Nyang gi chos 'byung*, on the contrary, affirms that the prince ascended the throne when his father was still alive (Bod, 168, 1):

Then, when he reached the age of twelve, the Prince expressed his view and pleaded with his parents saying, "I have pledged in the presence of Amitābha to care for the spiritual and material wealth of the sentient beings of Tibet; but also the Bodhisattva Monkey has made the same promise and because of that, now in this snowy kingdom, the children of the Monkey and the Crag-Demoness have become brutes. For that reason it has not been possible to tame them with peaceful means; drastic orders and punishments are required and great power is necessary for that." Extremely pleased, [the parents] summoned all the subjects and requested the Prince to seat himself on the precious throne. The father, surrendering his political authority, appointed and enthroned him as the ruler of the whole kingdom.

The *Yar lung jo bo'i chos 'byung* affirms (Si, 51, 17):

> Either the father died thirteen years after his birth or the father
> himself enthroned him; [at any rate,] he was empowered as king
> at the age of thirteen.

Even though some discordant or uncertain opinions such as this one
exist, in actual fact most of the Tibetan historical and religious documents agree that Srong-btsan sGam-po ascended the throne when he
was a full twelve or thirteen years old.

King Srong-btsan sGam-po with his Nepalese wife Bal-mo-bza' (left) and
Chinese wife rGya-mo-bza' (right). Ra-sa 'Phrul-snang [Jokhang], Lhasa.

2.1. QUEENS AND CHILDREN OF THE DHARMARĀJA SRONG-BTSAN SGAM-PO

In their religious and historical treatises Tibetan scholars say that as a youth the Dharmarāja Srong-btsan sGam-po married first a Nepalese princess and then a Chinese one; however, since these two principal wives did not bear him children, he eventually took other women in marriage. For example, in the *rGyal rabs gsal ba'i me long* we read (Pe, 158, 16):

> Then, since neither Bal-mo-bza' nor rGya-mo-bza' gave birth to a son, he married Zhang-zhung-bza'. She had no sons as well and for that reason requested the construction of the Thim-bu lKog-pa Temple. This temple was built at lCags-kha-khong.
>
> Then he married Ru-yong-bza'. She also had no sons; for that reason she requested the construction of the Mig-mangs-tshal Temple. This temple was built at Go-sha-gling.
>
> Then he married Mi-nyag-bza'. She also had no sons; for that reason she requested the construction of the Kha-brag-gser Temple. This temple was built at mKhar-sna-gdong.
>
> Then he married Mang-bza' Khri-lcam, [choosing her] from the sTod, Lung, and Mang [tribes].

The text clearly indicates the names of the five princesses taken in marriage and specifies that they did not give him children, also saying that the first of the princesses was Bal-bza' Khri-btsun. In this regard the *Dar rgyas gsal sgron*, quoting from the old Bonpo source *Byams ma*, stipulates that before the Nepalese and Chinese consorts he had married a princess from Zhang Zhung (Thob, 669, 87, 1):

> As for his queens, the *Byams ma* says:
> "From Zhang Zhung [he] took in marriage Zhang-zhung-za Lig-ting-sman. [She] brought a statue the size of a one-year-old [child representing] gShen-rab, the Lord of the Teachings, the Buddha of Zhang Zhung. For that reason the Them-them [*sic*] Temple was built.
>
> From Nepal [he] took in marriage Bal-bza' Khri-btsun; [she] brought a silver *maṇḍala* of Byams-pa [Maitreya], the Buddha of Nepal. For that reason the Ra-sa 'Phrul-snang [Temple] was built.

From China [he] took in marriage rGya-za Ong-co;[39] [she]
brought the statue of an eight-year-old Śākyamuni [Thub-pa],
the Buddha of China. For that reason the Ra-mo-che Temple
was built."

The *bKa' chems ka khol ma* says (Kan, 270, 9):

The first queen [was] Pho-gong Mong-bza' Khri-btsun. She
[requested the construction of the] mKhar-brag Temple [which
was] built of wood, gold, silver, copper, and iron.
      After her [came] Zhang-zhung-bza' Khri-btsun. She [re-
quested the construction of the] Yer-pa Them-bu lKog-pa
Temple [which was] built of bricks, wood, gold, and silver.

According to this source Zhang-zhung-bza' was married just after
Mong-bza'. When Srong-btsan was young, he first established an alli-
ance with Zhang Zhung by giving his sister Sad-mar-kar in marriage
to King Lig-mi-rkya. The *Tun hong bod kyi lo rgyus yig rnying* [Old Tibetan
Chronicles of Dunhuang] say (PI 572, 398):

During the lifetime of this king, Zhang Zhung [and] the Tibetan
king [lDe-bu] became allies. After a joyful [salutatory] tourna-
ment, Queen [*btsan mo*] Sad-mar-kar left for the kingdom of
Lig-myi-rhya to marry her Zhang Zhung consort.

Fom this statement one can logically infer that when King Srong-btsan
sGam-po sent his sister Sad-mar-kar to be the consort of the Zhang
Zhung king the latter reciprocated by offering him Zhang-zhung-bza'
Lig-ting-sman as a spouse.
      Srong-btsan sGam-po decided to establish a close connection with
Zhang Zhung because at that time the kingdom of Zhang Zhung was
much more powerful than Tibet. The *Zhang zhung snyan rgyud kyi bon ma
nub pa'i gtan tshig* says (Dhi, 260, 1, 5):

As for [the time and] the kings, it was the era when King Lig-
mi-rgya of Zhang Zhung, King Pan-ra-ling of Mon, and King
Khri-srong lDe-btsan of Tibet were in power.

---

39   [Princess Wénchéng Gōngzhǔ 文成公主, died in 680.]

Prior to that period, when each of these kings was young, there were only three ministers [in Tibet], one for foreign affairs, one for internal affairs, and one ambassador [*phrin blon*].

When King Khri-srong lDe-btsan was in power, there were ten ministers for foreign affairs, ten ministers for internal affairs, and ten ambassadors, thirty in all. At that time the power of the king was great: he subdued the king of sTag-gzig Nor and built long wooden bridges so that the commercial routes of border countries that were blocked by wide rivers could be reached.

At that same time the Zhang Zhung king Lig-mi-rgya was in power. The military strength of Zhang Zhung consisted of 990 units of 1,000 soldiers [each] and besides that there were [also] the commanders of the Sum-pa 1,000 soldier units.

Tibet did not have more than forty-two or forty-three units of 1,000 soldiers [each]. The Tibetan king could not possibly have conquered the king of Zhang Zhung. The king of Tibet reflected [on the matter] and decided that he would defeat the king of Zhang Zhung with wicked and underhanded means.

Even if this text of the *Zhang zhung snyan rgyud* cycle mentions Khri-srong lDe-btsan instead of Srong-lde-btsan, that is certainly a mistake in writing. The *Tun hong bod kyi lo rgyus yig rnying* [Old Tibetan Chronicles of Dunhuang] say (PI 556, 61):

The son generated from the union of Slon-btsan Rlung-nam with Tshes-pong-za 'Bring-ma Thog-dgos was Srong-lde-brtsan.

Because of this authoritative source we can be confident that the name of the Dharmarāja Srong-btsan sGam-po was 'Srong-lde-btsan,' as we can be certain that the story of King Lig-mi-rkya is true, since it is clearly described in the *Zhang zhung snyan rgyud*.

The *Tun hong bod kyi lo rgyus yig rnying* [Old Tibetan Chronicles of Dunhuang] also say (PI 574, 433):

During the era of this king, the Zhang Zhung king was conquered. Political actions were undertaken; King Lig-myig-rhya of Zhang Zhung was defeated; and the whole of Zhang Zhung was subjugated.

The *Chronicles* unambiguously indicate that the Dharmarāja Srong-btsan sGam-po annihilated the power of the Zhang Zhung king Lig-mi-rkya and that Zhang Zhung was brought under the Tibetan dominion. The way that occurred can be understood by consulting the precise exposition contained in the *Zhang zhung snyan rgyud*. In this regard we can also understand that the *Zhang zhung snyan rgyud* was brought from Zhang Zhung to Tibet during the time of the Dharmarāja Srong-btsan sGam-po because from the moment of his conquest of Zhang Zhung no accounts of King Lig-mi-rkya's descendants ruling Zhang Zhung can be found, even if in the times of the Dharmarāja Khri-srong lDe-btsan and the master and king Khri Ral-pa-can some peoples of Outer Zhang Zhung [Zhang Zhung Phug-pa] still had not been brought under Tibetan dominion.

The *rGyal rabs gsal ba'i me long* and other sources indicate that the queens Ru-yong-bza', Mi-nyag-bza', and Mang-bza' Khri-lcam became the king's spouses only after Bal-bza' Khri-btsun and rGya-bza' Kong-jo. This is confirmed by the *Tun hong bod kyi lo rgyus yig rnying* [Old Tibetan Chronicles of Dunhuang] (PI 579, 14):

> Then after six years King Khri-srong-rtsan departed for heaven. He had been married to Queen Mun-cang Kong-co for three years.

Hence Srong-btsan sGam-po spent three years with Kong-jo before his death.

This means that rGya bza' Kong-jo met the Dharmarāja Srong-btsan sGam-po in the female Fire Sheep year (Tibetan 2564, 647 CE) when the king was seventy-eight and acted as the king's consort for three full years. Then, in the three years after marrying Kong-jo, the Dharmarāja Srong-btsan sGam-po would have married Zhang-zhung-bza', Ru-yong-bza', Mi-nyag-bza', and Mang-bza'; such a happening, apart from its ascription to a sudden magical increase in fortune, is considered extremely unlikely in the ordinary world.

The fact that the Dharmarāja Srong-btsan sGam-po married a young Chinese princess after he grew old is not impossible nor unthinkable; generally speaking it was often customary for kings of ancient times to marry many young spouses also when they were aged. However the Dharmarāja Srong-btsan sGam-po did not marry Bal-bza' Khri-btsun from Nepal and rGya-bza' Kong-jo from China after he had already reached an advanced number of years just for the pleasure of the senses, but for specific reasons related to Tibetan politics; it goes without saying that establishing family alliances was certainly an important part of those reasons.

In the past, King Gri-gum—the first of the so-called Two sTengs of Western Tibet [sTod-kyi sTengs-gnyis] who came after the Seven Khri of the Sky [gNam-gyi Khri-bdun]—had suppressed the teachings of Bon in order to prevent Tibet from falling under the strong ascendancy of Zhang Zhung. Even though the power of the Bon-gShens connected with Zhang Zhung was declining, at that time the only prevalent culture in the kingdom of Tibet was Bon, and for that reason King Gri-gum bTsan-po was not able to fulfill his wish. The Dharmarāja Srong-btsan sGam-po, counseled by that historical experience, married Bal-bza' and rGya-bza' in order to introduce the sacred Dharma from India and China together with all its various forms of relevant cultural expression. The relations harbored by Tibet with India and China improved. This is confirmed by the accounts contained in old historical sources.

For what concerns King Gung-srong, the *Lho brag chos 'byung* says (Pe, Vol. I, 245, 21):

> Gung-srong was born in the female Iron Snake year [when] the father was fifty-three.

If we consider this statement it becomes obvious that Queen Mang-bza' Khri-lcam, the mother of Gung-srong Gung-btsan, had been married for years before she had children. Details about Srong-btsan sGam-po's son Gung-srong Gung-btsan are scanty. Since Srong-btsan had no other sons, his nephew [*dbon sras*] Mang-srong Mang-btsan was installed on the throne; that would indicate that no other male offspring had been born although it is difficult to know. Historical information on any of the queens having begotten female children is also lacking.

Concerning the identity of the main cabinet ministers [bKa'-blon] of Dharmarāja Srong-btsan sGam-po, we gain a slight idea from the *lDe'u rgya bod kyi chos 'byung*, which says (Bod, 253, 17):

> Khyung-po sPu-stang Zung-rtse and Mong-khri lTo-ri sNang-tshab acted as ministers. Then, for twenty-one years, sTong-btsan Yul-bzung was in charge.

And from the *lDe'u chos 'byung chen mo*, which affirms (Bod, 108, 19):

> Khyung-po Su-sna Zu-tse and Mong-khri Do-re sNang-tshab acted as ministers. Mong was disgraced; after that 'Gar sTong-btsan Yul-gzungs was in charge for twenty years. gCo Dar-rgyal Mang-po-rje Srong-nam was also in charge for twenty-five years.

The issue of Dharmarāja Srong-btsan sGam-po's years of life and death will now be briefly examined. If Srong-btsan sGam-po was born either in the female Fire Ox year (Tibetan year 2534, 617 CE) or in the female Earth Ox year (Tibetan year 2546, 629 CE) of the first *sMe-phreng* of the fifteenth *sMe-'khor* and lived for eighty-two years, the year of his death should be either the male Earth Dog year (Tibetan year 2615, 698 CE) or the male Metal Dog year (Tibetan year 2627, 710 CE) of the intermediate *sMe-phreng*. In this respect the *Tun hong bod kyi lo rgyus yig rnying* [Old Tibetan Chronicles of Dunhuang] and other sources, such as the Old and New *rGya'i thang yig* [Chronicles of the Chinese Táng 唐 dynasty] and so on, clearly state that Srong-btsan sGam-po died in the Metal Dog year (Tibetan 2567, 650 CE) of the first *sMe-phreng* of the fifteenth *sMe-'khor*. That shows itself to be a serious contradiction and totally improbable, because if in the Metal Dog year mentioned in the *Tun hong bod kyi lo rgyus yig rnying* [Old Tibetan Chronicles of Dunhuang] and in the Old and New *rGya'i thang yig* [Chronicles of the Chinese Táng 唐 dynasty] Srong-btsan sGam-po was eighty-two, no year would be suitable for his birth other than the female Earth Ox year of the last *sMe-phreng* of the fourteenth *sMe-'khor* (Tibetan year 2486, 569 CE).

Without taking into account the different dates for the years of birth and death of the Dharmarāja Srong-btsan sGam-po established on the basis of the year of the teacher Buddha Śākyamuni's *parinirvāna*, in actuality only thirty-four or thirty-two full years separate the female Fire or female Earth Ox year, which are part of the first *sMe-phreng* of the fifteenth *sMe-'khor*, from the male Earth or male Iron Dog year of the same *sMe-'khor*, making it categorically impossible for him to have arrived at eighty-two years.

The great scholar dGe-'dun Chos-'phel writes in his *Deb ther dkar po* (Si, 111,11):

> Srong-btsan was born in the Fire Ox year. The Earth Ox year is considered the year when he was installed on the throne. If all the surviving stories of former generations have considered Chinese historical accounts valid and reckon [those years] as belonging to one single sixty-year cycle, a commanding reason must exist for that. Assuming that it is so, Srong-btsan was [then] born in the Fire Ox year which occurs 1161 years after the Buddha's *nirvāna*. When he was thirteen, he was installed on the throne. When he was eighteen, Sino-Tibetan relations were initiated. When he was twenty-five, he received Kong-jo as his bride. Therefore when the *Deb sngon* says that the Tibetans fought China for eight whole years or so, I think that those years should correspond to the ages eighteen through twenty-five of Srong-btsan's life. Then, at the age of thirty-four, in the Metal Dog year, he died.

The author does not explain the reasons determining that reckoning.

Most accomplished Tibetan scholars of the past have unanimously said that the Dharmarāja Srong-btsan sGam-po lived eighty-two years. In this regard, in his *Deb ther dkar po*, the great scholar dGe-'dun Chos-'phel affirms (Si, 111, 7):

> Also their saying that he lived until he was eighty is in fact purely based upon a tantric prophecy. If the meaning of the words of the Tantra is very different, [that meaning] is not apparent at the moment, so it will not be considered here.

However, the *lDe'u chos 'byung chen mo* says (Bod, 117, 21):

Eventually when he was eighty-four, having ruled the kingdom for sixty-nine years, he departed for heaven at Zal-mo'i-'tshal in 'Phan-yul [north of Lhasa].

This text maintains that he lived eighty-four years. The majority of other religious and dynastic histories say that the Dharmarāja Srong-btsan sGam-po lived until he was eighty-two; that can only be attributed to their faith in the Tantra which is something extremely hard to explain. At any rate, if they were basing themselves upon that particular prophecy, it would have been more appropriate to say that the Dharmarāja Srong-btsan sGam-po lived until he was eighty; there was no need whatsoever to say that he lived until he was eighty-two or eighty-four.

Many Tibetan scholars have identified the year of death of the Dharmarāja Srong-btsan sGam-po with the Earth Dog or Metal Dog year of the intermediate *sMe-phreng* of the fifteenth *sMe-'khor*. For example, the *Deb ther dpyid kyi rgyal mo'i glu dbyangs* says (Pe, 46,22):

> From that time 932 years have elapsed until the Water Sheep year of the present eleventh sixty-year cycle [*rab byung*].

As the text says, from the male Metal Dog year (Tibetan year 2567, 650 CE) until the Water Sheep year of the eleventh *rab byung*, which corresponds to the Water Sheep year of the intermediate *sMe-phreng* of the twentieth *sMe-'khor* (Tibetan year 3500, 1583 CE), 932 full years or just about 933 years have elapsed (3500-933=2567).

The establishment of the periods of ancient history is based on major sources, such as the *Tun hong bod kyi lo rgyus yig rnying* [Old Tibetan Chronicles of Dunhuang] and the like. Nevertheless, to develop a solid understanding of the periods mentioned in those sources, we must compare them precisely with the histories of the countries bordering Tibet, so that the question can be conclusively settled. That is why the eminent scholar dGe'-'dun Chos-'phel said, "all the subsisting stories of former generations have considered the Chinese historical accounts valid;" that is also the reason why the *Deb ther sngon po* and *Deb ther dmar po* refer to Chinese chronologies.

The *rGya'i thang yig rnying pa* [Old Chronicles of the Chinese Táng 唐 dynasty] say (Dha, 13, 17):

In the first year of reign of the Yuung-dbu'i [era] (Metal Dog year, 650 CE),[40] Thang Ka'o-tsung, grieved over Srong-btsan sGam-po's death, sent General Shon-dbyi'i Dren-ci [Xiànyú Kuāngjǐ 鮮于匡濟] to the [king's] mausoleum with a letter bearing the emperor's seal and containing verses of auspicious wishes in order that he might read them in public.[41]

The *rGya'i thang yig gsar ma* [New Chronicles of the Chinese Táng 唐 dynasty] say (Dha, 80, 11):

> In the first year of the reign of the Yuung-hu'e [era] (Metal Dog year, 650 CE), [the emperor] sent an envoy to Tibet from China to express condolences for the death of Srong-btsan sGam-po.

These citations testify that the year of death of the Dharmarāja Srong-btsan sGam-po is the Metal Dog year of the first *sMe-phreng* of the fifteenth *sMe-'khor* (Tibetan year 2567, 650 CE).

The *Tun hong bod kyi lo rgyus yig rnying* [Old Tibetan Chronicles of Dunhuang] say (PI 579, 14):

> Then, after six years, bTsan-po Khri Srong-btsan departed for heaven.

And also (ibid., 579, 16):

> It occurred in the year of the Dog [650-651]. The dead body of the grandfather, King Khri Srong-rtsan, was concealed in the mortuary chamber of Phying-ba and it remained there.

----

40 [The first year of the Yǒng huī 永徽 era (650-656) of the reign of Gāozōng 高宗 (r. 649-683), second emperor of the Táng 唐 dynasty (618-907).]

41 (永徽元年五月) (Yónghuī yuán nián wǔ yuè) 吐蕃贊普死 (Tǔfān Zànpǔ sǐ). 遣右武衛將軍 (qiǎn yòu wǔwèi jiāng jūn) 鮮于匡濟 (Xiànyú Kuāngjǐ) 齎璽書往弔祭 (jī xǐ shū wǎng diào sāng). (First month of the fifth year of the Yónghuī era.) The Tibetan bTsan-po died. General Xiànyú Kuāngjǐ 鮮于匡濟 of the Imperial Militant Guard of the Right entrusted with a missive was sent to pay a condolence call. 劉昫,《舊唐書. 高宗本紀》, 收入《四庫全書》(臺北：臺灣商務印書館 1986) 卷四頁 4. Liú Xù, *Jiù Táng Shū Gāozōng Běnjì* (*Old Book of Táng, Gāozōng Basic Annals*) included in the *Sì kù qúan shū* (Complete Library of the Four Treasuries) Táiwān Shāngwù Yìnshūgǔan, Táiběi, 1986, fascicle 4, p. 4.

The nephew, King Khri Mang-slon Mang-rtsan, was residing at Mer-ke. One year.

Thus the year of the Dog mentioned in this document can be definitively stated to be the Metal Dog year in question.

The *rGyal rabs gsal ba'i me long* says (Pe, 159, 4):

> The son was called Gung-ri Gung-btsan. Of incomparable lineage, he was born in the Brag-lha bKra-shis Divine Mansion in the female Metal Snake year.

If the son of Srong-btsan was born in the female Metal Snake year (Tibetan year 2538, 621 CE) and we concur with those who maintain that the Dharmarāja Srong-btsan sGam-po was born in the female Fire Ox year of the first *sMe-phreng* of the fifteenth *sMe-'khor*, the Dharmarāja should have fathered him when he was a full four or five years old. If on the contrary we assume that the son was born in the Metal Snake year of the intermediate *sMe-phreng* (Tibetan year 2598, 681 CE), he would have been born when the Dharmarāja was sixty-four or just about sixty-five years old; and if Gung-srong died when he was eighteen in the Earth Dog year (Tibetan year 2615, 698 CE), his death should have occurred simultaneously with that of his father. However, most of the dynastic chronicles relate that after the death of his son Gung-srong, the king father Srong-btsan ruled the kingdom again, but that too is a contradiction. Besides, the year 2615/698 corresponds to the nineteenth or twentieth reigning year of the Tibetan king Khri 'Dus-srong [670–704; r. 676–704 CE] and to the first year of the Chinese *Hrin li* [Shènglì 圣历] era.[42] The *Tun hong bod kyi lo rgyus yig rnying* [Old Tibetan Chronicles of Dunhuang] say (PI 583, 76):

> It occurred in the year of the Dog [698-699]. In the summer the king went to the north for sport. In the winter the Chief Minister Khri-'bring led [the army] to greater and lesser Tsong-ka [Tsong-ka Che-cung] and captured the great Chinese general

---

42 [The years 698-699 of the reign of Empress Wǔ Hòu 武后 (624-706), China's only empress, who renamed the Táng 唐 dynasty Zhōu 周 in 690 and ruled until 705.]

Thug-pu-shi. That winter mGar was reprimanded. The king went to Phar. One year.

All this evidence demonstrates the impossibility of identifying the year of Srong-btsan sGam-po's death with the Earth Dog year of the intermediate *sMe-phreng*. We can also easily understand that the only feasible year is the Metal Dog year.

As for the fact that the king had a younger brother called bTsan-srong, the *Tun hong bod kyi lo rgyus yig rnying* [Old Tibetan Chronicles of Dunhuang] say (PI 579, 7):

> King Srong-btsan, the elder brother, and bTsan-srong, the younger brother, were not in agreement.

The *Tun hong bod kyi lo rgyus yig rnying* [Old Tibetan Chronicles of Dunhuang] also say (PI 571, 98):

> Queen Sad-mar-kar left for the kingdom of Lig-myi-rhya to marry her Zhang Zhung consort.

It is certain that the sibling Sad-mar-kar was a younger sister of Srong-btsan sGam-po; that can be understood by taking into consideration the age of Srong-btsan.

In synthesis, saying that the Dharmarāja Srong-btsan sGam-po was born in the female Earth Ox year of the last *sMe-phreng* of the fourteenth *sMe-'khor* (Tibetan year 2468, 569 CE), lived until he was a full eighty-one or barely eighty-two years, and died in the male Metal Dog year of the first *sMe-phreng* of the fifteenth *sMe-'khor* (Tibetan year 2567, 650 CE) represents a thesis that totally corresponds with the inner truth of history and to the meaning expressed by all renowned dynastic and religious documents according to which Srong-btsan sGam-po lived for eighty-two years.

Concerning the tomb of the Dharmarāja Srong-btsan sGam-po, the *rGyal rabs gsal ba'i me long* says (Pe, 192, 22):

> His mausoleum was erected in 'Chong-po. Its length was about one league [*dpag tshad*]. It was square with a chamber at the center.
>
> The body of the great Dharmarāja was arrayed on a dais made of clay mixed with paper and silk. Having been carried

on a chariot in a cavalcade accompanied by music, the body was deposited in the grave.

The inside [of the grave] was adorned with small tiles decorated with jewels; [that is why] it became known as The Tomb-Adorned-Inside [Bang-so Nang-rgyan-can].

It is said that inside [the mausoleum] five temples were also built.

The construction of square tombs originated from there.

It is also said that its name was Maroon-Colored Mountain [sKu-ri sMug-po].

This description of its dimension, the aspect of the tomb, and so on make evident that funerary practices reached a high degree of development during the Intermediate Period.

3. THE THIRTY-SIXTH RULER OF TIBET: GUNG-SRONG GUNG-BTSAN

In the *Tun hong bod kyi lo rgyus yig rnying* [Old Tibetan Chronicles of Dunhuang] the name of this king is Gung-srong Gung-rtsan; most of the Tibetan annals and religious histories led by the *lDe'u rgya bod kyi chos 'byung* and the *lDe'u chos 'byung chen mo* contain a similar reading, Gung-ri Gung-btsan; in the *rGyal rabs me long rnam gsal* we find the reading Go-ri Gung-btsan; the *rGyal rabs bon gyi 'byung gnas* calls him Gong-srung Gong-btsan. Although different ways of writing his name, such as the ones mentioned above, can be found, it is possible that Go-ri represents a corrupted form of the Zhang Zhung word *gu-ra* which means virtue. It is also easily understandable that Gong-srung Gong-btsan is an inaccurate phonetic spelling derived from Gung-srong Gung-btsan.

Gung is an archaic Tibetan term that in the modern language has the same meaning as heaven and sky and certainly derives from the name of a famous female deity of the ancient Tibetan pantheon, the ancestress queen of the sky called A-phyi Gung-rgyal.

Srong is also an archaic Tibetan term meaning fair and wise and Gung-btsan can be rendered as Heavenly King [*gnam btsan*]. The name in its entirety can be read as "the heavenly king endowed with a wise nature and a mind that is as great and vast as the sky" [*nam mkha' ltar thugs rgya che la mdzangs pa'i rang gshis dang ldan pa'i gnam gyi rgyal po*].

Concerning the father and mother of Gung-srong Gung-btsan, the *Tun hong bod kyi lo rgyus yig rnying* [Old Tibetan Chronicles of Dun-huang] say (PI 556, 62):

> The son generated from the union of Srong-lde-brtsan with Mong-za Khri-mo mNyen-ldong-steng was Gung-srong Gung-rtsan.

The *lDe'u rgya bod kyi chos 'byung* specifies (Bod, 298, 19):

> After [Srong-lde-brtsan] married the Tibetan Mong-bza' Khri-lcam, the son Gung-srong Gung-btsan was born.

Most illustrious dynastic and religious histories, such as the *lDe'u chos 'byung chen mo*, the *Deb ther dmar po*, the *rGyal rabs gsal ba'i me long*, the *rGyal rabs me long rnam gsal*, the *lHo brag chos 'byung*, the *rGya bod yig tshang chen mo*, the *Deb ther dpyid kyi rgyal mo'i glu dbyangs*, the *lHa thog rgyal rabs*, and so on, clearly say that Gung-srong Gung-btsan was born the son of the Dharmarāja Srong-btsan sGam-po and his queen Mong-bza' Khri-lcam.

The *Yar lung jo bo'i chos 'byung* says (Si, 56, 8):

> The son of King Srong-btsan sGam-po and 'Bro-bza' Khri-mo 'Bring-stengs was Gung-srong Gung-btsan.

The *Dar rgyas gsal sgron* says (Thob-gsar, 669, 87, 6):

> The son of Srong-btsan sGam-po and 'Gro Khri-ma 'Gring-ting was Gung-srong Gung-btsan.

These two texts write the name of the queen in two different ways, but we can understand from the order of the words that it is the name of the same queen, because either 'Bro-bza' and Mong-bza' are the names of two different queens or else it is one single queen with two different names denoting the clan and the family to which she belonged: this is a point that needs to be investigated.

In the essay entitled *Chos ldan rgyal rabs kyi lo thigs 'khrul sel* [Removing Confusion in the Histories Concerning Buddhist Royal Lineages] (composed during a course on the Tibetan language taught at the Central Institute of Nationalities) it is written (7, 17):

> That being so, Mang-srong Mang-btsan was the son of Gung-ri Gung-btsan who was the younger brother of the Dharmarāja Srong-btsan sGam-po.

And also (ibid., 7, 17):

> It is considered that after Srong-btsan sGam-po died at thirty-four he did not have children of his own; so it was his nephew Mang-srong, the son of his brother, who was enthroned and who became generally known as "the Nephew [*dbon sras*] Mang-srong Mang-btsan." An excerpt from the Dunhuang Chronicles mentioned in the *Deb dkar* says, "Since Srong-btsan had no off-spring, a nephew was installed on the throne." For that reason it could be logically established that Gung-ri Gung-btsan was the younger brother of Srong-btsan and not his son.

Even if this would prove that Gung-srong Gung-btsan was not the son of Srong-btsan, the majority of Tibetan dynastic and religious histories are unanimous in saying, "Srong-btsan sGam-po's son was Gung-srong Gung-btsan." Besides, the *Tun hong bod kyi lo rgyus yig rnying* [Old Tibetan Chronicles of Dunhuang] affirm (PI 556, 61):

> The son of Slon-btsan Rlung-nam and Tshes-pong-za 'Bring-ma Thog-dgos was Srong-lde-brtsan. The son of Srong-lde-brtsan and Mong-za Khri-mo mNyen-ldong-steng was Gung-srong Gung-rtsan.

This clearly indicates that Gung-srong Gung-btsan was the son of Srong-btsan; on what basis can it be affirmed that he was the son of Srong-btsan's brother?

The *Deb ther dkar po* says (Si, 108, 15):

> Since Srong-btsan did not have any sons, a nephew was installed on the throne.

This affirmation can only derive from the [Old and New] *rGya'i thang yig gsar rnying*, because it never appears in the *Tun hong bod kyi lo rgyus yig rnying* [Old Tibetan Chronicles of Dunhuang]. In this regard, also the assumption that Mang-srong is the son of a brother because he is designated as nephew [*dbon sras*] is unsuitable: the term *dbon po* means also son of the son, and even when it is interpreted as nephew, it does not necessarily imply that it refers to the son of a brother. Traditionally speaking, the enthronement of the son of a king would always take place upon the king's death, but the son of Srong-btsan sGam-po had died long before with no other suitable heirs for the throne at that time; hence the son of the son, Mang-srong Mang-btsan, was installed on the throne. Due to these circumstances the specific designation of nephew has been attributed to this king.

The *rGyal rabs gsal ba'i me long* says (Pe, 159, 4):

> The son was called Gung-ri Gung-btsan. Of incomparable lineage, he took birth in the Brag-lha bKra-shis Divine Mansion in the female Metal Snake year.

In particular, the *lHo brag chos 'byung* affirms (Pe, Vol. I, 245, 21):

> Gung-srong was born in the female Iron Snake year [when] the father was 53.

These citations show not only the year of birth of King Gung-srong Gung-btsan, but also prove that the year of birth of this king was the female Metal Snake year of the first *sMe-phreng* of the fifteenth *sMe-'khor* (Tibetan year 2538, 621 CE).

The *Nyang gi chos 'byung* affirms (Bod, 299, 18):

> The son of King Srong-btsan sGam-po was Mang-srong Mang-btsan. When that king was nineteen [he] saw the son Gung-srong Gung-btsan. Then the father died. The grandfather seized power. The son of that [Gung-srong Gung-btsan] was 'Dus-srong Mang-po-rje Rlung-nam 'Phrul-gyi rGyal-po.

According to this source, the son of the Dharmarāja Srong-btsan sGam-po was King Mang-srong Mang-btsan, the son of Mang-srong Mang-btsan was Gung-srong Gung-btsan, and the son of Gung-srong Gung-btsan was 'Dus-srong Mang-po-rje. The eminent scholar Bu-ston

Rin-chen-grub (1290-1364) adheres to that source and in his *Chos 'byung gsung rab rin po che'i mdzod* affirms (lHa, 125, 2):

> The son of that king (son of Mong-bza' Khri-btsun, in power for five years, died at eighteen) was Mang-srong Mang-btsan. His son was Gung-srong Gung-btsan (seized power at fifteen, died at twenty-four). His son was 'Dus srong Mang-po-rje Rlung-nam 'Phrul gyi rGyal-po.

The religious history of Klong-chen-pa says (Delhi, Vol. 1, 460, 230, 3):

> The son of that king was Mang-srong Mang-brtsan. His son was Gung-srong Gung-brtsan.

The *rGyal po bka'i thang yig* says (Pe, 114, 18):

> The son of gNam-ri Srong-btsan was Srong-btsan-sgam.
> The son of that [one] was Mang-srong Mang-btsan.
> The son of that [one] was Gung-srong Gung-btsan.
> The son of that [one] was Rlung-nam 'Phrul-gyi rGyal-po.

The *rGyal rabs 'phrul gyi lde mig* says (Delhi, 9, 17, 5):

> Mong-gza' Khri-lcam generated Mang-srong Mang-btsan. He ascended the throne when he was thirteen, remained in power for five years, and died when he was eighteen. The son Gung-srong Gung-btsan had not been born yet, so it became necessary for the father king to seize power once again. In the *Me long ma* the positions of Mang-srong and Gung-srong are reversed; the *Bu ston chos 'byung* is correct since it lists them exactly as above.

The perspective of this text is that the *Me long ma* is wrong while Bu-ston is right and is derived from the *rGyal-po bka' thang* and the *Nyang gi chos 'byung*. Nevertheless, most dynastic and religious histories clearly state that the son of Srong-btsan was Gung-srong Gung-btsan. Moreover, the authoritative *Tun hong bod kyi lo rgyus yig rnying* [Old Tibetan Chronicles of Dunhuang] say (PI 579, 16):

> It occurred in the year of the Dog [650-651]. The dead body of the grandfather, King Khri Srong-rtsan, was concealed in

the mortuary chamber of Phying-ba and it remained there. The nephew King Khri Mang-slon Mang-rtsan was residing at Mer-ke. One year.

And also (PI 581, 15):

> It occurred in the year of the Mouse [676-677]. In the summer the bTsan-po was residing at Sha-ra in sPrags. Khri Mang-slon departed for heaven in the winter from Tshang-bang-sna. The bTsan-po son, Khri 'Dus-srong, was born at lHa-lung in sGregs.

These citations indicate that the king nephew Mang-srong Mang-btsan was installed on the throne after the death of the Dharmarāja Srong-btsan sGam-po and that the son of Mang-srong Mang-btsan was 'Dus-srong Mang-po-rje. In this respect the *rGya'i thang yig rnying ma* says (Dha, 14, 4):

> Since the son of Srong-btsan died young, the grandson [*dbon sras*] was invited to ascend the royal throne.

Also this textual source in saying that the son of the Dharmarāja Srong-btsan sGam-po Gung-srong Gung-btsan died at a young age and that his grandson Mang-srong Mang-btsan was installed on the throne is in agreement with the Dunhuang documents.

To summarize the fundamental point, it is evident that the *lHo brag chos 'byung* is unmistaken in stating that King Srong-btsan sGam-po fathered Gung-srong Gung-btsan when he was fifty-two and that Gung-srong Gung-btsan was born in the female Metal Snake year of the first *sMe-pheng* of the fifteenth *sMe-'khor* (Tibetan year 2538, 621 CE); this date should be accepted as the correct one.

Regarding the time at which Gung-srong Gung-btsan ascended the throne, the *lDe'u chos 'byung chen mo* affirms (Bod, 118, 9):

> He ruled after he reached the age of thirteen. He remained in power for five years.

The *Ne'u sngon byung gi gtam* says (Dha, 10, 5, 6):

Gung-srong ruled after he reached the age of thirteen. He held the power for five years.

The *Yar lung jo bo'i chos 'byung* says (Si, 56, 10):

When he was thirteen he was installed on the throne.

The *rGyal rabs gsal ba'i me long* says (Pe, 163, 5):

Gung-ri Gung-btsan reached the age of thirteen and then seized power.

The *lHo brag chos 'byung* says (Pe, Vol. I, 245, 22):

When he was thirteen he was installed on the throne.

The *Deb ther dpyid kyi rgyal mo'i glu dbyangs* says (Pe, 45, 13):

When he was thirteen he was enthroned.

As these citations point out, most of the renowned religious and dynastic histories agree that Gung-srong Gung-btsan was raised to the throne at the age of thirteen. This means that he was born to his father Srong-btsan sGam-po in the female Metal Snake year (Tibetan year 2538, 621 CE), when the latter was a full fifty-two or barely fifty-three years old and that he ascended the throne when he reached the full age of thirteen in the male Wood Horse year (Tibetan year 2551, 634 CE). If he was enthroned at just thirteen instead of having reached the full age of thirteen, the date should correspond to the female Water Snake year (Tibetan year 2550, 633 CE); however, that was a year with impediments [*dgung skeg*] for Gung-srong Gung-btsan and an obstacled year is indisputably not when a king would be installed on the throne.

The activities carried out by the Dharmarāja Srong-btsan sGam-po during the nine years that preceded his death are described succinctly in the *Tun hong bod kyi lo rgyus yig rnying* [Old Tibetan Chronicles of Dunhuang]. Apart from that, historical data before that period are exiguous and is why we have limited information about Gung-srong Gung-btsan. For that reason the activities carried out by Srong-btsan sGam-po during the first part of his life as well as the general situation of Tibet at that time remain unknown. The Old and New *rGya'i thang yig* inform us that Srong-btsan sGam-po established new relations between China and Tibet toward the end of his life. Only since then, scattered elements concerning the history of Tibet began to be recorded in Chinese documents.

Since information about the first part of Srong-btsan sGam-po's life is lacking in the [Old and New] *rGya'i thang yig gsar rnying* and other sources, the best that can be done is rely on what has been conjectured about his life and on the scant records of that period of Tibetan history available in the hope that accurate accounts in some heretofore lost biographies will eventually be found.

For what concerns the queens and children of Gung-srong Gung-btsan, the *Grags rgyal bod kyi rgyal rabs* says (sDe, TA, 597, 2):

> He (Gung-srong Gung-btsan) married Wa-zhwa-bza' Mang-po-rje. Their son was Mang-srong Mang-btsan.

The *Yar lung jo bo'i chos 'byung* says (Si, 56, 15):

> The son of the Lord (Gung-srong) and 'A-zha-bza' Kho-'jo Mong-rje Khri-dkar Ti-shags was Mang-srong Mang-btsan.

The *Dar rgyas gsal sgron* says (Thob, 669, 87, 6):

> The son of that (Gung-srong Gung-btsan) and of 'A-zha-bza' Kho-jo Mong-rje Khri-dkar Ting-shags was Mang-srong Mang-btsan.

The *lHo brag chos 'byung* says (Pe, Vol. I, 245, 23):

> [He] married the princess 'A-zha-bza' Mong-rje Khri-dkar and the son Mang-srong Mang-btsan was born.

The *rGya bod yig tshang chen mo* says (Si, 170, 17):

> The son of that king (Gung-srong Gung-btsan) and 'A-zha-bza' Khos-jo Mo-rje was Mang-srong Mang-btsan.

The *Deb ther dpyid kyi rgyal mo'i glu dbyangs* says (Pe, 45, 13):

> [He] married the princess 'A-zha-bza' Kho-'jo Mong-rje Khri-dkar Ti-shags and the son Mang-srong Mang-btsan was generated.

Even if the quoted sources present different readings for the name of King Gung-srong Gung-btsan's consort, they all agree that she was an 'A-zha-bza' [a princess from the powerful 'A-zha or Tuyuhun Mongolian kingdom, 285-670 CE] and that her son was Mang-srong Mang-btsan.

The name of this and other queens are written in various manners mainly due to the fact that the original name of the person or of the clan was not Tibetan.

Most dynastic and religious histories do not reveal whether Gung-srong Gung-btsan had other sons apart from Mang-srong Mang-btsan. Nevertheless, in the *lDe'u chos 'byung chen mo* we read (Bod, 118, 19):

> The younger brother of Mang-srong was called 'A-zha Tsha-mer-lde. Exiled to the border plains, he hung [himself].

Hence, there was another prince besides Mang-srong Mang-btsan called Tsha-mer-lde who was the younger brother of Mang-srong and who hung himself following a political punishment.

For what concerns the identity of the chief ministers of Gung-srong Gung-btsan, the *lDe'u rgya bod kyi chos 'byung* says (Bod, 299, 3):

> Myang Mang-po-rje Zhang-snang and sNubs-tsan To-re Lang-snang acted as ministers.

The *Grags rgyal bod kyi rgyal rabs* says (sDe, TA, 197, 2):

> Zhal-'bro acted as his [minister].

The *Yar lung jo bo'i chos 'byung* says (Si, 56, 9):

> The ministers were Nyang Mang-po-rje Zhang-snang and gNubs-btsan To-re.

The *lHo brag chos 'byung* says (Pe, Vol. I, 246, 1):

> The ministers were Myang Mang-po-rje Zhang-snang and sNubs-btsan To-re.

The *rGya bod yig tshang chen mo* says (Si, 170, 12):

As for the ministers, these were Mang-po-rje Zhang-snang and sNubs-btsan Do-re.

Most of these famous religious and dynastic histories agree that the chief ministers of Gung-srong were Mang-po-rje Zhang-snang and gNubs-btsan To-re.

Regarding the number of years Gung-srong Gung-btsan remained in power and the year in which he died, the *lDe'u chos 'byung chen mo* affirms (Bod, 118, 10):

He ruled for five years. He died when he was nineteen and his father was still alive.

The *Ne'u sngon byung gi gtam* says (Dha, 10, 5, 6):

He ruled for five years and died when he reached the age of eighteen.

Most of the Tibetan religious and dynastic histories, such as the *Yar lung jo bo'i chos byung*, the *Deb ther dmar po*, the *rGyal rabs gsal ba'i me long*, the *Chos 'byung mkhas pa'i dga' ston*, the *rGya bod yig tshang chen mo*, the *Deb ther dpyid kyi rgyal mo'i glu dbyangs*, the *lHa thog rgyal rabs*, and so on, adhere to the *Ne'u sngon byung gi gtam* in maintaining that Gung-srong Gung-btsan ruled for five years and died when he was eighteen.

With the exception of the *lDe'u rgya bod kyi chos 'byung* and the *lDe'u chos 'byung chen mo* which affirm that Gung-srong Gung-btsan lived until the age of nineteen, all other sources say that he lived until he was eighteen. In particular, the *rGyal rabs gsal ba'i me long* and the *lHo brag chos 'byung* say that Gung-srong Gung-btsan was born in the female Metal Snake year of the first *sMe-phreng* of the fifteenth *sMe-'khor* (Tibetan year 2538, 621 CE); that he ascended the throne in the male Wood Horse year (Tibetan year 2551, 634 CE) which was also the year the Nepali princess Bal-bza' Khri-bstun arrived in Tibet; that he died in the male Earth Dog year (Tibetan year 2555, 638 CE); and that the father king Srong-btsan sGam-po ruled for a full twelve or barely thirteen years until the male Metal Dog year (Tibetan year 2567, 650 CE).

The *Nyang gi chos 'byung*, the *Bu ston chos 'byung*, and the *rGyal rabs 'phrul gyi lde mig* mention the names of the father bTsan-po Gung-srong

Gung-btsan and the son Mang-srong Mang-btsan but in reverse order and other than that are silent in regard to their lifespans and details concerning their reigns.

Many dynastic and religious histories call this king a half-king [*phyed*]. Tibetan annals show examples of lineages that are defined variously as "the very joyful three-and-a-half lineages" [*shin tu skyid po'i gdung rabs phyed dang bzhi*] or "the joyful eight-and-a-half lineages" [*skyid po'i gdung rabs phyed dang dgu*]. This particular king was in power for five years; after he died, the king father ruled again as he had before. In most royal dynasties a prince would be enthroned and would govern as king only after the death of the king father; Gung-srong Gung-btsan was in power while his father was still alive and hence was called a half-king.

For what concerns the tomb of King Gung-srong Gung-btsan, the *rGyal rabs gsal ba'i me long* relates that (Pe, 163, 10):

> His tomb was built at Don-mkhar-mda'. It was situated on the left side of gNam-ri Srong-btsan ['s grave]. It was called Gung-chen Gung-ri. So it is said.

4. THE THIRTY-SEVENTH RULER OF TIBET: KHRI MANG-SRONG MANG-BTSAN

In the *Tun hong bod kyi lo rgyus yig rnying* [Old Tibetan Chronicles of Dunhuang] this king is called Khri Mang-slon and Mang-slon Mang-rtsan. According to the ancient Tibetan system, the royal gShen would attribute an imposing name to the monarch which consisted of a mixture of Zhang Zhung and Tibetan terms: in this case the Zhang Zhung word *khri* corresponds to deity [*lha*] or Nature of the Mind [*thugs nyid*]; *mang* corresponds to splendor of the red coral [*dmar po bye ru'i 'od mdangs*]; *slon* corresponds to the Tibetan self-perfected [*lhun grub*]; and *rtsan* corresponds to the word *btsan* of later times. In the archaic Tibetan language this last word had three meanings depending on the context: it could be a verb meaning to sharpen [*rno ba*], an adjective meaning acute or keen [*rnon po*], or a noun meaning king. In modern Tibetan the name of this king can be rendered as Self-perfected Divine Red

Light [*lha 'od dmar lhun grub*], or King of the Self-perfected Red Light ['Od-dmar Lhun-grub rGyal-po] which is quite similar to the name of an ancient Zhang Zhung king called King Coral Light [Bye-ru 'Od-kyi rGyal-po]; this king had a glowing notably ruddy complexion and this characteristic was accordingly reflected in his name.

The king eventually became known as Khri Mang-srong Mang-btsan; the syllable *slon* of the original name was substituted by *srong*, meaning fair [*drang ba*] and wise of mind [*thugs rgyud mdzangs pa*] in archaic Tibetan because this distinguished and easy to pronounce term was also part of the name of this king's father.

Regarding the designation of nephew [*dbon sras*] attributed to Mang-srong Mang-btsan, in the essay entitled *Chos ldan rgyal rabs kyi lo thigs 'khrul sel* [Removing Confusion in the Histories concerning Buddhist Royal Lineages] (composed during a course on the Tibetan language taught at the Central Institute of Nationalities) it is written (7, 2):

> Most dynastic annals and chronicles refer to this king as the Nephew Mang-srong Mang-btsan; this is an issue that needs to be investigated. *dBon sras* is a generic term for relatives of the paternal line and a commonplace name indicating nephews and younger relatives of laymen and clergy. *dBon sras* is the son of a relative and is the honorific form for *tsha bo* [nephew]: all Tibetans who know the language correctly are aware of that. Calling Mang-btsan *dbon sras* clearly demonstrates that he was the son of a relative and I think no reason whatsoever exists to insist on saying that he must have been the son of Srong-btsan.

Therefore, although it is correct to include in the conventional designation of *dbon po* relatives and nephews of the paternal lineage, it can be affirmed only that Mang-srong Mang-btsan was the son of Gung-srong Gung-btsan, who was the son of Srong-btsan sGam-po; no religious or dynastic history says that he was the son of Srong-btsan sGam-po and I do not see any difference when the son of a son or the son of a relative is called *dbon po*.

For what concerns the place and time of Khri Mang-srong Mang-btsan's birth, the *lDe'u rgya bod kyi chos 'byung* says (Bod, 299, 5):

The father (Gung-srong Gung-btsan) died when his son Mang-btsan was still a child. Mang-srong was born in the Dog year.

The *lDe'u chos 'byung chen mo* says (Bod, 118,13):

Then, in the Dog year, his (Gung-srong Gung-btsan's) son Mang-srong Mang-btsan was born.

These two sources say that Khri Mang-srong Mang-btsan was born in a Dog year but do not specify the elements or any other relevant details. The *Grags rgyal bod kyi rgyal rabs* says (sDe, TA, 198, 5):

Mang-srong was born in the male Fire Dog year.

This text shows that the element of that year was Fire. Most of the Tibetan chronicles, such as the *Ne'u sngon byung gi gtam*, the *Yar lung jo bo'i chos 'byung*, the *Deb ther dmar po*, the *rGyal rabs gsal ba'i me long*, and so on, agree on that. However, they also identify the year of birth of the Dharmarāja Srong-btsan sGam-po with the female Fire Ox year of the first *sMe-phreng* of the fifteenth *sMe-'khor* (Tibetan year 2534, 617 CE); but according to that reckoning the male Fire Dog year (Tibetan year 2543, 626 CE) corresponds to a time when the Dharmarāja Srong-btsan sGam-po would have reached the full age of nine. Therefore, it would have been impossible that the Dharmarāja generated his son Gung-srong Gung-btsan in that year, let alone for the latter to have generated his.

The Fire Dog year of the intermediate *sMe-phreng* (Tibetan year 2603, 686 CE) is not a possibility as well, since that year corresponds to the time in which Khri 'Dus-srong Mang-po-rje reached the full age of ten. Hence it can be concluded that the element of the Dog year in which Khri Mang-srong Mang-btsan was born was not Fire.

The *Deb ther sngon po* says (Si, Vol. I, 75, 5):

Mang-srong Mang-btsan was enthroned when he reached the age of thirteen.

This clearly indicates that Mang-srong Mang-btsan reached the full age of twelve, or that he was barely thirteen when the Dharmarāja Srong-btsan sGam-po died. According to this historical source the year of death of Srong-btsan sGam-po was the Metal Dog year (Tibetan year 2567, 650 CE). If from that date we count back and subtract twelve full years (2567-12=2555; 650-12=638), we reach the male Earth Dog year (Tibetan year 2555, 638 CE); this is also the year in which his father Gung-srong Gung-btsan died. We can be certain of that because the *Nyang gi chos 'byung* says (Bod, 269, 18):

> The son of King Srong-btsan sGam-po was Mang-srong Mang-btsan. That king died when he was nineteen, just after having seen his son Gung-srong Gung-btsan.

This source presents the names of father and son in reverse order, but apart from that it is a clear confirmation that the son was born when the father died. The *rGya bod yig tshang chen mo* says (Si, 170, 17):

> The son of that Lord (Gung-srong Gung-btsan) and of 'A-zha-bza' Khos-jo Mo-rje was Mang-srong Mang-btsan. He ruled for a period of thirteen to fifteen years.

This source's viewpoint is not different from that of the *Deb ther sngon po*. The perspective of the *Deb sngon* according to which Khri Mang-srong Mang-btsan was born in the male Earth Dog year is completely coherent from an historical perspective. The *Tun hong bod kyi lo rgyus yig rnying* [Old Tibetan Chronicles of Dunhuang] say (PI 579, 16):

> It occurred in the year of the Dog [650-651]. The dead body of the grandfather, King Khri Srong-rtsan, was concealed in the mortuary chamber of Phying-ba and it remained there. The nephew, King Khri Mang-slon Mang-rtsan, was residing at Mer-ke. One year.

The *Chronicles* indicate that in the Dog year the remains of Khri Srong-btsan sGam-po were kept secret and placed in a mortuary chamber at Phying-ba. This demonstrates that the Dharmarāja died in that year, and also, by implication, that Khri Mang-srong Mang-btsan was enthroned. We can be certain that the Dog year in question was the male Metal Dog year of the first *sMe-phreng* of the fifteenth *sMe-'khor* (Tibetan year

2567, 650 CE) because the *rGya'i thang yig rnying ma* says (Dha, 13, 17; mTsho 138, 3):

> In the first year of the reign of the Yuung-dbu'i [era] (Metal Dog year, 650 CE), Thang Ka'o-tsung, grieved by Srong-btsan sGam-po's death, sent General Shon-dbyi'i Dren-ci [Xiànyú Kuāngjǐ 鲜于匡济] to the [king's] mausoleum with a letter bearing the emperor's seal and containing verses of auspicious wishes in order that he might read them in public.

The *Thang yig gsar ma* says (Dha, 80, 11):

> In the first year of the reign of the Yuung-hu'e [era] (Metal Dog year, 650 CE), [the emperor] sent a representative to Tibet from China, in order to express condolences for the death of Srong-btsan sGam-po.

The proof that the true year of birth of Khri Mang-srong Mang-btsan was the male Earth Dog year (Tibetan year 2555, 638 CE) lays precisely in these citations.

Concerning the time in which Mang-srong Mang-btsan ascended the throne, the *lDe'u rgya bod kyi chos 'byung* says (Bod, 299, 6):

> Within one cycle of [twelve] years [his] grandfather died. He ruled for fifteen years.

The *lDe'u chos 'byung chen mo* says (Bod, 118, 13):

> Then, within one cycle of [twelve] years, after his grandfather died [he was enthroned and] remained in power for fourteen years.

This source clearly shows that Mang-srong Mang-btsan was enthroned when the grandfather Srong-btsan sGam-po died in the Dog year that occurred twelve full years after the Dog year in which Mang-srong Mang-btsan was born. The *Grags rgyal bod kyi rgyal rabs* says (sDe, TA, 198, 5):

> Within one cycle of [twelve] years the grandfather died. Mang-srong held power for fifteen years.

This text also indicates that Mang-srong Mang-btsan was enthroned and the grandfather Srong-btsan sGam-po died when twelve full years had elapsed from the male Earth Dog year of Mang-srong's birth.

In this respect, also the *Ne'u sngon byung gi gtam*, the *Yar lung jo bo'i chos 'byung*, the *Deb ther dmar po*, the *rGyal rabs gsal ba'i me long*, the *Deb ther sngon po*, the *lHo brag chos 'byung*, and the *rGya bod yig tshang chen mo* agree that Mang-srong Mang-btsan was enthroned when he was a full twelve years old. The certainty that the Dog year in which Mang-srong Mang-btsan ascended to the throne is the male Metal Dog year (Tibetan year 2567, 650 CE), the year in which the Dharmarāja Srong btsan sGam-po died, is once again provided by the already cited *Tun hong bod kyi lo rgyus yig rnying* [Old Tibetan Chronicles of Dunhuang] (PI 579, 16):

> It occurred in the year of the Dog [650-651]. The dead body of the grandfather, King Khri Srong-rtsan, was concealed in the mortuary chamber of Phying-ba and it remained there. The nephew, King Khri Mang-slon Mang-rtsan, was residing at Mer-ke. One year.

As for the queens and children of Khri Mang-srong Mang-btsan, the *Grags rgyal bod kyi rgyal rabs* says (sDe, TA, 197, 5, 2):

> [...] Mang-srong Mang-btsan. His maternal uncle [*zhang*] was Tshe-spong. The son of Mang-srong Mang-btsan and 'Bro-pa Khri-chen Khri-ma lod was 'Dus-srong Mang-po-rje Rlung-nam.

The *Yar lung jo bo'i chos 'byung* says (Si, 57, 7):

> The son of the Lord (Mang-srong) and 'Bro-za Khri-pa Khri-ma-lod was 'Dus-srong Mang-po-rje Rlung-nam 'Phrul-gyi rGyal-po.

The *Dar rgyas gsal sgron* says (Thob, 669, 87, 7):

> The son of Man-srong Mang-btsan and 'Gro-bza' Khri-se Khri-ma-lod was Rlung-srong 'Phrul-rgyal.

The *rGyal rabs gsal ba'i me long* says (Pe, 194, 4):

[He] married the princess called 'Bro-bza' Khri-ma-lod.

And also (ibid., 195, 3):

> The son of Mang-srong Mang-btsan was 'Dus-srong Mang-po-rje Rlung-nam 'Phrul-gyi rGyal-po.

The *lHo brag chos 'byung* says (Pe, Vol. I, 292, 1):

> [He] married Princess 'Bro-bza' Khri-lod.

And concerning the birth of her son 'Dus-srong Mang-po-rje, the same text affirms (ibid., 292, 20):

> Seven days after the father died in the Water Mouse year, 'Dus-srong Mang-rje Rlung-nam 'Phrul-gyi-rgyal was born.

The *rGya bod yig tshang chen mo* says (Si, 171, 5):

> The son of the Lord (Mang-srong) and 'Bro-bza' Khri-po Khri-ma-lod was 'Dus-srong Mang-po-rje Rlung-nam 'Phrul-gyi rGyal-po. [He was born in the] female Water Bird year.

The *Deb ther dpyid kyi rgyal mo'i glu dbyangs* says (Pe, 49, 14):

> The son of that Lord who married 'Bro-bza' Khra-bo Khri-ma-lod was 'Dus-srong Mang-po-rje Rlung-nam 'Phrul-gyi rGyal-po.

These sources do not cite the names of queens other than the one above; that name is written in slightly different manners, but the changes are not significant. They also mention 'Dus-srong Mang-po-rje as the only son; however, the *Tun hong bod kyi lo rgyus yig rnying* [Old Tibetan Chronicles of Dunhuang] say (PI 582, 49):

> It occurred in the year of the Mouse [688-689]. The bTsan-po was residing at Nyen-kar. In the summer the council convened at Zu-spug. In the winter dBon Da-rgyal Khri-zung convened [the council] at Tshur-lung in Zhogs. Princess Khri-mo-stengs set forth to govern the Dags-yul. One year.

And also (PI 582, 51):

It occurred in the year of the Ox [689-690]. The bTsan-po was residing at Thang-bu-ra in Nyen-kar. Princess Khri-bangs departed to become the bride of the lord of 'A-zha.

The *Chronicles* indicate clearly that two sisters, one called Khri-mo-stengs and one called Khri-bangs, left to marry the lord of Dwags-po and the lord of 'A-zha.

For what concerns the chief ministers of Khri Mang-srong Mang-btsan, the *lDe'u rgya bod kyi chos 'byung* says (Bod, 299, 6):

'Gar sTong-btsan Yul-gzung acted as minister from the time of [Mang-srong's] grandfather until the time of the nephew. Also 'Chims Mang-bzher Ngan-po was a minister for a few years.

The *Yar lung jo bo'i chos 'byung* says (Si, 57, 2):

The ministers were 'Gar sTong-btsan Yul-bzung and 'Chims Mang-gnyer.

The *Deb ther sngon po* says (Si. Vol. I, 75, 6):

With the support of Minister mGar, he ruled for fifteen years.

In fact, most of the dynastic and religious chronicles, in accord with the above-mentioned *lDe'u* [*rgya bod kyi chos 'byung*] and [*Yar lung jo bo'i*] *chos 'byung*, say that Minister mGar was the chief minister during the lifetime of the grandfather and of the grandson.

Concerning the length of Khri Mang-srong Mang-btsan's rule and the time of his death, the *lDe'u rgya bod kyi chos 'byung* says (Bod, 299, 6):

He ruled for fifteen years.

And also (ibid., 299, 8):

Mang-srong died in the Mouse year.

The *lDe'u chos 'byung chen mo* says (Bod, 118, 14):

He ruled for fourteen years. At the age of twenty-seven he died at Bar-snang in gTsang.

This source says that he remained in power for a full fourteen years or for approximately fifteen years and died when he was twenty-seven; also the *Yar lung jo bo'i chos 'byung*, the *Deb ther dmar po*, the *rGyal rabs gsal ba'i me long*, the *lHo brag chos 'byung*, and the *rGya bod yig tshang chen mo* agree with this perspective.

The *Deb ther sngon po* says that Mang-srong Mang-btsan ascended the throne when he was thirteen and ruled for fifteen years; therefore it is in agreement with the *lDe'u chos 'byung*. It also says (Si, Vol. I, 75, 11):

> He seized power when he was thirty and died in the female Earth Rabbit year when he was forty-two.

The text relates information merely drawn from Chinese chronicles without offering any perspective of its own. It is clearly impossible to reconcile these two versions according to which Khri Mang-srong Mang-btsan lived for either twenty-seven or forty-two years.

The *Tun hong bod kyi lo rgyus yig rnying* [Old Tibetan Chronicles of Dunhuang] say (PI 579, 16):

> It occurred in the year of the Dog [650-651]. The corpse of the grandfather, King Khri Srong-rtsan, was concealed in the mortuary chamber of Phying-ba and it remained there. The nephew, King Khri Mang-slon Mang-rtsan, was residing at Mer-ke. One year.

Since the *Tun hong bod kyi lo rgyus yig rnying* [Old Tibetan Chronicles of Dunhuang] contain yearly records of events relating to Khri Mang-srong Mang-btsan from the male Metal Dog year (Tibetan year 2567, 650 CE), the year in which he reached the full age of twelve or was approximately thirteen, until, but not including, the male Fire Mouse year (Tibetan year 2593, 676 CE) when he was thirty-seven or approximately thirty-eight, no purpose exists in trying to seek more in this textual source about his lifespan and length of reign; even if it were necessary, it would produce no results.

The *Tun hong bod kyi lo rgyus yig rnying* [Old Tibetan Chronicles of Dunhuang] are also not mistaken in reporting the time of King Mang-srong Mang-btsan's death. They say (PI 581, 15):

It occurred in the year of the Mouse [676-677]. In the summer the king resided at Sha-ra in sPrags. In the winter Khri Mang-slon left for heaven from Tshang-bang-sna.

The *Chronicles* show that Khri Mang-srong Mang-btsan died in the male Fire Mouse year (Tibetan year 2593, 676 CE) of the intermediate *sMe-phreng* of the fifteenth *sMe-'khor*.

The *rGya'i thang yig rnying ma* says (Dha, 16,16; mTsho, 144, 3):

In the fourth year of the dByi'i Hphin era (Yì Fēng 仪风, Earth Rabbit year, 679 CE) King Mang-srong Mang-btsan died.

The *rGya'i thang yig gsar ma* says (Dha, 90,16; mTsho, 22,7):

In the fourth year of the Yi'i Hphing era (Yì Fēng 仪风, Earth Rabbit year, 679 CE) King Mang-srong Mang-btsan died.

According to these sources, during the fourth year of the Yi'i Hphing (Yì Fēng 仪风) era[43] which corresponds to the female Earth Rabbit year (Tibetan year 2596, 679 CE) of the intermediate *sMe-phreng* of the fifteenth *sMe-'khor*, Khri Mang-srong Mang-btsan died. If that is the case, it would appear that the king died when he was forty-one or about forty-two years old, this date showing a three or four year gap with respect to the date recorded in the *Tun hong bod kyi lo rgyus yig rnying* [Old Tibetan Chronicles of Dunhuang].

The Old and New Chronicles of the Chinese Táng 唐 dynasty [*rGya'i thang yig gsar rnying*] say that King Khri Mang-srong Mang-btsan died in the female Earth Rabbit year because at that time the royal successor had not as yet been born and also because at the time of Khri Mang-srong Mang-btsan's death the Chinese and Tibetan armies were engaged in an intense military conflict; it is certain that the circumstances of the king's death were kept secret for about three years or so. In this respect the *rGya'i thang yig gsar ma* says (Dha, 86, 2):

In the second year of the Hrang Yon era[44] (Wood Pig year, 675 CE), Tibet reached a peaceful settlement with the chief

---

43 [The years 676-679 of the reign of the Táng 唐 emperor Gāozōng 高宗.]
44 [The 上元 Shàngyuán era (674-676) of the reign of the Táng 唐 emperor Gāozōng 高宗.]

minister called Thu'u-hon Bhi-la'i and in the hope of establishing harmony with the Turks [Drug-gu] a nuptial agreement was
offered to the Tang emperor; but the emperor did not accept it.

The next year (Fire Mouse, 676 CE) the Tibetan army invaded the area that included Hra'an-Kra'u (Le'o-Tu'u [present day
Ledu], an area situated at the eastern border of Lake Kokonoor),
Ku'o-kra'u (in the southeastern part of Lake Kokonoor), Hō-
kra'u (A-mdo Ka-chu), and Hphang-kra'u (situated at the southeastern border of Lake Kokonoor) and massacred the local
officals, having attacked with a contingent of over 10,000 yaks
and horses.

Therefore the court of the Tang emperor instructed Minister
Kro'u-wang-zhon, who had been appointed generalissimo of the
expeditionary army at Tha'o-Kra'u, and Minister Li'u-hran-li'i
to engage on the battlefield with an army led by twelve commanders.

Similarly, Zhang-wang-ling [of the Right Guard] was ap-
pointed generalissimo of the expeditionary army at Le'u-kra'u.
The army of the Left Guard was led by the commander-in-chief
Si'i-sbi Ho'o-li and by Minister Sho'o-tshe'i. The [generals] of
Wang rank [Wáng 王 princes] of the two Guards engaged the
Tibetan army in battle, but they were not at a competitive level.

Tibet invaded the area of Tes-kra'u (situated at the eastern
border of Lake Kokonoor) and took by force the two districts
of rMi-kung and bsTan-gling (situated on the western side of
Len-than County in Gansu).

In addition to that, with the invasion of Hru'u-kra'u, also
that region was lost in Tibet's favor. The border garrison of
that area was defeated.

Then the commander sNe-ka'o-zhon [who was leading that
garrison] joined Minister Li'u-ring-ku'e at Tha'o-hō to erect a
defense, but they did not succeed.

Tibet, allied with the western Uigurs, invaded the area of
An-shi (a subject territory of Dunhuang in Gansu).

Once again, an edict was issued by the Tang court: Minister
Li'i-cing-shon was instructed to lead the army at Tha'o-Kro'u.
Li'u-ring-ku'e was requested to join the replacement [troops] at
the western border of the Yellow River [rMa-chu]. Hra'an-kra'u

was appointed deputy general. They were all asked to manifest their military courage and strength.

Furthermore, Li'i-sha'u-yi'i, the governor general of Yi'i-kro'u (Sichuan Province, Kong-wu'u County), and Thu'o-wang-hpheng, the governor general of Su'u-kra'u (Sichuan Province, Shi'i-brang County), were also ordered to conduct the army from the southern side of the Cang'an Mountains (situated in the western part of Sichuan Province) and to engage in battle with Tibet as had been done in the past.

The Tibetan army was defeated at Lung-kri (on the eastern side of Lake Kokonoor). General Li'i-cing-shon was leading [the army administered by] Minister Li'u-hrin-li. They fought the Tibetan army on the shores of Lake Kokonoor and Minister Li'u-hrin-li fell into the hands of Tibet. General Li'i-cing-shon, leading the remaining troops, erected a defense at Dreng-hpheng-gleng (the eastern border of Qinghai Province).

The Tibetan troops were not able to go after them, but assaulted the Chinese military encampment; in response, a contingent of five hundred soldiers ready to sacrifice their lives from the troops subordinate to the Tang general of the Left Guard, He'i-tshe'i-khrang-kris, assailed the Tibetan encampment at night. The Tibetan troops, terrorized, started to fight and kill each other. [The survivors] fled, [leaving behind] a large number of casualties. It was only in this way that the rest of the [Chinese] army under the guidance of the Tang general Li'i-cing-shon was able to escape.

This extended citation illustrates the political situation of Tibet at the time of Khri Mang-srong Mang-btsan's death. His son 'Dus-srong Mang-po-rje had not been born yet, so it appears totally plausible that under those crucial circumstances the death of the bTsan-po was kept secret for a few years.

As for the tomb of Mang-srong Mang-btsan, the *rGyal rabs gsal ba'i me long* says (Pe, 194, 12):

The tomb of Mang-srong was on the left. Also that tomb was filled with precious jewels. Its name was sNgo-gzhe Hral-po.

We can be sure that it was built on the left side of the tomb of the grandfather Srong-btsan sGam-po because the *lDe'u rgya bod kyi chos 'byung* says so (Bod, 378,5):

> Mang-srong was buried to the left of Srong-btsan. The [tomb's] name was sNgo-bzher Hral-po.

5. THE THIRTY-EIGHTH RULER OF TIBET: 'DUS-SRONG MANG-PO-RJE

The *Tun hong bod kyi lo rgyus yig rnying* [Old Tibetan Chronicles of Dunhuang] call this king Khri 'Dus-srong and 'Dus-srong Mang-po-rje; as already pointed out, in ancient Tibetan usage the royal gShen created a name for the king consisting of a combination of Zhang Zhung words and archaic Tibetan terms intended to provide a magnificent name with a profound meaning. The name of this king was certainly created following that custom: the Zhang Zhung word *khri* is rendered in Tibetan with deity/divine or as nature of the mind; *'dus*, sometimes also written *'du*, is an archaic Tibetan term meaning excellence; *srong* means of wise mind [*thugs rgyud mdzangs*] and endowed with courage [*snying stobs dang ldan pa*]; in the modern Tibetan language the name would be rendered as Divinely Wise and Excellent.

Mang-po-rje was a distinguished name in the past meaning 'respected by all,' akin to that of the Tibetan word *'phags pa* which translates the Sanskrit *ārya* [noble].

Different documents write the name of this king in diverse ways: the *Nyang gi chos 'byung* has 'Dus-srong Mang-po-rje Glong-nam 'Phrul-gyi rGyal-po; the *Grags rgyal bod kyi rgyal rabs*, Dur-srong; the *Ne'u sngon byung gi gtam*, 'Du-srong; and the *Bu ston chos 'byung*, 'Dus-srong Mang-po-rje Blo-nam 'Phrul-gyi rGyal-po. The reading presented by the *Yar lung jo bo'i chos 'byung*, the *Deb ther dmar po*, the *lHo brag chos 'byung*, the *rGya bod yig tshang chen mo*, and the *Deb ther dpyid kyi rgyal mo'i glu dbyangs* is 'Dus-srong Mang-po-rje Rlung-nam 'Phrul-gyi rGyal-po. The *rGyal po bka'i thang yig* simply has Rlung-nam 'Phrul-gyi rGyal-po; the *rGyal rabs gsal ba'i me long*, 'Dur-srong Mang-po-rje Rlung-nam 'Phrul-gyi rGyal-po; and the *Legs bshad rin po che'i mdzod*, Blung-srong 'Phrul-btsan. Of these various versions, the ones to single out are Khri 'Dus-srong and 'Dus-srong Mang-po-rje.

It is easy to understand that Rlung-nam 'Phrul-gyi rGyal-po is an epithet that designates with high praise a supernatural, miraculous king endowed with a knowledge as vast and profound as the sky and with wisdom and activities as swift as the wind. The spellings Glong-nam, Blo-nam, and Blung-nam found in the *Nyang gi chos 'byung*, the *Bu ston chos 'byung*, and the *Legs bshad rin po che'i mdzod*, or Dur-srong and 'Dur-srong found in the *Grags rgyal bod kyi rgyal rabs* and the *rGyal rabs gsal ba'i me long* are merely mistakes perpetuated throughout history. For many centuries Tibetans have copied ancient documents by hand and words that were somewhat alike in pronunciation have occasionally been reproduced in the wrong manner. Thus, we should take into consideration the fact that copied manuscripts may contain misprints and be cautious about that.

As for the time and place of 'Dus-srong Mang-po-rje's birth, the *lDe'u chos 'byung chen mo* says (Bod, 119, 1):

> Mang-srong died before his son 'Dus-srong Mang-po-rje Rlung-nam 'Phrul-gyi rGyal-po was born. The latter was born in the Mouse year at lHa-lung in sGrags.

Also the *lDe'u rgya bod kyi chos 'byung* says that the year of birth of 'Dus-srong Mang-po-rje was the Mouse year, but it does not specify the element of that Mouse year.

On the contrary, the *Grags rgyal bod kyi rgyal rabs* says (sDe, TA, 198, 6):

> Dur-srong was born in the male Water Mouse year after his father passed away.

This textual source affirms that the element of the birth year of 'Dus-srong Mang-po-rje was Water. Most of the Tibetan dynastic and religious chronicles, such as the *Ne'u sngon byung gi gtam*, the *Yar lung jo bo'i chos 'byung*, the *Deb ther dmar po*, the *rGyal rabs gsal ba'i me long*, the *lHo brag chos 'byung*, and the *rGya bod yig tshang chen mo*, traditionally accept this source and acknowledge that the year of his birth was the Water Mouse year. This year should correspond either to the male Water Mouse year of the first *sMe-phreng* of the fifteenth *sMe-'khor* (Tibetan year 2569, 652 CE) or to the Water Mouse year of the intermediate *sMe-phreng* (Tibetan year 2629, 712 CE). The *Tun hong bod kyi lo rgyus yig rnying* [Old Tibetan Chronicles of Dunhuang] say (PI 581, 15):

> It happened in the year of the Mouse [676-677]. In the summer the bTsan-pho was residing at Sha-ra in sPrags. In the winter, Khri Mang-slon departed from Tshang-bang-sna for heaven. The bTsan-pho son, Khri 'Dus-srong, was born at lHa-lung in sGregs.

Historically speaking, the male Fire Mouse year of the intermediate *sMe-phreng* of the fifteenth *sMe-'khor* (Tibetan year 2593, 676 CE) is either too early or too late for Khri Mang-srong Mang-btsan's death and his son 'Dus-srong Mang-po-rje's birth.

The *Bu ston chos 'byung* says (lHa, YA, 125, 2):

> His son 'Dus-srong Mang-po-rje Rlung-nam 'Phrul-gyi rGyal-po (born in the female Water Bird year)...

This date of the female Water Bird year (Tibetan year 2590, 673 CE) is closer to the date maintained in the *Grags rgyal bod kyi rgyal rabs*, although it antecedes it by three full years.

For what concerns the year in which 'Dus-srong Mang-po-rje was enthroned, the *lDe'u rgya bod kyi chos 'byung* says (Bod, 299, 10):

> When ['Dus-srong Mang-po-rje] was not yet born, the father Mang-srong died. He was born in the Mouse year at sGrags.

'Dus-srong Mang-po-rje was born in the Fire Mouse year (Tibetan year 2593, 676 CE), which is the year of his father's death. The *lDe'u rgya bod kyi chos 'byung* says that the political affairs of the country were principally in the charge of Minister 'Gar sTong-btsan Yul-gzung (Bod, 299, 6):

'Gar sTong-btsan Yul-gzung acted as minister from the time of [Mang-srong's] grandfather until the time of the nephew.

Through political arrangements, the minister ruled in the name of King 'Dus-srong Mang-po-rje in a manner that the *lDe'u chos 'byung chen mo* describes as simultaneous [*cig char srid bzung*]; this information is also found in many other renowned religious and dynastic records, such as the *Grags rgyal bod kyi rgyal rabs*, the *Ne'u sngon byung gi gtam*, the *Yar lung jo bo'i chos 'byung*, the *lHo brag chos 'byung*, and the *rGya bod yig tshang chen mo*.

The *rGya'i thang yig rnying ma* [Old Chronicles of the Chinese Táng 唐 dynasty] say (Dha, 16, 6; mTsho 144, 3):

> In the fourth year of the dByi'i Hphin era (Earth Rabbit year, 679 CE) King Mang-srong Mang-btsan died. The year following that (Metal Dragon year, 680 CE), his son 'Dus-srong Mang-btsan was enthroned at the age of eight. All the country's political power was in the hands of the son of the Minister mGar, Ching-ling.

The *rGya'i thang yig gsar ma* [New Chronicles of the Chinese Táng 唐 dynasty] say (Dha, 90, 16; mTsho, 22, 7):

> In the fourth year of the Yi'i Hpheng era (Earth Rabbit year, 679 CE) King Mang-srong Mang-btsan died. His son Chi'i-nu'u Shes-lhun ('Dus-srong Mag-po-rje) ascended to the royal throne. The chief Tibetan minister Cin-ling (mGar-btsan sNya-sdom-bu) held political power.

The *rGya'i thang yig gsar rnying* [Old and New Chronicles of the Chinese Táng 唐 dynasty] describe the conflicts between Tibet and China that arose at the time of Khri Mang-srong Mang-btsan's death. Due to those critical conditions the circumstances of the king's death were kept secret for three years. This is the reason why both *Chronicles* say that Mang-srong died in the Earth Rabbit year (Tibetan year 2596, 679 CE), that is to say, three years later than the date provided by the Dunhuang Chronicles, the Fire Mouse year (Tibetan year 2593, 676 CE). It is also quite possible that the two *Chronicles* surreptitiously added

a few years to the real age of 'Dus-srong Mang-po-rje since they say
that the prince was eight years old at the time of his enthronement.

As for the queen and offspring of 'Dus-srong Mang-po-rje, the
Yar lung jo bo'i chos 'byung says (Si, 58 ,6):

> The son of this sovereign ('Dus-srong Mang-po-rje) and
> mChims-bza' bTsan-me-tog was Khri-lde gTsug-brtan.

This source does not provide any other information; also other religious and dynastic sources relate approximately the same, although they
write the name of this queen in different ways: the *rGyal rabs gsal ba'i
me long* calls her mChims-bza' bTsun-mo-tog; the *lHo brag chos 'byung* has
mChims-bza' bTsan-mo-tog; the *rGya bod yig tshang chen mo*, 'Chims-bza'
bTsan-la Me-tog; and the *Deb ther dpyid kyi rgyal mo'i glu dbyangs*, mChims-
bza' bTsan-mo rDog-ge. With the exception of the *rGya bod yig tshang
chen mo*, all sources agree that the consort of 'Dus-srong Mang-po-rje
was a princess of the mChims clan. The names bTsan-me-tog found
in the *Yar lung jo bo'i chos 'byung* and bTsan-mo-tog found in the *Chos
'byung mkhas pa'i dga' ston* show most affinity with her true personal name.

The *Tun hong bod kyi lo rgyus yig rnying* [Old Tibetan Chronicles of
Dunhuang] speak of one queen and of her son Khri-gtsug lDe-brtsan
(PI 556, 65):

> The first son of 'Dus-srong Mang-po-rje and mChims-za
> bTsan-ma-thog Thog-steng was Khri-lde gTsug-brtsan.

However, they also say (PI 583, 72):

> In the year of the Monkey [696-697] the bTsan-po was residing
> at Zrid-mda'. Chief Minister [mGar] Khri-'bring established an
> 'A-zha administration at 'O-kol in Sil-gu-cin in the land of the
> 'A-zha. In the winter Mang-nyen bZhi-brtsan convened [the
> council] at 'O-bar-tshal. Many people were summoned from
> [the side of] Princess Mang-mo-rje. One year.

I wonder whether the Princess Mang-mo-rje mentioned here could be
the sister of 'Dus-srong Mang-po-rje.

For what concerns the chief ministers of 'Dus-srong Mang-po-rje, the *lDe'u rgya bod kyi chos 'byung* says (Bod, 299, 20):

'Gar bTsan-gnya' lDem-bu and 'Gar Khri-'bring acted as ministers for ten years.

The *lDe'u chos 'byung chen mo* says (Bod, 119, 4):

During the time of those ministers there were seven men of exceptional strength:

rNgog Ring-la Nag-po carried a baby elephant from Nepal on his back;

rNgog Gling-kham could lift a young yak;

Ca-rgod lTongs-btsan gripped a lion by the mane;

mGos-stag Chung-btsan could whirl over his head the whole skin of a deer filled with sand;

Cog-ro 'Brong-shor could catch hold of a wild yak running downhill and throw it to the ground;

gNon rGyal-mtshan sNang-grags could strike several birds [at once] with a multi-pointed arrow and cut off [pieces of their bodies];

gNon Khri-gdas Yus-byin could hurl wild horses from a precipice and pull them back up again.

The names of those seven powerful men also appear in the *lDe'u rgya bod kyi chos 'byung*, although some are slightly different: they are called rNgog Ring-la Nag-po, rNgog Gling-gam, sBas-rgod lDong-btsan, 'Gos g.Yag-chung, Cog-ro 'Brong-shor, gNon rGyal-mtshan, and gNon Khri-lde Yul-byin. The *Yar lung jo bo'i chos 'byung* says (Si, 57, 9):

The ministers were 'Gar bTsan-gnya' lDom-bu and dBas sTag-ra Khong-lod.

Also this text, like the *lDe'u chos 'byung*, mentions the seven powerful men and calls them rNgog Ring-la Nag-po, rNgog Gling-kham, gNon rGyal-mtshan, dBas-rgod mDongs-btsan, mGos g.Yag-chung, Cog-ro 'Brong-shor, and gNon Khri-bdun g.Yu-byin.

The *rGyal rabs gsal ba'i me long* gives the same names of the ministers as in the *Yar lung jo bo'i chos 'byung* and the following names for the seven powerful men: rNgog Ring-la Nag-po, rNgog Gling-kham, sNon rGyal-mtshan, dBas-'dong-sgong, 'Gos-g.yag-chung, Co-ro 'Brong-sher, and sNon-khri-bdun g.Yu-byin.

The *lHo brag chos 'byung* records that the ministers were Bu-gnya' bTsan-ldem-bu of mGar and dBas Ta-ra Khod-lod and offers the following names for the seven powerful men: rNgog Ring-la Nag-po, rNgog Gling-kham, gNon rGyal-mtshan, sBas-rgod mDongs-can, mGos g.Yag-chung, Cog-ro 'Brong-gshor, and gNon Khri-bdun g.Yu-byin.

The *Deb ther dpyid kyi rgyal mo'i glu dbyangs* mentions them in a similar way.

The *rGya bod yig tshang chen mo* describes these seven powerful men in a slightly different manner (Si, 171, 10):

> A-rgod lDong-btsan could hold a white lion by the ears.
>
> Mon Khri-bzang could bind two adult tigers together with an iron chain and carry them about, filling space with their roars.
>
> lDo-don Dam-yang Dag-'phags could lift and carry thirteen big teak timbers with a load of iron on top of them.
>
> lCog-ro Zangs-dkar held the Lhasa stone pillar at his waist as if spinning thread on a spindle.
>
> rNgog-rings Nag-po carried a live baby elephant from Nepal.
>
> mGos-shag-chung filled the skin of a doe with salt and whirled it over his head.
>
> gNon rGyal-mtshan rNam-grangs could shoot his arrows three times farther [than anyone] and could leap back and forth over a river.

Even if these narratives show some differences, the respective identities of the men can be clearly envisioned.

Concerning the number of years during which 'Dus-srong Mang-po-rje remained on the throne and the year of his death, the *lDe'u rgya bod kyi chos 'byung* says (Bod, 299, 20):

> He lived until he was twenty-nine.

And also (ibid., 300, 1):

> He died in lJang in the Dragon year.

If he was born in the male Fire Mouse year (Tibetan year 2593, 676 CE) and the full twenty-eight or about twenty-nine years in which he lived also include the duration of his reign, the full twenty-eighth year of his life (2593+28=2621, 676+28=704) should correspond to the male Wood Dragon year (Tibetan year 2621, 704 CE). The *lDe'u chos 'byung chen mo* says (Bod, 119, 14):

> In the Dragon year when he was twenty-nine, he was killed by the Hor [Turkish tribes] in the land of 'Jang. It is said that Cog-ro Khong-khri and Cang-dkar Sor-bzhi [tried to] retrieve his corpse, but obtained only a part of the right leg.

From what this source affirms, he most probably died on the battlefield.

Most of the religious and dynastic histories, such as the *Yar lung jo bo'i chos 'byung*, the *Deb ther dmar po*, the *rGyal rabs gsal ba'i me long*, the *lHo brag chos 'byung*, and the *rGya bod yig tshang chen mo*, say that 'Dus-srong Mang-po-rje ruled until he was twenty-nine and then died in the land of lJang. It is not certain whether the land of lJang mentioned is the same land of 'Jang of the *lDe'u chos 'byung*, because the *Tun hong bod kyi lo rgyus yig rnying* [Old Tibetan Chronicles of Dunhuang] say (PI 584, 95):

> It happened in the year of the Dragon [704-705]. In the spring rGyal gTsug-ru was born at Kho-brang-tsal. In the summer the bTsan-po father was residing at Yo-ti Cu-bzangs in rMa-grom and the mother Khri-ma-lod was residing at 'O-dang in Yar-'brog. The council was convened at Brag-sgo. In the winter the bTsan-po went to Mywa for a political campaign, but departed for heaven.

The *Chronicles* state that in the spring of the male Wood Dragon year (Tibetan year 2621, 704 CE) Khri-lde gtsug-brtan was born and that in the winter the king died on his way to a political campaign, but do not say anything about his going to the land of 'Jang and being killed there by the Hor.

The *rGya'i thang yig rnying ma* [Old Chronicles of the Chinese Táng 唐 dynasty] say (Dha, 21, 11, mTsho, 149, 19):

In the second year of the imperial dBan Su'i era (Fire Bird year, 697 CE),[45] the Tibetans sent a legation with the gift of a thousand horses and over two thousand ounces [*srang*] of gold to request a bride for the bTsan-po. The Thang [Táng 唐] emperor consented. At that time the Bal-yul (Ne-pho-lo) subjects of southern Tibet staged a revolt. bTsan-po 'Dus-srong Mang-btsan led the army in person in the direction of Bal-yul (Ne-pho-lo), [but] died en route.

The *rGya'i thang yig gsar ma* [New Chronicles of the Chinese Táng 唐 dynasty] say (Dha, 98, 9; mTsho, 32, 15):

In the first year of the imperial Wang Su Yi Thon Then era (Fire Monkey year, 696 CE), the gift of great quantities of gold and silver was sent from Tibet to the court of the Thang [Táng 唐] emperor as a request for a bride for the bTsan-po.

In the preceding year (Wood Sheep year, 695 CE), the bTsan-po of Tibet ('Dus-srong Mang-po-rje), personally leading [an army of] ten thousand cavalry troops, invaded the Chinese territory of Shi'i Kra'u (situated within Su-hphan County in Sìchuān 四川 Province) and fought four times with Dreng Ta' Tshe, the governor-general of that area, but the Thang [Táng 唐] won. Then the vassals of southern Tibet rebelled; the king himself, leading the army, went to subdue [the revolt], but died on the battlefield.

These two texts say that 'Dus-srong Mang-po-rje died on the battlefield in either the Fire Monkey or the Fire Bird year, making it difficult to determine how and when he actually died. However, the *Tun hong bod kyi lo rgyus yig rnying* [Old Tibetan Chronicles of Dunhuang] clearly record the yearly activities of the king and since no other sources are more authoritative than this one, it is evident that the date we should consider as the most suitable for 'Dus-srong Mang-po-rje's death is the

---

45 [According to Chinese sources, the Wànsuì era corresponds to the years 696-697 of the reign of the Second Zhōu 周 dynasty empress Wǔ Hòu 武后. The years are divided into two parts: the first part is called Wànsuì Dēngfēng 萬歲登封 and lasted from 20 January to 21 April 696; the second part is called Wànsuì Tōngtiān 萬歲通天 and lasted from 22 April 696 to 28 September 697.]

male Wood Dragon year of the intermediate *sMe-phreng* of the fifteenth *sMe-'khor* (Tibetan year 2621, 704 CE).

Concerning the tomb of 'Dus-srong Mang-po-rje, the *rGyal rabs gsal bai' me long* says (Pe, 196, I):

> The tomb of 'Phrul-rgyal was situated to the left of Mang-srong. It became known as the Tomb of the Holy Mountain [Bang-so lHa-ri-can]. It was built by the Hor people. Its name was Seng-ge brTsig-pa. So it is said.

The text says that the tomb was built by the Hor people; this fact must surely have some relation with the accounts of the king dying in battle.

6. THE THIRTY-NINTH RULER OF TIBET: KHRI-LDE GTSUG-BRTAN

This king is generally known as Khri-lde gTsug-brtan and as Mes Ag-tshoms. According to the *Tun hong bod kyi lo rgyus yig rnying* [Old Tibetan Chronicles of Dunhuang], he was originally called rGyal-gtsug-ru and was given the name Khri-lde gTsug-brtsan at the age of eight.

His first name, Khri-lde gTsug-brtan, is a combination of Zhang Zhung and archaic Tibetan terms: the word *khri* means deity or divine and the nature of the mind; *lde* means knowledge or wisdom; *gtsug* means eminent, supreme, or highest, and for that reason is the root of compound words such as the crown of the head [*spyi gtsug*], sciences or astrological sciences [*gtsug lag*], temple or monastery [*gtsug lag khang*], and so on; *brtan* means immutable and everlasting. In brief, in the Tibetan language of the present time, the name of this king can be understood to mean Nature of the Mind, Immutable Supreme Knowledge [*Thugs nyid mkhyen mchog 'gyur med*].

The reason for the name Mes Ag-tshoms [literally, Bearded Forefather] can be inferred from the *lHo brag chos 'byung* (Pe, Vol. I, 293, 18):

> Since he was a dignified elder and had a long beard, he was called Mes Ag-tshoms.

Concerning the time and place of birth of Khri-lde gTsug-brtan, the
lDe'u rgya bod kyi chos 'byung says (Bod, 300, 14):

> He was born in the Dragon year at Pho-brang lDan-mkhar.

The *lDe'u chos 'byung chen mo* says (Bod, 119, 19):

> Khri-lde gTsug-btsan, son of 'Dus-srong Mang-po-rje, was born
> in the spring of the Dragon year at Pho-brang Lan-khar.

These two sources clearly say that the year of birth was a Dragon year,
but do not specify the relevant element.

The *lDe'u chos 'byung chen mo* calls him Khri-lde gTsug-btsan and
also the *Nyang gi chos 'byung* refers to him with the same name; the *lDe'u
rgya bod kyi chos 'byung* calls him Khri-lde gTsug-brtan, which could seem
a variation in significance, but is simply a use of different words to
express the same meaning.

The *Grags rgyal bod kyi rgyal rabs* says (sDe, TA, 198, 1):

> Khri-lde gTsug-brtan was born in the spring of the Metal
> Dragon year at Pho-brang lDan-dkar.

These sources show that the year of birth was the Dragon year and
also that the element of that Dragon year was Metal.

The sDe-dge print edition of the text from which the last citation is drawn actually says, "He died ['das] at Pho-brang lDan-dkar,"
but if we read further down, the text mentions the year of his death:

> It is said that he died in the Water Horse year at Yar-'brog
> sBas-pa when he was sixty-three years old.

It is easy to understand that date as a copying error.

The *Ne'u sngon byung gi gtam*, the *Yar lung jo bo'i chos 'byung*, the *Deb
ther dmar po*, the *rGyal rabs gsal ba'i me long*, the *lHo brag chos 'byung*, the
rGya bod yig tshangs chen mo, and the *lHa thog rgyal rabs* also maintain that
Khri-lDe gTsug-brtan was born in the Metal Dragon year.

If the year of birth of Khri-lDe gTsug-brtan was the Metal
Dragon year, it should correspond either to the male Metal Dragon
year of the intermediate *sMe-phreng* of the fifteenth *sMe-'khor* (Tibetan

year 2597, 680 CE) or else to the male Metal Dragon year of the last
sMe-phreng of the fifteenth *sMe-'khor* (Tibetan year 2657 740 CE). But
if we compare and examine the history of Tibet and China, neither of
those two years function; besides, the *Tun hong bod kyi lo rgyus yig rnying*
[Old Tibetan Chronicles of Dunhuang] (PI 584, 95) say:

> It happened in the year of the Dragon [704-705]. In the spring
> rGyal gTsug-ru was born at Kho-brang-tsal.

The Dragon year mentioned in the *Chronicles* is certainly the male
Wood Dragon year of the intermediate *sMe-phreng* of the fifteenth
sMe-'khor (Tibetan year 2621, 704 CE), because the *Chronicles* contain
yearly records of the activities of the monarchs. The *Deb ther sngon po*
affirms (Si, 76, 4):

> Afterward, in the female Wood Snake year (705 CE), Dzung-
> dzung,[46] son of Chi Ka'u Dzung [Emperor Gāozōng 高宗]
> and of the Empress [Wŭ Zétiān 武则天] was installed on the
> throne. In that same year, also Khri-lde gTsug-brtan, the son
> of 'Dus-srong, was enthroned.

This text, drawing information from Chinese historical sources, provides similar evidence when it states that Khri-lde gTsug-brtan was
enthroned in that year. As already quoted above, the *Tun hong bod kyi lo
rgyus yig rnying* [Old Tibetan Chronicles of Dunhuang] say (PI 584, 97):

> In the winter the bTsan-po went to Mywa for a political cam-
> paign, but departed for heaven.

The father king Khri 'Dus-srong died in the winter of that year. It is
certain that he was enthroned in the year of his father's death, because
the *lDe'u chos 'byung chen mo* says (Bod, 119, 19):

> Khri-lde gTsug-btsan was born in the spring of the Dragon
> year at Pho-brang Lan-khar. At the end of the year the father
> died and [he] inherited the kingdom.

---

46 [Zhōngzōng 中宗, reigned in 684 and then from 705 to 710].

The *rGya'i thang yig rnying ma* [Old Chronicles of the Chinese Táng 唐 dynasty] say (Dha, 22, 2; mTsho, 150, 1):

> After that, the sons of the monarch contended for the royal throne and a long time passed when who was [actually] ruling was not sure. Then in the Wood Dragon year, 704 CE, the majority of people approved the appointment of Khri-lde gTsug-brtan, also known as Mes Ag-tshom, as king of the whole kingdom of Tibet. At that time he had reached the age of seven.

The *rGya'i thang yig gsar ma* [New Chronicles of the Chinese Táng 唐 dynasty] say (Dha, 99, 3; mTsho, 32, 19):

> The children struggled over the royal throne. Nevertheless, the ruler of Tshi-lu-zhu (Khri-lde gTsug-brtan) was appointed king by the people. At that time he was seven years old.

The fact that these sources speak of children competing for the royal throne strongly suggests that King 'Dus-srong Mang-po-rje had other children beside Khri-lde gTsug-brtan. The *lDe'u chos 'byung chen mo* says (Bod, 120, 20):

> The elder brother of this king [was] Pa-tshab Tsha-lha Bal-po. The younger brothers were Lod-po and Lod-chung. These three were exiled to the border plains.

Hence, there was an elder brother called Tsha-lha Bal-po who was the son of Pa-tshab-gza' and two younger brothers, respectively called Lod-po and Lod-chung. Even if Khri-lde gTsug-brtan had an elder brother, he was enthroned as soon as he was born; obviously this indicates that the ministers of that time contended strongly for political power. In this respect, the *Tun hong bod kyi lo rgyus yig rnying* [Old Tibetan Chronicles of Dunhuang] say (PI 584, 99):

> It happened in the year of the Snake [705-706]. bTsan-po rGyal gTsug-ru, the son, and the grandmother Khri-ma-lod were residing at Dron. lDeg-ren-pa' mNon-snang-grags, Khe-rgad mDo-snang, and others rebelled. At Bon-mo Na-la-tse,

the lDeg-ren-pa killed the adversaries. At Pong-lag-rang, they dethroned the elder brother bTsan-po lHa-bal-pho.

From this account, one can judge that the ministers belonging to the faction of lDeg-ren and Khe-rgad most probably banished the first-born lHa-bal-po from the kingdom, or else, as the *lDe'u chos 'byung chen mo* says, "exiled him to the border plains." Thus, while the supporters of lDeg-ren gNon-snang-grags and Khe-rgad mDo-snang were on the verge of expunging lHa-bal-po, the grandmother Khri-ma-lod and the ministers supporting her faction conferred power on the one-year-old rGyal-gtsug-ru, also known as Khri-lde gTsug-brtan. That until the king came of age the country was essentiallly ruled by the grandmother Khri-ma-lod and the chief ministers Mang-po-rje lHa-zung, dBas Khri-gzigs, and so on can certainly be deduced from what is written in the *Tun hong bod kyi lo rgyus yig rnying* [Old Tibetan Chronicles of Dunhuang].

The *rGya'i thang yig gsar rnying* [Old and New Chronicles of the Chinese Táng 唐 dynasty] say that Khri-lde gTsug-brtan had reached the age of seven when King 'Dus-srong Mang-po-rje died; if from the male Wood Dragon year of King Khri-lde gTsug-brtan's birth (Tibetan year 2621, 704 CE) we subtract seven full years (2621-7=2614; 704-7=697), we arrive at the female Fire Bird year (Tibetan year 2614, 697 CE); but the *Tun hong bod kyi lo rgyus yig rnying* [Old Tibetan Chronicles of Dunhuang] clearly list the yearly activities of the monarchs and show that the true year of birth of King Khri-lde gTsug-brtan was the male Wood Dragon year (Tibetan year 2621, 704 CE). No source is more reliable than this one and there is no need to look for another.

Concerning the time of King Khri-lde gTsug-brtan's enthrone-ment, the *lDe'u rgya bod kyi chos 'byung* says (Bod, 300, 15):

In the latter part of [his] life the father died. He ruled for thirty years.

The text has *tshe smad* [latter part of life], but what is actually meant is *tshe smang* or *tshe rmang* which indicates the early period of life; this can be recognized by taking into account the affirmation of the *lDe'u chos 'byung chen mo* that Khri-lde gTsug-brtan ascended the throne at the end of his first year of life when his father 'Dus-srong died.

Also other famous religious and dynastic histories, such as the *Grags rgyal bod kyi rgyal rabs*, the *Ne'u sngon byung gi gtam*, the *Yar lung jo bo'i chos 'byung*, and the *rGya bod yig tshang chen mo*, accept this view and say that Khri-lde gTsug-brtan was raised to the throne in the year of his birth because his father 'Dus-srong had died.

The *rGyal rabs gsal ba'i me long* says (Pe, 196, 7):

> Khri-lde gTsug-brtan was known as Mes Ag-tshom. He was born in the male Metal Dragon year at Pho-brang lDan-dkar. He seized the kingdom when he was ten years old.

This source adheres to the *Grags rgyal bod kyi rgyal rabs* in saying that the year of birth was the Metal Dragon year and also maintains that he was ten years old when he seized the throne; the *rGyal rabs 'phrul gyi lde mig* states this idea as well which, however, does not agree with historical timing for the reasons explained above.

The *lDe'u rgya bod kyi chos 'byung* says, "He ruled for thirty years." The *lDe'u chos 'byung chen mo* specifies his age and the year in which he died (Bod, 120, 17):

> At the age of fifty-five in the Pig year, he left his body at Yar-'Brog sBal-tshang.

Therefore he did not rule for thirty years.

Regarding the consorts and children of Khri-lde gTsug-brtan, the *sBa bzhed* simply mentions sNam-snang-bza' bZhi-stengs and Queen lJang-mo Khri-btsun who gave birth to lJang-tsha lHa-dbon; the latter married the Chinese princess rGya-bza' Gyim-shang Ong-jo [Jīnchéng Gōngzhǔ 金成公主, died in 739]; when he died she became the father's consort. Their son was Khri-srong lDe'u-btsan.

The *lDe'u rgya bod kyi chos 'byung* speaks only of a consort of Khri-lde gTsug-brtan called sNa-nam-mo sPyi-stengs. It also mentions a son called lJang-tsha lHa-dbon who married rGya-mo Ong-cong; when he died rGya-mo Ong-cong became the wife of his father and from their union Khri-srong lDe'u-btsan was born. The text does not specify which queen was the mother of lJang-tsha lHa-dbon.

The *Grags rgyal bod kyi rgyal rabs* says (sDe, TA, 197, 3),

Me-khri-lde took six wives; one of them, Gyim-phya Gon-ju, daughter of the Chinese lord Yag 'Byam, generated Khri-srong lDe-btsan.

This text informs us that there were six wives, but does not specify even one of their names.

The *Yar lung jo bo'i chos 'byung* says (Si, 59, 4):

> ... [H]aving married Queen lJang-mo Khri-btsun, a prince was born. He did not look like the child of human beings but rather like a divine [*lha*] child; for that reason he was given the name lJang-tsha lHa-dbon.
>
> Since [he found] no one suitable to marry in Tibet, he dispatched [a delegation] to escort Kong-jo, the daughter of the Chinese lord Wi Dzung.
>
> Angered that the daughter of the gNyags [clan] had not been chosen, gNyags Khri-bzang Yang-don murdered the prince before Kong-jo arrived.

And also (Si, 59, 11):

> From the union of the father with Kong-jo, Prince Khri-srong lDe'u-btsan was born.

Hence, according to those sources, Queen lJang-gza' Khri-btsun had lJang-tsha lHa-bon while Kong-jo had Khri-srong lDe'u btsan.

The account relating the assassination of lJang-tsha lHa-dbon by the gNyags is also affirmed in the *Deb ther dpyid kyi rgyal mo'i glu dbyangs* (Pe, 50, 19):

> Angered that the daughter of the gNyags [clan] had not been accepted, gNyags Khri-bzang Yang-'don killed the prince.

Also the *Yar lung jo bo* recounts a similar happening.

On the contrary, the *lDe'u rgya bod kyi chos'byung* says (Bod, 300, 7):

> lJang-tsha had become an imbecile.

And also (ibid., 300, 10):

> lJang-tsha lHa-dbon did not obtain the kingdom and was banished to the border plains.

The *rGyal rabs gsal ba'i me long* says (197, 23):

> (Kong-jo) arrived at the frontier of China and Tibet. In Tibet
> the ministers invited the prince. At night, they all raced horses
> in the moonlight, including the prince; but the horse unsaddled
> him and he died.

It is difficult to determine the actual story because the sources present
different versions.

Concerning the tomb of lJang-tsha lHa-dbon, the *rGyal rabs gsal
ba'i me long* says (Pe 198, 5):

> The tomb of lJang-tsha lHa-dbon was situated in front [of
> that] of his grandfather. It is said that it was circular in shape
> and that treasures were concealed in it.

It is evident that the tomb was built in front of the tomb of his
grandfather 'Dus-srong Mang-po-rje.

Regarding Khri-srong lDe'u btsan, the son of Khri-lde gTsug-
brtan, I quote a passage from an essay titled *Chos ldan rgyal rabs kyi lo thigs
'khrul sel* [Removing Confusion in the Histories Concerning Buddhist
Royal Lineages] (composed during a course on the Tibetan language
taught at the Central Institute of Nationalities) (16, 1):

> The *sBa bzhed* and the texts in agreement with this source relate
> the following: Khri-srong lDe'u-btsan was generated by Kong-
> jo; sNa-nam-bza' stole Kong-jo's child and pretended it was
> she who had given birth to him. The lord and the ministers
> were suspicious, but did not risk expressing their judgement
> on the matter. (Kong-jo) implemented some excellent Tibetan
> geomantic [*sa dpyad, fēngshuǐ* 风水] [practices] and before long,
> at the celebration for the first placing of a child's feet on the
> ground, while the two queens, [their] friends and relatives [*pha
> ming*], the ministers, and the subjects were all gathered together,
> the king placed a golden bowl filled with rice beer [*'bras chang*]
> in the hands of the son and asked him to give it to his ma-
> ternal uncle. The child put the precious bowl in the hands of
> the Chinese [relatives] and [said], "I am Khri-srong lDe-btsan,
> nephew [of the] Chinese [side of the family] [*rgya tsha*]." The

sNa-nam maternal uncle said, "I do not understand." Kong-jo, extremely pleased, said, "I, the maiden who came from China due to the karma of previous lives, have generated the incomparable son of the king," and so on.

These accounts, with their insistence in wanting to prove that Khri-srong was the nephew of the Chinese [side of the family], accomplish the exact contrary and convince one in fact that [actually] was not the case. They are like the old story according to which a royal consort expelled gas in the midst of a crowd and when she did so an attendant said, "Just now the royal consort expelled gas; but it was not her majesty who did it. It was me."

In the same manner it was said that the child generated by sNa-nam was not her child, but the child of the Chinese consort. If in a Tibet dominated by religion, where the king, the ministers, the retinue, and the subjects lived together in close circumstances, it was not possible to know even which one of the two queens had given birth and the truth had to be understood from a one-year-old child, how could have all the magnificent political feats possibly been accomplished, as well as friends protected, enemies destroyed, and the like? Traditional folktales which transform true history into distorted legends can at best elicit laughter from knowledgeable people.

In this excerpt what is said is the eloquent elucidation of a brilliant scholar which corresponds to the principles of history.

About the chief ministers of Khri-lde gTsug-brtan, the *sBa bzhed* mentions only gNyags Khri-bzang and reveals nothing else, while the *lDe'u rgya bod kyi chos 'byung* affirms (Bod, 300, 16):

Khu Mang-po-rje lHa-gzung had been appointed minister, but divisive talk began and Khu was reprimanded. sBas Khri-gzigs was minister for four years, 'Gro Cung-za 'Or-ma for twenty.

Concerning the reprimand that Khu Mang-po-rje lHa-gzung received, the *Tun hong bod kyi lo rgyus yig rnying* [Old Tibetan Chronicles of Dunhuang] say (PT 584, 99):

It happened in the year of the Snake [705-706]. bTsan-po
rGyal gTsug-ru, the son, and the grandmother Khri-ma-lod
were residing in Dron.

And proceed with (ibid., 102):

In the winter the bTsan-po rGyal-gtsug-ru and the grandmother
Khri-ma-lod were residing in Zhur. Khu Mang-po-rje lHa-gzung
was proclaimed chief minister. After that, at Gling-rings-tsal,
Khu Mang-po-rje lHa-gzung was reprimanded. dBa's Khri-gzigs
Zhang-nyen was proclaimed chief minister. [The king of] Se-rib
revolted. One year.

Thus, Khu Mang-po-rje was appointed chief minister in the female
Wood Snake year (Tibetan year 2622, 705 CE), when Khri-lde gTsug-
brtan was one year old, but was calumniated and fell in disgrace that
same year. The *Grags rgyal bod kyi rgyal rabs* says (sDe, TA, 197, 5, 2):

'Dus-srong Mang-po-rje was the son of that [Mang-srong
Mang-btsan] and of 'Bro-bza' Khri-chen Khri-ma-lod.

The consort of Mang-srong Mang-btsan belonged to the 'Bro clan;
therefore dBas, mChims, and 'Bro had the authority to admonish Khu
because they could count on the power of the grandmother Khri-ma-lod.
    The *Yar lung jo bo'i chos 'byung* says (Si, 58, 8):

The ministers were dBas sKyes-bzang sTong-btsan, mChims
rGyal-gzigs Shu-ting, and 'Brong Chung-bzang 'Or-mang.

The *rGyal rabs gsal ba'i me long* says (Pe, 196, 9):

sKyi-bzang sTong-btsan, mChims rGyal-shugs-steng, and 'Bro
Chu-bzang-'or were the three ministers.

The *lHo brag chos 'byung* says (Pe, Vol.I, 293, 16):

The ministers were sBas sKyes-bzang sTong-btsan, mChims
rGyal-gzims Shu-ting, and 'Bro Chu-bzang 'Or-ma.

The *rGya bod yig tshang chen mo* says (Si, 177, 12):

The ministers were sBas sKyes-bzang sTong-btsan, mChims rGyal-gzigs Shu-lde, and 'Bro Chu-bzang Hor-mang.

These sources provide the names of the three chief ministers, even if they do not record them in the same way. Maybe the one called sBas Khri-gzigs in the *lDe'u chos 'byung* could be identified with dBas-skyes-bzang, sKyi-bzang sTong-btsan, and dBas sKyes-bzang sTong-btsan in the *Yar lung jo bo'i chos 'byung* and other texts; furthermore, the one called mChims rGyal-gzigs Shu-ting could be identified with mChims rGyal-shugs-steng, mChims rGyal-gzims Shu-ting, and mChims rGyal-gzigs Shu-lde; and the one called 'Brong Chung-bzang 'Or-mang could be identified with 'Bro Chu-bzang-'or, 'Bro Chu-bzang 'Or-ma, and 'Bro Chu-bzang Hor-mang.

The *Nyang gi chos 'byung* says (Bod, 271, 8):

The three ministers mChims Khri-thog rJe-'bar, Cog Ro-skyes bZang-rgyal, and the maternal uncle of sNa-nam, Khrom-pa-skyes ...

The individuals mentioned here were the three powerful chief ministers who controlled the political scene during the second part of Khri-lde gTsug-brtan's life. They were the ministers who were adversaries of the Buddhadharma when Khri-srong lDe'u-btsan was young—the *Nyang gi chos 'byung* relates the troubles they caused in this respect—and who were immensely influential, especially during the first part of Khri-srong lDe'u-btsan's life.

The highly powerful grandmother Khri-ma-lod died in the male Water Mouse year (Tibetan year 2629, 712 CE) when Khri-lde gTsug-brtan reached the age of eight. The *Tun hong bod kyi lo rgyus yig rnying* [Old Tibetan Chronicles of Dunhuang] provide information in this regard and also mention the funerary rituals (Pl 586, 133):

In the year of the Mouse [712-713] during the summer, the bTsan-po was residing at Bal-pho. The grandmother was at Dron. [...] The king adopted the name Khri-lde gTsug-rtsan instead of rGyal gTsug-ru. The grandmother Khri-ma-lod died.

And also (ibid., 137):

It happened in the Ox year [713-714]. In the summer the bTsan-po was residing at brDzen-tang in Mal-dro.

And also (ibid., 139):

In the winter the bTsan-pho's court was residing at Brag-mar. The funerary rituals for the grandmother Khri-ma-lod were held at Pying-ba.

Concerning the date of Khri-lde gTsug-brtan's death, the *rGya bod kyi chos 'byung* says (Bod, 300, 20):

He died in the Pig year at 'Brog-sbal-tshang after [he] had attained the age of fifty-five.

Also the *lDe'u chos 'byung chen mo* says that he died in the Pig year. This Pig year would correspond to the female Earth Pig year of the last *sMe-phreng* of the fifteenth *sMe-'khor* (Tibetan year 2676, 759 CE). Regarding this year the *Tun hong bod kyi lo rgyus yig rnying* [Old Tibetan Chronicles of Dunhuang] simply say (PI 591, 256):

In the Pig year [747-748] the bTsan-pho's court was residing at Na-mar. [Delegates] were dispatched to each [area] to enact laws for the pasturelands and the uncultivated lands. At Khu-le, riding a horse ...

We do not know the activities carried out by Khri-lde gTsug-brtan in the time period that begins in the female Fire Pig year (Tibetan year 2664, 747 CE) in which he was forty-three and ends with the female Wood Sheep year (Tibetan year 2672, 755 CE) when he reached the age of fifty-one because the original manuscript is incomplete; however, the *Chronicles* do relate happenings in the female Wood Sheep year (PI 592, 12):

It happened in the year of the Sheep [755-756]. The soldiers pillaged the entourage of the father. They appointed commanders for the three 1,000 soldier units of sTong sar. The servants [and attendants] of Lang (Myes-zigs) and 'Bal (sKyes-bzang lDong-tshab) were banished and sent to mTong-sod. The two ministers Khri-bzang and Zhang sTong-rtsan plundered the

Te'u-cu stronghold. They reinstated [the military government of] rMa-grom [Upper Yellow River]. Zhang mDo-bzher was appointed general of rMa-grom. The ministers Khri-sgra, Mang-rtsan 'Pan-gang, mDo-bzher, and others convened the mDo-smad summer council at dBu-le Lam-nag. They led a military campaign at Te'u-cu. Zhang rGyal-zigs convened the winter council at Kog in Rag-tag. They appraised the [confiscated] possessions of the disgraced Lang and 'Bal. One year.

According to the following account, Lang and 'Bal murdered Khri-lde gTsug-brtan. In this regard the first twenty lines of the inscription on the southern side of a stone pillar situated in the back of the Zhol district of Lhasa read:

> During the time of King Khri-lde gTsug-rtsan, Ngan-lam Klu-Khong acted in a lofty way that was near the king's heart. 'Bal lDong-tsab and Lang Myes-zigs were the chief ministers, but [their] actions were far from the king's heart. They endangered the life of the bTsan-pho father, Khri-lde gTsug-rtsan, and [the king] died. [They came] close to imperiling the life of the bTsan-pho son, Khri-srong lDe-brtsan. [They] exacerbated the politics of the black-headed Tibetans. Klu-khong, judging 'Bal and Lang treacherous, informed the bTsan-pho son, Khri-srong lDe-brtsan. Their disloyalty turned out to be the case. They were disgraced. Klu-khong was near the heart [of the king].

This means that during the reign of King Khri-lde gTsug-brtan, Ngan-lam sTag-sgra Klu-khong offered his services in an honest manner, while 'Bal lDong-tsab and Lang Myes-zigs, despite their roles as chief ministers, acted as insurgents. They endangered the life of the bTsan-po father, Khri-lde gTsug-brtan, provoking his death, and also came near imperiling the life of the bTsan-po son, Khri-srong lDe'u-btsan. sTag-sgra Klu-khong brought the circumstances of the upheaval they created in the politics of the black-headed Tibetans and of their revolt to King Khri-srong lDe'u-btsan's attention, and the truth about their rebellion was discovered. They were condemned, and the good intentions of sTag-sgra Klu-khong were recognized. No details are presented as to what 'Bal and Lang actually did to the king, but that they created the circumstances to harm the king's life and caused his consequent death are clearly indicated, as is equally clear that these events occurred in the female Wood Sheep year (Tibetan year 2672, 755 CE) of the last *sMe-phreng* of the fifteenth *sMe-'khor*.

As we have seen the *lDe'u chos 'byung* says that Khri-lde gTsug-brtan lived for a full fifty-five years and died in the Pig year. The *Grags rgyal bod kyi rgyal rabs* affirms (sDe, TA, 198, I):

> It is said that having reached the age of sixty-three, [he] died at Yar-'brog sBas-pa in the Water Horse year.

According to this source he was born in the Metal Dragon year (Tibetan year 2597, 680 CE) and died sixty-two or about sixty-three years later (2597+62=2659; 680+62=742) in the birth year of Khri-srong lDe'u-btsan, that is to say, in the male Water Horse year (Tibetan year 2659 742 CE). Many historical and religious sources, such as the *Ne'u sngon byung gi gtam*, the *Deb ther dmar po*, the *rGyal rabs gsal ba'i me long*, the *rGya bod yig tshang chen mo*, and so on agree with this view. On the contrary, the *Yar lung jo bo'i chos 'byung* says (Si, 59,12):

> When [he was] twenty-three years old, [he] died at Yar-'brog sBal-tsha Na-khar.

This source maintains that he was born in the Metal Dragon year (Tibetan year 2657, 740 CE) and that he died twenty-three years later (2657+23=2680; 740+23=763) in the female Water Rabbit year (Tibetan year 2680, 763 CE), the year in which Khri-srong lDe'u-btsan reached the age of twenty-one. However, these dates are too early or too late when compared with the timing indicated by the *Tun hong bod kyi lo rgyus yig rnying* [Old Tibetan Chronicles of Dunhuang] and hence are not applicable. The *rGya'i thang yig rnying ma* [Old Chronicles of the Chinese Táng 唐 dynasty] say (Dha, 31, 8; mTsho, 179, 8):

> In the fourteenth year of the Than sPo'o era[47] (Wood Sheep year, 755 CE), bTsan-po Khri-lde gTsug-brtan died. His ministers requested his son Khri-srong lDe'u-btsan to accept the royal mandate.

---

47   [The Tiānbǎo 天寶 era of Emperor Xuánzōng 玄宗, 742-756.]

The *rGya'i thang yig gsar ma* [New Chronicles of the Chinese Táng 唐 dynasty] say (Dha, 103, 14; mTsho, 54, 14):

> In the fourteenth year of the Then Pa'o era (Wood Sheep year, 755 CE) the Tibetan bTsan-po Khri-lde gTsug-brtan died. His son Su'o Shi'i lHun-nam-btsan (Khri-srong lDe-btsan) was requested to ascend the royal throne. An envoy was dispatched to the Thang [Táng 唐] court on a peace-seeking mission.

These two excerpts confirm that the true year of death of Khri-lde gTsug-brtan is precisely the female Wood Sheep year (Tibetan year 2672, 755 CE) of the last *sMe-phreng* of the fifteenth *sMe-'khor*.

For what concerns the tomb of Khri-lde gTsug-brtan, the *rGyal rabs gsal ba'i me long* says (Pe, 201, 23):

> His tomb was built at Mu-ra-ri. It was placed to the left of 'Phrul-gyi rGyal-po['s tomb]. Its name was lHa-ri gTsug-nam.

7. THE FORTIETH RULER OF TIBET: KHRI-SRONG LDE'U-BTSAN

The name of this king consists of a combination of Zhang Zhung and Tibetan words: the Zhang Zhung word *khri* means deity or divine and supreme; *srong* is a Tibetan archaic term meaning honest [*drang ba*] and brave [*mdzangs pa*]; *lde* or *lde'u* is a commonly known Zhang/Bod word meaning wisdom [*mkhyen pa*] or knowledge [*shes pa*]; *btsan* is a Tibetan archaic term meaning keen [*rnon po*] or superior [*rab*]. In ordinary Tibetan language the name of this king could be rendered as the Divine Brave [King] with Superior Wisdom [*lha mdzangs mkhyen rab*].

Concerning the place and date of birth of the Dharmarāja Khri-srong lDe'u-btsan, the *lDe'u rgya bod chos 'byung* says (Bod, 301, 2):

> This king as well was born in the Horse year at Brag-dmar.

The *lDe'u chos 'byung chen mo* says (Bod, 121, 2):

> Then, in the spring of the Horse year, King Khri-srong lDe-btsan was born at Brag-dmar.

These two sources clearly indicate the year and the place of birth. In the *gTer byon bka' thang zangs gling ma* written by the master Nyang-ral Nyi-ma 'Od-zer (1124-1192) we read (gTer, KA, 33, 17, 5):

> Then, after nine months and ten days, the mother gave birth without difficulty in the Brag-dmar Palace. The royal child was born in the Horse year at sunrise on the day of the rGyal constellation of the spring season. With a perfect set of teeth and sapphire-hued hair swirled rightward on the crown of his head, he was as beautiful as a child of the gods. He was called Khri-srong lDe'u-btsan.

The *Nyang gi chos 'byung me tog snying po* says (Bod, 271, 20):

> Mes Ag-tshom gazed at the royal child Khri-srong lDe'u-btsan generated by his spouse, the Chinese Princess Gyim-shing Kong-jo.

These sources clearly indicate the name of the mother and father, the place, date, season, constellation, and time of his birth. In a similar fashion the *Padma bka'i thang yig* relates (Si, 341 , 4):

> Khri-srong lDe'u-btsan, king of Tibet, was born shortly after sunrise on the day of the rGyal constellation of the first month of spring of the Horse year.

These sources specify the year, month, constellation, and time of birth, but do not provide information about the element and the sixty-year cycle with which that Horse year is associated and to which it belongs; therefore it is difficult to establish the exact date through these excerpts. However, the *Ne'u sngon gyi gtam me tog phreng ba* informs us that (Dha, 11, 6, 3):

> Khri-srong was born in the spring of the Metal Horse [year] at Brag-dmar.

This Metal Horse year can only correspond to the male Metal Horse year of the last *sMe-phreng* of the fifteenth *sMe-'khor*, (Tibetan year 2647, 730 CE) or to the male Metal Horse year of the first *sMe-phreng* of the sixteenth *sMe-'khor* (Tibetan year 2707, 790 CE). Most well-known religious and dynastic histories and chronological tables, such as the

Grags rgyal bod kyi rgyal rabs, the *Ne'u sngon byung gi gtam*, the *Yar lung jo bo'i chos 'byung*, the *Deb ther dmar po*, the *rGyal rabs gsal ba'i me long*, the *Klu sgrub bstan rtsis*, the *rGya bod yig tshang chen mo*, and the *Baiḍūrya dkar po*, traditionally follow that approach. Nevertheless, analyzing well, we can immediately recognize that the male Metal Horse year of the first *sMe-phreng* of the sixteenth *sMe-'khor* (Tibetan year 2707, 790 CE) is not an applicable date. The *rGya'i thang yig rnying ma* [Old Chronicles of the Chinese Táng 唐 dynasty] says (Dha, 109, 11; mTsho, 91, 3):

> In the thirteenth year of the Can Krung era[48] (Fire Ox year, 797 CE), the Tibetan king died. His son Cus-kri-cin (Mu-ne bTsan-po) was enthroned.

In this case King Khri-srong lDe'u-btsan would have died at the age of seven. Also the male Metal Horse year of the last *sMe-phreng* of the fifteenth *sMe-'khor* (Tibetan year 2647, 730 CE) is not a feasible date: if Khri-srong lDe'u-btsan had been born in that year, as the *rGya'i thang yig gsar rnying* [Old and New Chronicles of the Chinese Táng 唐 dynasty] affirm, and enthroned when the father bTsan-po Khri-lde gTsug-brtan died in the female Wood Sheep year of the last *sMe-phreng* of the fifteenth *sMe-'khor* (Tibetan year 2672, 755 CE), he would have been twenty-five at the time of enthronement, a date certainly in thorough contradiction with the accounts in all dynastic histories.

The *Bu ston chos 'byung* says (lHa, 125, 6):

> An extraordinary son was born in the male Earth Horse year. When [the court] set out to [reach] 'Phang-thang to show him to the king, sNa-nam-bza' stole the child. She pretended he was hers and called him Khri-srong lDe-btsan.

This source maintains that the year of birth was the Earth Horse. Also the *Chos 'byung* of Klong-chen-pa and the *rGyal rabs 'phrul gyi lde mig* adhere to this view, but this date is also difficult to reconcile timewise because if as supposed the birth took place in the male Earth Horse

---

48 [According to Chinese sources the Jiànzhōng 建中 era of Táng 唐 Emperor Dézōng 德宗 (reigned 780-805) corresponds to the years 780-783, while the thirteenth year belongs to the Zhēngyuán 貞元 era (785-805).]

year of the intermediate *sMe-phreng* of the fifteenth *sMe-'khor* (Tibetan year 2635, 718 CE), the father Khri-lde gTsug-brtan would have been fourteen years old. Nor is the male Earth Horse year of the last *sMe-phreng* (Tibetan year 2695, 778 CE) a possible date: the proof for that is found in the *rGya'i thang yig gsar rnying* [Old and New Chronicles of the Chinese Táng 唐 dynasty] where it is clearly affirmed that King Khri-lde gTsug-brtan died and the son Khri-srong lDe'u-btsan was enthroned in the female Wood Sheep year (Tibetan year 2672, 755 CE) of the last *sMe-phreng*.

The *lHo brag chos 'byung* says (Pe, Vol. I, 297, I):

> Regarding the birth of the Dharmarāja Khri-srong lDe-btsan, the *sBa bzhed* says that he was born in the Rabbit year and that he took possession of the kingdom at the age of eight. The father was born in the Metal Dragon [year, 740 CE] and died at the age of sixty-three [Water Horse year, 802 CE]. If the son was born in the Earth Rabbit [year, 799 CE], only four years would have elapsed. If it is correct that he was enthroned when he was eight, he should have been born in the Wood Pig [year, 795 CE], but it appears that a scribal error occurred. Furthermore, most writings say that [Khri-srong lDe'u-btsan] was born in the male Metal Horse [year, 790 CE] and took possession of the throne when he was thirteen. If [these declarations are] true, then also the date of the Earth Horse [year, 778 CE] [provided] by Bu-ston appears to be thirteen years too early.

This source considers the male Metal Horse year an admissible date for Khri-srong lDe'u-btsan's birth. However, when Mu-ne bTsan-po's year of birth is discussed, it says (ibid., Vol. I, 404, 16):

> Secondly, Mu-ne bTsan-po was born in the male Water Tiger [year] when his father was thirty-four.

This source affirms that in the male Water Tiger year (Tibetan year 2679, 762 CE) the Dharmarāja Khri-srong lDe'u-btsan was thirty-four. If we assume that he was thirty-four years old, then the year of his birth should correspond to the male Earth Dragon year (Tibetan year 2645, 728 CE) of the last *sMe-phreng* of the fifteenth *sMe-'khor* (2679-

34=2645; 762-34=728). If we assume that he was a full thirty-three years old or about thirty-four (2679-33=2646; 762-33=729), then the year of his birth should correspond to the male Earth Snake year (Tibetan year 2646, 729 CE); therefore, the male Metal Horse year would not be suitable. It is for this reason that the *Deb ther dpyid kyi rgyal mo'i glu dbyangs*[49] severely criticizes dPa'-bo gTsug-lag Phreng-ba.[50]

In the astrological work of sMin-gling Lo-chen Dharmaśrī (1654-1717), titled *Nyin byed snang ba'i bu yig ngo mtshar phreng ba*, we read (Bod, 130, 16):

> In the Water Horse [year], Lord Khri-srong lDe'u-btsan was born.

The *Deb ther dpyid kyi rgyal mo'i glu dbyangs* says (Pe, 51, 20):

> The father [was] Khri-lde gTsug-brtan and the mother Kong-jo. King Khri-srong lDe'u-btsan was born in the Water Horse year [sixteenth year of the *rab byung*], called the *sna tshogs*, at the Brag-dmar Palace.

This source maintains that the Dharmarāja Khri-srong lDe'u-btsan was born in the male Water Horse year of the last *sMe-phreng* of the fifteenth *sMe-'khor* (Tibetan year 2659, 742 CE). This opinion is historically compatible: most religious and dynastic histories clearly show that the Dharmarāja Khri-srong lDe'u-btsan was thirteen years old when he ascended the throne after the death of King Khri-lde gTsug-brtan. If he was thirteen when bTsan-po Khri-lde gTsug-brtan died in the female Wood Sheep year (Tibetan year 2672, 755 CE), it can be established that the year of the Dharmarāja Khri-srong lDe'u-btsan's birth was the male Water Horse year (Tibetan year 2659, 742 CE). Additional proof can be obtained from the *Tun hong bod kyi lo rgyus yig rnying* [Old Tibetan Chronicles of Dunhuang] where we read (PI 590, 238):

> In the Horse year, in the summer, the bTsan-po's court was residing in mTshar-bu-sna. The Chinese envoy An-da-lang and

---

49 [Authored by the Fifth Dalai Lama Ngag-dbang Blo-bzang rGya-mtsho (1617-1682).]

50 [Author of the *lHo brag chos 'byung* (1504-1566).]

the envoy of the Black Mywa,[51] La-bri, paid homage. At Zlo, Shud-pu Khong-zung and Lang-gro Khong-rtsan calculated revenues and cash outflow and reported them in a register. Minister Mang-po-rje inspected the 'A-zha [jurisdiction] at Khu-nye Mon-gangs. bTsan-po Srong-lde-brtsan was born at Brag-mar. The mother [sNa-nam-bza'] Mang-mo-rje [bZhi-steng] died. One year.

The reason why the Dharmarāja Khri-srong lDe'u-btsan ascended the throne when he was thirteen is indicated by the *lDe'u rgya bod kyi chos 'byung* (Bod, 301, 3):

When he was thirteen, his father died.

Many religious and dynastic histories as well as chronological tables, such as the *bKa' thang shel brag ma*, the *Nyang gi bka' thang zangs gling ma*, the *Grags rgyal bod kyi rgyal rabs*, the *Ne'u sngon byung gi gtam*, the *Bu ston chos 'byung*, the *Klong chen pa'i chos 'byung*, the *Deb ther dmar po*, the *lHo brag chos 'byung*, the *rGya bod yig tshang chen mo*, the *'Brug pad dkar chos 'byung*, the *rGyal rabs 'phrul gyi lde mig*, and the *Klu sgrub bstan rtsis*, say that the Dharmarāja Khri-srong lDe'u-btsan ascended to the throne when he was thirteen.

The *Yar lung jo bo'i chos 'byung* affirms (Si, 59, 16):

Some dynastic histories say that he took power at the age of thirteen as soon as his father died. However the *sBa bzhed* maintains that he did so at the age of eight.

This text accepts the version of the *sBa bzhed*, as does the *rGyal rabs gsal ba'i me long*. However, the *sBa bzhed* also says (Si, 87, 15; Dha, 9, 4):

Later on, in the Rabbit year, Ong-jo gave birth to the prince.

And (ibid., 88, 15; 10, 8):

The prince at age four was residing at the 'Om-bu-tshal palace.

---

51 [The White and Black Mywa tribes occupied the region of present day Yúnnán 云南 Province (known as lJang in Tibetan). They were the Nánzhào 南詔 polity which Chinese Táng 唐 dynasty records show flourished in the eighth and ninth centuries.]

The *sBa bzhed*[52] does not mention that the king was enthroned when he was eight. Scholars have expressed different opinions concerning the authenticity of the *sBa bzhed*. It is said that three books existed that could be the original ones; nevertheless, the *sBa bzhed* we know is the one to which many annotations have been affixed at later times, as can be inferred from the following (Si, 160,11; Dha, 98, 4):

> The *gSung rab rin po che'i bang mdzod* [Treasury of Precious Teachings, that is, the *Bu ston chos 'byung*, compiled in the fourteenth century] affirms that [the words] *ston min* [dùn míng 頓明] and *rtsen min* [jiàn míng 渐明] are [transliterations of the] Chinese language. Therefore in Tibetan they have been rendered [respectively] as *cig char ba* [adherents of the instant enlightenment theory] and *rim gyis pa* [supporters of the gradual enlightenment theory].

A quotation in the *Bu ston chos 'byung* confirms that.

In brief, most of the Tibetan religious and dynastic histories maintain that the Dharmarāja Khri-srong lDe'u-btsan was thirteen when he was enthroned and that the year the father Khri-lde gTsug-brtan died was the female Wood Sheep year (Tibetan year 2672, 755 CE). In this regard the *Tun hong bod kyi lo rgyus yig rnying* [Old Tibetan Chronicles of Dunhuang] state (PI 592, 16):

> It happened in the year [of] the Monkey [756-757]. In the summer the bTsan-pho was residing at Zung-kar. The name proclaimed as bTsan-po was Khri-srong lDe-brtsan. He took the kingdom in his hands.

The *Chronicles* show that the Dharmarāja Khri-srong lDe'u-btsan took political power when he reached the full age of fourteen and on that occasion his previous name rGyal-gtsug-ru was changed to Khri-srong lDe'u-btsan. The *rGya'i thang yig rnying ma* [Old Chronicles of the Chinese Táng 唐 dynasty] say (Dha, 31, 8; mTsho 179, 8):

---

52 The Chronicles of sBa (dBa') compiled by dBa' gSal-snang, a contemporary of King Khri-srong lDe'u-btsan, present an account of the installation of Buddhism in Tibet.

In the fourteenth year of the Than sPo'o era[53] (Wood Sheep year, 755 CE), King Khri-lde gTsug-brtan died. His ministers requested his son Khri-srong lDe'u-btsan to accept the royal mandate.

The text clearly indicates that Khri-srong lDe'u acceded to the throne in the fourteenth year of the Chinese imperial Than sPo'o era (Tibetan year 2672, 755 CE), and if at that time he was thirteen years old, we can also deduce that his year of birth was the male Water Horse year (Tibetan year 2659, 742).

The different opinions expressed on the length of Dharmarāja Khri-srong lDe'u-btsan's reign can ultimately be reduced to three: the *lDe'u chos 'byung* and the sources that have the same view maintain that the Dharmarāja lived for fifty years; the *Nyang gi bka' thang zangs gling ma* and the sources that have its perspective maintain that he lived for sixty-nine years; and the *Padma bka' thang* and the sources that agree with it say that he lived for fifty-nine years.

Most scholars say that Khri-srong lDe'u-btsan was enthroned at the age of thirteen and that he remained in power until his death at either fifty-six, fifty-nine, or sixty-nine years of age; that being so, the Dharmarāja would have ruled for forty-three, fifty-six, or forty-six years. The *Deb sngon* says that the son of Khri-srong lDe'u-btsan, Mu-ne bTsan-po, was enthroned in the male Metal Monkey year (Tibetan year 2697, 780 CE) which corresponds to the time when the Dharmarāja was a full thirty-eight or about thirty-nine years old. Some historical documents indicate that the powerful king transferred the kingdom to his son Mu-ne when the Dharmarāja was engaging himself [fully] in the practice of Dharma. This circumstance and the viewpoint according to which Mu-ne bTsan-po ascended to the throne in the Metal Monkey year are mutually consistent.

If Mu-ne bTsan-po was ruling the kingdom while his father was still alive, it goes without saying that the final political decisions must have rested with the Dharmarāja until he died; that is why some historical documents relate that the son Mu-ne bTsan-po was installed on the throne after Khri-srong lDe'u-btsan's death. In reality it can be

---

53   [The Tiānbǎo 天寶 era of the Táng 唐 Emperor Xuánzōng 玄宗, 742-756.]

inferred that the Dharmarāja Khri-srong lDe'u-btsan ruled for a full twenty-three or about twenty-four years, that is to say, from the year in which he was thirteen years old until the male Metal Monkey year when he was a full thirty-eight or about thirty-nine years old.

Concerning the consorts of the Dharmarāja Khri-srong lDe'u-btsan, the *sBa bzhed* says (Si, 148, 16):

> He married five queens; since mChims-gza' lHa-mo-btsan and mKhar-chen-gza' mTsho-rgyal dedicated themselves to the practice of religion, no vestiges are left. 'Bro-gza' Khri-rgyal Mang-mo-btsan became ordained and received the name Byang-chub-rje; commemorating that is the dGe-rgyas Temple.[54]

And also (ibid., 149, 12):

> Queen Tshe-spong-gza' Me-tog-sgron had a child; for that reason she requested the edification of the Khams-gsum Zangs-khang Temple that was to resemble the [Samye] Central Temple of the father.
>
> [As for] Pho-yong-gza' rGyal-mo-btsun, the king took her as a wife because the Master [Padmasambhava] had prophesied that she would have died [had she remained only a] concubine of the king. She had one daughter.

In actual fact the Dharmarāja Khri-srong lDe'u-btsan had five wives. Mu-ne bTsan-po and the other children were the offspring of the first wife; Pho-yong-gza' had only a female child. The *bKa' thang shel brag ma* provides the names of two wives (Si, 342, 1):

> The two princesses Tshe-spong-gza' Ni-dmar-rgyan and 'Bro-gza' Byang-chub-sgron were received as wives.

The rediscovered Nyang text, *bKa' thang zangs gling ma*, says (gTer mdzod, KA, 34, 17, 2):

> Then the prince was enthroned. [The king] married three princesses: Her Majesty Tshe-spong-bza' dMar-rgyan; Her Majesty 'Bro-bza' Byang-chub-sman; and Her Majesty Pho-gyong-bza'.

---

54 [A temple built by her at bSam-yas.]

The majority of religious histories, such as the one of Klong-chen-pa and of dynastic histories, such as the *rGyal rabs gsal ba'i me long* and so on, take the standpoint of the *sBa bzhed* and of the above-mentioned chronicles.

The *Legs bshad rin po che'i mdzod* indicates that there were three main princesses (Pe, 223, 12):

> Khri-srong lDe'u-btsan had three wives: [the first two were the senior ones] rGya-bza' Kong-cu [and] Tshe-spungs-bza' dMar-rgyan; the younger one [was] 'Brom-bza' dKar-mo(-rgyal). 'Brom-bza' and rGya-bza' had no children; however, since they were well-disposed toward Buddhism they were highly influential. rGya-bza' had [also other] names: Pho-yangs-bza', Gyim-sham-bza', and so on.

Concerning the descendants of the Dharmarāja Khri-srong lDe'u-btsan, the *sBa bzhed* simply says that the three children of Tshe-spong-bza' Me-tog-sgron were Mu-ne bTsan-po, Mu-tig bTsan-po, and the youngest, Khri-lde Srong-btsan. The two [volumes of] *lDe'u chos 'byung*,[55] the religious history of Klong-chen-pa, and the *rGyal rabs 'phrul gyi lde mig* sustain the viewpoint of the *sBa bzhed*.

The *rGyal po bka'i thang yig* provides the names of the three children (Pe, 114, 22):

> [The consort of] Khri-srong lDe'u-btsan [was] lHa-yi Me-tog. Three sons were born [as] their descendants: Mu-ne bTsan-po, Mu-rum bTsan-po, and the Dharmarāja 'Jing-yon Sad-na-legs.

The *rGyal rabs gsal ba'i me long* provides the names of the three children as follows (Pe, 212, 23):

> Tshe-spang-gza' Me-tog-sgron generated three sons: Mu-ne bT-sad-po, Mu-rug bTsad-po, and Mi-mug bTsad-po Sad-na-legs.

The *Legs bshad rin po che'i mdzod* says (Pe, 223, 18):

---

55 [The *lDe'u rgya bod kyi chos 'byung* and the *lDe'u chos 'byung chen mo* authored by the scholar lDe'u Jo-sras (born eleventh century).]

[She had] three sons: the eldest was Mu-tig bTsan-po, the middle one was Mu-ne bTsan-po, and the youngest was Mu-thug bTsan-po.

Thus, although all these sources agree that there were three sons, they maintain different viewpoints as to their names and order of birth.

The *Grags rgyal bod kyi rgyal rabs* says (sDe, TA, 197, 5, 4):

Khri-srong lDe-btsan had four sons by his wife, the Princess Tshe-spong-bza' rMa-rgyal mTsho-skar: Mu-khri bTsan-po, who died when still young; Mu-tig bTsan-po, who attained liberation; Mu-ne bTsan-po, who ruled for one year nine months—since he was killed by his mother, he is considered a half king; and Khri-lde Srong-btsan, who inherited the kingdom.

This source maintains that the Dharmarāja Khri-srong lDe'u-btsan had four sons and shows the order in which they were born: the eldest was Mu-khri bTsan-po; the second was Mu-tig bTsan-po; the third was Mu-ne bTsan-po; and the fourth and youngest was Khri-lde Srong-btsan. Also the *Yar lung jo bo'i chos 'byung* adheres to the existence of four sons, but maintains that the eldest son was Mu-khri bTsan-po, the second Mu-ne bTsan-po, the third Mu-tig bTsan-po, and the youngest Khri-lde Srong-btsan. The *lHo brag chos 'byung* follows the *Grags rgyal*, while the *Deb ther dpyid kyi rgyal mo'i glu dbyangs* affirms (Pe, 67, 6):

dPa'-bo gTsug-lag, without understanding that Mu-khri bTsan-po and (Mu-ne bTsan-po) were two ways of expressing the same name, created the preposterous rumor that Mu-khri bTsan-po was the elder of the two.

This exemplifies criticism of the four sons' theory. However, since in actual fact the foremost supporter of that theory was Sa-skya-pa Grags-pa rGyal-mtshan [1147-1216] and not dPa'-bo gTsug-lag Phreng-ba [1504-1566], it is inappropriate to heap blame on the latter, also since nothing proves that one queen could not have generated more than three sons. dPa'-bo gTsug-lag Phreng-ba maintains that Mu-ne was born when the father Khri-srong lDe'u-btsan was thirty-four year old, while subsequent historical records say that he was born in the male

Wood Tiger year (Tibetan year 2691, 774 CE), a year in which the Dharmarāja was a full thirty-two years old; therefore it is extremely possible that a son could have been born before that time.

The *Tun hong bod kyi lo rgyus yig rnying* [Old Tibetan Chronicles of Dunhuang] say (PI 593, 38):

> It happened in the year of the Mouse [760-761]. In the summer the bTsan-po's court was established at Myang-sgrom. The bTsan-po's son was born.

If the *Chronicles* clearly mention that a son was born in the male Metal Mouse year (Tibetan year 2677, 760 CE) when the Dharmarāja Khri-srong lDe'u-btsan had reached the full age of nineteen, it is perfectly logical for the *Grags rgyal bod kyi rgyal rabs*, the *Yar lung jo bo'i chos 'byung*, and the *lHo brag chos 'byung* to relate the story of the birth of a son who was the eldest of four and was called Mu-khri bTsan-po.

The *rGya'i thang yig rnying ma* [Old Chronicles of the Chinese Táng 唐 dynasty] say (mTsho, 334, 12):

> In the fourth month of the thirteenth year of the Krin Yon[56] era (Fire Ox year, 797 CE) the king died. The eldest son was enthroned. He died after one year. His younger brother inherited the throne.

After the Dharmarāja Khri-srong lDe'u-btsan died, Mu-ne bTsan-po ruled for just one year, then died, and the throne was occupied by his younger brother. The younger brother in question cannot be the one called Mu-tig bTsan-po, who is reckoned the second born in the *sBa bzhed* and the third in the *Yar lung jo bo'i chos 'byung*, nor even the one called Mu-rug bTsad-po, who is deemed the middle one in the *rGyal rabs gsal ba'i me long* and other sources. Many religious and dynastic histories relate that this prince was denied the right to rule because he had killed the maternal uncle dBu-rings.

The forty-second king who ruled Tibet for six full years from the time of Mu-ne bTsan-po's death until Khri-lde Srong-btsan took the

---

56 [The Zhēngyuán 貞元 era of Táng 唐 Dézōng 德宗 imperial rule (785-805).]

throne can be none other than the Ju-tse bTsan-po mentioned in the *Deb ther dmar po* and the *Deb sngon*, or the Mu-rum bTsan-po in the *rGyal po bka'i thang yig*. This means that the Dharmarāja Khri-srong lDe'u-btsan had five sons, not four. Mu-rum bTsan-po would have come between Mu-ne bTsan-po and Khri-lde Srong-btsan: Mu-khri bTsan-po was the eldest; the second son was Mu-rug bTsan-po; the third was Mu-ne bTsan-po; the fourth was Mu-rum bTsan-po; and the fifth was Mu-tig bTsan-po or Khri-lde Srong-btsan. This is the perspective that emerges as butter from the churned milk of religious and dynastic histories.

Nevertheless, the issue of the number of Khri-srong lDe'u-btsan's children remains difficult to determine. When Mu-ne bTsan-po was born, the Dharmarāja had reached the full age of thirty-two or was about thirty-three; and since he did not have just one but many consorts, several sons and daughters could have been born one after the other. Most historical records base themselves on the celebrated names of the princes, Mu-ne bTsan-po, Mu-tig bTsan-po, Khri-lde Srong-btsan, Sad-na-legs, and so on. Other sources point to a number of names, Mu-ri bTsan-po, Mu-rug bTsan-po, Mu-rum bTsan-po, and so forth, which in reality have the same meaning. It is also extremely possible that the names of the children derive from the names of the king's various wives.

Generally speaking, not only the offspring of an unofficial consort could be ignored as a descendant in a lineage, but also many sons and daughters of some of the king's wives could be excluded, meaning either some brothers and sisters were adjudged insignificant, or that numbers of them were chastised in some way. In this respect the *lDe'u chos 'byung chen mo* says (Bod, 104, 13):

> At this time, since many competitors vied [for the role of] king, the sagacious minister [suggested] keeping one in the capital and expelling the others to the border plains.

The king may have had many children, but the reason for the little information presented by historical documents rests on circumstances such as the ones indicated by this text. Hence, it is meaningless to insist and say, "These are [all] the sons and daughters of Khri-srong lDe'u-btsan." Nonetheless, having introduced the preceding historical data and recognizing that definite names represent an indispensable element, at this time and in accordance with the prevailing outlook, I have come to the conclusion that the name of the eldest son was Mu-ne bTsan-po, that the name of the middle son was Mu-tig bTsan-po, and that the name of the youngest son was Sad-na-legs.

Concerning the identity of the chief ministers of the Dharmarāja Khri-srong lDe'u-btsan, the *lDe'u rgya bod kyi chos 'byung* says (Bod, 301, 9):

> During the earlier part [of the king's] life, the ministers were 'Chims Khri-thog-rje Thang-la-'bar and lCog-ro sKyes-bza' rGyal-gong; during the latter part [of the king's] life, the ministers were sBas gSal-snang, 'Gos Khri-bzang Yab-lhag, 'Chims rGyal-gzigs Klu-'theng, Ngam sTag-ra Klu-gong, and 'Chims 'Dom-bzher sPre-chung.

The *lDe'u chos 'byung chen mo* says (Bod, 121, 7):

> During the earlier part [of the king's] life, the ministers 'Chims Khri-thog-rje Thang-la-'bar, lCog-ro sKyes-gza' rGyal-gong, and Zhang Ma-zhang suppressed the Buddhadharma. Kā-chu and 'Khar-phrag were destroyed. Afterward, a law was sanctioned [forbidding] the practice of the Buddhadharma. Thereafter, fearing the king and [that] the punishment of [the Three] Jewels could befall them, [the ministers] expressed faith in the Buddhadharma and guided subjects toward it. sBa gSal-snang took their side and assisted [them]. Later on sBa gSal-snang bZher-zla-btsan, 'Gos Khri-bzang Yab-lhag, mChims rGyal-gzigs Klu-thong, Ngan-lam sTag-ra Klu-gong, and mChims mDo-bzher sPre-chung acted as ministers.

The *rGya bod yig tshang chen mo* says (Si, 198, 3):

> As for the ministers of that king, the ones who acted wisely were 'Gos Khri-bzang Yab-lhag, dBas rGyal-to-re, Khri gSum-rje sTag-sna, and gNyer sTag-btsan lDong-gzig. Zhang-rje rGyal-gzigs and sTag-sgra Klu-gong conquered foreign enemies. The history of the conquest of the Chinese bKra-shis Khri-sgo [capital Cháng'ān 長安] and so on is recorded on the exterior stone

pillar [at Zhol in Lhasa]. Khri gSum-rje sTag-sna implemented negotiations and treaties with China, the Gru-gu [Turks and Uighurs], and lJangs.

As for the time and place of death of King Khri-srong lDe'u-btsan, the *lDe'u rgya bod kyi chos 'byung* says (Bod, 358, 13):

[He] died at Zung-mkhar at the age of fifty-nine.

The *lDe'u chos 'byung chen mo* says (Bod, 132, 16):

In the end, when [he] reached the age of fifty-six, [he] died at Zung-mkhar-nang.

In this way we have two different ages, fifty-nine and fifty-six, for the number of years the Dharmarāja Khri-srong lDe'u-btsan had at his death. The *Padma bka'i thang yig*, which is earlier than the above-mentioned sources, says (Si, 601, 15):

[He] died at Zung-mkhar in the Dragon [year] [when he was] fifty-nine.

The *Deb ther dpyid kyi rgyal mo'i glu dbyangs* identifies the year of birth of the Dharmarāja Khri-srong lDe'u-btsan as the male Water Horse year (Tibetan year 2659, 742 CE), but in regard to the year of his death says (Pe, 66, 15):

In the male Metal Dragon year called rGyal-po rNam-gnon [the fourteenth year of the *rab byung*], all Tibetan subjects believed that the king passed into *nirvāṇa* [because he had been struck] by a heat illness.

It is evident that this source maintains the perspective of the *Padma bka'i thang yig*, since the Dharmarāja's death is identified with the male Metal Dragon year of the first *sMe-phreng* of the sixteenth *sMe-'khor* (Tibetan year 2717, 800 CE).

The *lDe'u chos 'byung chen mo* states that he died at fifty-six, but does not indicate the year of death and his birth year is mentioned only as Horse year without specifying the element; therefore it is difficult to determine the real perspective of this source. Nevertheless, when we compare it with the *rGya bod*, it appears that the Dharmarāja Khri-srong lDe'u-btsan was born in the male Water Horse year (Tibetan year 2659, 742 CE) and lived until he was a full fifty-five or about fifty-six years old (2659+55=2714; 742+55=797), that year corresponding to the female Fire Ox year of the first *sMe-phreng* of the sixteenth *sMe-'khor* (Tibetan year 2714, 797 CE).

The *Ne'u sngon byung gi gtam* says (Dha, 11 ,6, 3):

[He] reached the age of fifty-six. In the Wood Ox [year] [he] fell at (the bridge of) 'Khar-sdong-sna in Zung-mkhar and died.

Here the age of the Dharmarāja Khri-srong lDe'u-btsan is also fifty-six, but the year of death is identified as the female Wood Ox year; this identification obviously comes from the text itself which says that Khri-srong's year of birth was the Water Horse. Many Tibetan dynastic and religious histories as well as chronicles, such as the *rGyal rabs gsal ba'i me long*, the *Me long rnam gsal*, the *Klu sgrub bstan rtsis*, the *Baidūrya dkar po*, and so on, accept this perspective and maintain that he died in the female Wood Ox year when he was fifty-six (Tibetan year 2702, 785 CE).

The *bKa' thang zangs gling ma* says (gTer mdzod, KA, 142, 71, 3):

[His] death was [to have taken place] in the Ox year [when he was] fifty-six, but due to long life practice [he] was able to prolong [his life] for [another] thirteen years. Then, in the year of the Tiger [when he was] sixty-nine, the king departed for heaven.

Also the *Nyang gi chos 'byung* says that Khri-srong lDe'u-btsan lived until he was sixty-nine and then died in the Tiger year, without, however, specifying the element of that Tiger year; moreover it does not indicate the element of his year of birth, citing only that it was the Horse year. Therefore it is difficult to ascertain the true viewpoint of this text. Be that as it may, if we accept that the Dharmarāja Khri-srong lDe'u-btsan was born in the male Water Horse year (Tibetan year 2659, 742 CE) and lived for sixty-nine years, he must have died in the male Metal Tiger year (Tibetan year 2727, 810 CE). The hypothesis according to which the Dharmarāja Khri-srong lDe'u-btsan lived for sixty-nine years is the one that also the *Bu ston chos 'byung,* the *Klong chen pa'i chos 'byung,* and the *'Brug pad dkar chos 'byung* have habitually preferred.

The *rGyal rabs 'phrul gyi lde mig* says (Dhi, 11, 22, 3):

> The king was personally residing in the gNyug-ma-mthar Palace of Zung-mkhar. Then, in the Fire Tiger [year] [when he was] sixty-nine, [he] died.

Also this source maintains that the Dharmarāja lived until he was sixty-nine, but says that the year of death was the Fire Tiger year, doing so because it considers that the year of birth of the Dharmarāja was the male Earth Horse year (Tibetan year 2635, 718 CE). Nevertheless, that year corresponds to the time in which the thirty-ninth ruler of Tibet, Khri-lde gTsug-brtan, reached the full age of fourteen. Hence, it appears as a problematic counterpart of the general history of that period.

The *Yar lung jo bo'i chos 'byung* says (Si, 62, 12):

> Some dynastic histories affirm that the king who protected the Buddhadharma died at Zung-mkhar in the female Wood Ox year at the age of fifty-six.

And also (ibid., 63, 1):

> Some historical rediscovered texts [*gter-ma*] of the Teacher Padmasambhava say that the lifespan of King Khri-srong lDe'u-btsan was just fifty-six years; but the Teacher performed long life practices [for him, so his lifespan was] thrust thirteen years forward and he died when he was sixty-nine.

This source presents two options but leaves us in doubt because it does not express its own viewpoint. A similar idea is also found in the *lHo brag chos 'byung* (Pe, Vol. I, 404, 18):

> In the male Wood Mouse year at fifty-five, the father departed to meditate in the sMyug-ma-tshal Palace [in] Zung-mkhar.

At the end the text says (ibid., 466, 11):

> [He] died in the year in which [he] departed to meditate.

The *rGya bod yig tshang chen mo* says (Si, 198, 14):

> This [king] lived until he was fifty-six (probably not sixty-eight as it is also said) and died in the female Wood Ox year at Zung-mkhar.

Also these two texts hesitate and do not express a definitive opinion of their own like the *Yar lung jo bo*. In this case the one year difference clearly depends on what the reckoning is based: one text considers the ensuing year [fifty-six], the other the birth day year [fifty-five]. The *Tun hong bod kyi lo rgyus yig rnying* [Old Tibetan Chronicles of Dunhuang] speak about the Fire Pig year (Tibetan year 2664, 747 CE) in which the Dharmarāja reached the full age of five (PI 591, 256):

> In the Pig year [747-748] the bTsan-pho's court was residing in Na-mar. [Delegates] were dispatched to each [area] to enact laws for the pasturelands and the uncultivated lands. At Khu-le, riding a horse …

From this year until the female Wood Sheep year (Tibetan year 2672, 755 CE), which corresponds to the thirteenth year of the king's life, the *Chronicles* are silent. From the end of that Wood Sheep year until the male Fire Horse year (Tibetan year 2683, 766 CE), the year in which the Dharmarāja Khri-srong lDe'u-btsan reached the full age of twenty-four or about twenty-five, the *Chronicles* clearly record his history. The history of the male Fire Horse year is incomplete. The history that goes from this year to the next, the female Fire Sheep year (Tibetan year 2684, 767 CE), in which the Dharmarāja Khri-srong lDe'u-btsan reached the full age of twenty-five or about twenty-six, is incomplete; from the end of the short history of that Fire Sheep year until the female Metal Pig year (Tibetan year 2688, 771 CE), year in which the Dharmarāja Khri-srong lDe'u-btsan reached the full age of twenty-nine or about thirty, his history is recorded succinctly. From the end of the history of the Metal Pig year, which is also somewhat incomplete, until his fifty-fifth year some of the annual records of the king's continuing activities are missing. Nevertheless, the *rGya'i thang yig rnying ma* [Old Chronicles of the Chinese Táng 唐 dynasty] say (Dha, 109, 11; mTsho, 91, 3):

In the thirteenth year of the Can Krung era (Fire Ox year, 797 CE), the Tibetan king died. His son Cus-kri-cin (Mu-ne bTsan-po) was installed on the throne.

These sources provide us with the certainty that the real year of death of the Dharmarāja Khri-srong lDe'u-btsan was the female Fire Ox year of the first *sMe-phreng* of the sixteenth *sMe-'khor* (Tibetan year 2714, 797 CE). The text says, "His son Cus-kri-cin was installed on the throne." This may seem to indicate that an elaborate official ceremony was organized after the death of the king father for the legitimate enthronement of the son; but in fact, the *sBa bzhed* clearly tells us that the Dharmarāja Khri-srong lDe'u-btsan handed over the kingdom to his son Mu-ne bTsan-po when the latter was fifteen years old and also that the Dharmarāja himself left for Zung-dkar to practice meditation. It is therefore unquestionable that Mu-ne bTsan-po ruled Tibet for a period of eight full years, starting from the female Earth Snake year (Tibetan year 2706, 789 CE) in which he was fifteen until the year of the Dharmarāja Khri-srong lDe'u-btsan's death, which occurred in the female Fire Ox year (Tibetan year 2714, 797 CE).

As for the tomb of the Dharmarāja Khri-srong lDe'u-btsan, the *rGyal rabs gsal ba'i me long* says (Pe, 223, 8):

> His tomb was built at Mu-ra-ri. It was situated on the right side, behind [the tomb] of the father. [He] built it himself before he died. The name was 'Phrul-ri gTsug-snang. A single stone pillar stood close to it; [for this reason] the tomb became known as The Tomb with an Outer Ornament [Bang-so Phyi-rgyan].

8. THE FORTY-FIRST RULER OF TIBET: MU-NE bTSAN-PO

The name by which this ruler is generally known is Mu-ne bTsan-po: *mu ne* is a Zhang Zhung word meaning sky [*nam mkha'*] in Tibetan; *btsan-po* is an archaic Tibetan term that in the common Tibetan language signifies king or monarch [*rgyal po*]. Hence, the real meaning of this name is Heavenly Monarch [*nam mkha' btsan po*] or Heavenly King [*gnam gyi rgyal po*].

Concerning this monarch's time and place of birth, the *lDe'u rgya bod kyi chos 'byung* does not specify the year of birth; it simply says (Bod, 358, 16):

Mu-ne bTsan-po was born at Brag-dmar.

The *lDe'u chos 'byung chen mo* indicates the year of birth (Bod, 133, 4):

Mu-ne bTsan-po was born at Brag-dmar in the Tiger year.

The *Ne'u sngon byung gi gtam* specifies the element of that Tiger year; it says (Dha, 11, 6, 4):

Mu-ne bTsan-po was born at Brag-dmar in the Water Tiger [year].

Since this last source specifies that the year of birth was a Water Tiger year, many documents, such as the *Yar lung jo bo'i chos 'byung*, the *rGyal rabs gsal ba'i me long*, the *Chos 'byung mkhas pa'i dga' ston*, and the *rGya bod yig tshang chen mo*, adhere to this opinion and maintain that the year of birth of Mu-ne bTsan-po was the male Water Tiger year. However, I think that this year is hardly compatible with historical facts. If Mu-ne bTsan-po was born in the Water Tiger year of the last *sMe-phreng* of the fifteenth *sMe-'khor* (Tibetan year 2679, 762 CE), when the king father Khri-srong lDe'u-btsan had reached the age of twenty, the *Tun hong bod kyi lo rgyus yig rnying* [Old Tibetan Chronicles of Dunhuang] would have mentioned that fact in relation to the events in the kingdom of that year; but the *Chronicles* do not mention the birth of the king's son at all in that year. Rather, they relate how the councils were convened in the summer and in the winter and how the Tibetan army ransacked Chinese strongholds and attacked the Chinese capital. They say (PI 593, 45):

It happened in the year of the Tiger [762]. In the summer the bTsan-po's court was residing at Sa-byar. The summer council was convened at Bu-cung in Glag. The Chinese envoy Ang 'Do-shi and others paid homage. The mDo-smad council was convened at lHa-ri-mo in dBu-le. In the winter the bTsan-po's court resided at lCang-bu in Byar.

The winter council was convened at sKyi-bur. Minister Khri-sgra sTag-tshab convened the mDo-smad winter council at gTse. On the borders [officers with the rank of] commander of 1,000 units and above were given as reward a Chinese silk tribute.

In the latter part of the winter the Lord of China[57] died and a Chinese Lord[58] was newly installed. Since [the new Lord] found it incongruous to offer tributes of silk, maps, and so on [to Tibetans], political relations were damaged.

Zhang rGyal-zigs, Zhang-stong-rtsan, and others crossed the iron bridge at Bum-ling. They conducted an impressive campaign. [They] toppled many Chinese strongholds, such as 'Bu-shing-kun, Zin-cu, Ga-cu, and so forth. Zhang rGyal-zigs returned to Tibet.

Zhang rGyal-zigs, Minister sTag-sgra, Zhang sTong-rtsan, Zhang bTsan-ba, and others led the army to the capital [Keng-shi, Jīngshī 京師] [Cháng'ān 长安] and the capital was overthrown.

The Lord of China fled, [another] Chinese Lord was newly installed, and the army returned [to Tibet]. Zhang-rgyal-zigs went to Tibet for a major consultation. One year.

Even if the birth year of Mu-ne bTsan-po was a Tiger year, the element of that Tiger year could not be Water which can be inferred from the information above. If the birth year of Mu-ne bTsan-po was not the Water Tiger year, then it must have been the male Wood Tiger year (Tibetan year 2691, 774 CE), which comes twelve years later. The periods that elapsed from the birth of the Dharmarāja Khri-srong lDe'u-btsan that occurred in the male Water Horse year (Tibetan year 2659, 742 CE) until the female Fire Pig year (Tibetan year 2664, 747 CE) when the king reached the age of five and from the female Wood Sheep year (Tibetan year 2672, 755 CE) when the king reached the age of thirteen until the male Fire Horse year (Tibetan year 2683, 766 CE) when the king reached the age of twenty-four are only sketchily

---

57 [Emperor Táng Sùzōng 唐肅宗, reigned 756-762.]

58 [Emperor Táng Dàizōng 唐代宗, reigned 762-779.]

described in the *Tun hong bod kyi lo rgyus yig rnying* [Old Tibetan Chronicles of Dunhuang]. Apart from what is recorded in the *Chronicles,* no other sources can be relied upon in this regard because they are incomplete and even if the dates of birth of the Dharmarāja's children are shown, the manner is unclear.

8.1. Queens and Children of Mu-ne bTsan-po

The *lDe'u chos 'byung chen mo* says (Bod, 133, 5):

> When [he] reached the age of fifteen, [he] took over the king-dom. He ruled for one year nine months. [He] wanted sNa-nam rGyal-tsha lHa-snang, Shud-bu Khri-'bring Khong-btsan, and lDe-dman Gung-bzhir lDe-chung to be appointed ministers. [He] was at cross purposes with his mother and the mother killed him at the Yum-bu Castle when he was seventeen.

The text relates that Mu-ne bTsan-po "took over the kingdom when he reached the age of fifteen," but that does not correspond to historical facts; therefore, the Tiger year indicated by the [*lDe'u*] *Chos 'byung* [*chen mo*] must be the male Wood Tiger year (Tibetan year 2691, 774 CE). In this respect the *Deb ther sngon po* says (Si, Vol. I, 77, 9):

> In the male Metal Monkey year the eldest son of [Emperor] Tha'i Dzung,[59] Ding Dzung,[60] was raised to the throne. In that same year, Khri-srong lDe-btsan departed ['*das*] and the eldest son Mu-ne bTsan-po was raised to the throne.

This source clearly says that Mu-ne bTsan-po was enthroned in the male Metal Monkey year (Tibetan year 2697, 780 CE). At that time Mu-ne bTsan-po had just reached the age of six or was barely seven; and even if the *Deb sngon* says that year the Dharmarāja Khri-srong lDe'u-btsan departed [*gshegs*] and that after his departure the son was enthroned, a phrase that is as familiar in historical accounts as the

---

59 [Dàizōng 唐代宗, reigned 762-779.]
60 [Dézōng 德宗, reigned 779-805.]

mouth is to the hand, it cannot automatically be inferred from that sentence that Khri-srong lDe'u-btsan died. This is demonstrated by what the *sBa bzhed* relates (Si, 174, 4):

> Grief stricken, the king said "According to the words of the Ācārya [A-tsarya], my days cannot be prolonged." The king [was thought to take little responsibility], and an invitation was sent to the Paṇḍita[s]. The Ācārya Vimalamitra [Bi-ma Mi-tra, Dri-med bShes-gnyen] arrived and [the king] requested [him] to expound the Dharma of the Teacher Padmasambhava.
>
> [The king,] wishing to practice meditation, conferred power on the son Mu-ne bTsan-po and appointed Minister Zhang dBu-rings as the royal counselor, [directing the latter to] perform [his offices from] and reside in the Drum Storehouse of the middle building of the Central Temple [of bSam-yas].

And also (ibid., 175, 5):

> The father departed for Zung-dkar to practice meditation.

Most Tibetan histories usually say that the Dharmarāja Khri-srong lDe'u-btsan departed [*gshegs*] when he was fifty-six, implying that he left to practice secret instructions given by the Teacher Padma or to attain liberation.

Some of the hagiographical chronicles of Padmasambhava relate that the Dharmarāja handed over the kingdom to the son and departed to meditate. They reveal that for seventeen years, that is to say, from the male Metal Monkey year (Tibetan year 2697, 780 CE) in which the Dharmarāja Khri-srong lDe'u-btsan was thirty-nine up to the female Fire Ox year (Tibetan year 2714, 797 CE), the king had left to dedicate himself to spiritual practices, that spiritual practice became his main interest, and that he put political affairs in the hands of the son Mu-ne bTsan-po.

If we assume that Mu-ne bTsan-po was born in the Wood Tiger year, he was not even seven in the Metal Monkey year. Obviously the king father would never entrust a great political responsibility to a seven-year-old child; therefore it is plausible that Mu-ne bTsan-po was a full eighteen or about nineteen years old when he ascended to the throne in the male Metal Monkey year (Tibetan year 2697, 780 CE).

Some texts say that Mu-ne bTsan-po ruled either for one year nine months or for one year seven months, but that indicates only the duration of his kingdom after the death of the Dharmarāja Khri-srong lDe'u-btsan; it has nothing to do with the number of years in which Mu-ne bTsan-po ruled as a whole.

The *Nyang gi chos 'byung* says (Bod, 411, 8):

Then, when Mu-ne bTsan-po reached the age of twenty-five, he married Her Majesty Jo-mo Ru-yongs-za and ruled the kingdom.

This source clearly shows that he married and ruled when he reached the age of twenty-five; hence, the year of birth of Mu-ne bTsan-po must have been either the female Water Ox year (Tibetan year 2690, 773 CE) or, if we consider the full year, the male Water Mouse year (Tibetan year 2689, 772 CE). All viewpoints according to which the year of birth of Mu-ne bTsan-po was the Tiger year are incompatible. Also the *Ne'u sngon byung gi gtam* is of the same opinion as the teacher Nyang [author of the *Nyang gi chos 'byung*] (Dha, 11, 6, 4):

After [he] reached [the age of] twenty-five, he was bequeathed power. [He] continued to rule for one year nine months. [He] was killed by his mother at Yun-bu.

The *Yar lung jo bo'i chos 'byung* says (Si, 63, 10):

He ruled the kingdom for one year and nine months.

The *Deb ther dmar po* says (Pe, 38, 4):

[He] held power for one year nine months.

The above-mentioned sources say only that without giving further explanations.

The *Bu ston chos 'byung* says (lHa, 129, 7):

The son of that one, Mu-ne bTsan-po, took power in the male Water Tiger [year]. He built four large stūpas at bSam-yas. [He] thrice brought economic parity to the poor and rich Tibetan subjects. He ruled for one year seven months.

Here it is written that Mu-ne bTsan-po "took power in the male Water Tiger [year]." It is not clear if this statement is influenced by the traditional assumption that Mu-ne bTsan-po was born in the male Water Tiger year or if it is based upon certain causal factors that remain unexplained.

The *rGyal rabs gsal ba'i me long* says (Pe, 223, 16):

At the age of twenty-eight took power. Conquered kingdoms. Married Queen Ru-yong-bza' mDo-rgyal.

The age provided by this source needs to be examined. The text itself maintains that the Dharmarāja Khri-srong lDe'u-btsan was born in the male Metal Horse year (Tibetan year 2647, 730 CE); that he departed for heaven in the Wood Ox year (Tibetan year 2702, 785 CE) when he was fifty-six; and that his son Mu-ne bTsan-po was born in the male Water Tiger year (Tibetan year 2679, 762 CE).

If Mu-ne bTsan-po "took power when he was twenty-eight" and we calculate twenty-eight years from the Water Tiger year of his birth, we inevitably arrive at the female Earth Snake year (Tibetan year 2706, 789 CE); if we consider the full age of twenty-eight we arrive at the male Metal Horse year (Tibetan year 2707, 790 CE). Under these circumstances, the gap of five or about six years that elapsed from the time in which the Dharmarāja Khri-srong lDe'u-btsan died in the female Wood Ox year until the male Metal Horse year in which Mu-ne bTsan-po was enthroned cannot be ignored.

Since it is utterly impossible that a Sa-skya-pa scholar as great as the glorious Bla-ma Dam-pa bSod-nam rGyal-mtshan [1312-1375, author of the *rGyal rabs gsal ba'i me long*] did not know how to count years, we conclude that the problem is indubitably caused by the widely-held opinion according to which the year of birth of the Dharmarāja Khri-srong lDe'u-btsan was the male Metal Horse year.

The *lHo brag chos 'byung* says (Pe, Vol. I, 404, 20):

The son Mu-ne took power when he was twenty-three. The mother entrusted Princess Pho-yongs-bza' to her son because she was dear to her heart. Mu-ne married Princess Ru-yongs-bza' mDo-rgyal.

And also (ibid., Pe, Vol. I, 405, 14):

[He] ruled the kingdom for one year nine months.

This text assumes that the Dharmarāja Khri-srong lDe'u-btsan was born in the male Metal Horse year and that Mu-ne bTsan-po was born in the male Water Tiger year when the father was thirty-four; that is why it says that Mu-ne bTsan-po "took power when he was twenty-three." Except for the difference of one year, I do not see other contradictions in this viewpoint; but in the section dedicated to the Dharmarāja Khri-srong lDe'u-btsan it has already been demonstrated that the year of his birth was the male Water Horse year (Tibetan year 2659, 742 CE) and not the male Metal Horse year (Tibetan year 2647, 730 CE).

The *rGyal rabs 'phrul gyi lde mig* says that Mu-ne bTsan-po ruled for a period of seven years nine months (Dhi, 10, 23, 3):

> Some texts (such as the *Kam kam spyan snga'i chos 'byung*, and so on) say that the son ruled for seven years nine months which appears to be correct. It is also said that this king thrice balanced poverty and wealth equitably in Tibet. If we concur with the dates of the two *Chos 'byung* (of Bu-ston and of the [*rGyal rabs*] *gSal ba'i me long*), no time for accomplishing those three times would have existed.

The *Deb ther dpyid kyi rgyal mo'i glu dbyangs* says (Pe, 67, 8):

> The affirmation of the Dharma Master bSod-nam Grags-pa according to which not [enough] time would have existed [for Mu-ne bTsan-po] to balance poverty and wealth in Tibet three times in one year seven months is absurd. A benefactor may donate all necessary and desirable provisions to the poor, but cannot ignore the power of the karmic effects of previous actions, [or the one who gives would] quickly become destitute. Not only is this the case in finding equitable solutions to poverty and wealth, but also for all phenomena since everything is compounded and subject to destruction.

That is the text's viewpoint; and even though most religious and dynastic histories say that Mu-ne bTsan-po equalized poverty and wealth three times in one year seven months or in one year nine months, that would be a difficult thing to accomplish. We can understand that this is so from the time it takes us to accomplish even the smallest deeds.

The *rGyal rabs gsal ba'i me long* says (Pe, 224, 14):

> Poverty and wealth were balanced three times, but except for one year, the wealthy were as rich as before and the poor were as hungry as before.

The text says, "except for one year, the wealthy were as rich as before" [*lo re tsam ma gtogs phyug po rnams ni sngar ltar phyug*]; but how could such a thing happen in just one year and a few months? In a country as vast as Tibet at a time when people relied on horses for transport, one year and seven or more months would have certainly been insufficient for establishing and implementing an equitable balance between the poor and the rich. We should rather understand that during the seventeen years in which Mu-ne bTsan-po was on the throne, great deeds such as that one were accomplished.

Concerning the time of Mu-ne bTsan-po's death, the *lDe'u rgya bod kyi chos 'byung* simply says (Bod, 358, 17):

> The mother poisoned him.

The *lDe'u chos 'byung chen mo* affirms (Bod, 133, 7):

> [He] was at cross purposes with his mother and the mother killed him at the Yum-bu Castle when he was seventeen.

The text seems to indicate that he died when he was seventeen, but the actual situation is that Mu-ne bTsan-po was killed because of a conflict with his mother after seventeen years of governance.

The *Nyang gi chos 'byung* says (Bod, 414, 2):

> Then, since also Pho-yongs(-bza') rGyal-mo-btsun was dear to the king, at the time of [his] death, the father ordered, "Pho-yongs(-bza') will be married to the prince." For that reason Tshe-spongs-bza' Me-tog-sGrol was not happy on behalf of her

three sons. After the father died, Tshe-spongs-bza' considered killing Pho-yongs-bza'.

Using the pretext of affixing an ornament to the new hairstyle of Pho-yongs-bza', she approached her with the intention of stabbing her with a knife; [but she did not succeed] because the son Mu-ne bTsan-po protected [her] on the left side. The mother Tshe-spongs-bza', with cruel resolve, dispatched Minister Te-gu sTe-chung to Phyag-tshang to invite the son to the Yum-bu-mkhar Palace where [she gave him] poisoned food. Prince Mu-ne bTsan-po died at the age of twenty-seven, having ruled for twelve months.

The text says "after the father died"; this clearly indicates that at the time of, or soon after, the death of the Dharmarāja Khri-srong lDe'u-btsan, which happened in the female Fire Ox year of the first *sMe-phreng* of the sixteenth *sMe-'khor* (Tibetan year 2714, 797 CE), Mu-ne bTsan-po had been ruling for twelve months and that at the end of this period the mother fed him toxic food, which is the reason he died.

This text does not specify the year of birth of Mu-ne bTsan-po, so it is difficult to know in which year he died; but it says that Khri-srong lDe'u-btsan "departed for heaven in the Tiger year at the age of sixty-nine," pointing to the male Metal Tiger year (Tibetan year 2727, 810 CE), the year when Mu-ne bTsan-po, at the age of twenty-five, ascended the royal throne. If we count twenty-five years backward, the year of birth of Mu-ne bTsan-po would be either the female Wood Ox year (Tibetan year 2702, 785 CE) or if the whole year is counted, the male Fire Tiger year (Tibetan year 2703, 786 CE). This date is far too late if compared with the accounts related in the Chronicles of the Chinese Táng 唐 dynasty [*rGya'i thang yig*]; therefore the number twenty-seven given in this source is certainly a transcription error.

The *Ne'u sngon byung gi gtam* simply says (Dha, 11, 6, 5):

He was killed at Yun-bu by his mother.

The *Bu ston chos 'byung*, following the *lDe'u chos 'byung chen mo*, says (lHa, 130, 1):

When he was seventeen, the mother poisoned him and he died.

Concerning this viewpoint the *rGyal rabs 'phrul gyi lde mig* reads (Dhi, 11, 22, 4):

> The *Bu ston chos 'byung* says that Mu-ne bTsan-po was enthroned in the Water Tiger [year] and that he died at the age of seventeen after reigning one year seven months.

And also (ibid., 11, 22, 5):

> According to the first viewpoint, the son should have ascended to the throne when he was forty-five; therefore, the chronology of this religious history is incorrect in saying that the father died in the Fire Tiger [year] when he was sixty-nine.

This source acknowledges that the chronology is incorrect.

The *Yar lung jo bo'i chos 'byung* says (Si, 63, 13):

> When [Mu-ne bTsan-po] was twenty-nine, he was poisoned by his mother at the Yun-bu Palace and died.

This religious history acknowledges that Mu-ne bTsan-po ascended to the throne when he was twenty-eight. It also says, "Mu-ne bTsan-po was born in the male Water Tiger year at Brag-dmar," implying that the year of birth of Mu-ne bTsan-po was the male Water Tiger year (Tibetan year 2617, 762 CE); that Mu-ne bTsan-po was enthroned in the female Earth Snake year (Tibetan year 2706, 789 CE), when he was barely twenty-eight or in the male Metal Horse year (Tibetan year 2707, 790 CE), when he had reached the full age of twenty-eight; and that one year later, he died in the male Metal Horse year (Tibetan year 2707, 790 CE), when he was barely twenty-nine or in the female Metal Sheep year (Tibetan year 2708, 791 CE), when he had reached the full age of twenty-nine.

This text also maintains that the Dharmarāja Khri-srong lDe'u-btsan was born in the male Metal Horse year (Tibetan year 2647, 730 CE) and died in the female Wood Ox year (Tibetan year 2702 785 CE); this would mean that Mu-ne bTsan-po was enthroned four or five years after the death of his father (Tibetan year 2707, 790 CE), but that is incompatible from an historical point of view. In this respect, I think that the problem most probably stems from the conviction that the Dharmarāja Khri-srong lDe'u-btsan was born in the male Metal Horse year.

The *Deb ther dmar po* says (Pe, 38, 5):

> When [Mu-ne bTsan-po] was twenty-four he was killed by his mother; he died when his father was [still] alive.

This text clearly shows that when he died the father Khri-srong lDe'u-btsan was still alive. It also says that the father Khri-srong lDe'u-btsan died at fifty-six in the female Wood Ox year; and that the son Mu-ne bTsan-po, born in the male Water Tiger year, died at twenty-four in the female Wood Ox year; this implicitly establishes that both the king father and the king son died in the female Wood Ox year (Tibetan year 2702, 785 CE). In this regard the *rGyal rabs gsal ba'i me long* says (Pe, 224, 22):

> Since Queen Pho-yong-bza' rGyal-mo-btsun was the child of the queen mother rGya-mo-bza', the king father became greatly attached to her. When the father arrived at Zung-mkhar, he entrusted [her] to the son, so the son married her. When the father died, it is said that since Pho-yong-bza' did not remove her ornaments and did not mourn [his death], advancing pretexts for that [behavior], the mother Tshe-spangs-bza' was offended. [Thus] she entrusted and sent an assassin to kill [her], but the king son protected [her]. The mother developed a perverse idea: she invited [her] son [and offered] poisoned food [to him]. [Thus,] the king son Mu-ne bTsan-po died at the Yum-bu Palace at the age of twenty-nine, having ruled for one year nine months.

As we can see, many religious and dynastic histories present various accounts according to which Mu-ne bTsan-po died after his father; this is another case where the complication results from acknowledging the male Metal Horse year as the year of birth of the Dharmarāja Khri-srong lDe'u-btsan.

The *lHo brag chos 'byung* says (Pe, Vol. I, 405, 13):

> When [Mu-ne bTsan-po] was twenty-four in the Wood Ox [year], [he] died at the Yum-bu Palace.

This text mainly follows the *Deb ther dmar po* as far as the date of Mu-ne bTsan-po's death is concerned.

The *rGya bod yig tshang chen mo* says (Si, 199, 12):

> When [he] was twenty-nine, [he] died by poisoning.

This source is clearly in agreement with the viewpoint of the *Yar lung jo bo*.

The *rGyal rabs 'phrul gyi lde mig* says (Dhi, 11, 23, 1):

> When [he] was twenty-three, the mother Tshe-spong-bza' gave [him] poisoned food (out of spite against Princess Phong-'ong-gza'), and [he] died.

It may appear that this source does not follow the viewpoint of the *Deb ther mar po* because the latter says twenty-four, or else, the *Deb ther mar po* considers the twenty-three years as twenty-three full years.

Many opinions of this sort concern the date of Mu-ne bTsan-po's death, but regarding a definite year, the *rGya'i thang yig gsar ma* [New Chronicles of the Chinese Táng 唐 dynasty] say (mTsho, 334, 12):

> In the fourth month of the thirteenth year of the Krin Yon[61] era (Fire Ox year, 797 CE) the king died. The eldest son was enthroned. He died after one year.

Here it says "he died after one year." If that happened one year after the Dharmarāja Khri-srong lDe'u-btsan died in the Fire Ox year (Tibetan year 2714, 797 CE), it would definitely prove that Mu-ne bTsan-po died in the male Earth Tiger year (Tibetan year 2715, 798 CE). This hypothesis fully corresponds to the viewpoint traditionally expressed by most Tibetan dynastic and religious histories and by those historical documents which affirm that Mu-ne bTsan-po died one year seven months or one year nine months after the Dharmarāja Khri-srong lDe'u-btsan.

For what concerns the tomb of Mu-ne bTsan-po, the *rGyal rabs gsal ba'i me long* specifies (Pe, 225, 9):

---

61 [The Zhēngyuán 貞元 era of Táng 唐 Dézōng 德宗 imperial rule (785-805).]

[It] was [built] in front of the right side of [the tomb of] Ag-tshom. As for the name, it was called lHa-ri lDem-po.

9. THE FORTY-SECOND RULER OF TIBET: MU-RUM bTSAN-PO

The generally acknowledged name of this king is Mu-rum bTsan-po. The Zhang Zhung word *mu* means sky [*gnam*] and sky expanse [*mkha' dbyings*]. *Rum* is an archaic term well-known in Zhang/Bod; in the Zhang Zhung language proper it corresponds to *rkya*, while in Tibetan it means space or expanse [*klong*] or condition [*ngang*]. The name of this king, Mu-rum bTsan-po, translated in modern Tibetan would be mKha'-klong rGyal-po [King of the Sky Expanse]. Another name with which this king is known, Ju-tse bTsan-po, also derives from the Zhang Zhung language: the Zhang Zhung word *ju-tse* corresponds to base [*gzhi*] or root [*rtsa ba*] in Tibetan. Hence the name means King of the Origin [gZhi-rtsa'i rGyal-po].

Mu-rug bTsan-po or Mu-rub bTsan-po—where *rug* and *rub* represent variants of the Zhang Zhung word *ru* meaning power, hence, "Heavenly Powerful King" [gNam-dbang rGyal-po]—and Mu-rum bTsan-po have traditionally been acknowledged as mere synonyms, but in reality, Mu-rug bTsan-po or Mu-rub bTsan-po is the first elder brother of Mu-rum bTsan-po and the second elder brother of Mu-ne bTsan-po. In the *sBa-bzhed* and in the texts that agree with this source he is the one called Mu-tig bTsan-po. Mu-rum bTsan-po is the fourth of the five sons of the Dharmarāja Khri-srong lDe'u-btsan, all of whom had the distinctive word *mu* [*gnam*] in their names: Mu-khri bTsan-po, Mu-rug bTsan-po, Mu-ne bTsan-po, Mu-rum bTsan-po, and Mu-tig bTsan-po. In fact, also the Ju-tse bTsan-po of the *Deb ther dmar po* and of the *Deb ther sngon po* is to be understood as a variant of this king's name.

Let us see one example of how the *sBa bzhed* attributes the name Mu-tig bTsan-po to Mu-rug bTsan-po (Si, 174, 9):

> Queen Me-tog-sgron saw that power was conferred on the son Mu-ne bTsan-po and that the Minister Zhang dBu-rings, hav-

ing become the trusted counselor of the king, [was required to] perform [his offices from] and reside in the Drum Storehouse of the middle section of the Central [bSam-yas] Temple. She became enraged and suspicion caused her to think that power would certainly be bestowed on the sNa-nam faction. Hence she pleaded with Mu-tig bTsan-po. The Prince accompanied dBu-rings to the gate, unsheathed a small dagger, and killed him. The father said, "Where has the honorable minister gone?" Throwing away the blood-stained knife, [the Prince] said, "dBu-rings went far away" and ran to the middle building.

The king postponed his personal practice; but he was disquieted because he feared that the summer rains would arrive. Advice was requested of all the wise ministers and Minister 'Gos devised three judgements that created joy.[62] [The king] decided that Mu-ne bTsan-po was to receive the political power and that Prince [Mu-tig bTsan-po] was to be imprisoned in Mon at Lam-phrag Gang-chod[63] [of] Zhang-la-stong.

Most famous Tibetan dynastic and religious histories base themselves upon this source and usually present many accounts about the imprisonment of Mu-tig bTsan-po, the only difference being the place of imprisonment, which in the *lDe'u chos 'byung* is sKyed-tshal of Shangs

---

62 *zhal che dga' gsum*: the *lHo brag chos 'byung* specifies (Pe, Vol. I, 404, 5), The three judgements that created joy: after the speech of mGos it was declared, "Let him go to the Zur-mkhar [emperor's white] stūpas [of bSam-yas] to present his judgements." So he left on horseback. After he arrived there, he wrote [the following] words on the lower stone stūpa: When a king kills a subject, it is as if a mother was striking [her own child]: [the child has] no defense. When [he came to] the middle stūpa, he said, "[Here, I will write a] question" which delighted the royal father and son. He wrote: [How is it that] although someone is killed by another, the subjects do not object [and] the fact goes unnoticed[?]" (I think this is what is meant by the sentence *rgyal po 'bangs la mig ches te 'gro* that appears at this point.) Seeing the question, the subjects rejoiced. At the highest [stūpa he wrote:] If the king himself does not protect the law, he cannot impose it upon his subjects." Therefore the prince [was sentenced to] nine years of exile in the northern district of Zhang-la-stong. The sNa-nam-pa were happy about that. It is said that these were the three [judgements that created] joy.

63 *lam phrag gang chod*: this is perhaps a district of Zhang-la sTong-du Byin-pa or indicates a remote countryside.

and not Mon as the *sBa bzhed* specifies. In other ways they are more or less alike.

The *Deb ther dpyid kyi rgyal mo'i glu dbyangs* says (Pe, 67, 14):

> The middle one, Mu-rug bTsan-po. Usually, when the king and Minister Zhang [dBu-rings] [were to] hold talks on the conquest of two-thirds of the world, the son would arrive at the meeting place of the conference, [but once] dBu-rings, the son of Zhang, did not appear on time at the conference place. [That was because] the son had stabbed [him] with a small knife and killed [him]. Minister 'Gos expressed the three judgements that create fear[64] and the three judgements that create joy. The son was temporarily banished …

This text does not describe the circumstances related to the struggle among the princes for the throne, but in fact, even if in agreement with the *sBa bzhed*, it clearly suggests that the name of the prince who killed Zhang dBu-rings was Mu-rug bTsan-po.

If Mu-rug bTsan-po killed Zhang dBu-rings, the reason for his doing so should have been an important one. If he killed him only because "he did not appear on time at the conference place," even if some historical accounts traditionally say that the Tibetans were thorough savages because they were generated by a father monkey and a mother crag-demoness, could all Tibetans really be considered as being like that up to the time of Prince Mu-rug bTsan-po?

It is easy to see the reason why Mu-rug bTsan-po killed Zhang dBu-rings: he was the senior prince and yet, as the *sBa bzhed* clearly shows, Mu-ne bTsan-po had been enthroned and his chief minister Zhang dBu-rings had been appointed counselor of the king.

The *sBa bzhed* says (Si, 179, 1):

> Then, because [they wanted to] put an end to the power conferred on Mu-tig bTsan-po, with the pretext of inviting [him]

---

64   *zhal lce 'dar gsum*: the *dPyid kyi rgyal mo'i glu dbyang*s simply says these words without specifying what the three judgements were, but in fact I think that they can be understood as three frightening judgements which were suitably related to the three that produced joy.

back from Mon, the sNa-nam-pa killed [him] by crushing [his] chest.

When Mu-ne bTsan-po died, Mu-rug bTsan-po, the elder brother of Mu-rum bTsan-po, should have ascended to the throne; therefore, he was once again called back from Mon, but he did not reign because the sNa-nam-pa killed him: also this story is traditionally repeated by most Tibetan dynastic histories and historical documents. The sNa-nam-pa's murder is also mentioned in the *Yar lung jo bo'i chos 'byung* (Si, 63, 13):

sNa-nam startled the horse and the horse [unsaddled him and] killed [him].

Basing themselves upon this source, also the *lHo brag chos 'byung*, the *rGyal rabs 'phrul gyi lde mig*, and the *lHa thog rgyal rabs* contain brief repetitions of the story.

Even though it is indubitable that Mu-rug bTsan-po remained in prison for several years as a punishment for having killed Zhang dBu-rings, this account according to which he was invited back from Mon and killed by the sNa-nam-pa because supposedly he was going to seize the throne after Mu-ne bTsan-po's death is certainly preposterous: this is proven by the edict inscribed on the stone pillar placed by Khri-lde Srong-btsan Sad-na-legs, the youngest son of the Dharmarāja Khri-srong lDe'u-btsan, at the Zhwa Temple. Starting from the forty-eighth line, it reads:

I swear in front of the elder brother Mu-rug bTsan[-po], the Queens and relatives, the vassals, the political ministers, and also all the chief and secondary ministers of the maternal side. Erected as an eternal memorial.

As we can see, the elder brother Mu-rug bTsan-po was one of the witnesses mentioned in the Edict of the Oath.

The *rGya'i thang yig rnying ma* [Old Chronicles of the Chinese Táng 唐 dynasty] say (mTsho, 334, 12):

In the fourth month of the thirteenth year of the Krin Yon[65] era (Fire Ox year, 797 CE) the king died. The eldest son was enthroned. He died after one year. His younger brother inherited the throne.

In the female Fire Ox year (Tibetan year 2714, 797 CE) the Dharmarāja Khri-srong lDe'u-btsan died. According to the traditional system, the eldest son, Mu-ne bTsan-po, was enthroned. When Mu-ne bTsan-po died one year after, his younger brother was installed on the throne. It is impossible that this younger prince was Mu-rug bTsan-po because the majority of the Tibetan dynastic and religious histories clearly say that Mu-rug bTsan-po was subjected to a legal punishment, neither is it possible that it was the youngest prince Mu-tig bTsan-po/Khri-lde Srong-btsan because the *rGya'i thang yig gsar ma* [New Chronicles of the Chinese Táng 唐 dynasty] say (mTsho, 94, 9):

> In the twentieth year of the Krin Yon [era] (Wood Monkey year, 804 CE) the bTsan-po departed for heaven. The emperor entrusted the plenipotentiary of Kung-pu'u Hri-lang called Krang Can as his envoy to the funeral ceremonies. The younger brother of the bTsan-po took the throne.

Thus, the Chinese emperor sent a representative to the funeral ceremonies of Mu-rum bTsan-po and the younger brother of the king, Mu-tig bTsan-po/Khri-lde Srong-btsan was raised to the throne.

The *lHo brag chos 'byung* says (Pe, Vol. I, 105, 15):

> Then, it was ordered that the punished Prince Mu-tig bTsan-po be invited [back] from the north to be appointed. On the way, the sNa-nam-ba startled his steed, [the prince] fell from [the horse], and the horse killed him.

It is illogical for this text to claim that before the sNa-nam-ba killed him, the punished Prince Mu-rug bTsan-po, here called Mu-tig bTsan-po, had to return from the north as fit to sit on the throne, because the inscription quoted above demonstrates that he was present at the

---

65 [The Zhēngyuán 貞元 era of Táng 唐 Dézōng 德宗 imperial rule (785-805).]

placement of the stone pillar of the Zhwa Temple after his younger brother, the real Mu-tig bTsan-po, also known as Khri-lde Srong-btsan, was enthroned. If it was not Mu-rum bTsan-po the one who ruled the forty-second dynasty for six full years from the time in which the elder brother Mu-ne bTsan-po died in the male Earth Tiger year (Tibetan year 2715, 798 CE) until the time in which the youngest Prince Khri-lde Srong-btsan Sad-na-legs was enthroned in the male Wood Monkey year (Tibetan year 2721, 804 CE), who else would it have been?

The *rGya'i thang yig rnying ma* [Old Chronicles of the Chinese Táng 唐 dynasty] say (Dha, 54, 3):

> In the early part of the third month of the twentieth year of the Krin Yoon [era] (Wood Monkey year, 804 CE), the great minister Krang Can was dispatched from the Thang [Táng 唐] court to Tibet, in order to communicate [the emperor's] distress at the death of the Tibetan bTsan-po (Mu-rum bTsan-po) through three days of mourning.
>
> In the fourth month of the thirteenth year of the Krin Yoon [era] (the father) [of] that king died, so the eldest son was requested to occupy the royal throne, but after one year he died. The middle son (Mu-rum bTsan-po) took the royal throne and the Thang [Táng 唐] imperial court issued a decree according to which civil and military ministers above the Third Degree were to present their condolences.

This source clearly shows that Mu-rum bTsan-po ruled for six full years and died in the male Wood Monkey year (Tibetan year 2721, 804 CE).

In his authoritative *Deb ther dmar po*, Tshal-pa Kun-dga' rDo-rje (1309-1364), who correlated the history of China with that of Tibet, affirms (Pe, 22, 17):

> In the female Fire Ox [year] the Tibetan king died. Ju-tse bTsan-po was installed on the throne.

'Gos-lo[-tsa-wa] gZhon-nu-dpal (1392-1481) who also compared the history of China with that of Tibet in his learned *Deb ther sngon po* states (Si, Vol. I, 77, 10):

> After the death of Khri-srong lDe'u-btsan, the eldest son Mu-ne
> bTsan-po was appointed. He ruled for seventeen years and died in
> the female Fire Ox [year]. Ju-tse bTsan-po ascended to the throne.

These sources indicate that Ju-tse bTsan-po ascended to the throne
after Mu-ne bTsan-po died in the female Fire Ox year (Tibetan year
2714, 797 CE); regarding that, who else would have been suitable
apart from Mu-rum bTsan-po?

Tibetan dynastic and religious histories do not provide details
about the year of birth, the consorts, the sons, and the ministers of
this king; however, these issues can be determined in a rudimental way
through inferential reasoning. For example it can be logically inferred
that the year of birth of Mu-rum bTsan-po was the female Wood
Rabbit year (Tibetan year 2692, 775 CE), since no other suitable
time exists between the birth of the elder brother Mu-ne bTsan-po
which occurred in the male Wood Tiger year (Tibetan year 2691, 774
CE) and that of the younger brother Mu-tig bTsan-po, also known
as Khri-lde Srong-btsan, which occurred in the male Fire Dragon year
(Tibetan year 2693, 776 CE).

The *rGyal rabs gsal ba'i me long* contains affirmations related to Khri-
lde Srong-btsan that differ from those expounded in other Tibetan
dynastic and religious histories (Pe, 226, 4):

> When [he] reached the age of nineteen, [he] married Queen
> lHa-rtse. She gave birth to a child. When [the child] reached
> the age of thirteen, the father died.

Related here is certainly an account that refers to Mu-rum bTsan-po:
if we count eighteen full years or about nineteen years from the female
Wood Rabbit year (Tibetan year 269, 775 CE) in which Mu-rum
bTsan-po was born, we arrive at the female Water Bird year (Tibetan
year 2710, 793 CE). It is said that in that year he married a queen
called lHa-rtse who had a son. When the child was a full twelve or
barely thirteen years old, the father died. Since that year corresponds
to the male Wood Monkey year (Tibetan year 2721, 804 CE), he
must have married Queen lHa-rtse one year before he ascended to
the throne, because one year had to elapse from the time in which he
married until the birth of the son lDing-khri.

In synthesis, Mu-rum bTsan-po or Ju-tse bTsan-po, the forty-second ruler of Tibet, was born in the female Wood Rabbit year (Tibetan year 2692, 775 CE). He ascended to the throne in the male Earth Tiger year (Tibetan year 2715, 798 CE) when he was a full twenty-three years old; he remained in power for six whole years; and in the end, when he was a full twenty-nine years old, he died in the male Wood Monkey year (Tibetan year 2721, 804 CE).

Concerning the tomb of Mu-rum bTsan-po the *rGyal rabs gsal ba'i me long* says (Pe, 226, 13):

> It is said that his tomb was [placed] to the left [of the tomb] of 'Phrul-rgyal and that also that tomb was filled with precious jewels. Since [the tomb] of the mother was inundated, [his tomb] was placed [at a] high[er level]. The name was The Tomb of the Great King [rGyal-chen Bang-so].

The *Me long ma* says that this is the tomb of the son called lDeng-khri, but since this explanation is totally absent in other dynastic and religious histories, we can understand by implication that this lDeng-khri is Mu-rum bTsan-po, and also that this tomb is the tomb of Mu-rum bTsan-po.

10. THE FORTY-THIRD RULER OF TIBET: KHRI-LDE SRONG-BTSAN

Tibetan historians have different opinions concerning the name of this king; nonetheless, they call him either Khri-lde Srong-btsan or Mu-tig bTsan-po.

The name Khri-lde Srong-btsan is a combination of Zhang Zhung words and Tibetan archaic terms: in the Zhang Zhung language *khri* means deity, divine [*lha*] or superior [*mchog*]; *lde* means wisdom [*mkhyen pa*] or knowledge [*shes pa*]; *srong* is a Tibetan archaic word meaning honest [*drang po*] or just [*drang bden*]; *btsan* is also an archaic Tibetan word that can be interpreted as keen or sharp [*rnon po*]. In modern Tibetan Khri-lde Srong-btsan would be called mChog-mkhyen Drang-rnon, which means endowed with excellent or insurpassable wisdom, an honest heart, and a keen intellect.

Concerning the name Mu-tig bTsan-po, the *rGyal po bka'i thang yig* specifies (Pe, 117, 14):

> The Teacher gave [him] the name Mu-tig bTsan-po. The father, Khri-lde Srong-btsan; the minister of internal affairs, mJing-yon Sad-na-legs; the Chinese, Mu-ri bTsan-po.

This is what the text affirms. Nonetheless, Tibetan kings usually had one royal guard [sKu-gshen] to protect their lives and sometimes, together with the Bonpo who sheltered and insured the development of the royal lineage, one or two eminent Bonpo priests acted as advisors. In observance of the ancient custom, each would attribute a name to the children of the king after the lustral perfusion rite; thus it is absolutely certain that also the names of the children of the Dharmarāja Khri-srong lDe'u-btsan were all attributed in conformity with that custom. Although *mu tig* is the Tibetan term for a type of jewel [pearl] and the name might seem to be linked to that word, in reality its derivation is from the Zhang Zhung language: *mu* means sky [*nam mkha'*]; *mu khri* means deity [*lha*]; *tig* means one or unique [*gcig*]; and *btsan po* is the archaic Tibetan word for king [*rgyal po*]. In modern Tibetan Mu-tig bTsan-po means Unique Divine King [lHa-gcig rGyal-po].

Since the Dharmarāja Khri-srong lDe'u-btsan suppressed Bon and caused the Buddhadharma to spread and flourish, reasons for doubting the presence of royal Bonpo guards [sKu-gshen] at that time could exist. In reality, even at the time of the great diffusion and thriving of the Buddhadharma, one Bonpo royal guard would be assigned to keep the ancient traditions immaculate and to protect the king's life from the arising of risks. A confirmation of this practice is found in the *Gleng gzhi bstan pa'i byung khungs* which says (IsMEO, 18):

> The royal guards of Khri-srong lDe-btsan [were] sPe-ne Mu-dag [and] 'Bo-shod Kra-mo.

The *Legs bshad rin po che'i mdzod* says (Pe, 225, 4):

During the reign of that [king] (Khri-gtsug lDe-btsan), Buddhism flourished greatly. The royal guards were two: [the Tibetan] Bon-po Khyung-po sTag-sgra Dun-gtsug and the Zhang Zhung Bon-po Dun-tang rGyal-ba.

Concerning the royal guard of King Glang-dar-ma the *lDe'u chos 'byung chen mo* says (Bod, 140, 15):

[He] incriminated the royal expert of sacred formulas [*sku'i sngags mkhan*] and the royal guard [sKu-gshen].

As for the origin of the name mJing-yon Sad-na-legs, the *sBa bzhed* affirms (Si, 179, 4):

Then all the vassals discussed the matter concerning the empowerment of the younger sibling Khri-lde Srong-btsan. Someone said, "The prince has not [yet] come of age and cannot guide the subjects. Hence, let us entrust wise ministers with the formulation of the laws."[66] Someone else said, "In the past, when the father died and the prince had not [yet] come of age, power was handed to three ministers of the matrilinear line. They formulated laws [and the result was that] the divine religion [*lha chos*] was suppressed and great disputes arose which brought about Tibet's demise. Thus it is requested that the Prince be empowered [now] and that he guide the subjects with the counsel of wise ministers. Let the Prince be tested [to see] whether he is suitable or not." After the test was performed, the Prince was empowered at the age of four and reigned. Since the result of the test was positive, the Prince was called Sad-na-legs;[67] and on account of his sloping neck and powerful body he was also known as Glang-mjing-yon [Crooked-Necked Bull].

The acceptance of the above account by most dynastic and religious histories has contributed to the popularity also of the nickname.

---

66 *khrims bu chung*: this expression refers to circumstances in which the political responsibility had to be assumed by several ministers who would devise the foundations of a law by mutual consent.

67 [Literally, Good When Tested.]

As we have seen, the *rGyal po bka'i thang yig* says, "The Chinese called him Mu-ri bTsan-po," making this name a transliteration attributed to the monarch by the Chinese people, but that is impossible: no historical records exist according to which China named any of the Tibetan kings. It is in fact demonstrable that the name Mu-ri derives from the Zhang Zhung language with no connection whatsoever with Chinese.[68] Proof that this is one of the names of Mu-tig bTsan-po is found in the *Gleng gzhi bstan pa'i byung khungs*, which says (IsMEO, 18):

Mu-ri was also called Mu-tig bTsan-po.

The appellation Mu-tig bTsan-po, mentioned in the *sBa bzhed* and in sources that concur with that text, was the name attributed to the middle son of King Khri-srong lDe'u-btsan; relevant details can be examined in the section dedicated to Mu-rug bTsan-po.

The two *lDe'u chos 'byung* call this king by three different names: Khri lDe-btsan, Khri-lde Srong-btsan, and Sad-na-legs mJing-yon. Most of the acclaimed dynastic and religious histories, such as the *Grags rgyal bod kyi rgyal rabs*, the *Ne'u sngon byung gi gtam*, the *Klong chen pa'i chos 'byung*, the *Yar lung jo bo'i chos 'byung*, the *Deb ther dmar po*, the *rGyal rabs gsal ba'i me long*, the *Deb ther sngon po*, the *lHo brag chos 'byung*, the *rGya bod yig tshang chen mo*, the *rGyal rabs 'phrul gyi lde mig*, and the *bsTan rtsis gsal ba'i nyin byed*, habitually call him Khri-lde Srong-btsan.

The *Nyang gi chos 'byung*, the *Bu-ston chos 'byung* and other sources call this king Khri lDe-btsan, while the *Tun hong bod kyi lo rgyus yig rnying* [Old Tibetan Chronicles of Dunhuang] refer to him as lDe Srong-brtsan. It is easy to understand that the name Khri-lde Srong-btsan is an abbreviated form of three words belonging to two different readings: Khri lDe-btsan and lDe Srong-btsan.

The *Pad dkar chos 'byung* says (Dha, 332,165, 3):

---

68 [Cf. *A Lexicon of Zhangzhung and Bonpo Terms*, Bon Studies 11, Pasar Tsultrim Tenzin, Changru Tritsuk Namdak Nyima, Gatsa Lodroe Rabsal, edited by Yasuhiko Nagano and Samten G. Karmay, National Museum of Ethnology, Osaka, 2008, p. 188, fourth entry: *mu ri phyod = dbyings su bskyod pa*, to move in space, in the primordial sphere.]

Then, as prophesied in the sūtra of the compassionate Padma dKar-po, the name [of] Khri Ral-pa-can [became] Khri-lde Srong-btsan.

The text maintains that the name of King Ral-pa-can was Khri-lde Srong-btsan; the author calls Ral-pa-can, Khri lDe-btsan. The *Deb ther dpyid kyi rgyal mo'i glu dbyangs* says (Pe, 68, 7):

> Some dynastic histories call this king Khri-lde Srong-btsan; this error is not encountered in the *sGra sbyor bam po gnyis pa*[69] and other sources.

The text says that Khri-lde Srong-btsan is not the name of Mu-tig bTsan-po. Nonetheless, when reporting the commemorative words for the inauguration of the dKar-chung Vajradhātu [rDo-rje dByings] Temple built by Mu-tig bTsan-po, the *lHo brag chos 'byung* says (Pe, Vol. I, 409, 6):

> Written in gold on blue paper during the lifetime of the son Khri-lde Srong-btsan; lodged in a casket adorned with jewels; and [placed in the temple] erected in the spontaneously self-perfected Temple of bSam-yas as a companion emulating [the temple] of the father.

The second line of the inscription on the stone pillar of the Zhwa Temple commemorating the reward granted to Myang Ting-'dzin bZang-po [eighth-ninth centuries] reads:

> Bestowed upon the Buddhist monk Myang Ting-nge-'dzin as an eternal memorial by order of Khri-lde Srong-btsan, the transcendental divine ruler, king of the infinite sky.

These two examples show that Khri-lde Srong-btsan was one of the names of Mu-tig bTsan-po.

Concerning the place and date of birth of this monarch, the *lDe'u rgya bod kyi chos 'byung* says (Bod, 359, 8):

> This king as well was born at Brag-dmar in the Dragon year.

---

69 [*The Two-Volume Lexicon*, composed during the reign of this king, established rules and guidelines for translation.]

The *lDe'u chos 'byung chen mo* says (Bod, 133, 11):

> The younger sibling Khri-lde Srong-btsan was born in the
> Dragon year at sTon-brag-dmar.

These two sources maintain that this king was born in the Dragon year.
The *Nyang gi chos 'byung* says (Bod, 416, 17):

> [He] was born in the male Fire Dog year.

This text provides not only the year of birth, but also the element.
The *Ne'u sngon byung gi gtam* says (Dha, 11, 6, 5):

> The younger sibling Khri-lde Srong-btsan was born at sTon-
> brag-dmar in the Wood Dragon [year].

This source agrees with the *lDe'u chos 'byung* and also specifies that the
element of the year was Wood.
The *Bu ston chos 'byung* says (lHa, 129, 7):

> Mu-ne bTsan-po became the king in the male Water Tiger [year].

And also (ibid., 130, 1):

> He remained in power for one year seven months. At seventeen,
> the mother poisoned [him] and he died. Then the kingdom was
> handed over to [his] younger brother Khri lDe-btsan who was
> four years old.

The above quotations indicate that Mu-ne bTsan-po died in the female Water Rabbit year. If at that time the younger brother Khri-lde
Srong-btsan had reached the age of four, his year of birth must have
been either the male Metal Mouse year, or, if we consider four whole
years, the female Earth Pig year.
The *Yar lung jo bo'i chos 'byung* says (Si, 64, 1):

> The smallest brother was Khri-lde Srong-bTsan. He was called
> Sad-na-legs 'Jing-yon; he was born at Brag-dmar in the male
> Wood Sheep [year].

According to this source, the year of birth was the male Wood Sheep year.

The *Deb ther dmar po* says (Pe, 38, 9):

The fourth [was] Khri-lde Srong-btsan, born in the male Wood Dragon [year].

This text shares the view of the *Ne'u chos 'byung*.
The *lHo brag chos 'byung* says (Pe, Vol.1, 407, 5):

The fourth son, Khri-lde Srong-btsan, also known as lDing-khri, was enthroned at the age of twenty-three in the male Fire Tiger year.

Thus, when Khri-lde Srong-btsan ascended to the throne in the male Fire Tiger year (Tibetan year 2603, 786 CE), he had reached the age of twenty-three. In that case, the year of his birth would be the male Wood Dragon year (2603-22=2581; 786-22=764); this date perfectly accords with the opinion of the *Ne'u sngon byung gi gtam*. The *rGya bod yig tshang chen mo* is in agreement with this last source and says (Si, 199, 18):

The younger brother Khri-lde Srong-btsan was born at Brag-dmar in the male Wood Dragon [year].

In synthesis, three different opinions exist concerning this king's birth: the first one is that of the *lDe'u chos 'byung chen mo* which says that the birth occurred in the Dragon year, whereas Wood is indicated as that year's element by the *Ne'u sngon byung gi gtam*; the second opinion can be inferred from the *Bu ston chos 'byung*, because if we accept the reckoning presented in the two citations above [p. 198] he would have been born in the male Metal Mouse year; the [third and] last one is that of the *Yar lung jo bo'i chos 'byung* which maintains that he was born in the male Wood Sheep year. Let us consider the opinion of the *Bu ston chos 'byung*: if we assume that Khri-lde Srong-btsan was born in the Metal Mouse year, then the father Khri-srong lDe'u-btsan must have been a full eighteen years old at the time of his birth; that would mean that he was born before his third elder brother and that the father died when he was a full twenty-one or about twenty-two years old: this date cannot be reconciled chronologically. The male Wood Sheep year is not compatible either, although it concords with the time frame of the *Tun hong bod kyi lo rgyus yig rnying* [Old Tibetan Chronicles of Dunhuang], because it corresponds to the year before the enthronement of the father Khri-srong lDe'u-btsan; in this case no suitable age but that of thirteen exists.

Even if from a historical viewpoint the Dragon year given by the *lDe'u chos 'byung* can be considered as a possible date, it is difficult to determine the element of that year. The majority of scholars who adopted the view of the *Ne'u sngon byung gi gtam* seem to favor the male Wood Dragon year (Tibetan year 2681, 764 CE). However, if Khri-lde Srong-btsan was born in that year, the *Tun hong bod kyi lo rgyus yig rnying* [Old Tibetan Chronicles of Dunhuang] should at least have recorded the event. Concerning the activities of the Dharmarāja Khri-srong lDe'u-btsan for that year, the *Chronicles* say (PI 594, 62):

> It happened in the year of the Dragon [764-765]. The bTsan-po's court was residing at lCang-bu in Byar. The summer council was convened at Bu-cung in Glag. Minister Khri-sgra sTag-tshab convened the mDo-smad summer council at sNig in Sla-shod. In Tibet a major consultation was taking place. Promotions and transfers of illustrious ministers were carried out. The white chrysoberyl insignia was conferred on Chief Minister sNang-bzher and he was appointed [*sic*] chief minister. On Zhang rGyal-zigs was bestowed the great turquoise insignia and he was praised because he declared himself satisfied with the jurisdiction of mGar-'dzi-rmun. Minister Khri-bzang was appointed as chief minister. On Zhang sTong-btsan was bestowed the turquoise insignia and he was proclaimed general of the four frontiers. One year.

As we can see, the *Chronicles* say nothing about the birth of the son. This proves that the year and element of birth of Khri-lde Srong-btsan is precisely that in which the Dharmarāja Khri-srong lDe'u-btsan became a full thirty-four years old, that is to say, the male Fire Dragon year (Tibetan year 2693, 776 CE).

Regarding the enthronement of Khri-lde Srong-btsan, the *sBa-bzhed* affirms (Si, 179, 12):

Let us prepare a test [to see whether] the prince is fit or not. Then the power was bestowed on the Prince when he was four years old. Since the test was successful the Prince was known as Sad-na-legs [Good When Tested].

Sad-na-legs was extremely young so it was necessary to proceed with a test in order to check his capability. The *rGya bod yig tshang chen mo* and the *Deb ther dpyid kyi rgyal mo'i glu dbyangs* concur in this view and maintain that Khri-lde Srong-btsan was four years old when he ascended to the throne. I will subsequently explain why it is correct to assume that the male Wood Monkey year (Tibetan year 2721, 804 CE) is the true year of Khri-lde Srong-btsan's enthronement.

If Khri-lde Srong-btsan was a full four years old in the male Wood Monkey year, he must have been born in the male Metal Dragon year (Tibetan year 2717, 800 CE); but since this year comes three full years after the death of the father Khri-srong lDe'u-btsan, this date cannot be accurate, since no child can be born without a father.

The *lDe'u rgya bod kyi chos 'byung* says (Bod, 359, 9):

When [he was] thirteen, his father died; afterward, he ruled the kingdom for eighteen years.

This text indicates that he was installed on the throne when he was thirteen. The *lDe'u chos 'byung chen mo* affirms (Bod, 133, 12):

After [he reached the age of] twenty-three, his father departed for heaven.

It is easy to understand that the thirteen of the *lDe'u rgya bod kyi chos 'byung* is a scribal error for twenty-three.

The *Nyang gi chos 'byung* says (Bod, 415, 5):

It was decided to test the prince [to see whether he was] suitable or not. Since the test was successful, he was empowered at the age of twenty-four.

One whole year's difference exists in the reckoning system of this text, but in fact this is not in disagreement with the viewpoint of the *lDe'u chos 'byung* which is also that of the *Grags rgyal bod kyi rgyal rabs* and the

Ne'u sngon byung gi gtam. Here the prince is an adult who had reached the age of twenty-four. If the reason for testing him was not his young age, it could have had to do with the shape of his body, which was reflected in the prince's sobriquet, Glang-mjing-yon [Crooked-Necked Bull]; that can be inferred from the context of the *Nyang gi chos 'byung.*

The *Deb ther sngon po* says (Si, Vol. One, 77, 12):

> In the male Wood Monkey [year], (Mu-ne bTsan-po) died. In that same year, Khri-lde Srong-btsan was raised to the throne.

By stating that he was enthroned in the Wood Monkey year (Tibetan year 2721, 804 CE), this text is entirely in agreement that Khri-lde Srong-btsan ascended to the throne when he was a full twenty-three years old.

The *lHo brag chos 'byung* says (Pe, Vol. One, 407, 5):

> The fourth son, Khri-lde Srong-btsan, also known as lDing-khri, was enthroned in the male Fire Tiger year at the age of twenty-three.

This source says that Khri-lde Srong-btsan was twenty-three in the male Fire Tiger Year, therefore assuming that the elder brother Mu-ne bTsan-po was born in the Water Sheep year and that Khri-lde Srong-btsan was born in the Wood Dragon year; consequently his twenty-third year is identified with the male Fire Tiger year. If according to this scheme the twenty-third year is calculated from the Wood Dragon year, the enthronement would correspond to the male Earth Tiger year (Tibetan year 2715, 798 CE).

The *Deb ther sngon po* and the *rGya'i thang yig gsar rnying* [Old and New Chronicles of the Chinese Táng 唐 dynasty] say that after the elder brother Mu-ne bTsan-po died, Mu-rum bTsan-po, also known as Ju-tse bTsan-po, was raised to the throne. We can see that this is not in contradiction with the perspective according to which Khri-lde Srong-btsan was enthroned only after Mu-rum bTsan-po, also known as Ju-tse bTsan-po, ruled for six full years from the male Earth Tiger year (Tibetan year 2715, 798 CE) until the male Wood Monkey year (Tibetan year 2721, 804 CE).

For that reason it can be determined that Mu-tig bTsan-po, also known as Khri-lde Srong-btsan, who was the youngest son of the Dharmarāja Khri-srong lDe'u-bTsan, ascended to the throne in the male Wood Monkey year (Tibetan year 2721, 804 CE) when he reached the full age of twenty-eight. That Mu-tig bTsan-po, also known as Khri-lde Srong-btsan, who was the younger brother of King Mu-rum bTsan-po, also known as Ju-tse bTsan-po, ascended to the throne after his elder brother died is proven by the *rGya'i thang yig gsar ma* [New Chronicles of the Chinese Táng 唐 dynasty] which state (mTsho, 94, 9):

> In the twentieth year of the Krin Yon [era] (Wood Monkey year, 804 CE) the bTsan-po departed for heaven. The plenipotentiary of Kung-pu'u Hri-lang called Krang Can was invested by the emperor as envoy to the funeral ceremonies. The younger brother of the bTsan-po took the throne.

The *lDe'u chos 'byung chen mo* counts the years of the reign of Khri-lde Srong-btsan as twenty-five, while the *Nyang gi chos 'byung*, the *Grags rgyal bod kyi rgyal rabs*, and the *Ne'u sngon byung gi gtam* say that he ruled for thirty-one years. The *Yar lung jo bo'i chos 'byung* says (Si, 64, 2):

> [When he was] twenty-four, after the elder brother died, [he] ruled for thirty-two years.

Thus, also with this calculation a difference of one full year exists, but in reality I think that this source is in agreement with the *Nyang gi chos 'byung*, and so on, and that it also adopts the view of the *Deb ther dmar po*.

In his *lDe'u chos 'byung chen mo*, mKhas-pa lDe'u says that the king ruled for twenty-five years, but in his *lDe'u rgya bod kyi chos 'byung*, composed at a later date, he affirms that the king ruled for eighteen years; this must have been the true conclusion of mKhas-pa lDe'u. The *Pad dkar chos 'byung* says (Dhi, 330, 165, 2):

> [He] ruled for seventeen years.

This source presents one reigning year less with respect to the *lDe'u rgya bod kyi chos 'byung*, but in fact the two reckonings can be considered equivalent and with a reasoned perspective that conforms to historical events. The *rGya'i thang yig rnying ma* [Old Chronicles of the Chinese Táng 唐 dynasty] say (mTsho, 253, 13):

> In the fourth month of the twelfth year of the Yon Hi era[70] (Fire Bird year, 817 CE), a deputy was dispatched from Tibet [Bhod] to announce the death of the king. The emperor charged the Yug We general Wu'u Khrung Chi, to whom Yus Hri Krung Khrin credentials had been supplied, with attending the funeral ceremonies as his envoy. The plenipotentiary of Ten Krung Si dByi Hri called Don Cun was appointed as subordinate envoy.

The *rGya'i thang yig gsar ma* [New Chronicles of the Chinese Táng 唐 dynasty] say (Dha, 111, 1; mTsho, 96, 6):

> In the twelfth year of the Yon Ho era (Fire Bird year, 817 CE) the Tibetan minister Chi'i Ran-le'i arrived to report the circum-stances of the Tibetan king's death. The Thang [Táng 唐] army general Wu'u Khrun Ci was dispatched to offer condolences. The throne was occupied by the new Tibetan king Kha'o Li'i Khu'o Chus (Khri Ral-pa-can).

An analysis of these sources reveals the following: in the male Wood Monkey year (Tibetan year 2721, 804 AD) at a full twenty-eight years of age, Mu-tig bTsan-po ascended to the throne after the death of his elder brother Mu-rum bTsan-po. He ruled for thirteen full years and died in the female Fire Bird year (Tibetan year 2734, 817 CE) when he reached the full age of forty-one.

Concerning the wives, children, and ministers of Khri-lde Srong-btsan, the *sBa bzhed* says (Si, 179, 17):

> [He] married 'Bro-bza' Ma-mo lHa-rgyal and appointed 'Bro Khri-gzung as minister.

This source gives the name of just one consort. Later it provides the names of five children (ibid., 187, 8):

---

70 [The Yúanhé 元和 era of the Táng 唐 Emperor Xiànzōng 憲宗 (reigned 805-820).]

His children were five: Khri-gtsug lDe-btsan, lHa-sras gTsang-ma, Khri Dar-ma 'U-dum-btsan, lHa-rje, [and] lHa-chen-grub.

In a similar fashion, both the *lDe'u rgya bod kyi chos 'byung* (Bod, 359, 14) and the *lDe'u chos 'byung chen mo* (Bod, 133, 20) say:

King Sad-na-legs had five children: after lHa-rje and lHun-grub died at an early age, there were Khri Ral-pa-can, gTsang-ma, and Dar-ma.

The two sources not only indicate the names of the five children, but also clarify that lHa-rje and lHun-grub were the eldest and that they died at a young age.

The *Nyang gi chos 'byung* gives the names of two queens (Bod, 415, 13):

[He] married Queen Pho-yongs-bza' lHa-btsun and 'Bro-bza' Mang-po lHa-rgyal.

And also (ibid., 416, 21):

That king had five sons: Khri gTsug-lde Ral-pa-can, lHa-sras gTsang-ma, Khri Dar-ma 'U-dum-btsan, lHa-rje lHun-grub, and Khri-chen 'De'u.

The text gives the names of the five children but does not specify who the queens were and to which queen the children belonged; moreover, while in the *lDe'u chos byung* lHa-rje and lHun-grub are considered two distinct brothers, here lHa-rje lHun-grub is the name of one single child and the other is called Khri-chen lDe'u; in reality, this idea is adopted from the *Bu ston chos 'byung*.

The *Grags rgyal bod kyi rgyal rabs* says (Sa-bKa, TA, 197, 5):

Of the three children born from the marriage with 'Bro-gza' lHa-rgyal Gung-skar-ma, the eldest [was] Khri bTsan-ma. [He] was exiled to lHo-bum-thang and then died, poisoned by 'Brom gza' Legs-rje and sNa-nam-gza' Me-rje-the'u. Since Glang-dar-ma was brainless, hideous, and monkey-headed, he was not enthroned. The younger one, Khri gTsug-lde Ral-pa-can...

Even if this text provides the names of just three children, it contains significant information, specifying who was the eldest, middle, and youngest among them and also the name of the queen who generated them. The name of the eldest of the three sons, Khri bTsan-ma is clearly a scribal error for Khri gTsang-ma, since the *Ne'u sngon byung gi gtam* says (Dha, 12, 6, 1):

> gTsang-ma, the eldest of the three, [was born in the] male Metal Dragon [year]. [He] did not become king [and] died [at] Bum-thang [in] lHo-brag.

The *Yar lung jo bo'i chos 'byung* says (Si, 64, 12):

> The five children of that Lord were gTsang-ma, Dar-ma, Ral-pa-can, lHun-rje, [and] lHun-grub.

The names of the five children mentioned here are also found in most religious and dynastic histories, such as the *Deb ther dmar po*, the *Chos 'byung mkhas pa'i dga' ston*, the *rGya bod yig tshang chen mo*, and the *rGyal rabs 'phrul gyi lde mig*.

The *rGyal rabs gsal ba'i me long* says (Pe, 226, 4):

> When [he] reached the age of nineteen, [he] married Princess lHa-rtse. She gave birth to a child. When the child reached the age of thirteen, the father died. The tomb was erected at Don-mkhar-mda'. At the age of fourteen, the son lDing-khri ascended to the throne. [His] first wife had three children; one of his secondary wives had two, lHa-rje [and] lHun-grub, [so] five [children] were born altogether.

The text says that when Khri-lde Srong-btsan Sad-na-legs reached the age of nineteen he married Queen lHa-rtse. That statement coincides with accounts that relate how Mu-rum bTsan-po was a full eighteen or about nineteen years old in the female Water Bird year (Tibetan year 2710, 793 CE) when he married Queen lHa-rtse who gave birth to the son lDing-khri and when the latter was a full eleven or about twelve years old, the father Mu-rum bTsan-po died and the father's younger brother ascended to the throne. That could appear problematic, but according to formulations in Tibetan religious and dynastic histories, all children and queens attributed to lDing-khri should be recognized as the queens and children of Khri-lde Srong-btsan Sad-na-legs.

Khri-lde Srong-btsan built the dKar-chung Vajradhātu [rDo-rje dByings] Temple at sKyid-shod. He introduced a law promulgating the supreme value of the sacred Buddhadharma among all ministers and subjects. The names of three queens are indicated among those who swore the oath. According to the edict quoted in the *lHo brag chos 'byung*, these three queens were (Pe, Vol. I, 411, 21):

> Her Majesty 'Bro-gza' Khri-mo-legs, Her Majesty mChims-rgyal-gza' Legs-mo-brtsan, and Her Majesty Cog-ro-gza' brTsan-rgyal.

And it also specifies (ibid., 414, 7):

> Some among the senior wife's three children, who were born first, and the junior wife's two children, who came last, died. In any case, two younger siblings died when they were small.

The *Deb ther dpyid kyi rgyal mo'i glu dbyangs* lists the children in this order (Pe, 69, 5):

> That king had five sons: gTsang-ma, lHa-rje, lHun-grub, Dar-ma, [and] Ral-pa-can.

If one examines the various religious and dynastic histories, the following emerges: of the four princesses married by Khri-lde Srong-btsan, the senior wife was called in at least four different ways, 'Bro-gza' Ma-mo lHa-rgyal, 'Bro-gza' Khri-mo-legs, 'Bro-gza' lHa-rgyal Gung-skar-ma, and 'Bro-gza' Mang-po lHa-rgyal. She had three sons, Khri gTsang-ma, Khri Dar-ma 'U-dum-btsan, and Khri-gtsug lDe-btsan. There were also three junior wives: Cog-ro-gza' brTsan-rgyal, Pho-yongs-gza' lHa-btsun, and mChims-rgyal-gza' Legs-mo-brtsan. It is certain that one of the three secondary wives gave birth to lHa-rje and lHun-grub, also known as lHa-rje lHun-grub, and to Khri-chen lDe'u; but because historical documents do not specify of which junior wife they were the children it remains a difficult point to ascertain.

The identity of the chief ministers of Khri-lde Srong-btsan can be determined through the following sources. The *sBa bzhed* says (Si, 179, 17):

'Bro Khri-gzung was appointed as minister.

The *lDe'u rgya bod kyi chos 'byung* says (Bod, 359, 11):

'Bring-gzung Ram-shags was minister for eight years. mChims-rtsang bZher-legs was minister for five years. sBa-mang-rje lHa-lod was minister for one year.

The *lHo brag chos 'byung* reports the words of the dKar-chung Edict and says (Pe, Vol. I, 412, 2):

The Buddhist monks Bran-ka Yon-Tan [and] Myang Ting-'dzin are included among the chief ministers in charge of religious affairs. Zhang-'bro Khri-gzu Ram-shags, Zhang mChims-rgyal bTsan-bzher Legs-gzigs, dBa'-blon Mang-rje lHa-lod, dBas-blon Khri-sum bZher-mdo-btsan, Zhang mChims-rgyal lHa-bzher Ne-shags, [and] Rlang-blon Khri-sum rJe-speg-lha are included among the chief ministers in charge of political affairs.

Concerning the time of Khri-lde Srong-btsan's death, the *lDe'u rgya bod kyi chos 'byung* says (Bod, 359, 10):

After [he] reached the age of forty, [he] died in the autumn of the Sheep year at Phu [in] sGrags.

The *lDe'u chos 'byung chen mo* says (Bod, 133, 17):

After [he] reached the age of forty-four, [he] died in the autumn of the Sheep year at Phu in sGrags.

These two texts differ by four years, but we should remember that the *lDe'u rgya bod kyi chos 'byung* was composed later. Even if it is certain that forty is the basic idea implied, if the year of death is identified with the female Wood Sheep year when Khri-lde Srong-btsan would have been a full thirty-nine or about forty years old or as in the *rGya'i thang yig rnying ma* [Old Chronicles of the Chinese Táng 唐 dynasty] his death is posited in the female Fire Bird year (Tibetan year 2734, 817 CE) when Khri-lde Srong-btsan reached the age of a full forty-one or about forty-two years, these ideas are generally compatibile.

The *Nyang gi chos 'byung* says (Bod, 416, 18):

> He] departed for heaven [at the age of] fifty-four in the Fire Bird [year].

The text relates that Khri-lde Srong-btsan died in the Fire Bird year (Tibetan year 2734, 817 CE) when he was fifty-four, that is to say, after he reached the full age of fifty-three. In accordance with that, the year of his birth should be the male Wood Dragon year (Tibetan year 2681, 764 CE) (2734-53=2681; 817-53=764), but given that the *Tun hong bod kyi lo rgyus yig rnying* [Old Tibetan Chronicles of Dunhuang] do not record a birth among the events that occurred in that year, it seems to me that his true year of birth should be identified with the male Fire Dragon year (Tibetan year 2693, 776 CE).

All the famous religious and dynastic histories, such as the *Grags rgyal bod kyi rgyal rabs*, the *Ne'u sngon byung gi gtam*, the *Yar lung jo bo'i chos 'byung*, the *Deb ther dmar po*, the *lHo brag chos 'byung*, and the *rGya bod yig tshang chen mo*, adhere to the conclusion presented in the *Nyang gi chos 'byung* and agree in identifying the year of death of Khri-lde Srong-btsan with the female Fire Bird year (Tibetan year 2734, 817 CE).

As for the tomb of Khri-lde Srong-btsan, the *rGyal rabs gsal ba'i me long* says (Pe, 225,16):

> His tomb was built at Don-'khor-mda'. The name was Kya-ri Kyang-ldem.

Although this is the real location of the tomb, the *Me long ma* says that this tomb is the one built for Prince Mu-tig bTsan-po who was killed by the sNa-nam-pa; however the *Nyang gi chos 'byung* clearly specifies (Bod, 414, 17) that the tomb of that prince was "built at rGya-bo Zang-zang." That settles the matter.

11. THE FORTY-FOURTH RULER OF TIBET:
KHRI-GTSUG LDE-BTSAN

The name with which this monarch is generally known, Khri-gtsug lDe-btsan, is a name that combines Zhang Zhung and Tibetan words. The Zhang Zhung word *khri* means *lha* [deity or divine] and *thugs* (mind or heart) in Tibetan; *gtsug* indicates the crown of the head, and by implication, the supreme [*ches mtho*] or superior [*mchog*]; in the Zhang Zhung language *tsug* means virtue and knowledge; in Tibetan *lde* means wise; *btsan* or *btsan po* is an archaic term meaning sharp or keen [*rnon po*] and *rab* [excellent]. Thus, if we were to consider the whole name in modern Tibetan, it would correspond to Thugs-mchog mKhyen-rab [Superior Mind with Excellent Knowledge].

Another name of this ruler is Ral-pa-can, because he had long, matted hair; when the two names are abridged he is known as Khri-ral.

The *Nyang gi chos 'byung* calls the king Khri-chen 'De'u, which is definitely a special name.

The *sBa bzhed* says (Si, 181, 10):

> When the elder brother Khri-gtsug lDe-btsan reached the age of ten, [he] was empowered and ascended to the throne.

Since this authoritative source considers him the eldest among the five children of Khri-lde Srong-bgtsan, several famous dynastic and religious histories, such as the *Nyang gi chos 'byung*, the *Ne'u sngon byung gi gtam*, the *Bu ston chos 'byung*, the *Klong chen pa'i chos 'byung*, the *Me long rnam gsal*, the *Bod kyi yig tshang*, the *rGyal rabs 'phrul gyi lde mig*, and the *lHa thog rgyal rabs*, have adopted the same view and have traditionally maintained the propriety of the ascension to the throne of King Khri-gtsug lDe-btsan Ral-pa-can shortly after the death of the father Khri-lde Srong-btsan because he was the eldest prince.

The two *lDe'u chos 'byung* are problematic sources concerning the era of King Khri-lde gTsug-btsan. For example, they give the names of the children of King Khri-lde Srong-btsan, recording them in the following order:

lHa-rje and lHun-grub died at an early age. Then there were Khri Ral-pa-can, gTsang-ma, and Dar-ma.

The *lDe'u rgya bod kyi chos 'byung* says (Bod, 364, 14):

> The elder one was killed, the younger one was exiled. [He] was murdered after having ruled for one-and-a-half years. The light of the Buddhadharma was buried for seven generations. It is said that also this king was born at 'On-ljang-rdo in the Sheep year.

This text provides the year of birth of Khri Dar-ma 'U-dum-btsan and at the same time it says "the elder one was killed;" but even if it says "elder brother" [*gcen po*], the "It is said" [*skad pa*] in the third line indicates that this is simply an explanation and a view not shared by the text, because the *lDe'u* itself proceeds by saying (Bod, 364, 16):

> ... [B]orn in the Sheep year at 'On-ljang-rdo. The father departed for heaven when [the son] was twelve.

With this statement the text clearly agrees that the father Khri-lde Srong-tsan died in the Sheep year. We have already seen that this year corresponds to the female Wood Sheep year of the first *sMe-phreng* of the sixteenth *sMe-'khor* (Tibetan year 2732, 815 CE) in the section dedicated to Khri-lde Srong-tsan. If Khri Dar-ma had reached the age of twelve when the father died, no other year is possible for his birth except for the female Water Sheep year of the first *sMe-phreng* of the sixteenth *sMe-'khor* (Tibetan year 2720 803 CE); hence the theory of the *lDe'u chos 'byung* is that Khri-gtsug lDe-btsan was the younger brother of Khri Dar-ma.

The *Grags rgyal bod kyi rgyal rabs* says (sDe, TA, 597, 5):

> Khri gTsang-ma was the eldest of the three sons generated from his (Khri-lde Srong-btsan's) marriage to 'Bro-bza' lHa-rgyal Gung-skar-ma.

And also (ibid., 597, 6):

> Since Glang-dar-ma was brainless, hideous, and monkey-headed, he was not enthroned. The younger one, Khri gTsug-lde Ral-pa-can...

The text not only shows that Khri Dar-ma was the elder brother and that Khri-gtsug lDe-btsan was the younger one, but also states the cause that prevented Khri Dar-ma from occupying the throne.

Many famous and authoritative religious and dynastic histories such as the *Yar lung jo bo'i chos 'byung*, the *Deb ther dmar po*, the *rGyal rabs gsal ba'i me long*, the *lHo brag chos 'byung*, the *rGya bod yig tshang chen mo*, the *Deb ther dpyid kyi rgyal mo'i glu dbyangs*, and the *Legs bshad rin po che'i mdzod* have endorsed this theory as a logical choice. The reason is to be found in Tibetan politics.

In previous times the life of the Dharmarāja Khri-lde gTsug-brtan was endangered; for that reason the young Dharmarāja Khri-srong lDe'u-btsan could not take political power in his own hands for many years. Eventually when he was able to firmly seize that power he suppressed Bon and punished many ministers who were supporters of that religion.

Khri Dar-ma was the elder prince and in principle had the right to be enthroned, but his stubborn and thick-headed character and his continuous ill-advised behavior caused him to be denied the kingship. That is why his younger brother Khri-gtsug lDe-btsan Ral-pa-can was enthroned. Khri-gtsug lDe-btsan Ral-pa-can was a fervent Buddhist and many ministers who adhered to Bon were not happy about that. In the end they managed to kill King Ral-pa-can through evil deception and to install Khri Dar-ma 'U-dum-btsan on the throne. He was not enthroned before then, even if in principle he was of a suitable age. His younger brother Khri-gTsug lDe-btsan had been exalted by the powerful Buddhist ministers due to his noble act of spreading of the Buddhadharma; thus, in a wicked act of reprisal, Khri Dar-ma 'U-dum-btsan allied himself with the Bonpo ministers and suppressed the Buddhadharma. The relentless killing of Buddhist ministers and Buddhist practitioners was generated by those causes and conditions.

Concerning the time and place of birth of King Khri-gtsug lDe-btsan, the *lDe'u rgya bod kyi chos 'byung* says (Bod, 359, 16):

[He] too was born at 'On-ljang-rdo in the Dog year.

And also (ibid., 362, 13):

Then, after [he] reached the age of forty-one, the younger
brother Dar-ma usurped the throne. The vassals killed him at
Lan-dkar in the Mouse year.

From this citation we gather that he was born in the male Wood Dog
year (Tibetan year 2711, 794 CE) when his father Khri-lde Srong-btsan
was eighteen years old and that he was killed when he was thirty-eight
in the male Water Mouse year (Tibetan year 2749, 832 CE); but if we
count about forty-one years or a full forty-one years backward from
the Mouse year, the year of birth should be either the Tiger year or
the Rabbit year; therefore it is not possible that the murder happened
in the Mouse year.

Also the *lDe'u chos 'byung chen mo* gives approximately the same
information about the year of birth; concerning the year of death it
says (Bod, 137, 14):

In the end, when [he] was forty, he died in the autumn of the
Sheep year at Phu in bsGrags.

The text clearly affirms that he died in the Sheep year at the age of forty.
If from any Dog year suitable for his birth we add about forty years, we
arrive at the Ox year; if we add a full forty years we reach the Tiger year;
therefore it is not possible that the murder happened in the Sheep year.

If we assume that the year of death was the Sheep year he must
have lived for a full thirty-three years. The *rGya'i lo rgyus thung cen* says
(Dha, 233, 10):

In the Earth Horse [year] (838 CE) the Tibetan King Yi Tha'o
(Khri Ral-pa-can) died. His younger brother Glang-dar-ma took
the royal throne.

Since no more than one year's difference exists, we can determine that
the Sheep year in which Khri-gtsug lDe-btsan died was the male Earth
Sheep year (Tibetan year 2756, 839 CE); and we can also determine
that the Dog year of birth is the male Fire Dog year (Tibetan year
2723, 806 CE), which corresponds to two full years after the enthronement of the father Mu-tig bTsan-po, also known as Khri-lDe
Srong-btsan Sad-na-legs.

This opinion corresponds to what the *Ne'u sngon byung gi gtam* affirms (Dha, 11, 6, 6):

> Khri-gtsug lDe-btsan Ral-pa-can was born at Phu in 'On-cang-mdo in the male Fire Dog [year].

The *Bu ston chos 'byung* does not give a year of birth, but concerning the year of death it says (lHa,130, 4):

> In the female Metal Bird [year, when] the king was thirty-six, [he] was attacked from behind by dBa'-rgyal To-re and Co-ro Legs-sgra who killed [him].

The text says that he was killed in the female Metal Bird year (Tibetan year 2758, 841 CE). This date is about two full years late with respect to the year in which he died; but in fact, the text says that the year of birth was the male Fire Dog year (Tibetan year 2723, 806 CE), in conspicuous agreement that the king lived for thirty-six years. Most religious and dynastic histories such as the *Klong chen pa'i chos 'byung*, the *Yar lung jo bo'i chos 'byung*, the *Deb ther dmar po*, the *rGyal rabs gsal ba'i me long*, the *lHo brag chos 'byung*, the *rGya bod yig tshang chen mo*, the *rGyal rabs 'phrul gyi lde mig*, the *Klu sgrub bstan rtsis*, and the *Deb ther dpyid kyi rgyal mo'i glu dbyangs* have adopted this viewpoint and have traditionally agreed that the ruler Khri Ral-pa-can, also known as Khri-gtsug lDe-btsan, was born in the male Fire Dog year (Tibetan year 2723, 806 CE).

The *Nyang gi chos 'byung* says (Bod, 417, 2):

> The elder brother Khri-gtsug lDe-btsan, the Ruler Ral-pa-can, emanation of the Lord of Secrets Phyag-na rDo-rje [Vajrapāṇi], was born in the male Water Dragon [year]. In the Fire Bird year, when he reached the age of twelve, he was enthroned.

The text identifies the year of birth with the Water Dragon year. According to this reckoning Khri-gtsug lDe-btsan should have been born in the male Water Dragon year (Tibetan year 2729, 812 CE) when his father Khri-lde Srong-btsan was a full thirty-six years old and should have been a full four years old when the father was enthroned. If Khri-gtsug lDe-btsan was enthroned at twelve, it is obviously impossible for the year in question to be the Fire Bird year: it should rather be the female Water Rabbit year (Tibetan year 2740, 823 CE) or, if we consider the entire year, the male Wood Dragon year (Tibetan year -2742, 824 CE). If he was enthroned at twelve in the Fire Bird year, then the words Water Dragon year appearing in the text in relation to the year of his birth are definitely a scribal error. If we count twelve years backward from the Fire Bird year of his enthronement (Tibetan year 2734, 817 CE), we receive the clear proof that the year of birth of Khri-gtsug lDe-btsan was the Fire Dog year.

Concerning the time in which Khri-gtsug lDe-btsan Ral-pa-can was enthroned and reigned, the *sBa bzhed* says (Si, 181, 10):

> When the elder brother Khri-gtsug lDe-btsan reached the age of ten, he was empowered and [started to] rule.

For this reason the *Klong chen pa'i chos 'byung* and other sources have traditionally adopted this viewpoint. The *lDe'u rgya bod kyi chos 'byung* says (Bod, 359, 16):

> When [he] was two years old, the father died. He took power when he was twelve.

The text says that the father died when he was two; however, the *lDe'u chos 'byung chen mo* (Bod, 134, 2) says:

> When [the son] was twenty-two, the father departed for heaven; he ruled for twenty-two years.

The *lDe'u rgya bod kyi chos 'byung* says "two" and omits "ten"; that is in contrast with the *lDe'u chos 'byung chen mo*, which says that the age of enthronement was twenty-two, therefore "twelve" is a scribal error. The *Nyang gi chos 'byung* shows how such kind of mistakes can occur (Bod, 417, 3):

> [He] reached the age of twelve and in the Fire Bird year ascended to the throne.

Most dynastic and religious histories, such as the *Ne'u sngon byung gi gtam* the *Yar lung jo bo'i chos 'byung*, the *Deb ther dmar po*, the *rGyal rabs gsal*] *me long,* the *lHo brag chos 'byung,* the *rGya bod yig tshang chen mo,* the *rGyal rabs 'phrul gyi lde mig,* and the *Klu sgrub bstan rtsis,* adopting the perspective of both the *lDe'u chos 'byung* and the *Nyang gi chos 'byung,* generally agree that Khri-gtsug lDe-btsan took power and was enthroned in the female Fire Bird year (Tibetan year 2739, 817 CE) at the age of twenty-two and that twenty-two years elapsed until he died in the female Earth Sheep year (Tibetan year 2756, 839 CE).

The *Bu ston chos 'byung* presents a different outlook and says (lHa, 130, 3):

He seized power when [he] reached the age of eighteen,

but it does not provide any explanation as to its meaning and origin.

Concerning the consorts, children, and ministers of Khri-gtsug lDe-btsan, the *sBa bzhed* says (Si, 181, 11):

He married Queen gCo-ro-bza' dPal-gyi Ngang-tshul-can, and so on. The minister for external affairs was sBa Mang-rje lHa-lod. The Mahāpaṇḍita dPal-gyi Yon-tan was the chief minister for religious affairs.

This source gives only the name of the first queen and adds "and so on," which obviously implies the existence of other consorts. Regarding the chief ministers, the *lDe'u rgya bod kyi chos 'byung* says (Bod, 359, 17):

[His] ministers were sBa Mang-rje lHa-lod and 'Bring-khri gSum-rje sTag-snang. Bran-ka dPal-gyi Yon-tan was [also a] minister.

Furthermore, the *lDe'u chos 'byung chen mo* mentions the building of temples requested by the queens, providing the names of three [of them]: Cog-ro-bza' dPal-gyi Ngang-tshul, mChims-bza' Yon-tan sGron-ma, and Tshes-spong-bza' Yum-chen bTsan-mo-phan.

The *Nyang gi chos 'byung* indicates the names of the five princesses he married (Bod, 417, 5):

[He] married five [women]: Cog-ro bza' dPal-gyi Ngang-tshul-ma, mChims-bza' Khyung-dkar-ma, sNa-nam-bza' A-rje Pho-legs, Tshe-spong-bza' lHun-gyi Bu-mo, [and] lHa-lung-bza' Me-tog-ma.

And also (ibid., 420, 8):

> The children born to the queens were carried away by water
> spirits [Chu-sman], so he had no offspring. The subjects were
> happy anyway.

The *Klon chen pa'i chos 'byung*, by saying that (Dhi, 212, 384, 3):

> [He] married five princesses, gCo-ro-bza' dPal-gyi Ngang-tshul-
> ma, and so on,

clearly attests to the fact that he had five queens. The proof that they
did not bear any children is provided by the *Deb ther dmar po* (Pe, 39, 18):

> Since this king had no descendants, King Glang-dar-ma was
> installed on the throne.

And by the *rGya bod yig tshang chen mo* (Si, 206, 6):

> Although [he] had five [consorts], mChims-bza' dKar-rgyal,
> sNa-nam-bza' Mang-po Khod-legs, Nyang-bza' mChog-gi lHa-
> mo, Tshe-spong-bza', [and] mDo-rgyal-ma, he did not have any
> progeny.

Concerning the time of death of Khri-gtsug lDe-btsan, the *sBa bzhed*
says that he died but does not say when (Si, 189, 8):

> The evil matrilinear ministers consulted each other, conspired
> to destroy the Dharma laws, and decided that the Dharma laws
> could not be abolished without the death of the king.
> Some said, "Ral-pa-can has no children. His younger brother
> Prince gTsang-ma favors the Dharma laws, so he is in power.
> Therefore the Dharma laws will not be destroyed."
> [Some] said, "Would we succeed if we exiled gTsang-ma? But
> in that case, the power of the Monk Minister who is [obviously]
> well-disposed toward the Dharma laws would be even greater.
> Therefore the Dharma laws cannot be destroyed."
> Having consulted each other, [they decided to] use calumny
> in order to destroy the Dharma laws. [They spread the rumor
> that] the Monk Minister and Ngang-tshul-ma fornicated se-
> cretly and [reported it to the king], requesting a severe punish-

ment. The Monk Minister had not yet attained the realization of the practice of the root *sādhanā* of the Iron Life-force [*lcags kyi srog pa rtsa sgrub pa*], so the rumor had a serious effect and he was killed.

Prince gTsang-ma was immediately ordained and after an extensive farewell ceremony was exiled to sPa-gro in Mon.

The merits of Tibet declined and the demons became stronger, influencing the hearts of all the black-headed people.

lCog-ro heard the news about the prince and became unhappy. While the king was drinking Chinese rice beer, a bribed accomplice[71] killed lCog-ro by twisting [his] neck.

The two *lDe'u chos 'byung* clearly mention the time of death, after having abundantly elaborated upon the treachery of the evildoers. When discussing the year of birth we have already seen that the two sources give the female Earth Sheep year (Tibetan year 2756, 839 CE) as the year of his death when he was a full thirty-three years old.

The *Ne'u sngon byung gi gtam* says (Dha, 11, 6, 7):

[He] died at thirty-six in the Iron Bird [year].

This source posits the female Iron Bird year (Tibetan year 2758, 841 CE) as the year of King Khri-gtsug lDe-btsan's death at the age of thirty-six. This date is two full years or about three years later than the one provided by the *lDe'u chos 'byung*, so the difference does not seem that large.

Several dynastic and religious histories such as the *Bu ston chos 'byung*, the *Klong chen pa'i chos 'byung*, the *Yar lung jo bo'i chos 'byung*, the *Deb ther dmar po*, the *rGyal rabs gsal ba'i me long*, the *lHo brag chos 'byung*, the *rGya bod yig tshang chen mo*, the *rGyal rabs 'phrul gyi lde mig*, the *Klu sgrub bstan rtsis*, and the *lHa thog rgyal rabs* adhere to this view and identify the year of death of King Khri-gtsug lDe-btsan as the female Iron Bird year (Tibetan year 2758, 841 CE).

---

71   *bya phu bgyis*: a person who engages in a conspiracy in exchange for remuneration or for the gain of an official ministerial rank.

Even so, the true year of death of King Khri-gtsug lDe-btsan is close to the date of the female Earth Sheep year (Tibetan year 2756, 839 CE) provided by the two *lDe'u chos 'byungs*.

The viewpoint according to which he ascended to the throne in the Fire Bird year (Tibetan year 2734, 817 CE) when he was a full eleven or about twelve years old and ruled for a full twenty-one or about twenty-two years is historically recognized and coincides quite well; although the *rGya'i lo rgyus thung cen* says (Dha, 233, 10):

> In the Earth Horse [year] (838 CE) the Tibetan King Yi Tha'o
> (Khri Ral-pa-can) died. His younger brother Glang-dar-ma took
> the royal throne.

The *lDe'u chos 'byung* says that he ruled for twenty-two years. If this time is reckoned as twenty-two full years, the year of death is the female Earth Sheep year, but if only the beginning of the year is considered, the twenty-second year would correspond to the male Earth Horse year (Tibetan year 2755, 838 CE). Therefore the real year of death of King Khri-gtsug lDe-btsan is certainly this one.

As for the tomb of Khri-gtsug lDe-btsan Ral-pa-can, the *rGyal rabs gsal ba'i me long* specifies (Pe, 234, 5):

> The tomb of the ruler Ral-pa-can was built on the left corner
> of Don-mkhar-mda'. That tomb as well was filled with precious
> jewels. It was called Khri-steng rMang-ri. So it is said.

12. THE FORTY-FIFTH RULER OF TIBET:
KHRI DAR-MA 'U-DUM-BTSAN

The real name of this king is Khri Dar-ma 'U-dum-btsan, but the name with which he is universally known is Glang-dar-ma. The reason for this appellation is recorded in the *lHo brag chos 'byung* (Pe, Vol. I, 425, 13):

> The subjects called him Glang-dar-ma [adult bull] because he
> was stubborn, of little understanding, and had a body with the
> form of a bull.

The *rGyal rabs 'phrul gyi lde mig* says (Dhi, 10, 25, 5):

> From then on, people called the king Bull. Calling [him] with
> the name of an animal: how appropriate.

The quotation shows that the designation of Bull was obviously attributed to this king on account of the innumerable misdeeds he performed, because he had a stubborn, obstinate character, and also because
he was dim-witted, "as dense as a bull" [*mi glen pa glang lta bu*], as the
ancient saying goes.

However, it is certain that the epithet Bull was not meant disre-
spectfully. The *sBa bzhed* says (179, 15):

> Because [he] had a crooked neck and a powerful body, he was
> also known as Glang-mjing-yon [Crooked-Necked Bull].

Since also Khri-gtsug lDe-btsan was styled Bull, it is possible that
people with a large body and great strength would be called with that
nickname. Furthermore, we know that attributing the names of animals
to people was not a sign of irreverence, because the Buddha himself
was called the Lion of human beings. In the lineage of the masters
and accomplished scholars of the illustrious 'Brug-pa [bKa'-brgyud]
tradition, a succession of individuals were called Lion. Also many
famous masters, like the great Indian logician dPal-ldan Phyogs-kyi
Glang-po [Dignāga, c. 480 – c. 540 CE], had animal names as part
of their designations.

Some people said that Khri Dar-ma 'U-dum-btsan disliked the
Buddhadharma and was devoted to Bon and for that reason he suppressed the Buddhadharma in order to implement the spreading of
Bon. However, there is no truth in that. This is demonstrated by the
lDe'u chos 'byung chen mo, which makes clear that the king punished even
his own royal guard [sKu-gshen] (Bod, 140, 15):

> [He] incriminated the royal expert of sacred formulas [*sku'i
> sngags mkhan*] and the royal guard.

Moreover, information about Khri Dar-ma's proclivity for heinous
deeds and all sorts of debauchery are related not only in Buddhist

histories, but also in Bonpo religious and dynastic histories. For example the *Legs bshad rin po che'i mdzod* says (Pe, 134, 19):

> Since Dar-ma suppressed the Buddhadharma and performed many senseless acts, he became known as Dar-ma the Monkey-Head.

The text indicates that Dar-ma destroyed the Buddhadharma, but does not speak at all about his subduing the Bon, suggesting that he might have actually contributed to the spreading of the Bonpo tenets. However, that would be an illogical proposition. The Bon had already been completely crushed at the time of King Khri-srong lDe'u-btsan and it was not an option to do that again.

Moreover as is known, each monarch used to have a Bon-gShen as a royal guard [sKu-gshen] in order to maintain a connection with the ancient tradition, but Khri Dar-ma discredited his own [protector], meaning that he was not at all interested in furthering the Bon teachings. The idea that Khri Dar-ma hated the Buddhadharma and was favorable to Bon is certainly due to the fact that the ministers who supported his enthronement were extremely hostile to the Buddhadharma.

Khri is a Zhang Zhung word that in Tibetan means *lha* [deity or divine]; *dar ma* [adult] is easy to understand, since it is well-known both as an old and a new Tibetan term. In the *Tun hong bod kyi lo rgyus yig rnying* [Old Tibetan Chronicles of Dunhuang] the name of this king is 'U'i-dum-brtan; this too is a designation related to the ancient Zhang Zhung language: *'u* comes from the Zhang Zhung word *u* or *u-yi*. The *lHo brag chos 'byung* calls the king U-dum bTsan-po for this precise reason: *u* means *gsang ba* [secret] in Tibetan; and *dum* means *rnam pa* [aspect or manifestation]. Hence, in modern Tibetan, his name would be gSang-rnam rGyal-po [King of the Secret Manifestation]. Not surprisingly, also this name was conferred by a Bonpo royal guard [sKu-gshen] in accordance with the ancient custom.

In order to determine the time of birth of this king, the crucial element that needs to be firmly established from the beginning is whether he was the younger or the elder brother of Khri-lde gTsug-btsan.

As we have seen in the section dedicated to the Forty-fourth Ruler of Tibet, Khri-lde gTsug-btsan, several religious and dynastic histories such as the *sBa bzhed*, the *Nyang gi chos 'byung*, the *Ne'u sngon byung gi gtam*, the *Bu ston chos 'byung*, the *Klong chen pa'i chos 'byung*, the *Me long rnam gsal*, the *Bod kyi yig tshang*, the *rGyal rabs 'phrul gyi lde mig*, and the *lHa thog rgyal rabs* assert that Khri Dar-ma was the younger brother of Khri-lde gTsug-btsan. Other Bonpo and Buddhist sources such as the *lDe'u chos 'byung*, the *Grags rgyal bod kyi rgyal rabs*, the *Yar lung jo bo'i chos 'byung*, the *Deb ther dmar po*, the *rGyal rabs gsal ba'i me long*, the *lHo brag chos 'byung*, the *rGya bod yig tshang chen mo*, the *Deb ther dpyid kyi rgyal mo'i glu dbyangs*, and the *Legs bshad rin po che'i mdzod* maintain that he was the elder brother of Khri-lde gTsug-btsan.

It is not necessary to discuss at this point the possibility that Khri Dar-ma was the younger brother of Khri-lde gTsug-btsan because its historical consistency is nil. Taking into consideration the probability that Khri Dar-ma was the elder brother of Khri-lde gTsug-btsan, we may start by quoting the *lDe'u rgya bod kyi chos 'byung*, which says (Bod, 364,16):

Also this monarch was born in the Sheep year at 'On-ljang-rdo.

The text simply indicates that the year of birth was the Sheep year without specifying the element of that year, but further in the text we read, "After he was twelve, the father departed for heaven." If Khri Dar-ma had reached the age of twelve when his father Khri-lde Srong-btsan died, we can discover the date of his birth by calculating twelve years back from the female Wood Sheep year (Tibetan year 2732, 815 CE) which corresponds to the year of death of the father Khri-lde Srong-btsan; in this way we arrive at the female Water Sheep year (Tibetan year 2720, 803 CE).

Only small differences are found when comparing *lDe'u chos 'byung chen mo* with *lDe'u rgya bod kyi chos 'byung*. However, since mKhas-pa lDe'u [1085-1171] first drafted the *lDe'u chos 'byung chen mo* and then proceeded to compile *lDe'u rgya bod kyi chos 'byung* which is a more detailed text, the historical gist should be looked for in the *lDe'u rgya bod kyi chos 'byung*. Any unclear or doubtful point in the latter text can be resolved by consulting the *lDe'u chos 'byung chen mo*; in this way it is possible to capture the original viewpoint of mKhas-pa lDe'u.

The *Yar lung jo bo'i chos 'byung* says (Si, 67, 2):

King Glang-dar-ma was born in the female Water Sheep year.

The *lHo brag chos 'byung* says (Pe, Vol. I, 425, 12):

Khri Dar-ma U-dum-btsan was born three years before Khri-ral in the female Water Sheep [year].

Through these two sources we obtain the element of the year of his birth.

A note in the *rGyal rabs gsal ba'i me long* says (Pe, 237, 7):

King Glang-dar-ma was born in the Ox year.

Also this dynastic history asserts that the younger brother Khri-lde gTsug-btsan was born in the male Fire Dog year and that Khri Dar-ma was his elder brother. In accordance with that, the Ox year birth of Khri Dar-ma would be that of the female Fire Ox (Tibetan year 2714, 797 CE): this date is earlier than the time of death of the forefather Khri-srong lDe'u-btsan. Furthermore, he should have been enthroned when he was forty-one in the male Earth Horse year (Tibetan year 2755, 838 CE), after the death of his younger brother Khri-gtsug lDe-btsan. In this regard the same note says (ibid., 237, 7):

He was enthroned in the Bird year.

There is no way to justify this date: it cannot correspond to the Fire Bird year (Tibetan year 2734, 817 CE) because that year his younger brother Khri-gtsug lDe-btsan ascended to the throne; nor can it be the Earth Bird year (Tibetan year 2746, 829 CE) because the text itself says that the younger brother Khri-gtsug lDe-btsan died in the female Metal Bird year [841 CE]. The same comment also states (ibid., 237, 8):

[He] died in the Tiger year at the age of thirty-eight.

If that was true, Khri Dar-ma should have died in the male Wood Tiger year (Tibetan year 2751 834 CE); but the text itself says that the younger brother Khri-gtsug lDe-btsan died at thirty-six in the female Metal Bird year, in which case this date would have been seven years too soon. Be that as it may, I see no point in further examining this totally incorrect calculation that seems ascertained by someone who could not even count years. In synthesis, the true year of birth of Glang-dar-ma 'U-dum-btsan was the female Water Sheep year of the first *sMe-phreng* of the sixteenth *sMe-'khor* (Tibetan year 2720, 803 CE).

Concerning the time of enthronement, the consorts, children, and ministers of King Khri Dar-ma, I begin by citing the *lDe'u rgya bod kyi chos 'byung* which says (Bod, 364, 16):

> After [Khri Dar-ma] was twelve, the father departed for heaven. [He] ruled for one year and a halfmonth. In the Tiger year, at the age of thirty-two, [he] was killed by lHa-lung dPal-gyi rDo-rje.

According to this text Khri Dar-ma was killed by lHa-lung dPal-gyi rDo-rje in the male Wood Tiger year (Tibetan year 2751, 834 CE). The time [the text] refers to in "After he was twelve the father departed for heaven" should correspond to the female Fire Bird year (Tibetan year 2734, 817 CE) which is the year of enthronement of the younger brother Khri-gtsug lDe-btsan. If at that time Khri Dar-ma was twelve, his year of birth should have been the female Wood Bird year (Tibetan year 2722, 805 CE); but since this date is two years later than the Sheep year birth of Khri Dar-ma cited by the same text, it is certain that the meaning implied was fourteen.

The text also says, "in the Tiger year, at the age of thirty-two, he was killed by lHa-lung dPal-gyi rDo-rje." The Tiger year in which he was thirty-two is the male Wood Tiger year (Tibetan year 2751, 834 CE); moreover, saying that Khri Dar-ma ruled only for one year and-a-half-month implicitly indicates that he was enthroned in the female Water Ox year.

The *Nyang gi chos 'byung* says (Bod, 428, 21):

> King Dar-ma 'U-dum-btsan-po seized political power at the age of nineteen. He was empowered as king. All the Tibetan vassals who were hostile to the Buddhadharma appointed the monkey-headed dBas-rgyal To-re who disliked the Buddhadharma as minister of internal affairs. sNa-nam rGyal-tsha Khri-'bum rJe-khra mGo-ba was appointed as the minister of foreign affairs.

This text says that Khri Dar-ma was enthroned when he was nineteen. It also considers Khri Dar-ma as the younger brother of Khri-gtsug lDe-btsan Ral-pa-can and asserts that in the female Fire Bird year (Tibetan year 2794, 877 CE) Khri-gtsug lDe-btsan died and Khri Dar-ma ascended to the throne. According to that, the birth year of Khri Dar-ma should have been the male Earth Tiger year (Tibetan year 2775, 858 CE). If that were the case, the year of birth of Khri Dar-ma and the year of death of Khri Ral-pa-can would be too far apart and would hardly coincide with the historical context: the root of the problem is the above-mentioned quotation saying that Khri Ral-pa-can "departed for heaven in the Fire Bird [year] at the age of fifty-four."

Therefore, the basic idea that needs investigating is whether he died at the age of fifty-four or at the age of thirty-five in the female Metal Bird year (Tibetan year 2758, 841 CE), or, as already noted, if we are dealing with an error made by the copyist. In this regard the *Grags rgyal bod kyi rgyal rabs* affirms what may prove to be conclusive (sDe, TA, 198, 5):

> In the female Metal Bird [year] Khri-gtsug lDe-btsan died.

The *Nyang gi chos 'byung* mentions the duration of Khri Dar-ma 'U-dum-btsan's reign (Bod, 440, 5):

> It is said that [he] was king for three years [or] eighteen months, from the age of nineteen until twenty-one.

If we accept that the year of death of Khri-gtsug lDe-btsan and the enthronement of Khri Dar-ma 'U-dum-btsan took place in the Fire Bird year, the year of death of Khri Dar-ma should be the Earth Pig year (Tibetan year 2796, 879 CE); but if we presume that those events occurred in the Metal Bird year, the year of death of Khri Dar-ma would be the Water Pig year (Tibetan year 2760, 843 CE). The *Grags rgyal bod kyi rgyal rabs* says that Khri Dar-ma was killed in the Dog year while the *rGya'i thung cen* says that Khri Dar-ma 'U-dum-btsan died in the male Water Dog year. Between the last two calculations a one year gap exists, although [a real difference] depends on whether the year is considered as completed or not.

The *Grags rgyal bod kyi rgyal rabs* says (sDe, TA, 199, 1):

The middle son, Glang-dar Monkey-Head [sPrel-mgo] [was born in the] Water Sheep year]. When he turned fifteen, the father died. When he was nineteen, the younger brother died. Then he ruled the kingdom: for [the first] six months he ruled poorly; at the end of the female Metal Bird [year] he abolished the sacred Buddhadharma. Then, in the seventh-and-a-half month he was [still] behaving [like an] evil king, yet vaguely promised to be forbearing. [He] ruled for one year [and] a half month. In the Dog year he was killed by the Bodhisattva dPal-gyi rDo-rje.

The text says, "When he was nineteen, the younger brother died," meaning that when he reached that age his younger brother Khri Ral-pa-can died; this is certainly a scribal error, because in a previous passage we read (ibid., 198, 4):

Khri-gtsug lDe-btsan Ral-pa-can was born in the male Fire Dog [year] at 'O-cang-de'u. When this brilliant [being, who was] the youngest of three [brothers], reached the age of twelve, the father died [and] he was enthroned. By the time he was twenty-four, he was ruling two-thirds of the world. It is said that this emanation of the Noble Vajrapāṇi [Phyag-na rDo-rje] died at thirty-six in the Metal Bird [year].

The text affirms that when Khri-gtsug lDe-btsan was twelve his father died and he ascended to the throne and that at that time his elder brother Khri Dar-ma had reached the age of fifteen. The full twenty-third or the ensuing twenty-fourth year of his reign from the Fire Bird year (Tibetan year 2734, 817 CE) in which Khri-gtsug lDe-btsan ascended to the throne corresponds to the female Metal Bird year (Tibetan year 2758, 841 CE); therefore the age at death of the younger brother should be corrected to thirty-nine. In this regard also the affirmation of the *Grags rgyal bod kyi rgyal rabs* quoted above, "at the end of the female Metal Bird [year] [Khri Dar-ma] abolished the sacred Buddhadharma" can be understood as a scribal error, because the *Ne'u sngon byung gi gtam* says (Dha, 12, 6, 2):

When [the elder brother] reached the age of fifteen the father died. The younger brother died at thirty-nine. Then [he] seized power.

The *Yar lung jo bo'i chos 'byung*, in a comparable statement, confirms the information contained in the *Ne'u sngon byung gi gtam*.

The *Klong chen pa'i chos 'byung* says (Dhi, Vol. 2, 233, 395, 4):

King Glang-dar-ma 'U-dum-btsan was enthroned when [he] was nine [*sic*]. [He] appointed the demon [The'u-rang] dBas rGyal-to-re as minister of internal affairs.

And also (ibid., 243, 300, 6):

It is also said that this king remained in power for three years, from the age of eighteen until the age of twenty-one. But another history says that he took power when he was eleven and that he was killed after having reigned for one year five-and-a-half months.

This source evidently follows the *Nyang gi chos 'byung*— "[He] took the kingdom when he was nineteen"—and therefore considers Khri Dar-ma as the younger brother of Khri-gtsug lDe-btsan. It also relates remarkable information according to which Khri Dar-ma lived until he was eleven, ascended to the throne when he was nine, and ruled until he was ten or until the first half of his eleventh year; but it is easy to discern that also this hypothesis is extremely improbable.

The *Deb ther sngon po* affirms (Si, Vol. I, 78, 10):

This female Earth Sheep [year] is the fourth year since Glang-dar-ma's enthronement. He also ruled in the following male Metal Monkey [year] and until the female Metal Bird [year]. In this Metal Bird [year] he abolished the Buddhadharma, and immediately after that was killed by dPal-gyi rDo-rje. For this reason scholars maintain that the era that came after the suppression of the Buddhadharma started in the Metal Bird [year].

In this regard the *Deb ther dmar po* says (Pe, 23, 5):

In the male Fire Dragon [year] the Tibetan king died. In that same year the younger brother called Tha-mu [Glang-dar-ma] ascended to the throne. Since he liked wine and behaved in an iniquitous manner, the whole kingdom of Tibet was disturbed.

According to this information about Tibetan history drawn from the Táng 唐 Chronicles, Khri-gtsug lDe-btsan died in the male Fire Dragon year (Tibetan year 2753, 836 CE) and Khri Dar-ma took the throne; this would indicate that Khri Dar-ma ruled for five full years from the male Fire Dragon year until the female Metal Bird year (Tibetan year 2758, 841 CE).

The *lHo brag chos 'byung* relates (Pe, Vol. 1, 425, 14):

In the Metal Bird [year], when [he] was thirty-nine, [he] ascended to the throne. [He] married two princesses, a senior one and a junior one. The minister was dBa's sTag-rna-can.

And also (ibid., 430, 4):

Thus, King Glang-dar-ma ruled for six years and died in the Fire Tiger [year] at the age of forty-four.

Adhering to the perspective of the *Deb sngon*, the *lHo brag chos 'byung* posits that Khri Dar-ma ruled for five full years or for barely six and that after ascending to the throne in the Metal Bird year, he was killed in the male Fire Tiger year (Tibetan year 2763, 846 CE). Concerning his descendants the text says (ibid., 430, 8):

Many documents recount as follows, "The next year, the female Fire Rabbit [year], the junior wife Tshe-spong-bza' bTsan-mo-'phan had a baby who was conceived in the year of the father's death [*lto bor*]. Fearing that the senior wife might kill or injure [him], she watched over [him] without ever extinguishing the lights. For that reason he was called gNam-lde 'Od-srung [The Heavenly King Protected by Light].

At that time the senior wife sNa-nam-bza' said, "Last night I gave birth to a baby who is [already] teething." After she showed [the baby] the ministers said, "Even though the teeth of the child born last night make a rustling sound [*tseg ge tseg*], he still depends [*brtan*] upon [his] mother [*yum*]." For that reason he was called Khri-lde Yum-brtan [The Heavenly King Who Depends on His Mother].

Yet if it were said that he could not be considered a scion of the royal lineage, Yum-brtan was most probably the ninth descendant in the family line of father, sons, and nephews. Even if [he] was not a descendant, the word of the mother is irrefutable. Therefore the two children of the senior and of the junior [queens] should be regarded as [belonging to] the same lineage. Documents [that] state [the contrary do so] merely on account of their preference for 'Od-srung.

The text indicates the names of the senior and of the junior queens of Khri Dar-ma and that two descendants were born in the female Fire Rabbit year; the designation *lto bor* is used precisely because they were still in their mothers' wombs when the father Khri Dar-ma was murdered by lHa-lung dPal-gyi rDo-rje.

Most religious and dynastic histories, such as the *rGya bod yig tshang chen mo* and the *rGyal rabs 'phrul gyi lde mig*, adopting the point of view of the *Grags rgyal bod kyi rgyal rabs*, traditionally maintained that Khri-gtsug lDe-btsan Ral-pa-can died in the female Metal Bird year (Tibetan year 2758, 841 CE) and that Khri Dar-ma took the throne. However, the *Deb ther dpyid kyi rgyal mo'i glu dbyangs* says (Pe, 75, 13):

Afterward, in the female Water Bird year called *blo ngan*,[72] the wicked minister sBas sTag-sna and others killed the king by twisting his neck.

And also (ibid., 76, 1):

Glang-dar-ma 'U-dum-btsan was empowered as king. sBas sTag-sna became the minister for internal affairs.

This source posits the female Water Bird year (Tibetan year 2770, 853 CE) as the year in which Khri Dar-ma ascended to the throne after Khri-gtsug lDe-btsan was murdered; in this regard the *Ne'u sngon byung gi gtam* says (Dha, 11, 6, 7):

---

72 [*blo ngan* is the name of the female Metal Bird year, the fifty-fifth year of the *rab byung*.]

In the male Water Horse [year] Khri-srong lDe-btsan ruled the
kingdom. In the female Fire Bird [year] Khri-lde gTsug-btsan
died. Until that time the sacred Dharma had flourished greatly
for ninety-nine years. For that reason [those years are known
as] the Generations of Happiness [sKyid-pa'i-rabs].

It would seem that the name Khri-lde gTsug-btsan attributed to Khri-
gtsug lDe-btsan Ral-pa-can is due to the ninety-nine years of the
Generations of Happiness; but Ne'u Paṇḍita asserts that Khri-srong
lDe'u-btsan was born in the male Metal Horse Year. If we count ninety-
nine years from his enthronement which occurred in the male Water
Horse year (Tibetan year 2659, 742 CE) when he was thirteen, we
arrive at the female Metal Bird year (Tibetan year 2758, 841 CE)
(2659+99=2758; 742+99=841), not to the Fire Bird year; therefore the year he meant is certainly the female Metal Bird year. That is
confirmed by what the text says afterward (ibid., 11, 6, 7):

It is said that [he] died in the Metal Bird [year] when [he] was
thirty-six.

To summarize the key historical points: according to the *Grag rgyal rgyal
rabs* and the sources that accept its view Khri Dar-ma 'U-dum-btsan
was born in the female Water Sheep year of the first *sMe-phreng* of the
sixteenth *sMe-'khor* (Tibetan year 2720, 803 CE).

Historical data drawn from the Táng 唐 Chronicles and presented in the *Deb ther dmar po* and in the *Deb ther sngon po* show that in
the male Fire Dragon year (Tibetan year 2753, 836 CE) Khri-gtsug
lDe-btsan Ral-pa-can died and Khri Dar-ma 'U-dum-btsan ascended
to the throne.

Khri Dar-ma ruled for five full years or about six. sBas sTag-sna
was the minister of internal affairs.

Khri Dar-ma married two princesses: the senior queen was sNa-
nam-gza', the junior one Tshe-spong-gza' bTsan-mo-'phan. The son
of the senior wife was Yum-brtan, that of the junior one 'Od-srung.

Even though Khri Dar-ma was the elder brother he was not enthroned because of his love for wine, his wrongdoing, and implicitly because the younger brother Khri-gtsug lDe-btsan was a fervent Buddhist.

Ever since this king ascended to the throne, all kinds of increasingly hostile attitudes toward the Buddhadharma were displayed. In particular, in the female Metal Bird year (Tibetan year 2758, 841 CE), Khri Dar-ma, putting concretely into practice the scheme he had been planning for four years, carried out the despicable action of suppressing the sacred Dharma. For that reason in the same year, he was murdered by lHa-lung dPal-gyi rDo-rje.

It is said that the two sons of Khri Dar-ma 'U-dum-btsan, Yum-brtan and 'Od-srung, were orphans because they were born after the king was murdered, meaning that they were born in the male Water Dog year (Tibetan year 2759, 859 CE). From then on Tibet disintegrated. The way in which the royal lineage was ruling Tibet remained unknown for the time being.

Concerning the tomb of Khri Dar-ma 'U-dum-btsan, since at that time uprisings were rampant all over the Tibetan kingdom, it appears that no opportunity for building his tomb arose. According to the *lHo brag chos 'byung* the circumstances were as follows (Pe, Vol. 1, 433, 4):

> In the ninth year after the insurrections, in the Fire Bird [year] the four [ministers] Shud-pu sTag-rtse and so on discussed the matter [and decided to] allocate the tombs. Most [of the tombs] were exhumed. gNyags [obtained and] disinterred the tomb of Don-mkhar-mda'. Shud-bu [obtained and] disinterred the tomb of Seng-ge-can. The tomb of 'Phrul-rgyal was [obtained and] disinterred by Greng 'Phyos-khu. sNgo-bzher sNyi-ba obtained [one], but was not able to excavate [it] completely. 'Bro [and] Cog obtained Srong-btsan [sGam-po's tomb], but did not disinter [it].

Statues of the three kings Srong-btsan sGam-po, Khri-srong lDe'u-btsan, and Khri Ral-pa-can. rGyal-rtse gTsug-lag-khang, Tibet. Photo: Fosco Maraini. Reprinted from *Prima della tempesta, Tibet 1937 e 1948*, Shang Shung Edizioni, 1990.

IV

Identifying the Written Language
of Tibet in the Later Period

Great scholars and practitioners of the Tibetan Buddhist tradition have universally proclaimed that Tibet did not have a written language, let alone a culture, before the advent of the Dharmarāja Srong-btsan sGam-po. They essentially defined the country as a region of darkness. That story has become exceedingly familiar to the Tibetan people.

1. DID THON-MI SAM-BHO-TA CREATE THE WRITTEN TIBETAN LANGUAGE OR NOT?

The *bKa' chems ka khol ma* says (Kan, 105, 3):

> Then, since King Srong-btsan sGam-po had become powerful in the world, all the monarchs of the bordering countries arrived to present their yearly tributes of foodstuffs and riches. They were told to bring only comestibles and riches and not to send written messages because no written language existed [in Tibet].
>
> Thus, in order that Tibet have a written language, many astute Tibetans were sent to India to learn one, but all of them died, either in clashes [with the Indians] or because the heat killed them. Therefore, among his sixteen ministers, the king

[chose] the brilliant and sagacious Thon-mi Sam-bho-ṭa and sent him [to India] with a full measure [*bre*, circa thirteen kilos] of gold dust to learn the written language.

When Thon-mi Sam-bho-ṭa arrived in the south of India, he encountered a Brahmin who was well-versed in the art of reading and writing called Li-byin Ti-ka. He offered the Brahmin half the gold and requested that he teach him the written language. The Brahmin said, "[Dear] Tibetan child, I know twenty different written languages. Which one would you [like to] study?"

The Brahmin took him to the ocean shore to show him a stone pillar which had twenty kinds of writing beautifully and distinctly carved on it. The young Tibetan [pointed to one of them and] said, "I will learn this one," and trained himself in that writing system [in order to create] a written Tibetan language.

The Indian written language had fifty letters; [Thon-mi Sam-bho-ṭa] included the vowels and consonants [*a li ka li*] and excluded the *Ka* [*sic*] series and the retroflexed series, because these had no phonetic equivalent in Tibetan.

As for the sixteen vocalic letters and [the vowels] *i, o,* and so on, he formulated them mentally and then transposed them verbally.

After he attuned the letters to the Tibetan language, [he realized that] a letter *ca* was needed for the word *gcig*, corresponding to the Indian *ekā* [*sic*, one], so he entered that letter; a letter *cha* was needed for the word *chos, dharma*, so he entered that letter; a letter *ja* was needed for the word *'jigs rten, loka* [world], so he entered that letter; a letter *zha* was needed for the word *zhes, nama* [name, so-called], so he entered that letter; then he entered the letter *'a* to indicate the length of the vowels. In this way he devised five-and-a-half Tibetan letters that did not exist in the Indian language.

In terms of pronunciation, he used a combination of letters to reproduce in writing the natural sounds of Tibetan words. In that regard, [he envisaged in the letters] *ga, da, ba, ma,* [and] *'a*, the five appropriate prefixes, and [in the letters] *ga, nga, da, na, ba, ma, 'a, ra, la, sa*, the ten appropriate suffixes.

He included [the letter] *ca* from [the name of] the Cog-ro region; [the letter] *za* from [the name of the kingdom of] Za-hor; [the letter] *zha* from Zhang Zhung; and [the letter] *'a* from [the name of the] 'A-zha [Principality]. [The letters] *cha* and *ja* arose [spontaneously] in [his] mind. He composed subscript letters with discernment and [further] auxiliary suffixes.

In the end, [he had] concentrated and transformed the fifty letters of the Indian language into the thirty Tibetan letters and in so doing he created, it was said, the five-and-a-half letters that did not exist in India. The half letter was the letter *'a*, thus called because it functioned mainly as a prefix and a suffix.

Thon-mi Sam-bho-ṭa became skilled in [the art of] reading and writing and was the foremost literatus and translator of Tibet.

The content of this brief account has assumed great importance and significance and it can be considered the precursor of a paradigm for most Tibetan dynastic and religious histories that in later times elaborated upon the topic.

The *lHo brag chos 'byung* contains another version of the creation of the Tibetan written language by Thon-mi (Pe, Vol. I, 180, 3):

> .... [t]he Great Vehicle [Mahāyāna] together with its manifold sacred Dharma teachings. [When he] returned to Tibet, celebrations were held in his honor. [Thon-mi] took the Sanskrit [Nāga-ra] and Kashmiri letters as a model [and] at the royal citadel [of] Ma-ru [sKu-mkhar Ma-ru] devised the shape of the letters.
>
> [He] created the headed letters [*dbu can*], taking as an example the divine Lañ-tsa [Lan-tsha] script, and the *zur can* [angled script],[73] [taking as an example] the Wartu-la [Vivarta] script of the Nāga.

The text describes the great hardships endured by Thon-mi to reach India, the meetings with the scholars, the way in which he studied with them, and, as we read here, his creation of the print script modeled after the Lañ-tsa [Lan-tsha] script, and the *zur can*, that is to say, the cursive [*dbu med*] script modeled after the Wartu-la [Vivarta].

Most religious and dynastic histories say that Thon-mi composed the printed script from the Lañ-tsa [Lan-tsha] and the cursive script

---

73 A form of Tibetan cursive script now called *'bru-tsha* or *sgur-rtsa* where the letters are all surmounted by a triangular shape.

from the Wartu-la [Vivarta], but do not specify how he composed the cursive [*dbu med*] script, although his invention of *zur can*, to which the text specifically refers, was considered a marvelous feat in the thinking of great scholars.

Since I have already explained that the natural source of the *dbu med* script is the *smar* script (*Light of Kailash* Volume Two, *The Intermediate Period*, Chapter IV), I will not dwell on the topic here.

At any rate, *zur can*, like *dbu can*, is written from left to right without traits crowning the letters, but with an extension on the left and right sides of the letters so as to produce a triangular shape at the top; given that the aspect of the letters can be perceived as more or less similar to that of the Indian Wartu-la [Vivarta], it is conventionally called *zur can*. This is also confirmed by the *rGyal rabs gsal ba'i me long* which says (Pe, 70, 2):

> [He] created the *zur can* script by modeling it after the Wartu-la script of the Nāga.

Religious and dynastic histories present slightly different points of view about the models utilized by Thon-mi Sam-bho-ṭa for creating the Tibetan script. In this regard, the two *lDe'u chos 'byung*, which are old sources, relate simply that Thon-mi created the Tibetan written language without specifying how he did it and which script he took as a model. The *Nyang gi chos 'byung* says (Bod, 172, 11):

> He created *dbu can* taking as model the Na-ga-ra-ma [script] and created *dbu med* taking as model the Bha-gru-ma [script].

The *Bu ston chos 'byung* says that Thon-mi created the new Tibetan written language following the Kashmiri script.

The *rGyal po bka'i thang yig* says (Pe, 116, 8):

> [He] transformed the Nā-ga-ra script into *gzabs ma* [*dbu can*] and the Wa-rdhu-la [Vivarta] script into *shur ma*.[74]

The *Deb ther dpyid kyi rgyal mo'i glu dbyangs* says (Pe, 21, 4):

---

74 [A half-printed half-cursive form of Tibetan script.]

[He] composed eight necessary treatises, namely, the Root Grammar in Thirty Verses [*Lung du ston pa rtsa ba sum cu pa*], the Grammar Guide to the Signs [*Lung du ston pa rtags kyi 'jug pa*], and so on, to clarify the signs and forms of the *dbu can* [script] created after the Lañ-dza [*sic*] and the *shar ma* [*dbu med*] created after the Wartu-la [Vivarta].

This last viewpoint has become noted.

The *Deb ther dkar po* elaborates on the topic in the following manner (Si, 97, 16):

> Let us examine briefly what dynastic histories and commentaries say about the origin of the Tibetan written language.
>
> Lord Bu-ston [Rin-chen-grub 1290-1364] and others presumed that Thu-mi created it by taking as example the Na-ga-ra script. Other scholars suggested that he created *dbu can* and *dbu med* by taking as a model respectively the Lañ-dza (a corrupted form of the so-called golden Rañ-dza [script]) and the (coiling) Wartu-la [Vivarta] [scripts].
>
> According to the Bon-pos, there was no written language before Srong-btsan, since the only widespread religion was Bon; but that is not true. Moreover, it is asserted that the so-called *spungs yig* [literally, bundled script] of sTag-gzig was modified into the ancient Zhang Zhung script; that the latter became *sman brag*; and that *sman brag* gradually turned into *dbu can*, *'bru ma* [capital letters], and so on.
>
> In any case, Thu-mi arrived in India when the country was ruled by the royal descendants of the Gupta [c. 240-550 CE]. The writings on copper plates and other artifacts preserved until now in various parts of India and produced at the time of Thu-mi's contemporary, the Indian king Harsha [reigned 606-647 CE], and at the time of Kumaragupta (gZhon-nu sBas-pa [reigned 414-455 CE]), Suryawarman (Nyi-ma'i Go-cha) [reigned 535-561 CE],[75] and so on are amazingly similar to Tibetan script. When seen from a short distance, [the Indian writing] appears to be Tibetan written by an inexperienced hand,

---

75 [King of Tarumanagara, Island of Java.]

someone who probably had not studied calligraphy and whose reading capacity was slight.

The way in which Thon-mi composed the Tibetan script was explained above all by the *bKa' chems ka khol ma*. Nevertheless, other famous religious and dynastic histories provided their own versions, and here I cite two of them as indicative examples. The *Nyang gi chos' byung* says (Bod, 172, 2):

> First of all Maheśvara [Śiva] composed the consonants Ka, Tsa, Ta, Ṭa Pa, Kha, Tsha Tha Śra, Ba, Kśa, Sha, A, and so on.
>   'Jam-dpal [Mañjuśrī] composed the vowels A, Ā, I, Ī, U, Ū, Ri, Rī, Li, Lī, E, Ē, O, Ō.
>   Then the grammarians composed the series of the thirty-two consonants, Ka, Kha, Ga, Gha, Nga, and so on [that correspond to] the sequence of the five elements.
>   [Thon-mi] omitted the sounds that did not exist in Tibetan, [namely,] the Gha section and the [other] aspirated letters, [as well as the letters that] had no substitute; [he] omitted the Nga section [and] the five reversed letters because his tongue [could] not sound [them]; [he] concentrated the sixteen vocalic letters within O and I and modified [them]: [he] changed the I into the *gi gu* [◌ྀ], the U into the *zhabs kyu* [◌ུ], the E into the *'greng bu* [◌ེ], the O into the *na ro* [◌ོ], and the A [implicit in the consonants] into the dot [*rtseg*] [that separates the syllables]. [He] assembled thirty consonants.

And also (ibid., 172, 12):

> *Ca* was entered because there was no suitable [Indian letter for writing the word] *gcig*, in Indian *eka* [one]. *Ja* was entered because there was no suitable [Indian letter for writing the word] *'jigs rten*, in Indian *loka* [world]. *Cha* was entered because there was no suitable [Indian letter for writing the word] *chos*, in Indian *dharma*. *Zha* was entered because there was no suitable [Indian letter for writing the word] *zhu ba*, in Indian *pitta* [the bile humor]. *'A* was entered because Tibetan did not have long vowels. [In that way,] Tibetan had five-and-a-half [letters] that the Indian language did not have. The sound [of the letters] was left as in the Indian language. Having attuned the sounds

with the letters, [he] wrote [them] down, so that they could appear as prose and verse.

[He composed the letter] A [ཨ] [by taking as inspiration] the trunk of an elephant, the form of the division stroke [*shad* ।], [the thunderbolt of] Indra, a lion's mane, [and] a king sitting on a throne.

[He then] divided [the letters] and wrote them down; [he] established the five prefixes, the ten suffixes, [and] the group with six limbs; [he] divided [the letters by] placing them one below the other [and by] separating them with the division stroke [*shad*]; what was spoken [could then be expressed] in [written] words. Modifying the thirty [Indian] letters, [he] created [the thirty Tibetan consonants].

The *rGyal rabs gsal ba'i me long* says (Pe, 68, 8):

[He evaluated] the fifty Indian letters one by one. [At first, he] included all of them, [since] none [would precisely] correspond to the [envisaged] use. Among thirty main letters, ten [could also be used as] prefixes and ten [as] suffixes. Taking those as a model and grouping them together, [he endeavored to] formulate the thirty Tibetan letters.

[He took] the letters one by one [and] gave them the appropriate shape. Ka, Kha, Ca, Cha, Ja, Nya, Ta, Tha, Pa, Pha, Tsa, Tsha, Dza, Wa, Zha, Za, Ya, Sha, Ha, [and] A [became] the twenty main letters. [Out of those, he considered] Wa [as] the letter that could also be done without.

Ga, Da, Ba, Ma, [and] 'A [he defined as] the five prefixed letters.

Ga, Da, Ba, Ma, 'A, Nga, Na, Ra, La, [and] Sa [he defined as] the ten suffixed letters.

Ga, Da, Ba, Ma [and] 'A [he defined as] the five essential letters.

Ka, Ga, Ta, Da, Na, Nya, Zha, Sha, [and] Ha [he defined as] the nine letters with a leg.

Ca, Cha, Ja, Zha, Za, [and] 'A [he defined as] the six letters not existing in India.

Ka, Ga, Nga, Da, Ta, Na, Pa, Ba, Ma, Ca, Ja, Nya, Tsa, Dza, La, [and] Ha [he defined as] the sixteen 'children' letters.

[He] devised seven 'mother' letters: Ka, Ga, Ba, Za, Ra, La, [and] Sa. [Furthermore, he defined] Ra, La, [and] Sa [as] the 'mothers of all' (namely, the three mothers of all the subscript letters).

[He attributed to the letter] La four specific mothers: Ka, Ga, Ba, [and] Za (meaning that La is the subscript letter for these four consonants).

[He attributed to the letter] La two specific children: Ca and Ha.

Tsa and Dza [became] the children of [the letter] Ra.

Kha, Cha, Tha, Pha, Tsha, Wa, Zha, Ya, Sha, [and] A [he defined as] the ten letters that would maintain their own place, [namely,] they could not act as mother or children letters, nor as prefixes or suffixes.

Ga [and] Ba [he defined as] wandering (that is, they could act both as mother and children letters and as prefixes and suffixes).

I, E, [and] O [became] the three [vowels that could be] suspended on top [of the consonants] like a hat. These three [could be used with] all the letters.

Below [the consonants], like a beautiful cushion, [he devised the] three [subscript letters]: Ya, Ra, [and] U.

[Thus,] seven letters appeared with a subscript Ya: Kya, Khya, Gya, Pya, Phya, Bya, Mya [and] eleven letters with a subscript Ra: Kra, Khra, Gra, Pra, Phra, Bra, Mra, Sra, Shra, Dra, [and] Hra.

[The vowel] U [could be used with] all the letters and also with the subscript [letters] Ya [and] Ra, [as in] Kyu, Khyu, [or] Kru [and] Khru.

[All the] prefixes, suffixes, and subscript letters [spontaneously] arose in [his] mind.

Starting from the time in which the precious teachings of the sacred Dharma appeared in the vast country of snowy mountains that is Tibet, the majority of scholars who were born there and became renowned have done their utmost to show the contrast between all the good that flourished in the country with the arrival of Buddhism and all the bad that existed before then, maintaining that before the arrival of the miraculous king and minister that caused the light of the sacred Dharma to shine over the country, Tibet was an obscure, uncivilized place and that the ancient Tibetans living there were all dimwitted and dull. They pointed out that the country had been lit by the radiant sun of the Holy Teachings, through the grace of the inconceivable and magnificent enlightened activity of Maitreya [Byams-pa], the compassion of the prodigious king and minister, and the share of merits accrued by all Tibetan beings, declaring that the country was an extraordinary field of conversion of the most sublime Avalokiteśvara, and that the Dharmarāja Srong-btsan sGam-po was an exceptional and totally unrivalled emanation of the Noble Great Compassionate One.

More than one thousand years have passed since the diffusion of the sacred Dharma teachings until now and during this time, most Buddhist scholars have condemned the ancient tradition in all possible ways while utterly praising the new one. Many long and short historical texts have been compiled on the basis of that perspective which has gradually become widespread, conditioning the minds of most Buddhist and non-Buddhist students who, unfamiliar with antiquity, consequently adopted that view as their own.

Even though most historians of the Later Period transmitted and supported that kind of account because they were all noted followers of Buddhism and were therefore concerned with its propagation, it would not be in the least inappropriate to consider their viewpoint as exactly that of the holy Dharma: the sacred Dharma came from the noble country of India; therefore that country was more remarkable and holy than others. Moreover, the compassion and enlightened activities of the Buddhas and Bodhisattvas are unlimited; therefore, the Noble Avalokiteśvara made Tibet his conversion field and sent his emanation in the embodied form of King Srong-btsan sGam-po so that the country could be converted.

However, no way to give credence to that story exists because its source and rationale are completely based upon delusion, faith, pure vision, aspiration, and conviction. Its foundation, submitted to a threefold scrutiny, cannot be reconciled with actual conditions and contextual circumstances. Since it is evident that this account cannot be universally accepted, a thorough investigation in this regard becomes necessary.

There is no certainty whatsoever that a Tibetan written language was newly devised after the Dharmarāja Srong-btsan sGam-po sent Thon-mi Sam-bho-ṭa to India, nor that the teachings of the sacred Dharma and various relevant forms of cultural expression spread and developed in Tibet after they were brought from India and China because Srong-btsan sGam-po was an emanation of the Noble Avalo-kiteśvara and because he was endowed with immeasurable love and compassion for his Tibetan subjects trapped in a cage of darkness.

It is impossible that the idea generally elaborated in Tibetan his-tories—according to which, before that time, Tibet was an uncivilized country where most Tibetans lived as a horde of ignorant and stupid brutes—was also embraced by the Dharmarāja Srong-btsan sGam-po. Why? Because since a small child, he had limitless access to the Five Branches of Learning and he also had an extensive knowledge of the real *Sems Bon* (the essential teachings of Bon of the Total Perfection [rDzogs-chen]).

Therefore, cognizant of the fact that the light of Bon culture, like the sun and the moon, was shining over all of Tibet, he could not have regarded Tibet as a barbarous country. We know that Srong-btsan sGam-po had an extensive knowledge of those teachings because his oral and secret instructions related to the Avalokiteśvara cycle display in their essence the principles of rDzogs-chen.

We can find several oral instructions of the Dharmarāja Srong-btsan sGam-po in the *lHo brag chos 'byung* (Pe, Vol. 1, 250, 9):

> All kinds [of phenomena appear as] diverse; nevertheless, [they] are one's own mind.
> The [state] without object is beyond the intellect.
> [That which is] beyond the intellect is free from [discursive] activity; it abides in the condition of [that which is] as it is.
> [This] nonabiding [state] is the supreme relaxation.
> The person who realizes [that this is] so
> calls View [that which] transcends [all] extremes [and is] sepa-rated from mental fabrications;
> calls Meditation [that which is] not separated from the self-luminous presence;

calls Conduct [all that which is] not separated from the [real] sense;

calls Fruit [all that which is] beyond acceptance and rejection.

And also (ibid., 250, 22):

[That person] calls Awakening the self-liberation [of] conceptuality;

calls Sacred Teachings [that which] guide sentient beings onto the Path;

calls Community [*dge-'dun, saṃgha*] [all those who] integrate nonaction in their mind;

calls Nonaction the effortless relaxation in one's own Natural State.

And also (ibid., 251, 10):

All designations are [simply] names. Give up attachment to names. They are devoid of [inherent] existence.

All thoughts are the conceptual mind. Give up and abandon the fabrications of the mind.

'Give up' is a word. Throw away and abandon attachment to words.

'Abandon' is a concept. Dissolve concepts into space.

'To conceal' is a good thought.

[The Natural State is] equanimity[76] beyond [concepts of] good and bad, full awareness beyond [concepts of] hidden and concealed, vividness beyond [concepts of] coming and going, total freedom beyond acceptance and rejection, serenity beyond partiality and distinction, radiance beyond sending and receiving, brilliancy beyond clarity and obscuration, evenness beyond wandering and oblivion, [and] purity without wavering. View it as the state that is beyond the conceptual mind. View it as the meaning that is beyond words.

View it as the dimension beyond good and bad.

View it as the Mind beyond outside and inside.

---

76   *khad de ba*: a mental state totally devoid of conceptualization, usually called *had de ba*, which represents the state of total absence of all mental concepts such as "this is good" and "this is bad" that immediately follows a sudden experience of shock or fear.

View it as the Tantra beyond Father and Mother [distinctions].
View it as the meaning beyond duality.
The so-called meaning is beyond the conceptual mind.
Do not adhere to the beyond [as well]: view it as the Condition
separated from [all] descriptions.
When [it is] observed, there is nothing to be seen.
By remaining without looking, the Real Condition will be
realized.
By letting go of [the need for] accomplishment, the Mind-itself
will be realized.
By relaxing without grasping, one will be liberated in one's own
Real Condition.

And also (ibid., 254,19):

Remain undistracted in the Condition beyond effort.
Seal the dualistic mind in the dimension of space.
Rest in your own condition [of] instant presence without [look-
ing] at the [real] sense [as] an object of meditation.

A few excerpts of the *Twelve Little Tantras* from the Aural Transmission
teachings of Zhang Zhung [*Zhang zhung snyan rgyud kyi rgyud bu chung bcu
gnyis*] show how his instructions actually reflect the principles expounded
in those old Bonpo rDzogs-chen scriptures (Dhi, 171, 2, 5):

There is nothing to investigate with respect to the real sense.
There is nothing to meditate with respect to the real sense.
There is no conduct [to be adopted] with respect to the real sense.

And also (ibid., 173, 3, 6):

To look at the profound state [of] the Total Perfection is not
investigating [and thinking] 'this is it.'
Since by investigating [it] will not be seen, not seeing itself
[is] the best seeing.
As to the View of Kun-tu bZang-po, [it] cannot be explained
as 'this [is it]' or [as] 'it manifests in this way' or 'it appears in
that way.'

And also (ibid., 174, 3, 3):

Meditation referring to the profound state [of] the Total Perfection is not meditating [and thinking] 'this [is it].'

Through meditation [the profound state] does not become clear; without meditation, [the profound state is] neither cleared nor obscured.

The contemplation of Kun-tu bZang-po [is] fresh, natural, [and] unaltered; [it is] remaining in one's pristine, unaltered condition, without meditating and wandering [with the mind].

And also (ibid., 174, 3, 6):

To conduct oneself with respect to the profound state [of] the Total Perfection is not to behave [in some way, thinking] 'this [is it].'

Without separation from the View [and] Meditation, totally spontaneous [and] undiversified, the integrated conduct is the [real] Conduct.

Srong-btsan sGam-po's introduction from India and China of the sacred Dharma and related cultural expressions reminds us of the popular saying "the victory banner surmounts the ornament." A further development of a previously existing culture presumes the existence of circumstances that would allow for such a change; but since it was postulated that no culture whatsoever existed in Tibet before then, how would it have been possible to undertake such an introduction from border countries?

The *lHo brag chos 'byung* says (Pe, Vol. 1, 178, 8):

Do not depend on the written language of another place. The written language of Tibet proper is what is necessary.

These words signify that it was considered essential for Tibet to have its own specific written language without having to depend on that of other regions, specifically, the written language of Zhang Zhung. It does not at all imply that before then no written language existed in Tibet, but it does automatically explain why the text continues, "Do not depend on the knowledge of another place. A Tibetan culture proper is what is necessary."

The written language used in Tibet before Thon-mi A-nu, Minister of the Dharmarāja Srong-btsan sGam-po, introduced the new one was the so-called *smar yig* of Zhang Zhung; the source of that written language was Zhang Zhung, and also its spelling was largely related to the Zhang Zhung idiom. This can be understood by consulting texts on Zhang Zhung grammar and also the orthography of the *Tun hong bod kyi lo rgyus yig rnying* [Old Tibetan Chronicles of Dunhuang] that are now readily available.

Some scholars of later times doubted that Thon-mi Sam-bho-ṭa composed "The Root Grammar in Thirty Verses" [*lung du ston pa rtsa ba sum cu pa*] and "The Grammar Guide to Signs" [*lung du ston pa rtags kyi 'jug pa*] and posited that for the most part they must be subsequent compositions. The main rationale for this opinion is based on the numerous structural discrepancies that can be pinpointed between the Dūnhuáng [敦煌] documents and the model adopted in the two grammars by Thon-mi. This rationale is not a correct one because with the system created by Thon-mi it was not possible to modify in its entirety the grammatical model of the Zhang Zhung *smar* that was previously diffused in Tibet. Besides, the metrics naturally show that a great familiarity with the antecedent system was still present.

Furthermore, the *Nyang gi chos 'byung* affirms that a basis for the Tibetan written language already existed from former times (Bod, 165, 5):

> It has also been claimed that the Tibetan written language appeared during the time of Khrim-so Bud-btsan-po.

It is possible that Thon-mi Sam-bho-ṭa created the new Tibetan written language by modeling it on the Nā-ga-ra and Kashmiri scripts, as the *lHo brag chos 'byung* maintains, or that he may have created it by adopting the Gupta script, as the *Deb ther dkar po* affirms. At any rate, it is certain that all Tibetans have always considered with the necessary gratitude the unrivalled kindness shown by the prodigious minister when he created the printed and cursive scripts, now so familiar to us, and when he composed the two (originally eight) grammars that we have at present, without which the translation of the Indian Buddhist teachings into Tibetan could not have started, and so on.

However, an unequivocal distinction must be made between expressing due gratitude for the feats of Thon-mi Sam-bho-ta and determining that the country of Tibet was a region of darkness deprived of any form whatsoever of culture and written language prior to the time of the Dharmarāja Srong-btsan sGam-po and his wondrous minister Thon-mi Sam-bho-ta. That is extremely important.

2. ZHANG ZHUNG CULTURAL INFLUENCE AND THE POLITICAL STATUS OF THE TIBETAN KINGS

Thirty-four dynasties occurred between the time of the first Tibetan king gNya'-khri bTsan-po until that of the Dharmarāja Srong-btsan sGam-po; this was the Intermediate Period during which the Tibetan and the Zhang Zhung kingdoms co-existed. Comparing the beginning of the new Tibetan kingdom and the history of the Intermediate Period with the Zhang Zhung history of the Early Period, we can see that the former is extremely short.

Moreover, since all the cultural foundations of the Intermediate Period were precisely rooted in the Bon of Zhang Zhung and in its various cultural expressions, also the political status of the Tibetan kings was inevitably dependent on the Bon of Zhang Zhung, and above all on the powerful kings of Zhang Zhung who were its patrons. For these reasons some Tibetan kings tried to reduce Zhang Zhung interventions and endeavored to cautiously limit the power of the authoritative Bon-gShens who were active in Tibet; that can be deduced from the numerous accounts written in this regard.

This state of affairs commenced at the time of the eighth Tibetan monarch Gri-gum. The *Legs bshad rin po che'i mdzod* says (Pe, 185, 20):

> Minister Li-btsan-bzher said, "Great Lord! If the Bon-pos become too powerful, they will have the [same] authority as Your Majesty."
>
> Minister Zing-pa Ratna pleaded with the king as follows, "Oh Lord! Give the order for the banishment of the gShen-pos."

The Indian beggar Ratna Siddhi who was wandering through-out the kingdom said, "Now the [power of the] king and [that of] the gShen-pos are in equilibrium, but [if this condition persists,] during the lifetime of the children and grandchildren political authority will be in the hands of the Bon-pos."

Those and other [similar] calumnies were spread to divide the king and the gShen-pos.

And also (ibid., 186, 10):

Then the king said, "Summon all the gShen-pos." When they arrived the king said, "My political authority and your religious authority are two [separate matters]. mNga'-ris [Province] can-not contain both of them. Hence, I request that lHa-bon sGo-bzhi, Ge-khod This-'phen, and gCo Gyim-bu Lan-tsha remain as my personal bodyguards. All the others will leave the Four Ranges of Tibet."

As stated, King Gri-gum inflicted severe damage on the Bon-gShens. Fear of losing to the Bon-gShen power was certainly the reason behind that measure. The *Legs bshad* relates the causes and conditions that cre-ated that concern (Pe, 184, 12):

[The] third [aspect is concerned with] the abolishment of Bon correlated with the periods of dominion of specific kings and gShen-pos.

The *dBang chen* says, "When King Gri-rum bTsan-po lost his mind, slanderous rumors circulated about the king and the gShen-pos."

The *Phyi rgyud* says, "lDe Gyim-tsha rMa-chung was accom-plished in powerful Guardian practice; since he became extremely proud of [this] ability, discord arose between him and the king."

Thus, even if it is explained that the main reason seemed to be the might of the important Bon-gShens, it is implicit that also those key Bon-gShens had actually a reason for fearing that their strong individual power could be lost to the king. That notwithstanding, it is certain great caution had to be exercised because the Bon-gShens of that time automatically reflected the influence of Zhang Zhung; when the Tibetan king inflicted damage on the Bon-gShens, he had to consider that factor seriously.

Gri-gum bTsan-po was not the only Tibetan king who experienced those circumstances; it is quite possible that other kings of the thirty-four dynasties had to deal with the same concerns, although history has been silent on that account. In any case, although King Gri-gum inflicted severe damage on the Bon-gShens, he lacked the indispensable knowledge and necessary requisites for controlling Tibetan politics. Thus he was eventually murdered by Lo-ngam and the Tibetan kingdom found itself in the grievous situation of being ruled by his assassin.

There is no doubt that the Dharmarāja Srong-btsan sGam-po was totally aware of his political position when he decided to kindle the flames of the sacred Dharma in Tibet. It is precisely because he had a distinct knowledge of the conditions necessary for remaining in power that he sent his daughter Sa-mar-kar in marriage to King Lig-mi-rkya of Khyung-lung. This is confirmed by the *Tun hong bod kyi lo rgyus yig rnying* [Old Tibetan Chronicles of Dunhuang] (PI 571, 388):

> During the lifetime of this king, Zhang Zhung [and] the Tibetan king [lDe-bu] became allies. After a joyful [salutatory] tourna- ment, Queen [*btsan mo*] Sad-mar-kar left for the kingdom of Lig-mi-rhya to marry her Zhang Zhung consort.

The learned dGe-'dun Chos-'phel [1903-1951] and other scholars thought that Queen Sa-mar-kar was a sister of King Srong-btsan sGam- po because they assumed that he was born in the Fire Ox year of the first s*Me-phreng* of the fifteenth s*Me-'khor* (Tibetan year 2534, 617 CE). As a matter of fact, the word *btsan mo* can equally refer to the sister or the daughter of a king.

Examining Srong-btsan's deeds and positing, as the *Deb ther sngon po* does, that the year of his birth was the female Earth Ox year of the last s*Me-phreng* of the fourteenth s*Me-'khor* (Tibetan year 2486, 569 CE), we can automatically discern that before taking in marriage the Nepalese and Chinese princesses,[77] he already had other consorts and several male and female children. Moreover, the *Byams ma* relates (rGyud, TSHI, 72, 3):

> [He] married Zhang-zhung-bza' Lig-ting-sman. [She] brought a statue the size of a one-year-old [child portraying] gShen-rab, the Lord of the Teachings, the Buddha of Zhang Zhung. For that reason a request for the construction of the Theg-chen Temple was advanced.

The marriage with the Zhang Zhung princess granted close kinship ties between Zhang Zhung and Tibet.

In that regard, the above-mentioned quotation, "Do not depend on the knowledge of another place. A Tibetan culture proper is what is necessary" [p. 245] can be accurately interpreted if we consider what all the dynastic histories and annals have said, not without reason, about the Tibetan king first establishing ties with the king of Nepal by taking in marriage a Nepalese princess and then renewing ties with the Táng 唐 emperor by taking in marriage a Chinese princess, essentially for the purpose of introducing the sacred Dharma and its various relevant cultural expressions into Tibet.

Those ties represented an opportunity for King Srong-btsan sGam-po to realize his intentions. [Moreover] the Ten Divine Virtues [*lha chos dge ba bcu*] and the Sixteen Moral Rules for Laypeople [*mi chos gtsang ma bcu drug*][78] were purposely promulgated in order to establish new foundations that would distinguish the Tibetan written language and the Tibetan culture from that of Bon or Zhang Zhung.

Gradually, after the power of the Zhang Zhung king was destroyed, the whole territory of Zhang Zhung became a Tibetan colony, marking the beginning of the Later Period; the historical events that conclude the Intermediate Period are clearly related in the *Tun hong bod kyi lo rgyus yig rnying* [Old Tibetan Chronicles of Dunhuang].

------

77 [Bhrikuti Devi, Tib. Bal-mo-bza' Khri btsun, princess of the Licchavi Kingdom of Nepal; Wénchéng Gōngzhǔ 文成公主, niece of Emperor Tàizōng 太宗 (reigned 626-649).]
78 [See p. 264.]

On the basis of those causal factors, historians of later times have pronounced endless praise for the deeds of the bodhisattvic king and minister. Needless to say, those expressions of profound gratitude are justified and required; but if we do not acknowledge that appreciation for the kindness of previous kings and ministers without whom nothing to be grateful for would exist is also necessary, such declarations of praise become discreditable.

Those exaggerated displays of gratitude which greatly harmed the genuine history of Tibet confirm the words of the illustrious Sa-skya Paṇḍita [Kun-dga' rGyal-mtshan dPal-bzang-po, 1182-1251], "Even if one praises, in reality one is criticizing"; but also the adage "Someone who praises, even if he does not know how to praise, is better than someone who does not know how to criticize, but criticizes nonetheless."

Identifying the Civilization
of Tibet in the Later Period

The reign of Srong-btsan sGam-po marks the beginning of the
Later Period of the history of ancient Tibet. It is the new epoch
during which Zhang Zhung and Tibet were unified and the time during
which the diffusion in Tibet of the prodigious and diversified Indian
and Chinese cultures had begun.

When the two great rivers of the immense and diverse Indian and
Chinese cultures streamed together toward [that kingdom], the nature
of the development of the already rich, full-fledged, and splendid ancient culture of Tibet, clear and deep like Lake Manasarovar, acquired
a new shape, like a river flowing toward the ocean. We know that the
vast and profound Tibetan culture was already developed in its own
right, because at the present time we are still concretely putting its
aspects into practice.

Most Tibetan Buddhist scholars maintained that a written language
was not utilized in Tibet before the arrival of the Dharmarāja Srong-
btsan sGam-po. According to that view, Tibet did not at all possess a
vast and profound culture. However, throughout the various dynasties
that succeeded one another from the first king gNya'-khri bTsan-po
until lHa-tho-tho-ri sNyan-shal the Tibetan government ruled by way
of *sGrung, lDe'u,* and *Bon.* These three aspects represent the distinct

cultural features of Tibet in those times. Their importance is discussed in Volume Two, dedicated to the Intermediate Period.

King lHa-tho-tho-ri gNyan-btsan received the *sPang skong phyag brgya pa* [*Sakśipūraṇasudraka*, The Hundredfold Homage for Mending Breaches], the *mDo sde za ma tog* [*Za ma tog bkod pa'i mdo*, *Kāraṇḍavyūhasūtra*, The Sūtra Designed as a Jewel Chest], and other sacred items. That event corresponds to the first appearance of the Buddhadharma in Tibet. At that time two famous Indian doctors, Bi-byi dGa'-byed and Bi-lha dGa'-mdzes-ma, arrived in Tibet and propagated the medical science. The invitation of these two physicians by the Tibetan King lHa-tho-tho-ri sNyan-btsan is described in the secret hagiography of the venerable g.Yu-thog rNying-ma Yon-tan mGon-po [the Elder] [708-833] titled *gZi brjid rin po che'i gter mdzod* (Pe, 63, 21):

> After the glorious Bodhisattva lHa-tho-tho-ri'i sNyan-btsan heard that the two physicians [could] establish the teachings of the medical science in Tibet, [he] invited them to the Yum-bu Glang-mkhar Palace.

King lHa-tho-tho-ri sNyan-btsan offered his daughter lHa-lcam Yid-kyi Rol-cha to the doctor Bi-byi dGa'-byed. The two physicians remained in Tibet for two years. From the marriage of lHa-lcam Yid-kyi Rol-cha to Bi-byi dGa'-byed the doctor Dung-gi Thor-cog-can was born. The two physicians taught Dung-gi Thor-cog-can many sūtras, such as the *Rig pa rtsa'i mdo* [Root Sūtra of the Medical Science], the *'Tsho ba zas kyi mdo* [Sūtra for Nurturing Life through Food], the *sByor ba sman gyi mdo* [Medical Sūtra of Sexual Union], and the *rMa chas bzo'i mdo* [Sūtra for Healing Wounds], as well as many general works, root texts, commentaries, and explanations, including the synopses and the relevant procedures. Dung-gi Thor-cog-can became the personal physician of lHa-tho-tho-ri gNyan-btsan and of his son Khri-gnyan gZungs-btsan; until and including King dPal-'khor-btsan, the personal physicians of each Tibetan dynast were all descendants of Dung-gi Thor-cog-can. All these stories are clearly related in the above-mentioned text.

The *lDe'u chos 'byung chen mo* says (Bod, 108, 5):

During the time of this king (gNam-ri Srong-btsan), three [populations] of the border regions were subdued: the rGya [Chinese], the Gru-gu [Turks], and the Hor [Uighurs]. In Tibet, the first law edict [*khri rtse 'bum gdugs*] was formulated.

The *rGyal rabs gsal ba'i me long* says (Pe, 61, 17):

During the time of this king (gNam-ri Srong-btsan), medical and astrological [knowledge] were imported from China; the rGya [Chinese] and the Gru-gu [Turks] were conquered; salt was acquired from the northern regions; [and] the Khri-brtsigs 'Bum-brdugs Palace was built.

These two excerpts which mention the formulation of laws, the name of a palace, and so on show that various aspects of the Tibetan culture were gradually developing.

1. CHARACTERISTICS OF THE TIBETAN CIVILIZATION AFTER THE INTRODUCTION AND INTEGRATION OF INDIAN AND CHINESE CULTURAL PHENOMENA

During the lifetime of the Dharmarāja Srong-btsan sGam-po the minister Thon-mi Sam-bho-ṭa was sent to India. When the latter returned to Tibet, he established a new Tibetan written language, composing eight texts of Tibetan grammar. The translation into Tibetan of Indian and Chinese cultural topics was initiated. Spiritual teachers and learned scholars such as the Indian Ācārya Ku-sa-ra and the Brahmin Shang-ka-ra [Śaṇkara], the teacher Li-byin, the Nepalese master Shī-la Mañdzu, the Kashmiri teacher Ta-nu-ta, and the Chinese master Hwa-shang Ma-hā De-ba were invited. Thon-mi Sam-bho-ṭa, rDarmā-ko-sha, Arya A-lo-ka, Ye-shes-dpal, lHa-lung rDo-rje-dpal, and others worked as translators. All sorts of texts concerning medical science, the Kriya Yoga Tantras, and canonical literature were translated into Tibetan.

In particular, following the directive of the Dharmarāja, Thon-mi Sam-bho-ṭa opened the chest of the famous *gNyan po gsang ba* [Powerful Secrets] and translated into Tibetan the *sPang skong phyag brgya pa*

[*Sakśipūraṇasudraka*, The Hundredfold Homage for Mending Breaches]; the *mDo sde za ma tog* [*Za ma tog bkod pa'i mdo, Kāraṇḍavyūhasūtra*, The Sūtra Designed as a Jewel Chest]; the liturgical formula [*gzungs, dhāraṇī*] of the Cintāmaṇi [Wish-fulfilling Gem, the Six Syllable Avalokiteśvara Mantra]; different liturgical formulas derived from the Sūtras; and also the twenty-one Sūtras and Tantras of the Great Compassionate One. All these deeds are clearly related in the *bKa' chems* [*bka' khol ma*, The Royal Testament by Srong-btsan sGam-po].

At a time that Srong-btsan sGam-po's conquests were spreading far and wide, many different cultural expressions were taken as models that resulted in an improvement in the overall Tibetan level of knowledge. In that regard the *lHo brag chos 'byung* affirms (Pe, Vol. I, 184, 3):

> From the eastern [countries of] China and Mi-nyag various models of craftsmanship and astrology were introduced.
>
> From the pure southern [country of] India the sounds of the sacred Dharma were translated.
>
> The treasuries of food, cattle, and riches of the Sog-pos and Bal-pos [Nepal] were revealed in the west.
>
> From the northern [countries of the] Hor and the Yu-gur [Uighurs] various models of laws and services were introduced.
>
> After establishing control over the four directions and acquiring the riches of the border countries, [Tibet] dominated half the world.

The text cites the promulgation of several laws and regulations, including the thirty-six most valuable laws of Tibet, namely:

- the Six Major Laws [*bka'i khrims yig chen po drug*];
- the Six Major Recommendations [*bka' gros chen po drug*];
- the Six Insignia of Official Rank [*yig tshang drug*];
- the Six Symbols [*bka'i phyag rgya drug*];
- the Six Requisites [*rkyen drug*];
- the Six Garments Denoting Heroism [*dpa' mtshan drug*].

The Fifteen National Laws [*rgyal khrims bco lnga*] focused upon:

- the Three Deeds to be performed [*mdzad pa gsum*];
- the Three Deeds not to be performed [*mi mdzad pa gsum*];

- the Three Praises [*bstod pa gsum*];
- the Three Blames [*smad pa gsum*];
- the Three Sufferings not to be inflicted [*mi mnar ba gsum*].

In addition to these laws, there were Seven Major Laws [*khrims chen bdun*] related to the practice of the Ten Divine Virtues [*lha chos dge ba bcu*] and the Sixteen Moral Rules for Laypeople [*mi chos gtsang ma bcu drug*].

As for the Six Major Laws [*bka'i khrims yig chen po drug*], the *lDe'u rgya bod kyi chos 'byung* specifies (Bod, 270, 5):

The Six Major Laws were:
- the first edict decreed by Srong-btsan sGam-po [*khri rtse 'bum bzher gyi khrims*];
- the second edict decreed by Srong-btsan sGam-po [*'bum gser thang sha ba can gyi khrims*];
- the model laws for the kingdom [*rgyal khams dpe blang gi khrims*];
- the rules of justice [*mdo lon zhu bcad kyi khrims*];
- family laws [*khab so nan khrims*];
- the law of royal injunctions [*bka' lung rgyal khrims*].

The *lHo brag chos 'byung* presents different readings for some of these laws: instead of *'bum gser thang sha ba can gyi khrims*, it calls the second edict decreed by Srong-btsan sGam-po *'bum gser thog sha ba can gyi khrims*; instead of *khab so nan khrims*, it call family laws *khab so nang pa'i khrims*; instead of *bka' lung rgyal khrims*, it calls the law of royal injunctions *dbang chen bcad kyi khrims*.

The same text also provides a brief explanation about the meaning of *khri rtse 'bum bzher gyi khrims*, the first law decreed by Srong-btsan sGam-po (Pe, Vol. I, 185, 11):

With this law the king indicated the chieftains [*khos dpon*] who would be appointed as ministers.

He appointed mGar sTong-btsan Yul-bzung as Chief Minister of Tibet; Khyung-po Bun-zung-ce as Chief Minister of Zhang Zhung; Hor-bya Zhu-ring-po as Chief Minister of Sum-pa; dBang-btsan bZang-dpal-legs as Chief Minister of the cavalry; and Cog-ro rGyal-mtshan gYang-gong as Chief Minister of mThong-khyab.

Regarding the second law decreed by Srong-btsan sGam-po [*'bum gser thang sha ba can gyi khrims*], the same text specifies (ibid., 191, 17):

> The second law was called *'bum gyi gser thog sha ba can*. It defined weights and measures for grains and so forth: pints [*bre*], ounces [*srang*], handfuls [*phul*], *khyor* [two-palm measure], drams [*zho*], *nam*, and *se* [1/100 *zho*].

The Model Laws for the Kingdom [*rgyal khams dpe blang gi khrims*] are explained in detail in the *mKhas pa'i dga' ston*; some ideas presented in the *Deb ther dpyid kyi rgyal mo'i glu dbyangs* do not correspond exactly to the contents of the *mKhas pa'i dga' ston*, but that they were valid laws and regulations imported from other countries adapted to meet the specific needs of the Tibetan empire is easy to understand.

Concerning the Rules of Justice [*mdo lon zhu bcad kyi khrims*], the *lHo brag chos 'byung* says (Pe, Vol. I, 193, 14):

> These laws establish that the sentence for a dispute that involves a superior party and an inferior one does not favor the former to the detriment of the latter.

Concerning Family Laws [*khab so nan khrims*], the *lHo brag chos 'byung* says (Pe, Vol. I, 193, 23):

> These laws define the rights and happiness of two parties in relation to three [institutions:] marriage [*khab*], custody [*so*], and ordination [*nang*].
>
> For example in the case of two honorable [parties], if a child is born in one household and [accidentally] falls into a river and is swallowed by a fish, if the servant of another householder living downstream catches the fish and the child is still alive, the second householder gains right of custody of the child. If the first householder hears that and argues against it requesting justice to the king, [the king] will assign alternate yearly custody to each party, so that they may both fulfill their wish and hope for having children. If [other] children are born to each householder, they will be shown to the king; the king will give the children the titles of both noble families. Each child will carry its own title separately. If later on the children take

religious vows, they will be recognized as fully ordained monks belonging to two families.

The law of royal injunctions [*bka' lung rgyal khrims*] is explained by the *lHo brag chos 'byung* in the following way (Pe, Vol. I, 193, 16):

> It defines the impartial punishment mandated by the king when the responsibility of two parties is involved, taking as a model the general law of Maheśvara [*dbang chen bcad kyi spyi khrims*] [and in particular] the case of the Brahmin Dandi [Bram-ze dByug-pa-can]. The Brahmin borrowed the ox of a certain householder. When [he] gave it back, [he simply] left it in the corral and returned home without saying a word. The householder saw that the ox was back, but left [it] there without tethering [it]. The ox escaped and [the householder] carried a complaint before the king because his ox was lost. The king said, "The Brahmin returned the ox, but did not speak; therefore, [his] tongue will be severed [as punishment]. The householder saw [that the ox had been returned] but did not secure [it]; therefore, [his] hand will be severed [as punishment]."

The *lDe'u rgya bod kyi chos 'byung* presents the Six Major Recommendations [*bka' gros chen po drug*] (Bod, 269, 20):

> Cherishing the person of the king and [hospitably] offering curd and meat; oppressing the lDong [Mi-nyag] and sTong [Sum-pa] [tribes] and keeping the servants obedient; not letting the help escape so that they become belligerent [*rgod*] and not heeding women too much; being vigilant on the borders and not flogging the horses to race when unnecessary; defeating enemies abroad and making friends at home; earnestly practicing virtues and abandoning nonvirtues.

The *lHo brag chos 'byung* refers to these recommendations with slightly different words; it says, "nurturing the body of the king and [being hospitable by] repeatedly offering curd and meat" instead of "cherishing the person of the king and [hospitably] offering curd and meat;" "subjugating belligerent servants and keeping servants obedient" instead of "oppressing the lDong [Mi-nyag] and sTong [Sum-pa] [tribes] and keeping servants obedient;" "safeguarding the borders and the orchards of the subjects and not overworking draft horses when unnecessary" instead of "being vigilant on the borders and not flogging the horses to race when unnecessary."

The *lDe'u rgya bod kyi chos 'byung* mentions five of the Six Insignia of Official Rank [*yig tshang drug*] (Bod, 270, 12):

> Gold and turquoise, alloy, copper, and iron.

The *lHo brag chos 'byung* mentions all of them (Pe, Vol. I, 190, 15):

> Gold and turquoise for the highest, silver or alloy for the intermediate, and copper and iron for the lowest. Each of the six insignia existed in big and small [sizes]; thus there were twelve in all.

The Six Symbols [*bka'i phyag rgya drug*] are described in the *lDe'u rgya bod kyi chos 'byung* (Bod, 270, 14):

> The symbol of the [king's] command is the casket. The symbol of the law is the banner [*ru mtshon*]. The symbol of the country is the royal palace. The symbol of religion is the temple. The symbols of the heroes are tigers and leopards. The symbols of the learned are books.

The *lHo brag chos 'byung* shows minor differences to describe these symbols: it says "the symbol of heroism is the banner" instead of "the symbol of the law is the banner"; and "the symbol of heroes are tiger skin garments [*stag slog*]" instead of "the symbols of the heroes are tigers and leopards."

It is highly possible that banners, tiger skin garments, books, and so on were awarded as tokens of distinction, although reference is also made to the learned and heroes. Therefore I think that in this case the idea of the *lDe'u chos 'byung* better conforms to reality and that the symbols should actually be understood as represented by seals linked to official ranks of the specific chief ministers, thus displaying the images of a casket, banner, castle, temple, tigers and leopards, and so forth.

The Six Requisites [*rkyen drug*] are described by the *lDe's chos 'byung* as follows (Bod, 267, 12):

> [For what concerns] eminent people, the requisites for [appointing] ministers of the maternal lineage will be [faith in] the Buddhadharma and the credentials [awarded by the king]. [For what concerns] people of low extraction, the conditions of their status will be [determined by activities, such as] weaving and Bon. The requisite for learned ones will be writings.
>
> Lack of talents[79] will denote the corrupt ones. The requisite for bravery will be [hunting] tigers and leopards [*gung*]. Fox skin hats will denote cowards.

The *lHo brag chos 'byung* shows only two differences: it says "the requisite for eminent people will be [faith in] the divine Dharma" instead of "the requisites for [appointing] ministers of the maternal lineage will be [faith in] the Buddhadharma and the credentials [awarded by the king];" and "stealing will denote the corrupt ones" instead of "lack of talents will denote the corrupt ones."

According to the *lDe'u rgya bod kyi chos 'byung*, the Six Garments Denoting Heroism [*dpa' mtshan drug*] are (Bod, 270, 18):

> The tiger skin upper garment and the tiger skin skirt, big and small tassels [*zar*], tiger skin and leopard skin [fur coats].

The *lHo brag chos 'byung* has "*zer chen zer chung gnyis*" instead of "big and small tassels" [*zar chen zar chung gnyis*], and "*gam ras stag slog*" [garments of cotton and tiger skin] instead of "tiger skin and leopard skin [fur coats]" [*stag slag gzig slag gnyis*]; "the tiger skin upper garment and the tiger skin skirt" [*stag stod dang stag smad*] evidently consisting of an upper garment or mantle [*stod g.yogs*] and a lower garment or skirt [*smad sham*] made of tiger skin; "big and small tassels" are big and small ornamental strands applied to the left and right sides of the garment: all these articles were bestowed in recognition of the bravery of courageous individuals. The phrase "*zer chen zer chung gnyis*" of the *lHo brag chos*

---

79   *stag kya*: I think this expression may refer to young men who possess masculine features, but are totally lacking in male capacities.

'*byung* indicates big and small tassels traditionally applied to clothing and woven with multicolored thread to form a rainbow pattern or other similar designs; *gam ras* could represent a variant of *gab ras*, that is to say, garments made with cotton [*ras*] of excellent quality and with hidden [*gab*] or invisible seams or stitches.

The Three Deeds to be perfomed [*mdzad pa gsum*] are described in the *lDe'u rgya bod kyi chos 'byung* as follows (Bod, 275, 17):

> Creating happiness at home, having defeated foreign enemies; assembling a retinue, having made friends at home; working for the attainment of Buddhahood, having practiced the divine Dharma.

The *lDe'u rgya bod kyi chos 'byung* also describes the Three Deeds not to be performed [*mi mdzad pa gsum*] (ibid., 275, 20):

> Teaching servants the divine Dharma, [which is] the prerogative of eminent people; exchanging esoteric teachings, which are the cause of Buddhahood, for riches [instead of] holding [them] in [one's] heart; [allowing a] servant to become a lord [and to this end] remaining distant to the point of not even praising the child of a servant.

The last of these three deeds is clarified in the *lHo brag chos 'byung* (Pe, Vol. I, 191, 23):

> When [a morally superior person] praises an ignoble one, [it is] ruinous [for] both. For that reason a servant [should] not become a lord.

The Three Praises [*bstod pa gsum*] as described in the *lDe'u rgya bod kyi chos 'byung* (Bod, 276, 3):

> If heroes are not rewarded with tiger [skin garments], their heroism is meaningless. If learned persons are not rewarded with official recognition, their intellectual faculties will die. If people who do good are not praised with joy, there is no juice [*ru ma*] in [their] doing good.

The *ru ma* [juice] alluded to here refers to the yeast [*phab rtsi*] necessary for making beer and to the ferment [*ru rtsi*] for making yoghurt.

As for the Three Censures [*smad pa gsum*], the *lDe'u rgya bod kyi chos
'byung* says (Bod, 276, 7):

> If censure for cowardice [is] not [expressed] by [giving] fox [skin
> hats], there will be no difference between a hero and a coward.
> If thorough measures are not taken against the vile, there will
> be no difference between a virtuous [person] and a dishonest
> [one]. If punishments are not inflicted when crimes [are com-
> mitted], evildoers will be uncontrollable.

Instead of "if thorough measures are not taken against the vile, there
will be no difference between a virtuous [person] and a dishonest
[one]" [*ngan pa la nan thur ma byas na / mdzangs ngan gyi shan mi phyed*], the
lHo brag chos 'byung says, "If thorough measures are not taken against
negligence, efforts to be conscientious will never be made" [*ngan la nan
tur ma byas na / nam yang dran shes rem mi 'gyur*]; *nan tur* indicates the need
for repeatedly pointing out faulty behavior.

As for the Three Sufferings not to be inflicted [*mi mnar ba gsum*],
the *lDe'u rgya bod kyi chos 'byung* says (Bod, 276, 10):

> When hardship is inflicted on the father and mother who are the
> givers [of] life, [karmic] retribution will result together with the
> scorn of others; therefore, this is a suffering not to be inflicted.
>
> If hardship is inflicted on favorite sons and grandsons, even
> enemies will feel shame; therefore, this is a suffering not to be
> inflicted.
>
> Damaging the farm labor of a husband and wife to the point
> of impoverishing a whole family is a suffering not to be inflicted.

Instead of "If hardship is inflicted on favorite sons and grandsons"
[*mchan gyi bu tsha mnar na*], the *lHo brag chos 'byung* says, "If hardship is
inflicted on one's own favorite sons" [*rang gi mchan gyi bu mnar na*], but I
think that the sentence can be understood as referring to all the young
male and female children without distinction.

The Seven Major Laws [*khrims chen bdun*] according to the *lHo brag chos 'byung* (Pe, Vol. I, 192, 13):

> The so-called six or seven major laws include the law against murder [which sanctions] compensation for murder and rewards those who can prove that the defendant intended to commit murder; the law against stealing [which establishes] a hundred-fold repayment when items linked to the Three Jewels are stolen, an eightyfold repayment when the king's riches are stolen, and an eightfold repayment when possessions of the subjects are stolen; the law against adultery [which] assesses blame and punishment for rape; the law against falsehoods [to ensure that] vows [taken with] the tutelary deities as witnesses are kept; and [the law which determines] the control of alcohol intake which is [also] one of the five acknowledged Buddhist commandments. In addition [laws also prohibit] revolt by the subjects and the excavation of tombs.

The Ten Divine Virtues [*lha chos dge ba bcu*] become such when the ten nonvirtuous actions are abandoned. The three nonvirtuous actions of the body are killing, stealing, and sexual misconduct. The four non-virtuous actions of the voice are lying, slandering, using harsh words, and frivolous speech. The three nonvirtuous actions of the mind are covetousness, malevolence, and holding erroneous [doctrinal] views.

According to the *Deb ther dpyid kyi rgyal mo'i glu dbyangs*, the Sixteen Moral Rules for Laypeople [*mi chos gtsang ma bcu drug*] are (Pe, 22, 2):

> Worshipping the Three Jewels; practicing the sacred Dharma; honoring [one's] father and mother; respecting good families and the elders; assisting relatives and friends; helping neighbors; being honest and sincere; following the example of well-mannered people; making adequate use of victuals and riches; repaying benevolence; not falsifying weights and measures; not being indolent; not being envious; not obeying women; being well-spoken and polite; being forbearing and generous.

The Tibetan civilization flourished on the basis of those important laws and the political power connected with them became increasingly secure.

In addition, the *Yar lung jo bo'i chos 'byung* says (Si, 52, 7):

In the female Wood Sheep year [the Potala Palace was built on] the Red Hill [dMar-po-ri]; [it was] built with a perimeter of eight miles [*rgyang grags*] and a height of nine storeys. Also built were 999 strongholds.

The construction of the great Potāla Palace was initiated in the female Wood Sheep year (Tibetan year 2552, 635 CE) when the Dharmarāja Srong-btsan sGam-po was sixty-six or about sixty-seven years old.

Furthermore, the *lDe'u chos 'byung chen mo* says (Bod, 115, 12):

During the second part of [his] life, after having taken the Dharmarāja's throne, the king introduced the tradition of the Buddhist Law. He took in marriage Bal-mo-bza' Khri-btsun from Nepal. She wished to build the Miraculous Temple ['Phrul-snang], and they invited the Nepalese [expert] Bha-ta-ha to lay the foundations. The geomantic situation of Tibet was in-auspicious because the country was lodged on [the body of] a demoness lying on her back. Since [building the temple would have fatally] struck the demoness in the heart, [the expert] was reluctant to proceed.

The *lDe'u rgya bod kyi chos 'byung* says (Bod, 284, 21):

To restrain the reclining demoness, the Khra-'brug [Temple] was built on the left side [corresponding to her] left shoulder with [the temple of] Good Fortune [bKra-shis] and [the temple for] Increasing Merits [dGe-'phel] built (as its two subsidiary temples).

On the right [shoulder, the] dBu-ru bKa'-stsal [Temple was built together] with the Temple of Immutable Virtue [Mi-'gyur dGe-ba'i gTsug-lag] (as its subsidiary).

On the river side [situated] on the right, corresponding to [her] right hip, (the Bye-ma Temple was built) [together] with the Virtuous Abode of Awakening [Byang-chub dGe-gnas] (as its subsidiary).

On the left [hip] in Ru-lag, the Grom-pa-rgyang [Temple] was built [together] with the Temple of the Pure Law [rNam-dag Khrims-kyi lHa-khang] (as its subsidiary).

However, because it was still impossible to subjugate [her], four Taming Border Temples were erected: the Temple of mKho-mthing (in lHo-brag), to [hold down her] left elbow; the Bu-chu Temple of Kong-po, to [hold down] the right [elbow]; the Tre'i Ka-brag [Temple], to [hold down] the left knee, [and] the sPra-dun-rtse [Temple], to [hold down] the right [knee].

[Nonetheless, subjugating her had not been achieved]. Hence, four Further Taming Border [Temples were built]: to hold down the palm of [her] left hand, the Klong-thang sGron-ma Temple [was built] in Khams; to [hold down the palm of her] right [hand], the dPal-char Klu-gnon was built at mTshal-byi [in the] north [together with] (the Tshangs-pa Rlung-gnon Temple); to [hold down] the sole [of her] right foot, the Yid-'ong dGe-rgyas was built in Mang-yul; for the left [sole], the Bum-thang Temple was erected near the sKyer-chu [River in] Mon.

[However,] since overpowering [her] had not been attained, eight [sic] Further Taming Temples were built: Kwa-chu Thogs-med [in] rGya-gor; Klong-thang dPal-'byung in mDo-khams; Ke-ru dPal-'byung in 'A-zha; Sha-Indra in Li-yul [Khotan]; dBang-chen brTsegs-pa in Mang-yul; Bu-chu g.Yung-drung brTsegs-pa in Kong-po; [and] dPal-bo rGyas-pa [near the] sKyer-chu [River] in sPa-gro [Bhutan].

To the Four Further Taming [Temples] [four] accessory ['phy-ong] [temples were added, bringing their number to] eight: in the east, the Myang-ka-chu Temple was added to the Temple of the Immutable Vajra [rDo-rje 'Gyur-med lHa-khang] [placed] on the forehead of the white lion; in the south, the rMa-sha-rma Temple was added to the Temple of Bum-rtse-lung [placed] on the fangs of the whitish-grey tiger; in the west, the Myang-sprin Temple was added to the Mang-yul Byang-sprin Temple [placed] on the beak of the red bird; in the north, the gShen-gsas Temple was added to the sPra-dun-rtse Temple [placed] on the black tortoise.

After that, four temples were built in the intermediary direc-tions: these were the Temple of 108 Lig-tig [Malachite Stones] in the northeast; the Kong-chu Temple in the southeast; the Kho-mthing Temple in the southwest; and the Padma g.Yung-drung Temple in the northwest.

Then, eighteen [*sic*] Further Taming [Temples] were constructed: the Gling-chung, sKam-chung, and Ko-chu Temples
were built in order to control the [astrological] aspects of the
sun, the moon, the planets, and the constellations of the eastern
direction; the Bum-thang and Klong-rtse Temples were built so
that ascetics could perform rituals for the Fire Deities [Me-lha];
the dGe-re, dGyer-chu, and Hor-chu Temples were built so that
the female mountain spirits [*gnod sbyin mo*] could be served and
relied upon; the De-shang Temple and the Hab-shang Temple
were built at the border between Tibet and Nepal; the Gangs-bar
Temple was built to allay the concern that Lake Manasarovar
might overflow, creating complications for Tibet; the sPra-dun-
rtse Temple was built to block the sight of Mount Kailash
[Gangs Ti-rtse] to allay the concern that the elevation of the
mountain would hide the sides of all the others;[80] the Temple
of Nub-ri [Western Mountain] was built for the arrival of the
future [Buddha] Maitreya; the Temple of Khyung-lung dNgul-
mkhar was built in order to control the limits of the earth
and of the sky; the Khri-se Temple of Mang-yul was built for
the benefit of Shaivist practitioners; the Glang-po [Elephant
Temple] of Li-yul was built to commemorate the Parinirvāṇa
of the Buddha.

The *lDe'u chos 'byung chen mo* clarifies the meaning of the sentence "the
sPra-dun-rtse Temple was built to block the sight of Mount Kailash
to allay the concern that the elevation of the mountain would hide
the sides of all the others" [*spra dun rtse'i lha khang ni / gangs ti rtse mthos
nas ri thams cad la dngos bzhi med dogs pa'i ched du gangs mi mthong ba la bzhengs*]
(Bod, 116, 20):

> A concern [was raised regarding the possibility that] the sight
> of Mount Kailash [Gangs-ri Ti-se] might disturb the [other]
> mountains; the Temple of sPra-dum [*sic*] [was built] in order
> to block the vista of Mount Kailash.

The 'Phrul-snang Temple requested by the princess from Nepal [Bal-
mo-bza'] and the Ra-mo-che Temple requested by the princess from

---

80   *dngos bzhi med* means that the four sides of a mountain are not clearly visible.

China [rGya-bza'] have become extremely famous constructions. None-theless, they were not the only queens who asked that temples be built: Zhang-zhung-bza' Li-tig-sman, Mong-bza' Khri-lcam, Ru-yong-bza' rGyal-mo-btsun, and lDong-bza', known also as Mi-nyag-bza' Khri-btsun, each requested the construction of a temple. Several historical documents mention the temples erected by the queens. Concerning the temple of Zhang-zhung-bza' Li-tig-sman, the *bKa' chems ka khol ma* says (Kan, 270, 11):

> The Yer-pa Them-bu lKog-pa Temple of Zhang-zhung-bza' Khri-btsun was built and enhanced with bricks, wood, gold, and silver.

The *lDe'u rgya bod kyi chos 'byung* says (Bod, 298, 16):

> Lig-tig-mig, the daughter of King Lig-mi, was invited from Zhang Zhung; this queen erected four commemorative temples at the four corners of Srong-btsan's [kingdom].

The *lDe'u chos 'byung chen mo* says (Bod, 117, 8):

> Zhang-zhung-bza' Shi-Ku built the Brag-lha'i-rtse [Temple].

The *Bod kyi yig tshang gsal ba'i me long* says (Dha, 81, 2, 5):

> Zhang-zhung-bza' built the Lhasa Kha-brag Temple.

The *Nyang gi chos 'byung* says (Bod, 252, 11):

> lHa-gcig Mig-sman, the daughter of King Ling-dmig-bkra of Zhang Zhung, built the lKog-pa'i Thugs-dam [Temple].

The *Byams ma chen mo skyon gi 'jigs skyobs ma* says (bKa', TSHI, 35, 3):

> Zhang-zhung-bza' Lig-tig-sman was welcomed from the country of Zhang Zhung. She brought a statue the size of a one-year-old [child representing] the Lord of the Teachings gShen-rab, the Buddha of Zhang Zhung, and requested the building of the Theg-chen Temple.

The *rGyal rabs gsal ba'i me long* says (Pe, 158, 17):

[He] married [the princess] called Zhang-zhung-bza'. Because she had not borne a child, the Thim-phu sKog-pa Temple was built. The temple had iron doors.

The *lHo brag chos 'byung* says (Pe, Vol. I, 240, 4):

Zhang-zhung-bza' Li-thig-sman built the Them-bu bKog-pa Temple.

The *rGya bod yig tshang chen mo* says (Si, 163, 5):

Zhang-zhung-bza' Li-tig-man [built] the Khram-bu lKog-ma [Temple].

As we can see, although most of the quoted texts show slightly different readings for the name of the temple, they agree that the temple built by Zhang-zhung-bza' was the Them-bu lKog-pa. In this regard whether the Brag-lha'i-rtse mentioned in the *lDe'u chos 'byung chen mo* and the Lhasa Kha-brag Temple mentioned in the *Bod kyi yig tshang* are one and the same, or if the Theg-chen Temple mentioned in the *Byams ma* is a different name for the Them-bu lKog-pa are points that need to be investigated.

Concerning the temples built by Mong-bza' Khri-lcam, the *bKa' chems ka khol ma* affirms (Kan, 270, 9):

The mKhar-brag Temple of the first queen Pho-gong Mong-bza' Khri-btsun was built and enhanced with wood, gold, silver, copper, and iron.

The *Bod kyi yig tshang* says (Dha, 81, 2, 5):

Mong-bza' Khri-lcam built the Brag-lha [Temple] and also the Yer-pa Temple.

The *Nyang gi chos 'byung* says (Bod, 252, 10):

Mong-bza' Khri-lcam built the Lhasa mKhar-brag for personal spiritual practice.

The *rGyal rabs gsal ba'i me long* says (Pe, 159, 7):

The Pang-du Temple and a stūpa were built at the sacred site of Yer-pa on a rock resembling a sitting 'Phags-ma sGrol-ma [Ārya Tārā] as a personal practice place for the mother and the son. [The temple was built on her lap (*pang*)]. After the consecration, the father performed an aspiration prayer [saying,] "This will be the life vein [*srog rtsa*] of the Teaching, equal to the Ra-sa 'Phrul-snang [Jo Khang] Temple."

The *lHo brag chos 'byung* says (Pe, Vol. I, 240, 9):

Mong-bza' Khri-lcam built the Yer-pa Temple.

The *rGya bod yig tshang chen mo* says (Si, 163, 6):

Mong-bza' Khri-lcam built the temples of Yer-pa.

As we can see, except for the *Nyang gi chos 'byung*, the remaining religious and dynastic histories quoted here agree about the builder of the Yer-pa Temple.

Concerning the temples built by Ru-yong-bza' rGyal-mo-btsun, the *bKa' chems ka khol ma* says (Kan, 270, 13):

Queen [*khri btsun*] Ru-yong-bza' rGyal-mo-btsun built the mGon-po Kun-tu-zhal [Revolving-Head Mahākāla] Temple at Brag [Yer-pa]. When she decided to build the Brag-phug Temple on the lCags-po-ri [Hill in Lhasa], she offered a measure of salt for each stone until [the temple] was completed.

The *Bod kyi yig tshang* says (Dha, 81, 2, 5):

Ru-yong-bza' built the Thim-bu lKog-pa Temple.

The *rGyal rabs gsal ba'i me long* affirms (Pe, 158, 18):

Then [he] married [the princess called] Ru-yong-bza'. Because she had not borne children, the Mig-mangs-tshal Temple was built. The temple was located at Go-sha-gling.

The *lHo brag chos 'byung* relates (Pe, Vol. I, 240, 7):

Ru-yongs-bza' built the lHa-klu-phug [Temple] by dislodging the self-originated [images of] deities [*lha*] and Klu [Nāga] from the caves [*phug*] at Brag; eighty units [of] salt were used. [She] offered a measure of salt for each segment of cut stone until the rock images were excavated from the [site] of the temple.

It is not clear what the text means by "eighty units [of] salt were used" [*tshwa la brgyad cu sde'i dus*]. My interpretation is that eight measures of liquid salt were thrown [*tshwa la brgyad chu 'debs*] because liquid salt could penetrate deeper into the natural cavities so that the perimeters of the spontaneous images could be distinguished.

The *rGya bod yig tshang chen mo* claims (Si, 163, 6):

Ru-yong-bza' rGyal-mo-btsun [built] the lHa-klu-phug [Temple of] Brag.

As we can see, all above-mentioned texts differ in indicating the temple built by this queen.

Concerning the temples of lDong-bza' also known as Mi-nyag-bza', the *bKa' chems ka khol ma* reports (Kan, 270, 17):

lDong-bza' Khri-btsun, daughter of Li-lcam-lha, built the Mig-mangs-tshal Temple [made of] earth, stones [and] wood and enhanced with colored paintings.

The *Bod kyi yig tshang* asserts (Dha, 81, 2, 6):

Mi-nyag-bza' built the Mig-mangs-'tshal Temple.

The *rGyal rabs gsal ba'i me long* declares (Pe, 158, 20):

Then [he] married [the princess] called Mi-nyag-bza. Since also this queen had borne no children, the Kha-brag gSer-gyi lHa-khang [Golden Temple] was built. The temple was located at mKhar-sna-gdong.

The *lHo brag chos 'byung* says (Pe, Vo I, 240, 10):

Agreement seems to exist [that] Ru-yongs-bza' built the Mig-mangs-tshal Temple and [that] Mi-nyag-bza' built the Lhasa mKhar-brag Temple; but since the number of queens has been reported many times as five, if Ru-yongs-bza' and Mi-nyag-bza' were to be considered the same [person], [the actual construction of] mKhar-brag must have occurred under this [king's] fourth successor.

The opinion of the *Bod kyi yig tshang* seems valid; however, the cause of the two different names can be better understood if we consider the likely possibility that lDong-bza' and Mi-nyag-bza' were simply two ways of indicating the same name, given that the Mi-nyag belonged to the lDong clan.

The *lDe'u chos 'byung chen mo* explains briefly how the Dharmarāja Srong-btsan sGam-po built three supports for the whole territory of Tibet together with the ministers and the subjects (Bod, 117, 5):

> Of the 108 temples that the king promised to build, forty-two were completed [during his lifetime]. The foundations [of the first] of the remaining temples which had not been built [then] were laid at Bla-phu so that they could be erected afterward.

The *Deb ther dmar po* says (Pe, 36, 14):

> During the lifetime of this king ('Dus-srong Mang-po-rje), tea, a great number of musicians, and the Seven Powerful Men [rTsal-po-che'i Mi-bdun] appeared.

Thus at that time tea was cultivated, new musical traditions flourished, and the Seven Powerful Men who were skilled in various sports made their appearance. In this regard the *rGyal rabs gsal ba'i me long* specifies that some forms of art were already widespread at the time of the Dharmarāja Srong-btsan sGam-po (Pe, 64, 22):

> By the time he reached adulthood, the gifted prince had become expert in the Five Traditional Sciences [*rig pa'i gnas lnga*] [grammar, logic, craftsmanship, healing, and spirituality] and also in art, astrology, and workmanship. The ministers remarked, "This Lord of ours is endowed with multifold skills. His mind is profound [*sgam*]." So they called him Srong-btsan sGam-po.

As we can understand, the name sGam-po derives from the skills developed by the king in all those sciences before he was enthroned.

Knowledge of various sports was also widespread at the time of King Khri-lde gTsug-brtan; that can be inferred from many instances, including the one of the Tibetan minister playing polo [*spo lo*] with the Chinese minister g.Yang Kring mentioned in the *rGya'i thang yig rnying ma* [Old Chronicles of the Chinese Táng 唐 dynasty] (Dha, 23, 1):

> In the eleventh month of the third year of the Cin Lung era (Earth Bird year, 709 CE),[81] Zhang-tsan-thu'u, the chief minister of the Tibetan bTsan-po, arrived [in China] to escort [Princess] Cin Khrin Kong Jo. During the reception offered by Tang Krun Tsung, the daughter of Tang Krun Tsung and her husband g.Yang Kring played polo in the garden; also the emperor and the ministers participated in the entertainment.

Many religious and dynastic histories—such as the *lDe'u rgya bod kyi chos 'byung*, the *rGyal rabs gsal ba'i me long*, the *lHo brag chos 'byung*, the *rGya bod yig tshang chen mo*, and the *Deb ther dpyid kyi rgyal mo'i glu dbyangs*—mention the Seven Powerful Men [*rTsal-po-che'i Mi-bdun*]. While the sources present some minor differences in their accounts, in essence the information they provide is consistent; as an indicative example, the *lDe'u rgya bod kyi chos byung* contains a clear description of those men (Bod, 299, 12):

> rNgog Ring-la Nag-po carried a baby elephant from Nepal on his back.
>
> rNgogs-gling-gam [was able to] hoist a four-year-old yak in the air.
>
> sBas-rgod lDong-btsan captured lions.
>
> 'Gos g.Yag-chung [was able to] whirl a deer skin filled with sand over his head.
>
> Cog-ro 'Brong-shor could stop a wild yak from hurtling downhill and drag it to a halt.
>
> gNon-rgyal-mtshan [was able to] shoot a hawk with a multi-pointed arrow which would then remain fixed in the sky as if a divination had been cast.

---

81 [The Jǐnglóng 景龍 era (707-710) of the second reign of Emperor Zhōngzōng 中宗 (705-710) of the Táng 唐 dynasty (618-907).]

gNon Khri-lde Yul-byin [was able to] shove an untamed
horse off a cliff and pull it back up [again].

The various sports requiring great strength that flourished in Tibet at
that time, in particular whirling a deer skin filled with sand over the
head, are truly amazing feats even for our times when the sports culture is advanced and features many superlative sportsmen and women.

The *lHo brag chos 'byung* briefly describes the deeds of King Khri-lde
gTsug-brtan (Pe, Vol. I, 294, 8):

> When Bran-ka Mu-le Ka-sha and gNyags Dznyā-na Ku-ma-ra
> were sent to India to obtain the Buddhadharma, they heard that
> the two paṇḍitas Sangs-rgyas gSang-ba and Sangs-rgyas Zhi-
> ba were meditating on Mount Kailash. [They tried to] invite
> [the paṇḍitas to Tibet] but [they] declined. So [they] requested
> [and received] from the two masters the detailed exegesis of the
> [Vinaya] Sūtra series, the *gSer 'od dam pa* [the Sūtra of the Sacred
> Golden Light], plus some Kriya and Ubhayā [U-pa] Tantras.
> [They] brought the texts [to Tibet] and offered [them] to the
> king as objects of veneration. [King Khri-lde gTsug-brtan] built
> five temples to contain [them] at Lhasa mKhar-brag, Brag-dmar
> mGrin-bzang, mChims-phu Nam-ral, Brag-dmar Ka-ru, [and]
> Ma-sa-gong.

The *rGyal rabs gsal ba'i me long* says (Pe, 197, 3):

> The *gSer 'od dam pa* [the Sūtra of the Sacred Golden Light] and
> the detailed exegesis of the Vinaya series were translated from
> the Chinese language by Kem-shi. Pe-ci Tsandra-shrī translated
> many medical texts.

The *Deb ther dpyid kyi rgyal mo'i glu dbyangs* affirms (Pe, 50, 11):

> Ordained monks were invited from Li-yul [Khotan] and shown
> respect. However, Tibetans were not ordained [at that time].

When g.Yu-thog Yon-tan mGon-po was young, he was the personal
physician of King Khri-lde gTsug-brtan. During the last part of his
life he was the personal physician of the Dharmarāja Khri-srong lDe'u-
btsan.

At that time there were nine famous proficient physicians in Tibet: g.Yu-thog Yon-tan mGon-po, Bi-li Legs-mgon, 'Ug-pa Chos-bzang, Che-cher Zhig-po, Mi-nyag Rong-rje, Brang-ti rGyal-bzang, gNyag-pa Chos-bzang, sTod-sman Grags-rgyal, and mTha'-bzhi Dar-po. Also other physicians were invited: these were the great Indian doctor Śāntigarbha, the Chinese sTong-gsum Gang-ba, the Khotanese Ma-hā De-ba, the Nepalese Da-na Shī-la, the Kashmiri Khu-na Badzra, the Mongolian Na-la Shan-dir, Khyom-ru-rtse from Dol-po, the Turk-ish Seng-ge 'Od-can, and Shi-la-na from Khrom. Since each of these doctors transmitted his own specific medical knowledge, the Tibetan medical science became enriched and comprehensive. In this regard, the biography of g.Yu-thog Yon-tan mGon-po elucidates clearly and in detail how the teachings of the Tibetan medical science reached the apex of their development due to the encampment he organized in the Kong-po Valley to collect herbal ingredients and also to his formation of study sessions at the beginning of autumn on the Four Medical Tantras [rGyud bzhi] and on other medical texts containing the methodologies and disquisitions of various specialists, doctors such as Zla-ba'i rGyal-po and others.

Activities for the diffusion of the teachings flourished and ex-panded like summer lakes during the lifetime of the Dharmarāja Khri-srong lDe'u-btsan. The minister Sang-shi brought back from China the dGe ba chu'i mdo [the Sūtra of the Ten Virtues], the rDo rje gcod pa [Skt. Vajracchedikā Prajñāpāramitā Sūtra, the Diamond Sūtra], the Sa la'i ljang pa'i mdo [the Sūtra of the Śāla Tree], and other texts. The Lo-tsā-bas Sang-shi, rGya Me-mgo, and the Kashmiri A-nanta translated them from the Chinese into the Tibetan language.

Moreover, also the Chinese scholar Hwa-shang Ne-le and the scholars Dar-chen Ha-ra and Yi-pa Bha-bo traveled to Tibet to work together with the Tibetan Lo-tsā-bas Bhi-la Shong-kun, Dar-chen-dpal, and others to translate several astrological and medical texts into Tibetan from the Chinese language. All these facts are clearly mentioned in the lDe'u rgya bod kyi chos 'byung, the lHo brag chos 'byung, the Deb ther dpyid kyi rgyal mo'i glu dbyangs, and other sources.

The Dharmarāja Khri-srong lDe'u-btsan invited in succession the great Indian Paṇḍita Śāntarakṣita [mKhan-chen Zhi-ba-'tsho, 725-788] and the great Master Padmasambhava and built the temples and shrines of the glorious bSam-yas, the Unchanging and Spontaneously Perfected Temple [Mi-'gyur lHun-gyis Grub-pa'i gTsug-lag-khang].

Twelve fully ordained disciples of the Indian Mahāpaṇḍita Śāntarakṣita were invited to Tibet. They taught the Sanskrit, Chinese, Nepalese, Zahori, Kashmiri, and Khotanese languages to many intelligent young Tibetans, such as Pa-gor Be-ro-tsa-na; mChims Śākya Pra-bha; sBa Khri-gzigs; 'Khon Klu-dbang Srung-ba; gTsang Legs-grub; Bran-ka Mu-tig; Rlangs Khams-pa Go-cha; rMa Rin-chen-mchog; La-gsum rGyal-ba Byang-chub; sBa gSal-snang; sBa Khri-bzher; Seng-gong lHa-lung-gzigs; sNa-nam rDo-rje bDud-'joms; Shud-bu dPal-gyi Seng-ge; rTsangs Rin-chen Legs-grub; Glang Ka-ta-na; rTsangs De-wandra; Shud-bu Khong-sleb; Zhang-lha bSe-btsan; and Ngan-lam rGyal-ba mChog-dbyangs. Most of them became prodigious translators.

In the presence of the Mahāpaṇḍita Śāntarakṣita, seven were chosen as the first Tibetan ordained monks [Sad-mi-bdun]. They are identified by the *Pad dkar chos 'byung* as follows (Dhi, 324, 162, 2):

> Seven men were ordained to test the feasibility of establishing monkhood in Tibet. Their preceptor was Bo-dhi-satwa [Śāntarakṣita].
>
> The three elders among the candidates were sBas Ratna Rakṣi-ta, known as Rin-chen Srung-ba [Guardian of the Precious Jewel]; sBas Dznyā-nandra Rakṣi-ta, known as Ye-shes dBang-po Srung-ba [Guardian of the Supreme Wisdom], an important Buddhist scholar and great benefactor of Tibet who became the successor of Bo-dhi-satwa after the latter's death; and Rat-nendra Rakṣi-ta, known as Rin-chen dBang-po Srung-ba [Guardian of the Supreme Precious Jewel].
>
> Glang Su-ga-ta Warma Rakṣi-ta, known as bDe-bar gShegs-pa'i Go-cha Srung-ba [Armor-like Protector of the Sugata] was middle-aged.
>
> The three young ones were dPa'-gor Be-ro-tsa-na Rakṣi-ta, known as rNam-par sNang-mdzad Srung-ba [Guardian of Vairocana], who greatly contributed [to the understanding of]

the essence of the supreme teaching; 'Khon Nā-gendra Rakṣi-ta, known as Klu'i dBang-po Srung-ba [Guardian of the King of Nāgas]; and rTsangs De-bendra Rakṣi-ta, known as lHa'i dBang-po Srung-ba [Guardian of the King of Gods].

The great Indian masters Vimalamitra [Dri-med bShes-gnyen], Śāntigarbha, and Viśuddhasiṃha, who were invited later, translated many Buddhist texts together with the Tibetan Lo-tsā-bas and the Seven Chosen Ones [Sad-mi-bdun] in the Translation Temple [sGra-sgyur Lo-tsā'i-gling of bSam-yas].

When Master Dharmakīrti was invited, the Yogatantra Vajradhātu *maṇḍala* and other empowerments were bestowed at the Māra-Taming Mantra Temple [bDud-'dul sNgags-pa'i-gling].

The Kashmiri Paṇḍita Jinamitra, Dānaśīla, and others imparted the Vinaya rules in the Temple of the Pure Law [rNam-dag Khrims-khang-gling].

The Chinese masters, Hwa-shang among others, practiced meditative absorption in the Temple of Unwavering Meditation [Mi-g.yo bSam-gtan-gling].

Enunciation and study of the Dharma were carried out in the Temple of Vairocana [Be-ro-tsa-na'i-gling].

Grammar was taught in the Temple of Pure Messages [brDa-sbyor Tshangs-pa'i-gling].

Treasures were placed in the Temple of Pehar [Be-har-gling].

Since meditation centers were established at Yer-pa, Chu-bo-ri, and other locations, many accomplished Tibetan yogis and yoginīs began to frequent them, such as the famous twenty-five main disciples of Guru Padmasambhava.

The translators sKa-ba dPal-brtsegs, Klu'i dBang-po, and others, residents at the lDan-dkar Palace, compiled a catalog [*dkar chag*] of all texts previously translated in Tibet; this became known as the lDan-dkar-ma Catalog.

The most illustrious and active Lo-tsā-bas of that time were Vairocana, lDan-ma rTse-mang, and the Kashmiri A-nanta, who were known as the three elders; gNyags Dznyā-na Ku-mā-ra, 'Khon Klu'i dBang-po, and rMa Rin-chen-mchog, who were known as the three middle-aged ones; and sKa-ba dPal-brtsegs, Cog-ro Klu'i rGyal-mtshan, and Zhang Ye-shes-sde, who were known as the three young ones.

At one point, since disagreement arose among Tibetan scholars concerning the gradual approach [*rim gyis pa*] [to enlightenment] sustained by the Indian Mahāpaṇḍita Śāntarakṣita [725-788] and the sudden approach [*cig char ba*] promoted by the Chinese Master Hwa-shang Mahāyāna, the teacher Kamalaśīla [flourished 740-795] was invited from India to settle the doctrinal dispute.

The Dharmarāja Khri-srong lDe'u-btsan compiled extensive works, such as the *bKa' yang dag pa'i tshad ma bam po bdun pa* [Sevenfold Epistemological Volume on the True Words of the Buddha], as well as many shorter ones. The great Lo-tsā-ba Vairocana and other scholars composed a variety of treatises. All those works are described in the historical chronicles and in the major Tibetan dynastic and religious histories and there is no necessity to elaborate upon them in this context.

During the reign of Mu-ne bTsan-po, inequalities in prosperity were eliminated three times; this is recorded in all Tibetan histories.

Khri-lde Srong-btsan Sad-na-legs built the dKar-chung Vajradhātu Temple in the lower valley of the sKyid River [sKyid-shod]. He invited Paṇḍitas Vimalamitra [Dri-med bShes-gnyen], Dznyā-na Se-na, the Nepalese Huṃ-ka-ra, Pra-dznyā Dharmā, Śākyasiṃha, Surendrabodhi, Jinamitra, Dānaśīla, and Buddhasiṃha and honored the previous great translators. Many texts were translated into Tibetan such as the *dKon mchog sprin* [Skt. *Ratnameghasūtra*, the Cloud of Jewels Sūtra], and the *Lang kar gshegs pa'i mdo* [Skt. *Laṅkāvatārasūtra*, Ascent onto Lanka Sūtra], as well as many other sūtras and tantras from the Buddhist canon and treatises from the collection of Indian commentaries.

During the lifetime of his son, Khri-gtsug lDe-btsan Ral-pa-can, international scholars such as the Ācārya Jinamitra, Surendrabodhi, Śīlendrabodhi, Dānaśīla, Bodhimitra, the Tibetan scholars Ratna Rakṣita and Dharmatāśīla, and the translators Dznyā-na Se-na, Dza-ya Rakṣita, Mañjuśrīvarma, Ratnendraśīla, and so forth translated into Tibetan a great number of sūtras, tantras, treatises, and commentaries from the languages of India, Orgyan, Za-hor, Kashmir, Khotan, China, and Bru-sha.

Khri-gtsug lDe-btsan Ral-pa-can decreed the use of rules that established lexical homogeneity in text translation [*skad gsar bcad*] and prohibited the translation and diffusion of the highest Yogatantra cycles, especially those of the Mother Tantra, although they were deemed appropriate in the sphere of practice of individual yogins. Previously translated texts were also systematized according to the script revision prescribed by the king and two more sets of the translated words of the Buddha [*bka' 'gyur*] with their commentaries and treatises [*bstan 'gyur*] were added to the lDan-dkar-ma Catalog, namely, the mChims-phu-ma and the 'Phang-thang-ma. The history of their placement in the dKor-mdzod [the Pe-kar-gling Temple of bSam-yas] and other relevant events are clearly recorded in most religious and dynastic histories and also in the Twofold Volume on Word-Combination [*sGra sbyor bam gnyis pa*] contained in the "CO" section of the Derge Tenjur [sDe-dge bsTan-'gyur].

Furthermore, the so-called Seven Wise Ministers [*'phrul blon mdzangs pa mi bdun*] were greatly honored for their contribution to the progress of civilization in the snowy country of Tibet. Their names and deeds are listed in famous dynastic and religious histories, such as the *lDe'u chos 'byung*, the *Ne'u sngon byung gi gtam*, the *lHo brag chos 'byung*, and the *rGya bod yig tshang chen mo*, albeit with some slight differences.

According to the *lDe'u chos 'byung*, the first of the wise ministers was Ru-las-skyes, son of 'Dreng; the second was Khu lHa'u mGo-dkar; the third was Thon-mi Sam-bho-ṭa; the fourth was sNyags Khri-bzang Yang-ston; the fifth was Khri-bzang Yab-lhag; the sixth was Mon Khri-to-re sNang-tshab; the seventh was gNyer sTag-btsan lDong-gzigs; and the eighth or seventh-and-a-half one was Princess Ong Chung from China.

According to the *Ne'u sngon byung gi gtam*, the first wise minister was gNyer sTag-tshal lDong-gzigs; the second was Khri Do-re sNang-tshab, son of Mong; the third was Ru-las-skyes, son of 'Breng; the fourth was Thon-mi Sam-bho-ṭa; the fifth was lHa-bu mGo-dkar, son of Khu; the sixth was Khri-bzang Yab-lhag; and the seventh was Khri-bzang Yab-brten, son of rNgogs.

According to the *lHo brag chos 'byung mkhas pa'i dga' ston*, the first wise minister was Ru-las-skyes; the second was lHa'u mGo-dkar; the third was Khri-dor sNang-btsun, son of Mong; the fourth was Thon-mi Sam-bho-ṭa; and the fifth was Khri-bzang Yang-ston, son of sNyags. The text does not mention the sixth and the seventh ones.

According to the *rGya bod yig tshang chen mo*, the first of the wise ministers was Ru-las-skyes, son of 'Dzeng; the second was lHa-bu mGo-dkar, son of Khu; the third one was Khri Do-re'i sNang-tshab, son of Mong; the fourth was Thon-mi Sam-bho-ṭa; the fifth was Khri-bzang Yab-don; the sixth was Khri-bzang Yab-lhag; and the seventh was sTag-tshab lDong-gzigs, son of gNyer. Regarding the order of their appearance, if the first five ministers listed in the *lHo brag chos 'byung mkhas pa'i dga' ston* are combined with the sixth one mentioned in the *rGya bod yig tshang chen mo* and with the seventh one in the *lDe'u chos 'byung*, we can see that a great correlation of historical facts exists.

Concerning the first of the Seven Wise Ministers ['phrul blon mdzangs pa mi bdun], the *lHo brag chos 'byung* says (Pe, Vol. I, 164, 2):

> The first changes [appeared with] Ru-las-skyes. As innovative acts [he] produced charcoal from burned wood; with charcoal, ore [was] fused [so that] gold, silver, copper, and iron [could be] obtained. He invented the yoke by carving holes in wood. He dug up the earth and built irrigation channels. Yoking together a pair of draft animals, [he transformed] meadows into fields [for] cultivating. [He] raised bridges over water [where] crossing was difficult. That is when ploughed crops appeared for the first time.

Ru-las-skyes was the minister of the tenth Tibetan monarch sPu-de Gung-rgyal.

Concerning the second wise minister, the *lHo brag chos 'byung* affirms (Pe, Vol. I, 165, 5):

> The first [of] the Six Legs [Legs-drug] was called I-sho-legs. His minister was lHa'u mGo-dkar. The paternal uncle was the son of Ru-las-skyes. [He] was the second of the Seven Wise Ministers ['phrul blon mdzangs pa mi bdun]. As innovative acts [he established the sizes of] fields by calculating [the number of] pairs of oxen

yoked together [necessary to plow them] [*dor kha*]. For the nomads [he] determined the number of animals that would form a herd of cattle. [He] channeled water flowing from the upper part of the valleys into trenches. Plowing [of] irrigated fields in the lower part of the valleys became common at this time.

As for the third wise minister, the *lHo brag chos 'byung* relates (Pe, Vol. I, 171, 4):

> At this time (the era of King sTag-ri gNyan-gzigs) Khri-dor sNang-btsun, son of Mong, created weight measurements [*bre phul srang*] for butter and cereals. [If] two [persons] wished [to], [they could] trade [goods]. [If] two [persons] agreed [about the confines of] mountain passes and valleys, [they could] coordinate [their activities]. Before that time, commerce and weight measurements did not exist in Tibet. For that reason [he] became known as the third of the Seven Wise Men.

Concerning the fourth wise minister, the same text reveals (ibid., 184, 11):

> Thon-mi became known as the fourth of the Seven Wise Men because [he] created the first written language [of] Tibet.

Concerning the fifth one, the same text asserts (ibid., 184, 12):

> Moreover, in terms of innovative acts, Khri-bzang Yang-ston, son of sNyags, relocated mountain dwellings in the valleys, built fortresses on high summits, and created towns. Until that time Tibetan houses were built [only] on mountains. For that reason he is the fifth of the [Seven] Tibetan Wise Men.

Concerning the sixth one, the *rGya bod yig tshang chen mo* specifies (Si, 237, 5):

> Khri-bzang Yab-lhag, the sixth Wise One, appeared during the time of the Dharmarāja Khri-srong lDe-btsan.

This textual source evidently attests that the sixth Wise One was Khri-bzang Yab-lhag and that he was a minister during the lifetime of the Dharmarāja Khri-srong lDe'u-btsan but credits him with the same innovations that the *mKhas pa'i dga' ston* ascribes to the fifth Wise One.

Therefore one has to turn to the *lDe'u chos byung chen mo* to discover his actual achievements (Bod, 114, 20):

> [The sixth Wise One] was Khri-bzang Yab-lhag. [He] positioned bodyguards in the four directions to protect the king. [He] established an army of 22,000 warriors to defeat enemies. Since [he] fixed the levels of compensation for people, future ministers did not have to ponder [about that matter] any longer. Before that time reparation and compensation did not exist in Tibet.

Concerning the seventh Wise One, the *lDe'u chos byung chen mo* affirms (Bod, 115, 5):

> The seventh Wise One was gNyer sTag-bstan lDong-gzigs. [He] classified together [*dgye ru sdebs*][82] *mdzo po* [male cross between a yak and a cow], *rtol po* [male calves born from a female *mdzo* and a bull], *be'u* [crosses between a female yak and a bull], [as well as] sheep, [and] assigned one cow, one bull, [and] cattle [*gnag*] to [each] household. [He established the collection of] grass in bundles so that plants [grown during the] summer [could be available as] forage in the wintertime. Before that time no laws [regulated] the distribution of cattle.

The *rGya bod yig tshang chen mo* specifies the time during which sTag-tshab lDong-gzigs appeared (Si, 231, 10):

> The seventh Great Wise One, sTag-tshab lDong-gzigs, son of gNyer, appeared during the lifetime of Khri-lde Srong-btsan 'Phrul-rgyal.

It is difficult to ascertain what the *lDe'u chos 'byung* actually means when it describes the deeds of the seventh Wise Minister. In this regard the *Ne'u sngon byung gi gtam* relates (Dha, 9, 5, 1):

> One of the Wise Ones was gNyer sTag-tshal lDong-gzigs. As for his deeds, [he created the] law [regulating] the distribution [of] one cow, one bull, [and] cattle [*gnag*], goats, [and] sheep to [each] household. [He established the collection of] grass in bundles so that plants [grown during the] summer [would be available as]

---

82   [For the translation of this term see discussion below.]

forage in the wintertime. [He] converted grassy meadows into [cultivated] fields and afterward built houses. Before that time no harvesting [of] grass [and] crops existed in Tibet.

The *rGya bod yig tshang chen mo* communicates nearly identical information (Si, 229, 15):

[He created the] law [regulating] the distribution [of] cows, bulls, *'bri* [female of the yak], yaks, goats [and] sheep. [He established the collection of] grass in bundles so that plants [grown during the] summer [would be available as] forage in the wintertime. [He] converted grassy meadows into [cultivated] fields and supervised the management [of pastural areas] on the mountains. Before that time no harvesting [of] grass [and] crops existed in Tibet.

It is not certain whether the two above-mentioned sources refer to the promulgation of a law according to which every family should have had cows, bulls, *'bri* [female of the yak], yaks, goats, and sheep or if the law measured the allocation of those animals or else, if it determined penalties for inadequate appreciation of their market value.

Still, with respect to the same deed described in those two texts, the meaning of the *lDe'u chos 'byung* is even more cryptic. The *lDe'u chos 'byung* says, "[He] classified together [*dgye ru sdebs*] *mdzo po* [male cross between a yak and a cow], *rtol po* [male calves born from a female *mdzo* and a bull], *be'u* [crosses between the female of the yak and a bull], [as well as] sheep." Crosses between yaks and cows are called *mdzo* or *mdzo po* while crosses between female yaks [*'bri*] and bulls are called *'bri mdzo*. Although extremely useful for plowing and transporting and valued for rural activities, these animals are sterile. *rTol po* are the calves of a female *mdzo* and of a yak or bull which, if they survived, were for the most part utilized for the same toil as a *mdzo*, although without supplementary food and milk it was difficult for them to subsist. If a female and a male *rtol po* produce offsprings, the latter have less chance of survival than their parents. Even if these two types of animals were appreciated for the work they performed, they were useless for reproduction.

Since livestock growth was the main concern, my interpretation is that *mdzo po* and *rtol po* were considered of equal value as the male and female calves of a cow and of a *'dri* or as male and female sheep. Furthermore, I think that the intended meaning of *dgye ru sdebs* is "grouping for barter" [*brje ru sdebs*] and referred to a new trading system according to which animals with the same value could be exchanged, such as for example one *mdzo* for one calf or one sheep or one *rtol* for one calf or one sheep. "[He] assigned one cow, one bull, [and] cattle [*gnag*] to [each] household [*ba re glang re gnag re khyim du btsal*]" could refer to the promulgation of a new law requesting each Tibetan family to maintain a cow, a bull, and cattle [*gnag*]—that is to say, a *'bri* or a yak—so that their number could be increased.

The *lDe'u chos 'byung chen mo* describes the contribution of the eighth or seventh-and-a-half Wise One (Bod, 115, 9):

> The eighth Wise One, the Chinese [Princess] Ong Chung, established the differentiation between the garments of men and women and between male and female activities. She assigned bows [and] arrows to men [and] the spindle to women. Before that time such distinctions did not exist.

Whether they are counted as seven, seven-and-a-half, or eight, the Wise Ones represented a way of describing the progress of Tibetan civilization. Those who overlook the pre-existing civilization of Zhang Zhung could think that the civilization of the ancient Tibetan people developed precisely in that way only because of the admirable innovations of those enterprising spirits.

2. THE TEN CULTURAL SCIENCES OF TIBET

A current way of identifying aspects of Tibetan culture is as the Ten Cultural Sciences [*rig gnas bcu*].

2.1. The Five Major Cultural Sciences

The Five Major Cultural Sciences [*rig pa'i gnas chen po lnga*] are:

2.1.1. the science of arts and crafts [*bzo ba rig pa*];

2.1.2. the science of healing [*gso ba rig pa*];

2.1.3. the science of language [*sgra rig pa*];

2.1.4. the science of logic [*gtan tshigs rig pa*]; and

2.1.5. the science of inner meaning [*nang don rig pa*].

2.2. The Five Minor Cultural Sciences

The Five Minor Cultural Sciences [*rig pa'i gnas chung lnga*] are:

2.2.1. astrology [*skar rtsis*];

2.2.2. poetics [*snyan ngag*];

2.2.3. metrics [*sdeb sbyor*];

2.2.4. lexicography [*mngon brjod*]; and

2.2.5. drama [*zlos gar*].

Orthodox historical views have alleged that Tibet was a savage country lacking all sciences before their importation from India, Orgyan, Za-hor, Nepal, Li [Khotan], and Bru-zha, or China, as in the case of craftsmanship, medicine, and astrology. In so doing, this view has gradually lulled into somnolence the true history of the civilization of ancient Tibet. The causes of this phenomenon have already been elaborated upon in the chapter dedicated to the origin of the ancient Tibetan civilization [Volume One, Chapter V] and I will not tire the reader by repeating them here.

2.1.1. The Science of Arts and Crafts [*bZo ba Rig pa*]

Some specific examples of the historical background of the Five Major Cultural Sciences [*rig pa'i gnas chen po lnga*] are presented below starting with the first, the science of arts and crafts [*bzo ba rig pa*]. The *bKa' chems ka khol ma* affirms (Kan 84, 8):

> After Lord gNya'-khri bTsan-po arrived at bTsan-thang sGo-bzhi in Yar-lung, the palace was erected [*pho brang btab*]. Not built of earth and stones, the palace was a tent made of the skins of herbivorous wild animals, such as deer and *'brong* [wild yaks], and those of carnivorous animals, such as tigers and leopards.

The text refers to the palace as a tent made of hides which does nothing other than call attention to a lack of knowledge and ability in building castles.

The *rGya bod yig tshang chen mo* briefly describes how the Potala Palace was constructed (Si, 155, 13):

> The Nepali Princess [Bal-bza'] supplied many precious jewels [to build the citadel] so that enemy troops could not inflict injury and the king would not be harrassed.
>
> After male and female gNod-sbyin [Yakṣa spirits] were bound into servitude, a thirty-two tier brick wall-like fence was erected on dMar-po-ri [hill].
>
> Similar to Laṅkāpurī—the capital of the land of the Srin-po [Rākṣasa demons]—the stronghold had 999 pinnacles and openings. Each building had four shafts with red banners. Guards were positioned under the eaves above the four principal doors in the four directions. Five sentinels kept constant watch on the building's roof.
>
> On its southern side inside the bulwark, a nine-storied bastion named the Mongolian Palace [Pho-brang Sog-po] was the king's most important building. These two [structures] were connected by a silver bridge of coiled iron chains.
>
> The bastion and the bulwark were furbished with parapets, doors [with] handles, [yak] tail fans, tiles, projecting beams, pediments, small bells with clappers of precious stones, [and] fringes [made of] nets of pearls.

The text candidly implies that without the jewels of the Nepalese princess the Tibetans could not have afforded the costs of such a palace and had she not brought with her Nepalese workers capable of creating such a huge structure when she came to Tibet, Srong-btsan sGam-po would most certainly have pitched a skin tent as [his] residence on dMar-po-ri. With a similar outlook, the *Nyang gi chos 'byung* specifies that the workers involved were only of Nepalese origin (Bod, 237, 7):

> The Nepalese masons transported the stones from gSang-phu; [they] did the construction [work].

And also (ibid., 249, 10):

> The king charged the Nepalese artists with the following: "Paint
> a deity on the southern side of the shrine hall." The artists
> arranged small bowls, brushes, colored lacquer, and other ma-
> terials at the foot of a pillar featuring a tree leaf motif around
> its capital.

The text ignores the hardships, efforts, and perseverance endured month
after month and year after year by the Tibetan workers, craftsmen,
and laborers that contributed to the construction of the Potala Palace
of the king of Tibet and of all the temples and shrines of the Ra-sa
'Phrul-snang [Jokhang], the Ra-mo-che, and so on. It is possible that
the declarations of the majority of dynastic and religious histories that
the Tibetans specialized in craftsmanship were religious artists and
carpenters miraculously emanated from the king or that the constructions appeared spontaneously because of a prodigious manifestation
by the king were made with the virtuous intention of inspiring faith
and admiration in the charismatic king. For example the *lHo brag chos
'byung* reports (Pe, Vol., 1, 234, 11):

> At that time the king put to work 5,000 sculptors [who] mani-
> fested from [his] body. [They] took the Indian He-dun Bi-har
> [Temple] as a model. The ground laid out [for their work] was
> that of a medium-sized ocean-going vessel.

And also (ibid., 234, 11):

> In one day the emanations built the ground floor of the Ra-sa
> [Temple] with bricks.

And also (ibid., 234, 15):

> In the morning 300 emanated craftsmen were put to work;
> [they] served [as] carpenters.

Nevertheless, what certainty is there that Tibetan workers and laborers
did not endure numberless hardships and inconceivably arduous toil?

The *Legs bshad nor bu'i phreng ba* identifies the origin of the Tibetan science of arts and crafts and describes the historical background for the creation of the first Buddha images (Dhi, 16, 8, 1):

> The text composed by the son of the sage [*drang srong*] A-tri titled *Ri mo'i mtshan nyid tshangs pa'i tshad yig* [Characteristics of a Picture According to Brahmā] says that a long time ago when the life of human beings was less than 100,000 years the human king called 'Jigs-thul [Fear Subduer] appeared. Since he ruled the earth with justice, the duration of human life increased [again] to 100,000 years and [life] became joyous.
>
> The king carried out intense ascetic practices [*dka' thub*] and thus attained the eight qualities of mastery[83] and became extremely accomplished in the knowledge of all scriptures so that [when] Brahmā [sent] armies with divine weapons to the human world they were not able to destroy it.
>
> At that time the beloved son of a Brahmin died unexpectedly. The Brahmin said to the king, "It seems you are not ruling with justice [after all]. [One of] your subject[s] has met with an untimely death: my son has been taken [from me] by force. If [my] son is not returned [to me], I will commit suicide right here."
>
> Thus the king guided the Brahmin, leading [him] into the presence of King Yama, the Lord of Death [whose] blazing radiance [was] like [that of] the sun.
>
> After paying homage, [they] requested the release of the Brahmin's son. [The Brahmin said,] "[If] I do not get [him back,] I will terminate my life." [Also] the king [pled with Yama to] release [the son], but Yama said over and over again, "Impossible."
>
> Finally they readied themselves for battle [and fought]: weapons rained down [on] both sides. The king defeated the retinue of Yama, deluging them with [his] divine weaponry, so that Yama [himself intervened,] brandishing a staff; also the king wielded [his] staff adorned with the head of Brahmā menacingly.

---

83 *dbang phyug gi yon tan brgyad*, the qualities that realize all desires: subtle form, visible form, lightness, omnipresence, accomplishment, clarity of mind, and firm concentration.

All the worlds were panic-stricken. Brahmā appeared and said, "Stop your fighting. Yama is not to be blamed. Draw a picture of the Brahmin's boy." Accordingly the king drew [the picture]. Brahmā animated [it] and presented [it] to the Brahmin.

[The king] subdued [the chief of] the hungry ghosts called gCer-bu. [Brahmā] said, "Well done" and called him gCer-thul [Subduer of gCer]. Since the king was the first person to draw images, [Brahmā also] named him First Draftsman [Dang-por Bri-ba].

Brahmā ordered the king to pay [his] respects to Yama; the king complied and everyone was happy.

Later the king went to Brahmā's world and requested the technique [for] drawing images. The supreme mountain is Mount Meru [Ri-rab]. The chief of all beings born from an egg is the sky-soarer [eagle]. The chief of all human beings is the king. That is why the king learned the art of drawing those four images first and then perfected the skill of drawing everything. That is [also] related in the prophecy disclosed by Bi-shwa Karma.

And also (ibid., 17, 9, 4):

[As for representations of] the physical form of the Teacher, first came painted images and then carved reliefs. The painted images [have] two [sources]. The first was the image that King gZugs-can sNying-po [Bimbisara, 558 BCE–491 BCE] sent as a gift to King Uṭayana; looking at the image of the Teacher, the followers of the Vedas [Rig-byed-pa] were so amazed by its beauty that their eyes became like those of an inebriated person. The image taken as a model was that of the Teacher reflected in the water when the Teacher was dwelling near a river; [this became known as the Buddha] at the riverside [chu lon ma].

The second source is embodied by three large pearl embroideries that Mu-tig 'Khri-shing, the daughter of the king of Singa [Ceylon], sent to the Teacher, reciprocating His gift. The images depicted on the cotton fabric radiated light and among them was the clearly visible figure of the Buddha with his pure distinctive marks. [This image] became widespread in Kashmir [Kha-che] and Magadha [Yul-dbus].

Concerning the origin of sculpted images ['bur sku], the *Shes bya kun khyab* [The All-Encompassing Treasury of Knowledge][84] relates (Pe, Vol. I, 572, 8):

> When the Teacher was not [yet] gone, the [faithful] house-holder Dad-sbyin invited the *Samgha* [dge-'dun] to a midday meal. Beholding the magnificence of the Buddha in the first seat of the line, this [extremely generous] patron [known as the] Feeder-of-the-Destitute [mGon-med Zas-sbyin, Anāthapiṇḍada] pleaded, "If the Teacher allows [it, I would like to] request [that He] remain [here in order that a] statue [of him] be made." The request was granted and many statues of precious materials were created.
>
> Then, while the Bhagavān Buddha [bCom-ldan-'das] had gone to the land of the gods, the king of the City of Light [gSal-ldan-ma, Kāśī, Varanasi] ordered a sandalwood statue of the Buddha as a recipient for offerings. When the Teacher returned from [the land of] the gods, the statue [walked] six steps toward [him] in welcome.
>
> [Furthermore,] a request [came from] China for the Bhagavān Buddha to visit that country in order to create auspicious circumstances; [on that occasion a sandalwood statue] descended from the sky. Even today many *si thang* copies[85] in China of the so-called Sandalwood Buddha [Tsandan Jo-bo] can be found. Those were the first statues [to appear].

And also (ibid., 574, 22):

> At the time of the Buddha, King Bimpa Sā-ra [gZugs-can sNy-ing-po, Bimbisara] was ruling in Ma-ga-dhā.
>
> During the reign of King Ngang-tshul, the 'Phreng-'dzin [Asuramālādhara, gods holding their prayer-bead garlands] appeared on the Srig-dha Mountain in the region of Ma-ru.
>
> At the time of De-ba-pā-la, Wa-rendrar-dhī-mān and his son Bu-bitpā-lo appeared. They were residing at Bhanga-la. They were great experts in the art of painting and statue-making. The

---

84   [Author, 'Jam-mgon Kong-sprul Blo-gros mTha'-yas (1813-1899).]
85   *si thang*: statues modeled after the original and made with an alloy called *li ma*.

upholders of their tradition gradually became the [renowned] artists of Magadha. It is said that in the old Western world they were called the artists of the East.

And also (ibid., 575, 21):

It is recorded that the earliest model of images that marked the development of the painting and sculpting tradition in Tibet was the [clay] mold of the image of the Buddha near the river [*thub pa chu lon ma*] that sTag-tsang Lo-tsā received directly from the Mahābodhi [Temple] of Bōdh Gayā, blessed and carried by hand, wrapped in a clean cloth moistened with perfumed water. That model antedates the self-created holy images of the Khra-'brug [Temple in Yarlung], the self-created [image of] the Great Compassionate One of the Ra-sa [Jo Khang Temple], and other models [created] at the time of the emanation King Srong-btsan sGam-po as well as [all] statues [placed in the] Mahābodhi, the main bSam-yas [Temple], at the time of [King] Khri-srong.

Three types of creative arts developed in Tibet. They are classified and described as the arts related to body, voice, and mind.

Concerning art related to the body, the *Legs bshad nor bu'i phreng ba* says (Dhi, 18, 9, 7):

Two forms of art refer to the body: primary and secondary. The primary are the holy objects related to the Three Jewels or to the supports [of] Body, Speech, and Mind.

The supports of Enlightenment are those of the Body of Reality [*chos sku, dharmakāya*], of the Perfect Enjoyment Body [*longs sku, sambhogakāya*], and of the Emanation Body [*sprul sku, nirmāṇakāya*].

The supports of the Body of Reality are known as stūpas of which five [kinds] exist: those of spontaneously perfected nature; those which are unexcelled; those [derived from] blessings; those derived from accomplishments; and those of the single vehicles.

And also (ibid., 20, 10, 1):

The land and its inhabitants were exultant as a result of the exceptional deeds performed by the Teacher. Eight Stūpas, named

Stūpas of the Sugata [bDe-gshegs], were erected in order to mark and celebrate the anniversary of each event.

These were the Mass of Lotuses Stūpa [built to celebrate] the place, [that is to say,] the town [of] Kapilavastu, and the time, [that is to say,] the birth of the Teacher.

The Mahābodhi or Māra-Taming Stūpa, [built to celebrate] the place, [that is to say,] the king's court, and the time when [the Buddha] manifested total enlightenment.

The Stūpa of the Many Doors of Auspiciousness [*bkra shis sgo mangs*] or [of] the Wheel of Dharma [built to celebrate] the time [the Buddha] turned the Wheel of Dharma in Varanasi.

The Stūpa for Defeating the Extremists or [of] the Great Miracle [built to celebrate] the time when [the Buddha expounded] miraculous teachings at Śrāvastī.

The Stūpa of the Divine Descent [built to celebrate] the time [he] at [age] thirty-three was in summer retreat in the city [of] Kāśī and [his] mother descended from heaven to listen to [his] teachings.

The Stūpa [of] Loving Kindness and Reconcilement or [of] Marīcī ['Od-zer Can-ma], [built to celebrate] the time Devadatta [lHas-byin] created discord [among] the Samgha [*dge-'dun*] at the king's court and the Supreme Pair [mChog-zung] [Śāriputra and Maudgalyāyana] reconciled the controversy.

The Stūpa [of the] Blessing or [of] Complete Victory [celebrating] the time when [the Buddha returned from] his three-month [retreat] at Vaiśālī.

The Nirvāṇa Stūpa built at the time of [the Buddha's] death in the city [of] Kushinagar.

The supports for the Perfect Enjoyment Body are scroll paintings, statues, and appropriate clay images of the Five Buddha Families[86] and of the Eight Close Sons or main Bodhisattvas[87] clad in silk and adorned with jewels.

---

86   rNam-snang [Vairocana], Don-yon Grub-pa [Amoghasiddhi], Rin-chen 'Byung-ldan [Ratnasambhava], sNang-ba mTha'-yas [Amitābha], and Mi-bsky-od-pa [Akṣobhya].

87   'Jam-dbyangs [Mañjuśrī], Phyag-na rDo-rje [Vajrapāṇi], sPyan-ras-gzigs [Avalokiteśvara], Sa-yi sNying-po [Kṣitigarbha], sGrib-pa rNam-sel

Concerning the supports for the Emanation Body, the ordinary ones are the images of supreme emanation bodies clad as ordained persons; the extraordinary ones are the myriad of representations of the peaceful, joyful, and wrathful assemblies of deities of the Tantric *maṇḍalas*.

Concerning the supports for the Jewel of the Dharma or supports for the Voice, the *Legs bshad nor phreng* [The Jewel Garland of Elegant Sayings] says (Dhi, 21, II, 4):

> The *Ye shes rdo rje kun las btus* [Compendium of Vajra Wisdom] specifies that the main supports for the Voice or the Dharma are the manuscript volumes [*pusta ka'i glegs bam*] of the Sūtra series [with their] 84,000 approaches to the Dharma [and] the 33,000 [teachings] belonging to the Tantric series.

And also (ibid., 22, II, I):

> In regard to the written language, from among the sixty-four types of writing styles existing in India, such as Brāhmī, and so on, the Tibetan scholar Thon-mi Sam-bho-ṭa took as a model the Kashmiri written language for the thirty letters and the *bu drug*[88] created by him. From Thon-mi's model the calligraphic styles created by Khyung-po gYu-khri, Sum-pa gNod-sbyin and others gradually developed and spread, including capital letters [*gzab chen*] and minuscule letters [*gzab chung*]; the big and small broad letters [*'bru chen dang 'bru chung*]; and within the small broad letters, the Khotanese style [*li lugs*], the style [of the Tripiṭaka translator] lDan[-ma rTse-mang] [*ldan lugs*], the *Shar shar ma* [quick calligraphy],[89] and the abbreviated style [*dkyus yig*].
>
> The capital and minuscule letters [are used] for primary scriptures; the big broad letters [are used] for authoritative commentaries of the Indian paṇḍitas; and the small broad letters

---

[Sarvanīvaraṇaviṣkambhī], Nam-mkha'i sNying-po [Ākāśagarbha], Byams-pa [Maitreya], and Kun-tu bZang-po [Samantabhadra].

88 I think these correspond to the six reversed or retroflexed letters of the Sanskrit alphabet: ṭa, ṭha, ḍa, ṇa, ṣa, and kṣa.

89 [This is the style in which the Author compiled his manuscript.]

and the remaining ones [are used] for the mainstream Tibetan scriptural tradition.

[The ordinary supports are] mastery in the use of any of the appropriate inks and other superior [materials, such as] gold and silver for the big and small slanting calligraphy [*gco chen gco chung*], including in brief, a good training and study of [all] the various forms of handwriting.

The special supports for the Voice are the bell, the prayer beads for counting [mantras], and so forth.

Concerning the supports for the Jewel of the Saṃgha [*dge-'dun*], the same text relates (ibid., 22, 11, 4):

> As for the *Saṃgha*, [there is first] the Mahāyāna *Saṃgha* [represented by] the Bodhisattvas traversing the stages; [their supports] are the various types of pure attributes of the renunciants, such as [those] appearing on the body of Mañjuśrī, and usually, the attributes of a beautiful young [person], such as garments, ornaments, the five locks of hair, and the topknot.
>
> [The supports of the Hīnāyana *Saṃgha* of] the Śrāvakas are the beautiful attributes of the renunciants, such as the mendicant's staff, the alms bowl, [and] the book [*po ti*].
>
> [Those of the] Pratyekabuddhas are the slightly bent top of the head, and so on.

In synthesis, the main supports for the body are those of the three dimensions connected to the Three Jewels: for the Body, any suitable painting and statue of deities depicting their distinct manifestations, faces, arms, and attributes, as well as the various types of stūpas; for the Voice, texts, prayer beads for counting mantras, bell, and so on; and for the Mind, symbolic implements, such as the vajra and the dagger; within this category are also included different kinds of sacred dances, as well as all sitting and dancing postures, hand gestures, and gazes connected with yogic yantras. A support for the Body may be represented also by any appropriate mundane activity, such as building temples and houses, cooking, creating ornaments and sewing clothes, playing sports, theatrical performances, and dancing.

Concerning vocal activities, the *Legs bshad nor phreng* [The Jewel Garland of Elegant Sayings] says (Dhi, 23, 12, 2):

> There are primary and secondary activities for the Voice.
>
> Primary activities consist in honoring the Victorious Ones with songs of praise having six characteristics: melody; modulation [of the voice]; raising [the pitch of tunes]; lowering [the pitch of tunes]; increasing the [rhythm]; [and] decreasing the [rhythm]. These melodies include those of the Sūtra tradition previously known in Tibet; *yogic* melodies diffused since [the time of] the elder and younger translators; spiritual songs of the siddhas; and praising and invoking the peaceful and wrathful Dharma protectors.
>
> Expertise in making musical instruments [such as] small and big cymbals [*sil chol*],[90] large drums, round drums, drums that have skin-striking surfaces on both sides, Chinese string instruments [*pi wam*], flutes, conch shells, copper trumpets, long brass trumpets, and so on is an art related to the Body.
>
> Expertise in melodious singing and chanting represents an ordinary activity of the Voice.

Also activities related to the Mind are succinctly described in the *Legs bshad nor phreng* [The Jewel Garland of Elegant Sayings] (Dhi, 23, 12, 5):

> The primary activities related to the Mind consist in eradicating external misconceptions through study and reflection as well as internal misconceptions through meditation and, in particular, practicing discriminating knowledge or the knowledge that fully discerns phenomena; as said in the Treasury [of Abhidharma], "Afflictions that are not accurately investigated [with respect to their real nature can] on no account [permit] peace." These are the main activities of the Mind.
>
> The secondary activities of the Mind are said to be the above-mentioned eight kinds of examination (Dhi, 11, 6, 7: precious substances, land, garments, fruit trees, horses, elephants, men, and women), and in particular, the eight examinations of pos-

---

90   *sil chol*: small cymbals [*sil snyan*] and big concave cymbals known as *rol mo* or *shub chen*.

sessions which consist in that of precious substances [used as] supports for the Body, Voice, and Mind, that is to say, cymbals, bells, wind bells, clothes, silk brocade, lattices [*ling man*], bowls, tea, and so forth.

2.1.2. The Science of Healing [*gSo ba Rig pa*]

Concerning medical science, the *Legs bshad nor phreng* [The Jewel Garland of Elegant Sayings] briefly identifies its origin and development in India, China, and Tibet (Dha, Vol. I, 25, 13, 7):

> No Sūtras or Tantras among the Words of the Victorious One expound upon medical treatment as such.
>
> Nevertheless, ancillary Vinaya scriptures explain in great detail the way of administering the four basic types of remedies.[91]
>
> Furthermore, the Khye'u Chu-'bebs [Youth-Who-Brings-Water, Buddha Śākyamuni in a former birth] section of the *gSer 'od dam pa* [Sūtra of the Sacred Golden Light], the Mahāparinirvāṇa Sūtra, the Tantra of Vajra Ḍākinī [*rDo rje mkha' 'gro'i rgyud*], and in particular, the Kālachakra [*Dus kyi 'khor lo*] contain detailed explanations concerning methods for preserving the body, the most important of which [is considered] the yogic prāṇa practice [*rnal 'byor gyi rlung sbyor*], [followed by] ordinary remedies and longevity practices [*bcud len*]. [The explanations] also [discuss] remedies that the renunciants are able to find [naturally] in their own bodies and remedies in the external world for the wealthy, the three levels of longevity practices—higher, middle, and lower—as well as the yoga of the supreme corpse, greatest of the great [*chen po'i chen po ro chen*].
>
> One famous non-Buddhist [source exists] according to which the Vedas of long life were emanated from the central face of Brahmā and emerged from the depth of the ocean at the time of the first [five] powerful kings [of India].

And also (ibid., Vol. I, 28, 14, 2):

---

91 *sman rnam pa bzhi* correspond to medicines administered at the appropriate time, medicines well-suited for a limited period of time [*thun tshod*], seven-day medications, and life-saving medicines. These and other remedies associated with them are referred to as treatments suitable for use by fully ordained monks.

In China [the science of healing] developed due to the blessing of Mañjuśrī from the time of the Thang Ci-u [dynasty, Táng cháo 唐朝 618-907] and was expounded by kings and ministers, by Taoist and Buddhist priests, and so forth.

In Tibet, although a limited knowledge [about] what to adopt and what food [and] behavior to reject [already] existed from a former time, [medical science did not really flourish until] the Chinese Princess brought the so-called *sMan dpyad chen mo* [Great Book on Medicine] which was translated by Hwa-shang Ma-hā De-wa and rDarma-ko-sha.

Three physicians were invited at that time: Badzra Dhwa-dza from India, Hon Wong Hong Nge from China, and Ga-le-nos from Khrom of sTag-gzig. They translated several [texts] of their own traditions and composed the sevenfold volume titled *Thun mong du mi 'jigs pa'i mtshon cha* [Universal Fearless Weapons].

Afterward, also Gyim-shang Kong-jo [wife of Khri-lde gTsug-brtan, father of Khri-srong lDe'u-btsan, 704-755] brought many [other texts] of medicine and astrology [to Tibet].

The fundamental texts of the Tibetan medical science are the Four Medical Tantras [*sMan gyi rgyud bzhi*] which consist of the Root Tantra [*rTsa rgyud*], the Exposition Tantra [*bShad rgyud*], the Oral Instruction Tantra [*Man ngag rgyud*], and the Subsequent Tantra [*Phyi ma rgyud*]. As we shall see, different ways of considering the origin of these Four Tantras can be found.

The *lHo brag chos 'byung mkhas pa'i dga' ston* affirms (Pe, Vol. 2, 1521, 1):

The Four Medical Tantras, essence of all the oral instructions, [are] famous texts in Tibet [containing] all the instructions transmitted by the true *nirmāṇakāya* emanation g.Yu-thog mGon-po. [He] appeared six times in India.

And also (ibid., 1522, 5):

This itself is [the teaching taught by] the supreme *nirmāṇakāya* himself [Buddha]. [So] many medicinal herbs [grew] on the grassy hill [located] to the east of his dwelling [that the hill] resembled [Mount] sPos-ngad-ldang. On the southern side were warming medicinal herbs; on the northern side, high altitude and cooling medicinal herbs; the western [area] was conducive to [the growth of] forests: his abode [resembled] the medicine city of lTa-na-sdug [of Mount Sumeru].

It has been said that the narrative according to which the fourfold assembly of disciples [monks, nuns, laymen, and lay-women], the gods of the desire realm [such as] Kāmadeva [Yid-las-skyes], and disciples [abiding] in the wisdom of awareness requested the Buddha Supreme-Healer [Sangs-rgyas sMan-gyi-bla] [whose] mind [abides in the] *dharmakāya* to explain the Four Tantras and that the Buddha expounded them, serves as a basis for introducing pure vision to those who live in ordinary vision and who are in need of taming. I think that in terms of pure vision this is not a contradiction.

And also (ibid., 1522, 16):

Someone maintains that [the Four Tantras are a] transmission [of] the Medicine Buddha. [Some] say that [they are] teach-ings emanated from Śākyamuni [just] as [when the Buddha] manifested as Vairocana on the peak of Mount Sumeru and taught the Yogatantra. [Some] say that [they are a] rediscov-ered teaching [*gter ma*]. [Some say that] g.Yu-thog expanded [a previously] existent short [version of the] Four Root Tantras. Even if it is determined that [these Tantras] are the fruit of the *nirmāṇakāya*, if one properly examines the facts, no other texts contain similar instructions. Hence it is impossible that medical texts better than the Four Tantras exist in the world. [Teachings that] correspond to the Word of the Buddha should be honored, especially during these unfavorable times for Tibet.

The *Shes bya kun khyab* [All-Encompassing Treasury of Knowledge] ex-plains (Pe, Vol. I, 593, 18):

Several different opinions have been expressed concerning the [taxonomy of the] Four Tantras. Some maintain that they should belong either to the Canonical Transmission [of the words of the Buddha] [*bka' ma*] or to the Treatises [*bstan bcos*], while some say that they belong to both. Others say [that they should be considered only as] part of the Treatises. The best opinion is the one conveyed by the master [Tā'i Si-tu Paṇchen Karma] bsTan-pa'i Nyin-byed [1699-1774], confirmed by his disciples, who posited that in the external sphere they are the Word of the Victorious One; in the internal sphere, they belong to the continuum of the rediscovered texts; and in the secret sphere, they are the teachings of g.Yu-thog.

Furthermore, the *Legs bshad nor phreng* [The Jewel Garland of Elegant Sayings] (Dhi 31, 16, 1) declares:

> It has been said that the Four Medical Tantras appeared as the quintessence [of the mind] of the *nirmāṇakāya* manifestation g.Yu-thog-pa [at the] time appropriate [for] Tibet. The majority of followers like [to consider them] as the pure Word [of the Buddha]. The *rNying ma rgyud 'bum* says that they were retrieved from a *gter ma* location by a monk endowed with clairvoyance.

The *Legs bshad nor phreng* [The Jewel Garland of Elegant Sayings] also provides a superficial description of the nature of the Tibetan science of healing (Dhi, 31, 16, 1):

> All [related] topics can be expressed as a combination of three [factors]: the disease that needs to be cured and the patient; diagnosis and remedies; and nurses and physicians. Instead [the topics viewed in terms of] the eight aspects are the need to abandon the four faults while keeping in mind the four positive skills related to the [four elements, namely,] remedies and patients, and nurses and physicians.

2.1.3. The Science of Language [*sGra Rig pa*]

The *Shes bya kun khyab* [All-Encompassing Treasury of Knowledge] describes the earliest source of the science of language in the following manner (Pe, Vol. 1, 557, 16):

> The Root Tantra of Mañjuśrī says that the Victorious One prophesied the birth of the Brahmin Pāṇini [fourth century BCE] in the Dhi-ru-ka grove [of] the western Noble Land [Gandhara]. When [he] asked [a] palm reader [to tell him

whether he would] learn the science of words, [the palm reader responded] negatively. So [with a] small knife, he altered the lines on his hands and then studied with the best grammarians on earth.

Since [he] was still not satisfied with the level of [his] knowledge, he practiced the knowledge mantras [*rigs sngags*] of the worldly [deity] dBang-phyug [Śiva] [until he] saw the face [of] the Noble One. "What [is your] wish?" asked [the Noble One]. [He replied,] "I request a knowledge of grammar." Because of the Noble One's blessing, as soon as [the Noble One] pronounced the cluster of letters, A, I, U, and so on, he understood all the topics of grammar of the three worlds. He then composed the Pā-ṇi Byā-ka-ra-ṇa [Skt. *vyākaraṇa*, grammar] [in] 1,000 stanzas [*śloka*] and the 1,000 stanzas [of] the *Bye brag 'byed pa'i mdo* [Scripture that Shows the Difference].

And also (ibid., 559, 1):

[There is a] prophesy in the Subsequent Tantra of the Kālachakra about the birth of the master Tsandra-go-mī. He was born in eastern India [in a place] called Wa-rindra. He knew all the ordinary sciences [such as] grammar, logic, and so on without having studied them. At the age of seven, he was [already] able to challenge the antagonism of the heretics. He received teachings from Master Mya-ngan Med-pa [Nonsuffering]. [He] practiced and achieved the accomplishment [of] the knowledge mantras [*rigs sngags*] of Avalokiteśvara and Tārā and became a great paṇḍita.

And also (ibid., 559, 15):

In the same form as the eloquent commentary on the essential meaning written by Pā-ṇi-pa, [he] compiled a work called the Tsāndra Byā-ka-ra-ṇa in 700 stanzas [*śloka*] and twenty-four chapters [that contained] few abridged concepts, revealing a perfect understanding of the meaning of all that pertains to this kind of knowledge. He composed relevant ancillary texts on literary language as well.

And also (ibid., 560, 16):

During the reign of King Tsandan, the Lord of the gods [Indra] transmitted to the Brahmin Indra-dhuba the Indra Byā-ka-ra-na, that is to say, the Grammar of Indra, which explained the true grammatical topics in 25,000 stanzas [*śloka*]. Soon after, in order to fulfill the order of King bDe-spyod to learn that grammar, the Brahmin Sabta-warma practiced [meditation on] the six-headed Kumāra [gZhon-nu gDong-drug]. When he realized this attainment, [the god] asked [him], "What is your wish?" [He replied,] "I wish to learn the Indra Byā-ka-ra-na." As soon as [the god] said: "*Siddho warna samamnāya,*" [he] understood all the grammatical meanings and composed the Ka-lā-pa Byā-ka-ra-na. The grammar was [compiled following] the system of the Indra Byā-ka-ra-na. [He] also wrote many general and specific commentaries. The grammar was studied by numerous people also in Tibet. Shong-lo was the first person to translate it.

And also (ibid., 561, 7):

Furthermore, at the time of Paṇḍita sGo-drug-tsam, the Noble goddess Sarasvatī ['Phags-ma dByangs-can-ma] transmitted the Sa-ra-sva-ti Byā-ka-ra-na directly to Master A-nu-bhu-ti of the Brahmin caste [of the] southern [region of] Ma-hā-rāshṭa. The grammar became greatly diffused in India. [In] Tibet the commentary of the principal text was initially translated by Jo-nang rJe-btsun sGrol-ba'i mGon-po [Tāranātha, 1575-1634], relying on the Paṇḍitas Kṛṣṇa and Balabhadra. Commentaries were also compiled.

These excerpts identify the origin of the science of language and the root texts of the commentaries. About the necessity of studying the science of language, the *lHo brag chos 'byung* says (Pe, Vol. 2, 1509, 11):

[Grammar] is the most important [aspect] of all languages. It is a topic [that is an essential] part [of the curriculum] of [a] scholar, so that [one will not] be called [an] ox for being ignorant of it, and [also] so that eminent Indians will be impressed [by one's knowledge of] another language.

2.1.4. The Science of Logic [gTan tshigs Rig pa]

For what concerns the science of reasoning or science of logic, the *Shes bya kun khyab* [All-Encompassing Treasury of Knowledge] affirms (Pe, Vol. I, 562, 9):

> Many [works] have been produced [in this field of knowledge] such as the *rTog ge'i bstan bcos* [Treatise on Logic] compiled by the non-Buddhist teacher Drang-srong Gling-skyes and the *rTog ge'i tshig don brgyad ston pa'i bstan bcos* [Treatise Explaining the Eight Categories of Dialectical Sophistry][92] compiled by the Brahmin rKang-mig. However, since these treatises present shortcomings that have sparked controversies, [such as ones that] previously emerged in Buddhist texts, they have not been considered here. For this reason [logic] is particular because ordinary understanding or the mere [six] divisions of speech in debate cannot be compared with the real sense of the teachings.

And also (ibid., 562, 23):

> Regarding the teachings of this master, the first of the Buddhist texts was titled *rTsod pa grub pa* [Principles of Debate]. Some say that the author was Master Vasubandhu [dByig-gnyen, fourth century]. However, earlier Tibetan masters have posited that the author could not have been the younger brother [of Asaṅga] Vasubandhu because of the extensive criticism [of Vasubandhu contained] in the autocommentary of the *Tshad ma kun btus* [The Compendium of Valid Cognition, Skt. *Pramāṇasamuccaya*, by Dignāga, 480-540 CE], and [because] the venerable Vasumitra and other authors signed their works with Vasubandhu's name.

And also (ibid., 565, 5):

---

92 *rtog ge'i tshig don brgyad*: four classifications belonging to the categories of knowledge and four classifications belonging to the categories of the signifier, that is to say, the four distinctions into real and apparent for both direct and inferred knowledge, methods used by oneself to produce understanding or cognition, and the four distinctions into real and apparent for statements both of proof and confutation, methods used by others to produce recognition.

Some root texts and commentaries were translated in Tibet by sKa-ba dPal-brtsegs and Dran-pa Nam-mkha' during the earlier diffusion of the doctrine, such as [for example] the *gTan tshig thig pa* [Drop of Reasons, *Hetubindunāmaprakaraṇa*] and the *'Brel pa brtag pa* [Analysis of Relations, *Sambandhaparikṣāvṛtti*] within the Seven Treatises [*sde bdun*] [composed by Dharmakīrti, seventh century].

At the time of the later diffusion of the doctrine, the Compendium of Valid Cognition [*Tshad ma kun btus*] and other texts were translated by Zha-ma Seng[-ge] rGyal[-ba, eleventh century]. More extensive commentaries such as the *Tshad ma stong phrag bcu gnyis pa* [Twelve Thousand Stanzas on Valid Cognition] were first translated by rMa dGe-ba'i Blo-gros and [then] discussed by Khyung-po Grags-so and others; in that way the so-called old valid cognition [*tshad ma rnying pa*] flourished to a small degree.

rNgog Lo[-chen] Blo-ldan Shes-rab [1059-1109] rewrote those translations in a different style of calligraphy and completed the translation of the *rNam nges* [*Pramāṇaviniścaya, Tshad ma rnam par nges pa*, Ascertainment of Valid Cognition by Dharmakīrti] and of the *Rig thig* [*Nyāyabinduprakaraṇa, Rig pa'i thigs pa zhes bya ba'i rab tu byed pa*, Drop of Reasoning by Dharmakīrti]. [After] having extrapolated the main [principles of] the *rGyan* [*Abhisamayālamkāra, mNgon par rtogs pa'i rgyan*, Ornament of Clear Realization, by Maitreya, fourth century] and the positions of Dharmottara [Chos-mchog] [748-800], [he established a] new [tradition of] logic.

[His] successor, Phywa-pa Chos-kyi Seng-ge [1109-1169], composed two large and small compendia on the Madhyamaka [doctrine] [*dBu-ma*]. In particular, after having compiled the [root text and commentary called] *Tshad ma'i bsdus pa yid kyi mun sel rtsa 'grel* [The Compendium of Valid Cognition Dispelling Mental Darkness], [he] established the academic tradition of the Compendia.

As to the nature of the science of logic the *Legs bshad nor phreng* [The Jewel Garland of Elegant Sayings] affirms (Dha, 82, 41, 5):

The subject matter and its descriptions are extensive, but in synthesis [they can be defined as] ultimate valid cognition and conventional valid cognition. [They are also] known as the eight categories of dialectical sophistry: real and apparent statements of proof and consequence [*thal 'gyur*, Skt. *prasaṅga*]; real and apparent direct [knowledge] and inferred [knowledge]; or as subjective understanding, with the appearance of direct experience and inference, and extrinsic realization, with the appearance of statements of proof and refutation; or as affirmation and refutation.

In brief, this science has been traditionally recognized as a sharp weapon for defeating proponents of erroneous views concerning the fundamental nature of knowable phenomena by means of a syllogistic approach and the acceptance of statements of proof.

2.1.5. The Science of Inner Meaning [*Nang don Rig pa*]

The essential principle of this cultural science is linked to the sphere of individual self-awareness. It refers to one's own luminous nature that is profound, peaceful, and totally beyond the limits of mental conceptualization: the ultimate nature totally unconditioned by primary and secondary causes, beyond words, thoughts, and explanations, and beyond origin and cessation.

This nature is called in different ways according to the various vehicles: the Common Vehicle [*Thun mong gi theg pa*] calls it the Nature of Selflessness [*bdag med pa'i gnas lugs*]; the Vehicle of the Bodhisattvas [*Byang sems kyi theg pa*] calls it Transcendent Wisdom [*shes rab kyi pha rol tu phyin pa*]; the Mantra Vehicle, the Path of Transformation [*sNgags sgyur lam gyi theg pa*], calls it the Great Symbol [*phyag rgya chen po*]; and the Vehicle of the Primordial State [*rang grol a ti'i theg pa*], the Path of Self-Liberation, calls it Total Perfection [*rdzogs pa chen po*].

This is the supreme state of knowledge of Lord Buddha. This supreme state of knowledge has appeared as the sacred Dharma taught by Lord Buddha according to the spiritual capacity of individuals and as the noble Saṃgha, the members of which have contributed to the upholding, preservation, and diffusion of the sacred Dharma.

The history concerning the beginning of the diffusion in Tibet of the holy teachings of the Three Jewels during the lifetime of King Srong-btsan sGam-po and the flourishing of the Sūtra and Tantra teachings during the lifetime of the Dharmarāja Khri-srong lDe'u-btsan and his son following the encounter with Guru Padmasambhava and his disciples represents the essential content of all the narratives produced by the doctrinal schools which are found in Tibetan dynastic and religious documents. The implications of the numerous and extensive texts produced by those who wished to deepen their knowledge in this respect and which were compiled according to the doctrinal position adopted by the single authors are concretely present in the various fields of our senses. However, their study with an impartial attitude that does not fall into sectarianism would be auspicable.

The topics investigated through the science of the intrinsic meaning [*nang don rig pa*] are the quintessence of the Sūtra, Mantra, and Mind Series: the Sūtra Series comprises the Three Baskets [*sde snod gsum*, Skt. Tripiṭaka] of Sūtra, Vinaya, and Abhidharma; the Mantra Series includes the higher and lower Tantras; the Mind Series features the cycles of the Total Perfection. These series represent unique paths of skillful means related to the body, speech, and mind of individuals and are respectively styled the Path of Renunciation [*spang lam*], the Path of Transformation [*sgyur lam*], and the Path of Self-Liberation [*rang grol gyi lam*].

The three series are definitively acknowledged as the topics studied through the science of intrinsic meaning. In this regard the Old School of the Early Translations [*snga 'gyur rnying ma*] posited a classification into Nine Vehicles [*theg pa rim pa dgu*] which included the ordinary vehicle of Gods and Humans [*thun mong lha mi'i theg pa*], the vehicle of the Śrāvakas and Pratyekabuddhas [*nyan rang gi theg pa*], and the vehicle of the Bodhisattvas [*byang sems kyi theg pa*], as well as the extraordinary Mantra Series, namely, the series of the three Outer Tantras—Kriyā, Ubhayā, and Yoga—and that of the three Inner Tantras—Mahāyoga, Anuyoga, and Atiyoga.

Then, due to the emergence of specific doctrinal viewpoints, all sorts of schools [*grub mtha'*] and traditions emerged with their distinct ways of understanding, learning, and practicing the principles of the Sūtras and Tantras:

- the New Mantra School [sNgags gSar-ma] of the bKa'-brgyud-pas deriving from Mar-pa Chos-kyi Blo-gros (1012-1097);
- the illustrious New Mantra School [sNgags gSar-ma] of the Sa-skya-pas deriving from Sa-chen Kun-dga' sNying-po (1092-1158);
- the Old bKa'-gdams-pa School [bKa'-gdams rNying-ma] deriving from Lord Atiśa (982-1054);
- the great New bKa'-gdams-pa School [bKa'-gdams gSar-ma], known as Ri-bo dGa'-ldan-pa from its first monastery, deriving from the incomparable Tsong-kha-pa Blo-bzang Grags-pa (1357-1419);
- the Jo-nang-pa School deriving from Jo-nang Tāranātha (1575-1634);
- the Zhi-byed School [Zhi-byed-pa] deriving from Pha-dam-pa Sangs-rgyas (who arrived in Tibet in the year 1113) [and died around 1117 CE];
- the gCod tradition deriving from Ma-gcig Lab-sgron (1103-1201);
- the Bo-dong tradition deriving from the great Paṇḍita Bo-dong Phyogs-las rNam-rgyal (1376-1451);
- the Bu-lugs-pa School deriving from Bu-ston Rin-chen-grub (1290-1364);
- the (Reformed) Bon tradition deriving from mNyam-med Shes-rab rGyal-mtshan (1356-1416).

The general attitude when the philosophical tenets of different schools are studied is to consider the doctrines of the school we follow, regardless of its name, as correct and to regard those of other schools as fallacious. Even though such an approach implies a serious effort to refute the position of the other side, establish one's own position, and respond to the criticism of one's position, it can hardly assimilate the profound key point of the science of intrinsic meaning, which the great master Śāntarakṣita [Zhi-ba-mtsho, 725-788] once said was "the Transcendent Wisdom beyond words, thoughts, and explanations, the

Essential Nature, unborn [and] unhindered [like] space, the sphere [of] Self-revealing Primordial Wisdom [belonging] to each [sentient being], the Mother of the Victorious Ones of the three times."[93] Hence, I think it is extremely important to distance oneself from the prejudice of narrow scholastic sectarianism in order to bring to light the real sense.

These are the so-called Five Major Cultural Sciences. They represent the solid foundations of a perfect and organic civilization as well as the distinctive expressions of the admirable and comprehensive culture of Tibet.

2.2. The Five Minor Cultural Sciences [Rig pa'i gNas chung lNga]

According to a common saying, knowing astrology [*skar rtsis*], one will not be at a loss with numbers; knowing prose, one will not be at a loss with poetry [*snyan ngag*]; knowing metrics [*sdeb sbyor*], one will not be at a loss with verses; knowing lexicography [*mngon brjod*], one will not be at a loss with names; and knowing drama [*zlos gar*], one will not be at a loss with languages.[94]

2.2.1. Astrology [*sKar rtsis*]

Three distinct types of astrology flourished in Tibet: zodiacal astrology [*skar rtsis*], warfare astrology [*g.yul rgyal*, literally, to be victorious in battle], and elemental astrology [*'byung rtsis*]. Concerning the first one, the *Shes bya kun khyab* [The All-Encompassing Treasury of Knowledge] affirms (Pe, Vol. 1, 569, 2):

---

93   [*smra bsam brjod med shes rab pha rol phyin / ma skyes mi 'gag nam mkha'i ngo bo nyid / so sor rang rig ye shes spyod yul ba / dus gsum rgyal ba'i yum //*]

94   [The Author does not treat the topic of drama in this excursus. As a bibliographic reference see for example Antonio Attisani, "Tibetan Secular Theatre: The Sacred and the Profane," *PAJ: A Journal of Performance and Art*, PAJ 63 (Vol. 21, Number 3), September 1999, pp. 1-12.]

The science that predicts positive and negative effects and that differentiates time by reckoning the movement of planets and constellations was amply expounded and discussed in treatises compiled within non-Buddhist currents of the [Indian] sages rNga-bong, Garga, and others.

In spite of that, when the ninth [tenth] [Kalki king of Śambhala, Holder-of-the-Castes] Rigs-ldan rGya-mtsho rNam-rgyal [Samudra Vijaya] ascended the lion's throne, [barbarian teachings were spreading] in the land of Ma-kha [Mecca] [and when they reached] the western part of India the seventh barbarian teacher Mun-can sBrang-rtsi'i Blo-gros [Rāhu Madhumati, Mohammed] concealed philosophical astrology and taught a simplified method, so that [the movements of] planets, constellations, and so forth became incomprehensible.

During his reign, [the eleventh Kalki king of Śambhala, Holder-of-the-Castes] Rigs-ldan rGyal-dka' [Aja, d. 1027 CE] began to concretely apply the abridged reckoning system [byed rtsis] based upon the true teachings of the Condensed [Kālachakra] Tantra [bsDus rgyud, Laghutantra].

After that, in the Fire Rabbit [year, 1027 CE] the disclosure of the real meaning of the prophesy contained in the Kālachakra about the corruption of the non-Buddhist reckoning methods, which had become famous all over India, caused the beginning of a correct astrological reckoning. The time span from the presence of the barbarian [teachings] until that point is known as me mkha' rgya mtsho. The Fire Rabbit [year] cited above is recognized as the first year of the first rab byung.

Concerning warfare astrology, the same text says (ibid., 597, 21):

It is said that the Bhagavān [bCom-ldan-'das] explained [warfare astrology] upon the request of the Lord of the Gods [Indra] when in ancient times the Gods and the Asuras [lha dang lha min] were engaged in a battle. [He] manifested himself as Mahādeva Īśvara [lHa-chen-po dBang-phyug], the beloved mundane Lord of the outsiders [phyi pa].

In the land of human beings the dPal yul las rnam par rgyal ba'i rgyud [Tantra of the All-Victorious from the Noble Country] was first disseminated by Karmasiddha Utpala.

In Tibet [texts of warfare astrology] were translated by Jayā Ananda, the Paṇḍita from 'Dzum-lang, and by Shes-rab Rin-chen, the Lotsāba of Glo-bo [Mustang].

As for the astrology of the elements, the same source affirms (ibid., 587, 6):

> The origin of the so-called astrology of the elements ['byung rtsi] or black astrology [nag rtsis] is China. In this regard [it is narrated that] the first emperor sPa-Hu Hshi-dhī [Chin. Fúxī Dì, 伏羲帝] received a gold-colored turtle as a present from one [of his] subjects [who lived] at the seashore. After he observed and examined [the turtle], the symbols of the eight spar kha[95] appeared in [the emperor's] mind for the first time. On that basis [he] developed the astrological systems of the spar [kha] and sme [ba] in relation to the yearly cycles that were subsequently elaborated by accomplished kings, ministers, and sages who [were considered] emanations [of divine beings].
>
> In particular, Khong-spu-tsi, an emanation of Mañjuśrī known in Tibet as Kong-tse 'Phrul-rgyal,[96] devised countless systems of astrological calculations [rtsis] and healing rituals [gto], thus establishing a tradition that developed greatly in later times.
>
> Here in Tibet, this tradition was first initiated by the earlier and later Kong-Jo [Kong-jo sNga-phyis, that is to say, the Chinese princesses Wénchéng Gōngzhǔ 文成公主 (628-680/2 CE) and Jīnchéng Gōngzhǔ 金成公主 (?-739 CE)],[97] who brought texts of Chinese astrology.

The principal astrological topics are related to Indian astrology, for example, the collection of the five subject matters [rtsis su lnga bsdus],

---

95 *spar kha brgyad*: the Eight Trigrams [Chin. Bāguà 八卦], namely, Khen [Qián 乾 ䷀], Khon [Kūn 坤 ䷁], [Lí 離 ䷝], Kham [Kǎn 坎 ䷜], Gin [Gèn 艮 ䷳], Dwa [Duì 兌 ䷹], Zon [Xùn 巽 ䷸], and Zin [Zhèn 震 ䷲], which respectively symbolize Heaven, Earth, Fire, Water, Mountain, Lake, Wind, and Thunder.
96 [The Author affirms that identifying Kong-tse 'Phrul-rgyal with Khong-spu-tsi (Confucius, Chin. Kǒng Fūzǐ 孔夫子 551–479 BCE) is inexact and not pertinent. See Vol. I, chapter II, pp. 119-122.]
97 [They were the consorts of Srong-btsan sGam-po and Khri-lde gTsug-btsan Mes Ag-tshoms (b. 704 CE).]

namely, Rāhu [sgra gcan], the time of the change of years and months [lo 'pho zla 'pho], solar and lunar eclipses [nyi zla gza' 'dzin], the five planets [gza' lnga],[98] and the different signs of the zodiac [dus sbyor]; and to the manifold topics of Chinese elemental astrology such as the examination of the spirit classes that possess the earth [sa bdag gi rigs brtag pa]; natal horoscopes [tshe rabs las rtsis]; reckoning of hindrances for single years [skeg rtsis]; nuptial astrology [bag rtsis]; astrology of death [gshin rtsis]; and so on.

2.2.2. Poetics [sNyan ngag]

The Shes bya kun khyab [The All-Encompassing Treasury of Knowledge] briefly explains this cultural science as follows (Pe, Vol. I, 599, 19):

> Concerning poetics [and] rhetorical treatises, [it is said that the first ones, that is to say, the Vedas] appeared long ago when the life of all beings had a duration of 20,000 years. They were classified by Rṣi Vyāsa [Drang-srong rGyas-pa, third millennium BCE] and are acclaimed by [all] non-Buddhist philosophical theoreticians.
>
> Also many other treatises have been written by famous sages, such as the treatise [of] Bharata in more than 100,000 stanzas [śloka], praised by lords and commoners alike; the sNyan dngags sgom pa'i chos [Principles of Meditation in Poetics] written by Me-bzhin 'Jug-pa'i Bu-mo; the Rāmāyaṇa of Vālmīki [Grog-mkhar]; the Ashṭad-sha-pu-rā of Marke-ndra-ya; the Ra-ghu-waṃ-sha of Ra-ma-shra-ma [sic],[99] and so on. These did not appear in Tibet.
>
> In later times, Kālidāsa [Nag-mo'i Khol-po] wrote many exceptional poems such as the Poems of the Eight Messengers [Pho nya brgyad] [sic], [which include] the Cloud Messenger [Meghadūta, Tib. sPrin gyi pho nya], the epic Kumārasambhava [gZhon-nu 'byung-ba], and so on.

---

98   Mars, [mig dmar], Mercury [lhag pa], Jupiter [phur bu], Venus [pa sangs], and Saturn [spen pa].

99   [The Raghuvaṃśa is an epic poem on the Raghu dynasty composed by Kālidāsa.]

However, the work that incorporates the best of earlier creations is definitely the *rGyan gyi bstan bcos me long* [The Mirror Treatise on Poetics] written by the Brahmin paṇḍita Dandi [dByug-pa-can, seventh century] who was an authoritative expert in both Hindu and Buddhist philosophy. His work was the object of numerous and extensive commentaries, both Hindu and Buddhist.

Later on, the Sanskrit manuscript of the *Ṭīk chen* [Great Commentary] of Ratna-śrī and Ngag-dbang Grags-pa came into the hands of the lord rDarmā-ka-ra.

2.2.3. Metrics [*sDeb sbyor*]

The *Shes bya kun khyab* [The All-Encompassing Treasury of Knowledge] contains a clear explanation about this cultural science (Pe, Vol. I, 600, 16):

It is said that the first to expound rules about metrics was Ṛṣi Vālmīki [Drang-srong Grog-mkhar].

[The tradition narrates that a] Nāga had arrayed the sand on the ocean shore in rows[100] and an eagle began pecking [at it]. [The Nāga said,] "This is not animal food. Do not eat it," and proceeded to complete [his arrangement]. The eagle [said,] "Please forgive me," and [asked the Nāga] to become his master so that he would understand the meaning [of that display]. [The Nāga said,] "As you like," and allowed him to remain there. That [Nāga] was known as Ṛṣi Piṅgala [Drang-srong dMar-ser-can] or the Limitless King of Nāgas [Klu-rgyal lHag-ma-can].[101]

rGyal-ba'i-lha wrote commentaries on the scriptural tradition derived from him and disseminated its exposition and study. By identifying the eight good qualities [of speech], [he was able to] clarify the condensed verses [*tshigs bcad*], interpret the figures of speech [of] the scripture itself, and facilitate the progressive intoning of [the verses] in a distinct manner, [and thus created

---

100 *praptār*: a Sanskrit term that in Tibetan is rendered as 'placing objects in a row' [*gral sgrig pa*] or arranging objects in succession [*phreng du bsgrig pa*].
101 [He authored the *Chandaḥśāstra*, the earliest known treatise on prosody written in Sanskrit.]

a system] qualified by the eight good qualities [of speech], the accumulation [of breath], and repose.

The Omniscient of the Age of Strife Rin-'byung Zhi-ba composed an astounding work on metrics, including a root text and a commentary featuring the six applications [of breathing] [sDeb sbyor rin 'byung rtsa 'grel].

Many commentaries and figures of speech [were created in India, such as those] by the teacher dPal-ye-shes and also in Tibet, such as those by the Eighth Master [rJe-brgyad-pa, Kar-ma-pa Mi-bskyod rDo-rje, 1507–1554], sMin-gling Lo-chen [Dharmaśrī, 1654-1717], and others.

2.2.4. Lexicography [mNgon brjod]

Concerning this cultural science, the *Shes bya kun khyab* [The All-Encompassing Treasury of Knowledge] says (Pe, Vol. I, 601, 16):

> Many treatises on lexicography exist in India such as those composed by Me-dī-ni-ka-ra and Paṇḍita dPal-'dzin-sde and those composed by Hā-rā-ba-lī and Drag-po'i-'bangs; but the best [of all] is the [metrical dictionary of the Sanskrit language titled] The Treasury of Immortality [Amarakośa, 'Chi med mdzod] composed by the great master Amarasimha ['Chi-med Seng-ge, ca. 375 CE], who was accepted by Ārya as a disciple.
>
> Two Indian commentaries on this [work], the *rNam bshad bdud rtsi* [Nectar Exegesis] [and] the *Tshig gi zla ba* [Moon of Words], apply the principles of sounds according to the system of Pā-ṇi-pa.
>
> The Sanskrit manuscript reached the hands of the Omniscient Lord.
>
> The commentary written by Su-bhu-ti titled *'Dod 'jo* [Wish-granting] was employed in actual theatrical works [in order to establish metrical] counting units that did not exist in Tibet.

The *Legs bshad nor phreng* [The Jewel Garland of Elegant Sayings] says (Dha, 46, 23, 7):

> [Works on] the so-called minor sciences or five conventional sciences—grammar, poetics, metrics, lexicography, and drama—did not flourish before the time of the lord of Dharma [Chos-rje] Sa-skya Paṇḍita [1182-1251]. Then, even if diffused as

long ago as [the time of] Thar-lo Nyi-ma rGyal-mtshan, these works were not translated in Tibetan until Shong-ston rDo-rje rGyal-mtshan, the crown-ornament of [all] scholars, who, having studied with excellent teachers, namely, the Indian Paṇḍitas Lakshmi-ka-ra and Ma-hindra-bha-dra, made the first translations of numerous [texts on] grammar, poetics, and so on and revised the translation of many others.

These excerpts permit us to understand in a concise manner the viewpoints identifying the Five Major and Five Minor Cultural Sciences, their origins, the periods of their diffusion in Tibet, and other relevant information.

Bibliography[102]

"Klu sgrub bstan rtsis"
    bsTan rtsis gsal ba'i nyin byed
    Author: Mang-thos Klu-sgrub rGya-mtsho (1523-1596)
    Publishing house: Bod ljongs mi dmangs dpe skrun khang, Lhasa
    Publishing date: 1987

"Klong chen pa'i chos 'byung"
    Chos 'byung rin po che'i gter mdzod thub bstan gsal bar byed pa'i nyi 'od ces bya ba
    Author: Klong-chen-pa Dri-med 'Od-zer (1308-1363)
    Publisher: Dodrup Sangyey Lama, Delhi
    Publishing date: 1976
    Type: *dbu med* manuscript

"bKa' chems ka khol ma"
    (*gter-ma*)
    Revealer: Jo-bo rJe A-ti-sha (982-1054)
    Editor: sMon-lam rGya-mtsho

---

102 This bibliography, arranged according to the Tibetan alphabetical order, lists the three different genres of texts quoted in the present work, first with the abridged title, when that has been used, and then with the full title. Whenever possible or applicable, oral transmission texts [*bka' ma*], and treatises [*bstan bcos*] carry the name of the author and his dates, and/or the date of creation; aural transmission texts [*snyan rgyud*], and texts originated from pure vision [*dag snang*] carry the name of the compiler; *gter-ma* texts carry the name and dates of the original author, of the discoverer(s) [*gter ston*], and/or of the discovery; these are followed by the name of the owner, publisher, or editor(s), or that of the review (in case of articles), the name of the place of publication, or the name and place of the publishing house, the year of publication, and indications about the type of publication (manuscript, manuscript in *dbu med*, reproduction of manuscript, or xylographic edition). The same structure is followed in all volumes.

Publishing house: Kan su'i mi rigs dpe skrun khang, Lanzhou
Publishing date: 1989

"*sKal bzang mgrin rgyan*"
Sangs rgyas g.yung drung bon gyi bstan pa'i byung ba brjod pa'i legs bshad skal pa bzang po'i
mgrin rgyan zhes bya ba
Author: dPal-ldan Tshul-khrims (1902-1973)
Publishing house: Bod ljongs mi dmangs dpe skrun khang, Lhasa
Publishing date: 1988

"*Khrims yig blang dor gsal bar byed pa'i drang thig dwangs shel me long nyer gcig pa zhes pa'i*
le'u bcu drug pa"
in: *Bod kyi snga rabs khrims srol yig cha bdams sgrig* [Selection of ancient Tibetan
legal records] Gangs chen rig mdzod series, Vol. 7
Author: sDe-srid Sangs-rgyas rGya-mtsho (1653-1705)
Publishing house: Bod ljongs mi dmangs dpe skrun khang, Lhasa
Publishing date: 1989

"*Khro bo dbang chen ngo mtshar rgyas pa'i rnam bshad gsal ba'i sgron ma*"
Author: sKyabs-ston Ri-chen 'Od-zer (born 1353)
Publisher: Yongs-'dzin Sangs-rgyas bsTan-'dzin (born 1912)
Publishing house: New Thobgyal, Tibetan Bonpo Monastic Centre, Dolanji,
HP, India
Publishing date: 1973
Type: *dbu med* manuscript

"*Grags rgyal bod kyi rgyal rabs*"
in: *Sa skya bka' 'bum*, Vol. TA
Author: rJe-btsun Grags-pa rGyal-mtshan (1146-1216)
Publishing house: sDe dge lhun grub steng
Type: Woodblock print

"*Gleng gzhi bstan pa'i byung khungs*"
Author: Khyung-po Blo-gros rGyal-mtshan (fourteenth century)
Owner: Is.IAO (Istituto Italiano per l'Africa e l'Oriente), Rome, Italy
Type: *dbu med* manuscript

"*rGya bod yig tshang chen mo*"
rGya bod kyi yig tshang mkhas pa dga' byed chen mo 'dzam gling gsal ba'i me long
Author: sTag-tshang rDzong-pa dPal-'byor bZang-po
Compilation date: 1434
Publishing house: Si khron mi rigs dpe skrun khang, Chengdu
Publishing date: 1985

"*rGya'i thang yig rnying ma*"
rGya'i yig tshang nang gsal ba'i bod kyi rgyal rabs gsal ba'i me long
Trans. and editor: sTag-lha Phun-tshogs bKra-shis (born 1922)
Publication place: Dharamsala, HP, India
Publishing date: 1973

"rGya'i thang yig rnying ma"
   Thang yig gsar rnying las byung ba'i bod chen po'i srid lugs
   Trans. and editors: Don-grub-rgyal (1953-1985) and Khrin-chin-dbyin
   (Chen Jianjian)
   Publishing house: mTsho sngon mi rigs dpe skrun khang, Xining
   Publishing date: 1983

"rGya'i thang yig gsar ma"
   rGya'i yig tshang nang gsal ba'i bod kyi rgyal rabs gsal ba'i me long
   Trans. and editor: sTag-lha Phun-tshogs bKra-shis (born 1922)
   Publication place: Dharamsala, HP, India
   Publishing date: 1973

"rGya'i thang yig gsar ma"
   Thang yig gsar rnying las byung ba'i bod chen po'i srid lugs
   Trans. and editors: Don-grub-rgyal (1953-1985) and Khrin-chin-dbyin
   (Chen Jianjian)
   Publishing house: mTsho sngon mi rigs dpe skrun khang, Xining
   Publishing date: 1983

"rGya'i lo rgyus thung cen"
   rGya'i yig tshang nang gsal ba'i bod kyi rgyal rabs gsal ba'i me long
   Trans. and editor: sTag-lha Phun-tshogs bKra-shis (born 1922)
   Publication place: Dharamsala, HP, India
   Publishing date: 1973

"rGyal rabs 'phrul gyi lde mig"
   rGyal rabs 'phrul gyi lde mig, or *Deb ther dmar po'i deb gsar ma zhes bya ba*
   Author: Paṇ-chen bSod-nams Grags-pa (1478-1554)
   Publishing house: International Academy of Indian Culture, New Delhi
   Publishing date: 1968

"rGyal rabs bon gyi 'byung gnas"
   in: *Three Sources for a History of Bon*
   Author: Khyung-po Blo-gros rGyal-mtshan
   Compilation date: 1439
   Publisher: mKhas-grub rGya-mtsho
   Publication place: New Thobgyal, Tibetan Bonpo Monastic Centre, Dolanji,
   HP, India
   Publishing date: 1974

"rGyal rabs me long rnam gsal"
   rGyal rabs me long gsal byed nyung ngu rnam gsal
   Author: Ratna Gling-pa (1403-1478)
   Publishing house: Library of Tibetan Works and Archives, Dharamsala, HP,
   India
   Publishing date: 1985
   Type: *dbu med* manuscript

"*rGyal rabs gsal ba'i me long*"
  Author: Sa-skya-pa bSod-nams rGyal-mtshan (1312-1375)
  Publishing house: Mi rigs dpe skrun khang, Beijing
  Publishing date: 1981

"*rGyud bu chung bcu gnyis*"
  Zhang Zhung Aural transmission Cycle
  in: *History and Doctrines of Bonpo Niṣpanna Yoga*
  Upholder: Kun-tu bZang-po
  Teacher: Ta-pi Hri-tsa
  Compiler: Gyer-spungs sNang-bzher Lod-po (eighth century)
  Publishing house: International Academy of Indian Culture, New Delhi
  Publishing date: 1968

"*Chos 'byung dpag bsam ljon bzang*"
  'Phags yul rgya nag chen po bod dang sog yul du dam pa'i chos byung tshul
  dpag bsam ljon bzang
  Author: Sum-pa mKhan-po Ye-shes dPal-'byor (1704-1788)
  Compilation date: 1748
  Publisher: International Academy of Indian Culture, New Delhi
  Publishing date: 1975

"*'Jig rten mGon po'i gsung bzhi bcu pa*"
  in: *dGongs gcig yig cha*, Vol. I
  Author: sKyobs-pa 'Jig-rten mGon-po (1143-1217)
  Publishing place: Bir Tibetan Society, HP, India
  Publishing date: 1975

"*rJe btsun g.yu thog yon tan mgon po rnying ma'i rnam par thar pa bka' rgya ma gzi brjid rin
  po che'i gter mdzod ces bya ba*"
  in: *g.Yu thog gsar rnying gi rnam thar*
  Author: Jo-bo lHun-grub bKra-shis
  Publisher: Mi rigs dpe skrun khang, Beijing
  Publishing date: 1982

"*Nyang gi chos 'byung*"
  Chos 'byung me tog snying po
  Author: Nyang-ral Nyi-ma 'Od-zer (1124-1192)
  Publishing house: Bod ljongs mi dmangs dpe skrun khang, Lhasa
  Publishing date: 1988

"*Nyin byed snang ba'i bu yig ngo mtshar phreng ba*"
  rTsis gzhung nyin byed snang ba'i lag len bu yig ngo mtshar 'phreng ba
  Author: sMin-gling Lo-chen Dharma-śrī (1654-1717)
       Publisher: Dondup Tashi, Leh
       Publishing date: 1976

"*Tun hong bod kyi lo rgyus yig rnying*"
  in: Spanien, Ariane, and Imaeda, Yoshiro (eds.), *Choix de documents tibétains
  conservés à la Bibliothèque nationale*, Vol. II

Publishing house: Bibliothèque Nationale, Paris
Publishing date: 1979

"bsTan rtsis gsal ba'i nyin byed"
  See *Klu sgrub bstan rtsis*

"Thang yig gsar ma"
  See *rGya'i thang yig gsar ma*

"Thu'u bkan grub mtha" <Grub mtha' shel gyi me long>
  Thu'u bkan grub mtha' shel gyi me long
  Author: Thu'u-bkan Blo-bzang Chos-kyi Nyi-ma (1737-1802)
  Publishing house: Kan su'u mi rigs dpe skrun khang, Lanzhou
  Publishing date: 1984

"Dar rgyas gsal sgron"
  bsTan pa'i rnam bshad dar rgyas gsal ba'i sgron ma zhes bya ba
  in: *Sources for a History of Bon*
  Author: sPa-ston bsTan-rgyal bZang-po (1290-1364)
  Compilation date: 1345
  Publisher: bsTan-'dzin rNam-dag (born 1926)
  Publishing house: New Thobgyal, Tibetan Bonpo Monastic Centre, Dolanji,
  HP, India
  Publishing date: 1972

"Deb ther dkar po"
  Bod chen po'i srid lugs dang 'brel ba'i rgyal rabs deb ther dkar po zhes bya ba
  in: *mKhas dbang dge 'dun chos 'phel gyi gsung rtsom phyogs sgrig*
  Author: dGe-'dun Chos-'phel (1905-1951)
  Publishing house: Si khron mi rigs dpe skrun khang, Chengdu
  Publishing date: 1988

"Deb ther sngon po"
  Author: 'Gos-lo gZhon-nu-dpal (1392-1481)
  Publishing house: Si khron mi rigs dpe skrun khang, Chengdu
  Publishing date: 1984

"Deb ther dpyid kyi rgyal mo'i glu dbyangs"
  Gangs can yul gyi sa la spyod pa'i mtho ris kyi rgyal blon gtso bor brjod pa'i deb ther rdzogs
  ldan gzhon nu'i dga' ston dpyid kyi rgyal mo'i glu dbyangs zhes bya ba
  Author: V Dalai Lama Ngag-dbang Blo-bzang rGya-mtsho (1617-1682)
  Publishing house: Mi rigs dpe skrun khang, Beijing
  Publishing date: 1988

"Deb ther dmar po"
  Deb ther dmar po rnams kyi dang po hu lan deb ther
  Author: Tshal-pa Kun-dga' rDo-rje (1309-1364)
  Publishing house: Mi rigs dpe skrun khang, Beijing
  Publishing date: 1981

"Dri med gzi brjid"
'Dus pa rin po che'i rgyud dri ma med pa gzi brjid rab tu 'bar ba'i mdo
(*gter-ma*)
Revealer: Khyung-po Blo-ldan sNying-po (born 1360)
Publisher: bSod-nams rGyal-mtshan
Publishing place: New Thobgyal, Tibetan Bonpo Monastic Centre, Dolanji,
HP, India
Publishing date: 1978
Type: *dbu med* manuscript

"mDo 'dus"
lHa'i bon mdo 'dus pa rin po che'i rgyud (Sūtra Series, Vol. SA)
(*gter-ma*)
Revealer: A-tsa-ra Mi-gnyis (tenth century)
Publishing house: Si khron zhing chen mi rigs zhib 'jug su'o Bod kyi rig gnas
zhib 'jug khang, Chengdu
Type: Reproduction of *dbu med* manuscript

"lDe'u rgya bod kyi chos 'byung"
mKhas pa lde'us mdzad pa'i rgya bod kyi chos 'byung rgyas pa (Gangs chen Rig mdzod
Series, Vol. 3)
Author: Jo-sras lDe'u (twelfth century)
Publishing house: Bod ljongs mi dmangs dpe skrun khang, Lhasa
Publishing date: 1987

"lDe'u chos 'byung chen mo"
Chos 'byung chen mo bstan pa'i rgyal mtshan lde'u jo sras kyis mdzad pa
(Cover title: *lDe'u chos 'byung*)
Author: Jo-sras lDe'u (twelfth century)
Publishing house: Bod ljongs mi dmangs dpe skrun khang, Lhasa
Publishing date: 1987

"Ne'u sngon byung gi gtam"
sNgon gyi gtam me tog phreng ba
in: *Rare Historical Texts from the Library of Burmiok Athing*
Author: Ne'u Paṇḍi-ta Grags-pa sMon-lam (thirteenth century)
Publishing house: Library of Tibetan Works and Archives, Dharamsala, HP,
India
Publishing date: 1985
Type: *dbu med* manuscript

"Pad dkar chos 'byung"
Chos 'byung bstan pa'i padma rgyas pa'i nyin byed
in: *Kun mkhyen bka' 'bum* (Collected Works), Vol. KA and CHA
Author: Kun-mkhyen Padma dKar-po (1527-1592)
Publication place: Bhutan
Type: Woodblock print

"Padma'i bka'i thang yig"
    U rgyan gu ru padma 'byung gnas kyi skyes rabs rnam par thar pa rgyas par bkod pa zhes bya ba
    (gter-ma)
    Revealer: Yar-rje U-rgyan Gling-pa (born 1323)
    Publishing house: Si khron mi rigs dpe skrun khang, Chengdu
    Publishing date: 1987

"sPu rgyal gdung rabs kyi rtsa ba'i 'byung khungs skor la cung zad dpyad pa" (article)
    in: *Bod ljongs zhib 'jug* (magazine of the Tibetan Academy of Social
    Sciences), Vol. 2, Lhasa, 1986
    Author: Chab-spel Tshe-brtan Phun-tshogs (twentieth century)

"Bu ston chos 'byung"
    bDe bar gshegs pa'i bstan pa'i gsal byed chos kyi 'byung gnas gsung rab rin po che'i mdzod ces
    bya ba
    Author: Bu-ston Rin-chen-grub (1290-1364)
    Publishing house: Lhasa Zhol dpar ma
    Type: Woodblock print

"Bod kyi yig tshang"
    rGyal rabs sogs bod kyi yig tshang gsal ba'i me long
    in: *Rare Historical Texts from the Library of Burmiok Athing*
    Author: Ne'u Paṇḍi-ta Grags-pa sMon-lam (thirteenth century)
    Publishing house: Library of Tibetan Works and Archives, Dharamsala, HP,
    India
    Publishing date: 1985

"Bod kyi rus khungs thog ma'i tshan dpyod" (article)
    in: *mTsho sngon slob gso* [Qinghai Education], Vol. 6, Xining, 1983
    Author: A-mdo-ba Padma dBang-rgyal

"Bod kyi lo rgyus las 'phros pa'i gtam nor bu'i do shal"
    Author: Nam-mkha'i Nor-bu (born 1938)
    Publishing house: Library of Tibetan Works and Archives, Dharamsala, HP,
    India
    Publishing date: 1981

"Bod gna' rabs kyi rig gnas dang chos lugs mi rigs bcas kyi 'byung khungs skor gleng ba" (article)
    in: *Bod ljongs zhib 'jug* (magazine of the Tibetan Academy of Social
    Sciences), Vol. 2, Lhasa, 1984
    Author: Dung-dkar Blo-bzang 'Phrin-las (1927-1997)

"Bod mi'i 'byung khungs che long tsam brjod pa" (article)
    in: *Bod ljongs zhib 'jug* (magazine of the Tibetan Academy of Social
    Sciences), Vol. I, Lhasa, 1985
    Author: Reb-kong rDo-rje-mkhar

"Blon po bka'i thang yig"
    in: *bKa' thang sde lnga*
    (gter-ma)

Revealer: Yar-rje U-rgyan Gling-pa (born 1323)
Publishing house: Mi rigs dpe skrun khang, Beijing
Publishing date: 1986

"*sBa bzhed*"
bTsan po khri srong lde btsan dang mkhan po slob dpon padma'i dus mdo sngags so sor mdzad pa'i sba bzhed zhabs btags ma
藏族古典文史名著拔协增补本绎注
[Zàng zú Gǔ diǎn Wén shǐ Míng zhù Bá xíe Zēng bǔ běn yì zhù. Famous Works of Classical Tibetan History and Literature. Bá Xíe. Extended and annotated edition]
Author: sBa-gsal-snang (ninth century)
Publishing house: Si khron mi rigs dpe skrun khang, Chengdu
Publishing date: 1990

"*Ma ṇi bka' 'bum*"
(*gter-ma*)
Revealer: Grub-thob dNgos-grub (twelfth century)
Publishing house: mTsho sngon mi rigs dpe skrun khang, Xining
Publishing date: 1991
Type: Book

"*Mi nyag gi skor rags tsam gleng ba*" (article)
in: *Bod ljongs zhib 'jug* (magazine of the Tibetan Academy of Social Sciences), Vol. 3, Lhasa, 1986
Author: Reb-kong rDo-rje-mkhar

"*Me long rnam gsal*"
See *rGyal rabs me long rnam gsal*

"*Zhang zhung snyan rgyud kyi rgyud bu chung bcu gnyis*"
See *rGyud bu chung bcu gnyis*

"*Zhang zhung snyan rgyud kyi bon ma nub pa'i gtan tshigs*"
Zhang Zhung Aural transmission Cycle, Vol. PA
in: *History and Doctrines of Bonpo Niṣpanna Yoga*
Compiler: Gyer-spungs sNang-bzher Lod-po (eighth century)
Publishing house: International Academy of Indian Culture, New Delhi
Publishing date: 1968

"*Yar lung jo bo'i chos 'byung*"
Author: Yar-lung Jo-bo Shākya Rin-chen-sde (fourteenth century)
Compilation date: 1376
Publishing house: Si khron mi rigs dpe skrun khang, Chengdu
Publishing date: 1988

"*Legs bshad skal bzang mgrin rgyan*"
See *sKal bzang mgrin rgyan*

"Legs bshad nor phreng"
    Rig gnas lnga'i rnam dbye cung zad bshad pa legs bshad nor bu'i phreng ba blo gsal mgul rgyan zhes bya ba
    Author: Kālapāda, alias Dus-'khor Zhabs-drung (seventeenth century)
    Publishing house: Library of Tibetan Works and Archives, Dharamsala, HP, India
    Publishing date: 1981

"Legs bshad rin po che'i mdzod"
    Legs bshad rin po che'i gter mdzod dpyod ldan dga' ba'i char zhes bya ba
    Author: Shar-rdza bKra-shis rGyal-mtshan (1859-1933)
    Publishing house: Mi rigs dpe skrun khang, Beijing
    Publishing date: 1985

"Shes bya kun khyab"
    Theg pa'i sgo kun las btus pa gsung rab rin po che'i mdzod bslab pa gsum legs par ston pa'i bstan bcos shes bya kun khyab
    Author: Kong-sprul Yon-tan rGya-mtsho (1813-1899)
    Publishing house: Mi rigs dpe skrun khang, Beijing
    Publishing date: 1982

"Srid pa rgyud kyi kha byang"
    Srid pa rgyud kyi kha byang chen mo
    (gter-ma)
    Revealer: Khod-po Blo-gros Thogs-med (born 1280)
    Date of revelation: 1301
    Publisher: bsTan-'dzin rNam-dag (born 1926)
    Publication place: New Thobgyal, Tibetan Bonpo Monastic Centre, Dolanji, HP, India
    Publishing date: 1976

"Srid pa mdzod kyi mdo mkhor 'das khams kyi rtsa ba g.yung drung las rnam par dag pa'i rgyud"
    (Sūtra Series, Vol. KA)
    (gter-ma)
    Revealer: Gyer-mi Nyi-'od (twelfth century)
    Publishing house: Si khron zhing chen mi rigs zhib 'jug su'o Bod kyi rig gnas zhib 'jug khang, Chengdu

"gSol 'debs bar chad lam sel"
    (Padma bKa' thang)
    (gter-ma)
    Revealer: mChog-gyur bDe-chen Gling-pa (1829-1870)
    Publishing house: Si khron mi rigs dpe skrun khang, Chengdu
    Publishing date: 1987

"lHo chos 'byung blo gsar rna ba'i rgyan"
    dPal ldan 'brug pa'i gdul zhing lho phyogs nags ma'i ljongs kyi chos 'byung blo gsar rna ba'i rgyan ces bya ba
    Author: Brag-phug dGe-bshes dGe-'dun Rin-chen (born 1926)

Compilation date: 1972
Publishing house: sGrub sde nges don zung 'jug grub pa'i dga' tshal, Bhutan
Type: Woodblock print

"lHo brag chos 'byung"
Chos 'byung mkhas pa'i dga' ston, or *Dam pa'i chos kyi 'khor los bsgyur ba rnams kyi byung ba gsal bar byed pa mkhas pa'i dga' ston*
Author: dPa'-bo gTsug-lag Phreng-ba (1504-1566)
Editor: rDo-rje rGyal-po
Publishing house: Mi rigs dpe skrun khang, Beijing
Publishing date: 1986

Index of Tibetan and Zhang Zhung
Names and Terms

Index of Tibetan Textual Sources

Index of Sanskrit Names and Terms

Index of Chinese Names and Terms

CPSIA information can be obtained
at www.ICGtesting.com
Printed in the USA
BVHW071156010720
582722BV00001B/95